Shadows and Chivalry

C. S. Lewis and George MacDonald on Suffering, Evil and Goodness

Shadows and Chivalry
C. S. Lewis and George MacDonald on Suffering, Evil and Goodness

Winged Lion Press
Hamden, CT

First published 2006 by Paternoster
Paternoster is an imprint of Authentic Media
9 Holdom Avenue, Bletchley, Milton Keynes, MK1 1QR, UK

Winged Lion Press titles may be purchased for business or promotional use or special sales.

10-9-8-7-6-5-4-3-2-1

WINGED LION PRESS

ISBN-13 978-1-935688-01-3

For Momma,
lady of love,
and for Daddy,
my own dear knight of the sun.

Thank you for your chivalry.

Curtis "Gene" McInnis
(1942-2011)

CONTENTS

Foreword	vii
Preface	xi
Acknowledgements	xiii
Abbreviations	xv
Introduction	1

Chapter 1
The Land of Shadows — 5

Early Troubles for MacDonald	11
Early Troubles for Lewis	16
A Spirit in Bondage	22
More Troubles for MacDonald	31
Within and Without	36

Chapter 2
Silver Threads — 53

Omnipotence, Freedom, and Possible Worlds	55
The Mistress of the Silver Moon	61
The *Tao*	62
Dwarves and Other Skeptics	65
The Light of Reason	76
The *Tao* in Fiction	81
More Troubles	92
Encouragement	95
Faith and Feelings	113

Chapter 3
Death and Divorce — 128

Losing One's Shadow	132
Evil Fortune	138
Outside and Inside Evil	143
Choosing Goodness	151

Chapter 4
The Philosophy of Hell   **158**
The One Principle of Hell   164
Purgatory   169
Final Damnation?   171
The Substance of Hell   178
False Loves   188
Pictures of Hell   194
The Great Escape   203

Chapter 5
The Chivalry of God   **210**
Beyond Mere Morality   210
Beyond Mere Spirituality   213
A Useful Metaphor   216
False Gods   219
The Divine Sonship   232
A Lamb to the Rescue   235
A Lion to the Rescue   243
Pictures of God   252
The Art of Love   260
Good Hierarchy   270

Chapter 6
Inness   **278**

Afterword   **291**
Bibliography   **301**
Index   **305**

FOREWORD

Shadows and Chivalry is a unique and important book for students and scholars of George MacDonald and C.S. Lewis. It is unique because it identifies a foundation of ideas and images shared by these two great Christian authors which are repeated throughout their many books. For that reason, Jeff McInnis pays close attention to poems that initiated their publishing careers – the dramatic poem *Within and Without* published by MacDonald in 1856 and *Spirits in Bondage* by Lewis in 1919. Both poems present central images of light and shadows, doors and choices, suffering, death and otherworldly desire.

Drawing from the literary treasury of the Romantic imagination, both authors offer the idea of chivalry as a Christian ideal. Naturally, as Lewis did not begin writing as a Christian until after 1930, the imagery in his early poem from 1919 does not perfectly reflect the ideals of his post-Christian books. But Lewis always credited his initial 1916 reading of MacDonald's *Phantastes: A Romance* as instrumental in baptizing his imagination. So perhaps even here some influence is evident. Thus, *Shadows and Chivalry* is unique in tracing the early and later development of these primary themes, comparing how these ideas are presented in representative works of the authors.

By "shadows" the author's title refers to themes of suffering and death found in the authors' works. Perhaps the word "chivalry" is best reflected in the ideal of service. It is a word that epitomizes Christian responsibility each of these writers felt toward their readers. Chivalry is aptly presented by MacDonald in his novel *The Seaboard Parish* when describing the process by which a knight in the middle ages was taught to serve:

> "In America, the very name of servant is repudiated as inconsistent with human dignity. There is *no* dignity but of service. How different the whole notion of training is now from what it was in the middle ages! Service was honourable then. No doubt we have made progress as a whole, but in some things we have degenerated sadly. The first thing taught then was how to serve. No man could rise to the honour of knighthood without service. A nobleman's son even had to wait on his father, or to go into the family of another nobleman, and wait upon him

as a page, standing behind his chair at dinner. This was an honour. No notion of degradation was in it. It was a necessary step to higher honour. And what was the next higher honour? To be set free from service? No. To serve in the harder service of the field; to be a squire to some noble knight; to tend his horse, to clean his armour, to see that every rivet was sound, every buckle true, every strap strong; to ride behind him, and carry his spear, and if more than one attacked him, to rush to his aid. This service was the more honourable because it was harder, and was the next step to higher honour yet. And what was this higher honour? That of knighthood. Wherein did this knighthood consist? The very word means simply *service*. And for what was the knight thus waited upon by his squire? That he might be free to do as he pleased? No, but that he might be free to be the servant of all. By being a squire first, the servant of one, he learned to rise to the higher rank, that of servant of all. His horse was tended, this armour observed, his sword and spear and shield held to his hand, that he might have no trouble looking after himself, but might be free, strong, unwearied, to shoot like an arrow to the rescue of any and every one who needed his ready aid. There was a grand heart of Christianity in that old chivalry."

In the same novel, MacDonald describes a watercolor painting by Arthur Hughes (a friend and the primary illustrator of his books). The painting *The Knight of the Sun* (1860, now located at Ashmolean Museum in England), is reproduced on the cover of this book and was identified by MacDonald in a footnote located in his chapter entitled "The Studio." On the frame of the actual painting Hughes inscribed a line from MacDonald's poem *Better Things* (1857): "Better a death when work is done than earth's most favored birth." Here is MacDonald's exquisite description and explanation of the painting's meaning:

A dark hill rose against the evening sky, which shone through a few thin pines on its top. Along a road on the hill-side four squires bore a dying knight—a man past the middle age. One behind carried his helm, and another led his horse, whose fine head only appeared in the picture. The head and countenance of the knight were very noble, telling of many a battle, and ever for the right. The last had doubtless been gained, for one might read victory as well as peace in the dying look. The party had just reached the edge of a steep descent, from which you saw the valley beneath, with the last of the harvest just being reaped, while the shocks stood all about in the fields, under the place of the sunset. The sun had been down for some little time. There was no gold left in the sky, only a little dull saffron, but plenty of that lovely liquid green of the autumn sky, divided with a few streaks of pale rose. The depth of the sky overhead, which you could not see for the arrangement of the picture, was mirrored lovelily in a piece of water that lay in the centre of the valley.

[...] Here is a picture to my own heart; it is glorious. [...] you see it is evening; the sun's work is done, and he has set in glory, leaving his good name behind him in a lovely harmony of colour. The old knight's work is done too; his day has set in the storm of battle, and he is lying lapt in the coming peace. They are bearing him home to his couch and his grave. Look at their faces in the dusky light. They are all mourning for and honouring the life that is ebbing away. But he is gathered to his fathers like a shock of corn fully ripe; and so the harvest stands golden in the valley beneath. The picture would not be complete, however, if it did not tell us of the deep heaven overhead, the symbol of that heaven whither he who has done his work is bound. What a lovely idea to represent it by means of the water, the heaven embodying itself in the earth, as it were, that we may see it! And observe how that dusky hill-side, and those tall slender mournful-looking pines, with that sorrowful sky between, lead the eye and point the heart upward towards that heaven. It is indeed a grand picture, full of feeling—a picture and a parable."

Jeff McInnis has written a book that, as MacDonald might say, is "to my own heart." It presents a rich outline of the imaginative hearts of two revered Christian writers. It is a scholarly work that aids us in understanding and appreciating one specific slice of literature. But, perhaps of more importance, it also inspires the reader to practice the old chivalry which is the "grand heart of Christianity."

Robert Trexler, Publisher

⌘ X ⌘

PREFACE

This study is essentially two things: a story and an exploration. It is the story of one writer's influence upon another writer, and an exploration of what both men wrote about suffering, evil and goodness. Lewis's and MacDonald's writings have interested and helped me greatly over the years, and I hope that readers who are interested in either the story or the exploration find this summary interesting, and perhaps helpful. I particularly hope that it might be helpful in some small way to those who have struggled with the question that the study begins with: How can God be good when there is so much that is bad in the world? This kind of help, of course, is not to be confused with what may help those who are presently suffering or grieving. As Lewis says, prayer, human kindness, and the love of God are our only hope in these times.

I regret that I have not been able to quote here from more of MacDonald's and Lewis's books. My hope has been to produce a representative cross-section that includes every *kind* of work that they both wrote, covering the works they are most famous for (but not only in our time), as well as some of the lesser-known works. The general goal has been to cast my net as deep and as wide as I need to tell the particular story, and make the particular exploration, that this study attempts. The fact that this is only a summary, of course, means some very good fish have gone uncaught. But take your own net to the library or bookshop. Those fish are all still there, and they're much more delightful and fresh in their original state.

ACKNOWLEDGEMENTS

The errors and omissions here will all be mine, but I have many people to thank for helping to make this study as interesting and informative as it is. I would first like to thank Robert Trexler for his work in getting this to a wider audience, and most especially for his wonderful foreword. With its reference to MacDonald's words on knighthood in *The Seaboard Parish*, it is the perfect way to begin this study. The original study was simply incomplete without these words from MacDonald. Thank you for making it better in a very special way.

I would also like to thank again the School of English at the University of St. Andrews for the opportunity to attempt this study. In particular I would like to thank Dr. Christopher MacLachlan, my thesis supervisor. The value of his guidance and encouragement was inestimable. It will not be forgotten. Thanks also to the late Dr. Barbara Murray, whose supervision in Dr. MacLachlan's absence was greatly appreciated and delightfully received.

I am sincerely grateful to the post-graduate secretary, Mrs. Jill (Gamble) Keay, for her patience and help with what I am sure were too many questions. I would also like to thank Dr. MacLachlan and the School of English for the acquisition of MacDonald's complete works. Thanks also to Dr. Robert Keay at St. Mary's for discussions and answers to theological queries.

I would like to specially thank Dr. Kirstin Johnson for her help, discussions, and encouragement. Particularly important to this study has been her transcription of Lewis's notes in his own copies of MacDonald's *Unspoken Sermons*. Many thanks to her for allowing me to view these notes, and to Christopher Mitchell, curator of the Marion E. Wade Center at Wheaton College (Wheaton, Illinois) for making these copies of Lewis's available for viewing. Greg Johnson has also been a great encouragement and inspiration.

Many thanks also to Walter Hooper, whose painstaking efforts have made so much study on Lewis possible. I am also grateful for the research undertaken by the late William Raeper, who produced such interesting and important work on MacDonald before his tragic death in a plane accident years ago. My vigorous refutation of his argument concerning MacDonald's view of evil should in no way be confused with hostility toward the man. He has done all of us interested in MacDonald a great service, and his work ought to be respected.

I am also grateful to William Murchison, who never seems to tire of doing for me what is undeserved, and to Bill O'Neal for much of the same. I'm also grateful to the Intercollegiate Studies Institute for the initial funding that allowed me to embark on this project. Thanks also to Mrs. Annette Kirk and Mrs. Andrea Kirk Assaf for their encouragement, and to Russell Kirk and his books. It is also meet to formally acknowledge the authors themselves, George MacDonald and C.S. Lewis, who wrote the books I study here. Studying things shouldn't always destroy our ability to enjoy them, or be helped by them. The delight and gratitude run very deeply here, as it no doubt does with many who read this.

Sincere thanks also to my mother and father, whom I could never thank enough. Being so far away from them for so long was the least enjoyable part of doing this study, but I gently remind them that it was partly their fault. One morning, some years ago, I removed the Christmas wrapping that hid these words: *The Screwtape Letters*. Thank you for that book, the tattered remains of which I used for this study. Not the greatest of your gifts, by far, but greatly appreciated.

Jeff McInnis
Carthage
August 2012

ABBREVIATIONS

ABO	*The Abolition of Man*
AC	*Adela Cathcart*
AFH	*Alec Forbes of Howglen*
AL	*The Allegory of Love*
ANTH	*George MacDonald: An Anthology*
AQN	*Annals of a Quiet Neighbourhood*
AV	Authorised (King James) Version of the Bible
CFT	*The Complete Fairy Tales* (MacDonald)
CHR	*Christian Reflections*
CLET	*Collected Letters of C.S. Lewis, Volume 1* (Walter Hooper, ed.)
CR	*Compelling Reason*
CSL	*C.S. Lewis: A Biography*
DE	*David Elginbrod*
DOS	*Diary of an Old Soul*
EA	*England's Antiphon*
EC	*An Experiment in Criticism*
ELSC	*English Literature in the Sixteenth Century, Excluding Drama*
MLET	*An Expression of Character: The Letters of George MacDonald*

4L	*The Four Loves*
FSE	*Fern Seed and Elephants*
FAC	*Till We Have Faces*
GD	*The Great Divorce*
GDK	*God in the Dock*
GIB	*Sir Gibbie*
GK	*The Golden Key*
GOB	*A Grief Observed*
GMW	*George MacDonald and His Wife*
HB	*The Horse and His Boy*
HG	*The Hope of the Gospel*
HS	*That Hideous Strength*
LB	*The Last Battle*
LIL	*Lilith*
LLET	*The Letters of C.S. Lewis* (W.H. Lewis, ed.)
LM	*Letters to Malcolm*
LWW	*The Lion, the Witch and the Wardrobe*
PRC	*Present Concerns*
RAEP	*George MacDonald* (by William Raeper)

MC	*Mere Christianity*	PPL	*A Preface to Paradise Lost*
MIR	*Miracles*	REG	*The Pilgrim's Regress*
MN	*The Magician's Nephew*		
MOL	*Miracles of Our Lord*	RF	*Robert Falconer*
NEB	*New English Bible*	ROBB	*George MacDonald (by David S. Robb)*
NW	*At the Back of the North Wind*	RPS	*Reflections on the `Psalms*
ORTS	*A Dish of Orts*	SBJ	*Surprised by Joy*
OSP	*Out of the Silent Planet*	SC	*The Silver Chair*
P&C	*The Princess and Curdie*	SCL	*The Screwtape Letters*
P&G	*The Princess and the Goblin*		
PC	*Prince Caspian*	SIB	*Spirits in Bondage*
PER	*Perelandra*	US	*Unspoken Sermons*
PHA	*Phantastes*	VDT	*The Voyage of the Dawn Treader*
POE	*Poems*		
POR	*The Portent and Other Stories*	WG	*The Weight of Glory and Other Addresses*
PP	*The Problem of Pain*	WW	*Within and Without*

Notes on Quotations

* Unless otherwise indicated, italics in quotations are the authors'.
* All of my explanatory notes in quotations are surrounded by brackets [my note]. Breaks within a quotation, in which I skip from one part of a passage to another, are indicated by an ellipsis within brackets [...]. All other text within quotations, including ellipses with no brackets, is the authors'.
* Unless otherwise indicated, all Bible quotations are from the Authorised (King James) Version.

INTRODUCTION

On 7 March, 1916, a seventeen-year-old C.S. Lewis, already a man of many books, wrote to his friend Arthur Greeves: 'whatever the book you are reading now, you simply MUST get this at once'.[1] The book was a 1/1d. Everyman edition of *Phantastes: a Faerie Romance* that he had picked up at a train station bookstall. The author was George MacDonald, a Scottish writer of the previous century who specialised in serialised novels, fairy tales and fantasy. Both the book and the author would come to influence Lewis, if Lewis himself is to be believed, more than any other book or author he would ever read. Lewis, one of the twentieth century's most published and influential writers, had many literary heroes. But only MacDonald would he come to call 'my master'.[2]

'I fancy I have never written a book in which I did not quote from him', Lewis would write in an anthology of MacDonald's writing he edited thirty years after he first read *Phantastes*.[3] Or as he would write in his autobiography, 'George MacDonald had done more to me than any other writer'.[4] Lewis, the future creator of Narnia, historian of literature and highly influential medievalist, would never be affected more deeply by any one piece of literature than *Phantastes*, a book he almost never read: 'I had looked at the volume on that bookstall and rejected it on a dozen previous occasions [...] A few hours later I knew that I had crossed a great frontier'.[5]

The frontier he crossed in *Phantastes* was an imaginative threshold. At that stage in his life Lewis remembers being 'waist-deep in Romanticism' and willing to sink into whatever depths it might take him.[6] As he put it later, the danger was one of 'slithering down the steep descent that leads from the love of strangeness to that of eccentricity and thence to that of perversity'.[7] In MacDonald's *Phantastes* he found something different. 'If this new world was strange, it was also homely and humble', Lewis wrote.[8] 'If this was a dream, it was a dream in which one at least felt strangely vigilant [...] the whole book

---

1   C.S. Lewis (Walter Hooper, ed.), *C.S. Lewis: Collected Letters, Volume 1* (London: Harper Collins, 2000), pp. 169-170.
2   George MacDonald (C.S. Lewis, ed.), *George MacDonald: An Anthology* (New York: Simon and Schuster, 1996), p. xxxii. *Anthology* originally published in 1946.
3   ANTH, p. xxxii.
4   C.S. Lewis, *Surprised by Joy: The Shape of My Early Life* (San Diego: Harcourt, 1984) p. 213. First published in 1955.
5   ANTH, pp. xxxii-xxxiii.
6   ANTH, p. xxxiii.
7   ANTH, p. xxxiii.
8   ANTH, p. xxxiii.

had about it a sort of cool, morning innocence'.[9]

The goodness Lewis found in *Phantastes* was very different from the religion he had been acquainted with in his early years, the kind that he found so stuffy. As he wrote in the *Anthology*:

> I should have been shocked in my teens if anyone had told me that what I learned to love in *Phantastes* was goodness. But now that I know, I see there was no deception. The deception is all the other way round–in that prosaic moralism which confines goodness to the region of Law and Duty, which never lets us feel in our face the sweet air blowing from "the land of righteousness",[10] never reveals that elusive Form which if once seen must inevitably be desired with all but sensuous desire–the thing (in Sappho's phrase) "more gold than gold."[11]

This paper is in part an exploration of how MacDonald's rendering of goodness affected Lewis's writing. It is primarily a literary study, but as one's life cannot help but affect one's writing, it will also include a good deal of biographical information on both writers. This is especially appropriate in studying the idea of goodness, for both were unmistakably Christian writers: writers who believed in a God of goodness and who wrote stories with this in mind. This belief, however, did not come easily for either. Both men struggled seriously with the problem of evil in their own experience and thinking, and both took it seriously in their writing.

This paper must therefore descend to become a study of evil before it can become a study of goodness. Whether or not good can exist without evil is a metaphysical and theological question, one that MacDonald and Lewis both addressed in their writing. But it is a literary fact that neither man could write a book without mentioning both. Take the conflict between good and evil away from their books and you have little left to call a story. The literary worlds of MacDonald and Lewis, whatever the case may be in heaven, are places full of shadows as well as light.

---

9   ANTH, p. xxxiii.

10   See Bunyan's *Pilgrim's Progress*, Part 1 (paragraph 886): 'Now I saw in my dream, that the Pilgrims were got over the Inchanted Ground, and entering in the Countrey of Beulah, whose Air was very sweet and pleasant'. See Isaiah 62.4 for 'Beulah'.

11   ANTH, p. xxxiv. Lewis quotes from a fragment of Sappho, the Greek poet (ca. 600 B.C.).

INTRODUCTION

CHAPTER 1

THE LAND OF SHADOWS

Shades of the prison-house begin to close
Upon the growing Boy
 —Wordsworth, 'Intimations of Immortality'[1]

Oh, for ten years that I may overwhelm
Myself in poesy!
 —Gavin Douglas, *Palice of Honour*[2]

My God, my God, why hast thou forsaken me?
 —Matthew 27.46[3]

Lewis said goodness was the quality in *Phantastes* that attracted him most, and so it may have been, but there is another element in *Phantastes* that no doubt attracted Lewis: consolation for pain, suffering and other kinds of evil fortune.

Phantastes is the story of Anodos's adventures in Fairy Land—that is, if one can rightly call the book a story, and if one can call what happens in it a typical adventure. *Phantastes* is more a series of images or encounters. It can be argued that the individual stories or images themselves, seemingly unrelated to each other at first glance, overshadow whatever larger story there is. Anodos is the one character who connects all the images and events, and there is important development in his character, or at least his perception, along the course of his journey. But it is the individual dream-like encounters themselves, the stories within the story, that impress themselves most on the reader's mind.

One such encounter, in chapter nineteen, sees Anodos floating by boat to an island after a rather dreary and trying period in his journey through Fairy Land.[4] On the island he encounters something common to most of MacDonald's stories: an old woman in a cottage. In *Phantastes* MacDonald uses the woman and her cottage to address the realities of pain and suffering.

After knocking on the cottage door and being invited in by 'the sweetest

1   Quoted by MacDonald in *The Hope of the Gospel* (Whitehorn: Johannesen, 1995), p. 56. First published in 1892.
2   Quoted by Lewis in *English Literature in the Sixteenth Century, Excluding Drama* (Oxford: Clarendon Press, 1954), p. 78.
3   Quoted by MacDonald in *Unspoken Sermons: First, Second, and Third Series* (Whitehorn: Johannesen, 1997), p. 110 (beneath the title in 'The Eloi', first series). First series first published in 1867.
4   See George MacDonald, *Phantastes: A Fairie Romance* (Grand Rapids: Eerdmans, 1981), chs 18 and 19. First published in 1858.

voice I had ever heard', Anodos meets the particular kind of old woman that shows up again and again in MacDonald's fiction.[5] Her face is covered with innumerable wrinkles, her skin is as ancient parchment, and her form is 'tall and spare' but 'straight as an arrow'.[6] The woman's incredibly sweet voice and 'absolutely young' eyes, along with the wrinkles, make her seem old and young at once.[7] Anodos, engulfed by 'a wondrous sense of refuge and repose' in the woman's cottage, feels 'like a boy who has got home from school, miles across the hills, through a heavy storm of wind and snow'.[8] He almost acts upon a sudden urge to spring from his chair and kiss the old woman's lips. When she finishes her cooking and brings him food, he cannot help laying his head upon her bosom and 'bursting into happy tears'.[9] The old woman responds with an embrace and gentle words of comfort.

We begin to see here another quality in *Phantastes*, something other than goodness by itself, that may very well have resonated with a seventeen-year-old Lewis. The particular misfortune of losing one's mother as a child was an evil shared by both MacDonald and Lewis. MacDonald's mother, Helen MacKay MacDonald, died of tuberculosis in 1833, when George was eight years old.[10] Lewis lost his mother, Flora Hamilton Lewis, to cancer in 1908, when Lewis was nine.[11]

How fully MacDonald or Lewis ever recovered from their mothers' deaths is something a literary study can never answer with much certainty. How much the loss of their mothers affected their writings is also debatable, but it is very certain in Lewis's case that his mother's death was the first great tragedy of his life, and it is reasonable to believe that it played some role in the development of his early atheism. Lewis himself described the effect this way: 'With my mother's death all settled happiness, all that was tranquil and reliable, disappeared from my life. There was to be much fun, many pleasures, many stabs of Joy; but no more of the old security. It was sea and islands now; the great continent had sunk like Atlantis'.[12]

And so we may begin to see a possible link between Lewis and MacDonald that Lewis never mentions. In that first letter to Arthur Greeves about *Phantastes*, Lewis dismisses the first chapter of the book: 'You must not be disappointed at the first chapter which is rather conventional faery tale

---

5   PHA, pp. 128-129.
6   PHA, p. 129.
7   PHA, p. 129.
8   PHA, p. 129.
9   PHA, p. 129.
10 See William Raeper, *George MacDonald* (Tring: Lion, 1987), p. 22.
11 See R.L. Green and W. Hooper, *C.S. Lewis: A Biography* (New York: Harcourt Brace Jovanovich, 1976), pp. 24-25.
12 SBJ, p. 21.

style'.[13] But there may have been more in that first chapter to attract Lewis than he ever admitted. In it Anodos discovers a fairy woman in an old writing desk that once belonged to his father. Like the woman in the cottage he is to meet in Fairy Land, this fairy woman is at once old and young. After informing Anodos that he will find the way into Fairy Land on the morrow, she tells him to look into her eyes. 'Eagerly I did so', Anodos recounts.[14] 'They filled me with an unknown longing. I remember somehow that my mother died when I was a baby'.[15] Anodos then looks deeper and deeper into the fairy woman's eyes, 'till they spread around me like seas, and I sank in their waters'.[16] The ecstatic vision soon vanishes from Anodos's view, as does the fairy woman from whom it came. But it leaves Anodos saying to himself, '"Surely there is such a sea somewhere!"', to which a 'low sweet voice' replies, '"In Fairy Land, Anodos"'.[17]

However attractive Lewis found MacDonald's Fairy Land itself, it is reasonable to think that a story beginning in such a way would have an additional attraction to one who had lost his mother in childhood. A fairy land full of feminine and nurturing images, which MacDonald's Fairy Land certainly is, must have had a special appeal to both MacDonald the writer and Lewis the reader.[18]

But we must not be too quick to attribute Lewis's subsequent fascination with *Phantastes*, and with MacDonald's writing in general, to the imaginative consolation it may have provided regarding the loss of their mothers. It was not even this great loss in itself, according to Lewis, that led to his atheism. The loss of his mother did shatter his childhood idea of God as one who always granted whatever one wished or prayed for. Young Lewis had prayed for his mother's recovery and, after her death, for a more miraculous recovery. He had worked himself into a faith that his prayers would indeed be answered, for prayers offered without such faith, he had been taught, wouldn't be answered.[19] His disappointment at the failure of his prayers, though, brought on no great change in his religious views, for his religious views at that time, he recalls, were scarcely religious at all. The childhood faith that was shattered by his mother's death was not faith in a loving and good God. It was not even a faith that feared God. '[God] was [...] to appear neither as Saviour nor as Judge, but merely as a magician', Lewis wrote later. 'And when He had done what was required of Him I supposed He would simply—well, go away'.[20]

13   CLET, p. 170.
14   PHA, p. 8.
15   PHA, p.8.
16   PHA, p. 8.
17   PHA, p. 8.
18   See PHA, chs 4 (p. 29), 5 (pp. 36-39), 6 (p. 42), 10 (p. 65), 15 (pp. 112-116), 19, 21 (pp. 162-165), 24 (p. 181), 25 (pp. 184-185).
19   See SBJ p. 20.
20   SBJ, p. 21.

Lewis's disbelief in a good God, if Lewis himself is to be believed at all, was more than simply a reaction to the loss of his mother. Such doubt was more accumulative, even vague, in its development. Some of the seeds of this doubt were sown by his education and reading, most of which treated religion in a strictly anthropological manner.[21] But other seeds were more general, planted even before the death of his mother. Lewis believed the causes of this pessimism began with the clumsiness of his own hands. In his fifties, he described the psychological effect caused by his clumsiness this way:

> Perhaps I had better call it a settled expectation that everything would do what you did not want it to do. Whatever you wanted to remain straight, would bend; whatever you tried to bend would fly back to the straight; all knots which you wished to be firm would come untied; all knots you wanted to untie would remain firm. It is not possible to put it into language without making it comic, and I have indeed no wish to see it (now) except as something comic. But it is perhaps just these early experiences which are so fugitive and, to an adult, so grotesque, that give the mind its earliest bias, its habitual sense of what is or is not plausible.[22]

Another possible bias for Lewis was one he would have received from his father, whom he remembers giving 'highly coloured statements' about how adult life was to be 'an unremitting struggle in which the best I could hope for was to avoid the workhouse by extreme exertion'.[23] Lewis summed up such thinking in a conversation with his best friend at Malvern College (Worcestershire): 'Term, holidays, term, holidays, till we leave school, and then work, work, work till we die'.[24] All of these factors led him to a general pessimism that by his early teens had developed into a conscious atheism after having read writers like H.G. Wells and Sir Robert Ball,[25] who had impressed on his mind 'the vastness and cold of space, the littleness of Man'.[26] He had come to a very definite belief that 'the universe was, in the main, a rather regrettable institution'.[27] He had not yet read Lucretius, but he had come to feel the force of his 'great "Argument from Undesign"':

> *Nequaquam nobis divinitus esse paratam*
> *Naturam rerum; tanta stat praedita culpa.*

Or as Lewis translates it,

---

21 See SBJ, pp. 62-63.
22 SBJ, p. 64.
23 SBJ, pp. 64, 65.
24 SBJ, p. 65.
25 Sir Robert Stawell Ball (1840-1913), astronomer and mathematician, published *The Story of the Heavens* (1886), among other works.
26 SBJ, p. 65.
27 SBJ, p. 63.

> Had God designed the world, it would not be
> A world so frail and faulty as we see.[28]

He abandoned whatever faith he may have had in God 'with no sense of loss but with the greatest relief'.[29]

The reasons behind Lewis's early atheism are most clearly stated in the opening pages of his book *The Problem of Pain* where he paraphrases what had been his argument against a good God. Besides the vast emptiness of space, there is the vast history of Earth which has been relatively free of life for millions of years, and which may go on existing for millions of years 'when life has left her'.[30] Even within the tiny period of time when life does exist, it is a never-ending strife:

> It is so arranged that all the forms of it can live only by preying upon one another. In the lower forms this process entails only death, but in the higher there appears a new quality called consciousness which enables it to be attended with pain. The creatures cause pain by being born, and live by inflicting pain, and in pain they mostly die.[31]

This pain is magnified for humans, the 'most complex' of these creatures, who by their reason are enabled to foresee their own pain.[32] Thus 'acute mental suffering' precedes much of their pain, and they foresee their own death 'while keenly desiring permanence'.[33] Their reason also magnifies their ability to inflict pain and misery:

> It also enables men by a hundred ingenious contrivances to inflict a great deal more pain than they otherwise could have done on one another and on the irrational creatures. This power they have exploited to the full. Their history is largely a record of crime, war, disease, and terror, with just sufficient happiness interposed to give them, while it lasts, an agonised apprehension of losing it, and, when it is lost, the poignant misery of remembering. Every now and then they improve their condition a little and what we call civilisation appears. But all civilisations pass away and, even while they remain, inflict peculiar sufferings of their own probably sufficient to outweigh what alleviations they may have brought to the normal pains of man.[34]

And even the best civilisations, like humanity and all else, will come to an ignoble end:

---

28 SBJ, p. 65.
29 SBJ, p. 66.
30 C.S. Lewis, *The Problem of Pain* (New York: Macmillan, 1986), p. 13. First published in 1940.
31 PP, pp. 13-14.
32 PP, p. 14.
33 PP, p. 14.
34 PP, p. 14.

> The race is doomed. Every race that comes into being in any part of the universe is doomed; for the universe, they tell us, is running down, and will sometime be a uniform infinity of homogeneous matter at a low temperature. All stories will come to nothing: all life will turn out in the end to have been a transitory and senseless contortion upon the idiotic face of infinite matter.[35]

The conclusion, he had thought, was clear. Such a universe could not have been the work of a 'benevolent and omnipotent spirit': 'Either there is no spirit behind the universe, or else a spirit indifferent to good and evil, or else an evil spirit'.[36]

This was the kind of thinking that made Lewis an atheist by the time he encountered George MacDonald's comforting old woman and protecting beech trees. MacDonald himself was not an atheist, but this did not keep him from questioning God. Where Lewis's most straightforward account of pain and suffering comes in a philosophically flavoured book, MacDonald's clearest treatment of the problem can be found in his published sermons. MacDonald, planning for a clerical career after graduating from King's College in Aberdeeen, had worked for a short time as pastor to a dissenting congregation in Arundel before turning to a life of literature, teaching, public lecturing and other jobs. MacDonald's three series of *Unspoken Sermons*, first published in 1867, 1885 and 1889, were particularly important to Lewis.[37]

In one of the sermons from the second series, entitled 'The Voice of Job', MacDonald addresses human suffering. The Old Testament book of Job, perhaps the Bible's most conspicuous treatment of pain and suffering, tells the story of a man who suffers unbelievable amounts of bad fortune. It is no surprise, then, that MacDonald turns to the book when he, as a believer in a good God, confronts the same kinds of questions that helped make Lewis an atheist, or, as MacDonald would begin the sermon, the kinds of questions that all mankind asks:

> [Job] is a man seated among the ashes, covered with loathsome boils from head to foot, scraping himself with a potsherd. Sore in body, sore in mind, sore in heart, sore in spirit, he is the instance-type of humanity in the depths of its misery—all the waves and billows of a world of adverse circumstance rolling free over its head [...] Job, I say, is *the human being*—a centre to the sickening assaults of pain, the ghastly invasions of fear: these, one time or another, I presume, threaten to overwhelm every man.[38]

---

35   PP, pp. 14-15.
36   PP, p. 15.
37   See ANTH, p. xxx: 'My own debt to this book is almost as great as one man can owe to another'.
38   US, p. 328 (paragraph 1 in 'The Voice of Job', second series).

While asserting that Job's questioning is the questioning of all humanity, MacDonald notes that his questions are particularly painful and profound because they come from the mouth of one who also believes in a God of goodness. His perplexity, as opposed to the 'stony patience' of Prometheus,[39] is that of a child who somehow believes good of his Father:

> Job is nothing of a Stoic, but bemoans himself like a child—a brave child who seems to himself to suffer wrong, and recoils with horror-struck bewilderment from the unreason of the thing. Prometheus has to do with a tyrant whom he despises, before whom therefore he endures with unbewailing unsubmission, upheld by the consciousness that he is fighting the battle of humanity against an all but all-powerful Selfishness: endurance is the only availing weapon against him, and he will endure to the ever-delayed end![40]

Job is 'more troubled than Prometheus' because he believes in a good God at the heart of reality when the reality around him seems anything but good:

> He cannot, will not believe [God] a tyrant; but, while he pleads against his dealing with himself, loves him, and looks to him as the source of life, the power and gladness of being. He dares not think God unjust, but not therefore can he allow that he has done anything to merit the treatment he is receiving at his hands. Hence is he is of necessity in profoundest perplexity, for how can the two things be reconciled?[41]

An attempt to reconcile the two things—God's goodness and the world's evil—runs deeply throughout MacDonald's writing, as indeed a belief in God's goodness and personal experience of pain and suffering co-existed throughout his own life. To MacDonald's own story we must look, then, if we are to fully appreciate and understand his literature, just as the voice of Job cannot be fully appreciated without knowing something of the story of Job. Such knowledge will also help us understand his influence on Lewis, who became an atheist, as we have noted, because he could not reconcile the idea of a good God with the realities of pain and suffering.

Early Troubles for MacDonald

George MacDonald was born and raised in rural Aberdeenshire. It is this world of his boyhood that we see so much of in his realistic novels. As Lewis remarks in his anthology, 'All that is best in his novels carries us back to that "kaleyard" world of granite and heather, of bleaching greens beside burns that look as if they flowed not with water but with stout, to the thudding of

---

39   See Shelley's *Prometheus Unbound* (1820). See also Aeschylus's *Prometheus Bound* (ca. 465 B.C.).
40   US, p. 329 (par. 2 in 'The Voice of Job', second series).
41   US, pp. 329-330 (par. 2 in 'The Voice of Job', second series).

the wooden machinery, the oatcakes, the fresh milk, the pride, the poverty, and the passionate love of hard-won learning'.[42] This harkening back to his boyhood, by the way, is something that distinguishes MacDonald from Lewis. Lewis's fiction is never set in places that remind of his Ulster upbringing. What realistic settings there are (most of his stories are set in other worlds) have to do with life at a university college.[43] The only description of his early years comes in the pages of his autobiography *Surprised by Joy*. In most all of MacDonald's novels, however, one gets a Burns-like dose of rural sincerity. The greatest instance of such sincerity in MacDonald's young life, and the inspiration for the title character of his first novel, *David Elginbrod*,[44] was his father, George MacDonald Sr. Whereas Lewis's own father left him with the impression that life was little more than never-ending strife, MacDonald's father impressed his son with an idea of what God's goodness must be like.

It is clear in his writing that MacDonald thought the father-child relationship, a heavenly father's loving relationship with the children that he creates from his own heart, was at the core of reality.[45] In *Sir Gibbie* MacDonald admits how difficult it is for some to grasp such a truth when their earthly fathers fail to show such heavenly love, as when we read of Ginevra's problems with prayer: '[she] tried to say her prayers, but found it very difficult, for, do what she might to model her slippery thoughts, she could not help, as often as she turned herself towards him, seeing God like her father, the laird'.[46] MacDonald himself had no such problem. By all accounts his relation with his father helped, rather than hindered, his belief in a good God.[47]

And just as his father's character helped to form his image of a good and loving God, so his father's example may have helped to shape his son's attitude towards evil fortune. The evidence shows that he met pain with stout courage, as when his leg had to be amputated above the knee due to tuberculosis. As his grandson Greville would record, 'He refused the stupefying dose of whisky [used before the days of chloroform] and did not even have his face covered, preferring to watch the gory proceedings'.[48] George Sr. even joked about it in years to come, claiming that '"It is a fact, sir, that I have a leg on each side of the Bogie"', and that '"The Defiance [the mail coach] runs between my legs every day"'.[49] His amputated leg had been buried in a churchyard on the other side of a road in Huntly. George Sr. also joked about his lack of a leg in order to pacify

---

42   ANTH, p. xxiii.

43   See C.S. Lewis, *That Hideous Strength: A Modern Fairy-Tale for Grown-Ups* (New York: Macmillan, 1986). First published in 1945.

44   See RAEP, p. 22.

45   See, for example, 'Abba Father!', US, pp. 275-295; and HG, p. 152.

46   George MacDonald, *Sir Gibbie* (Whitehorn: Johannesen, 1996), p. 252. First published in 1879.

47   See US, pp. 284-285 (par. 26 in 'Abba, Father!', second series); ANTH, p. xx.

48   RAEP, p. 21.

49   RAEP, p. 21.

a dangerous mob during some of the worst days of the potato famine in 1846. A rumour had spread that the MacDonalds were keeping a store of grain until already high grain prices rose even higher. He met the angry crowd in Huntly town square where protesters had amassed a bonfire with an effigy of George Sr., complete with wooden leg, thrown on top. With passions at their highest and the fire about to be lit, George Sr. noticed a blunder: "'Bide a wee, lads... afore ye set the corp alow [aflame]. Ye've fastened the timmer leg to the wrang hurdie [hip]'". And then, leaning on his walking stick, added gravely, "'Noo, ye's gang on wi' yer ploys wi' a guid conscience, an' burn yer auld freen!'".[50] The crowd's anger turned to laughter and cheers. Afterwards they followed him to his barns to see that they were as empty as everyone else's.

MacDonald's father, however, would serve as more than an example. He would do what he could to comfort his son, whose early life was filled with pain of its own. As George would later write, 'In my own childhood and boyhood my father was the refuge from all the ills of life, even sharp pain itself'.[51] MacDonald was often ill as a boy. On one occasion he was kept in bed for four months and bled from the arm.[52] He enjoyed much outdoor play and adventure but oftentimes his body could not keep up. MacDonald's entire life, as we shall see, can be characterised as what he had time to do between, or during, recurring bouts of illness.

Two of George's brothers died in childhood or infancy. The death of James MacDonald at the age of eight was blamed in part on the treatment he received from a brutal schoolteacher named Colin Stewart. One of George's other brothers, Charles Francis, remembers on more than one occasion having to be carried out of school 'in a dead faint' from the thrashings he received from Stewart's tawse. On another occasion Stewart imprisoned nineteen of his pupils in the school house after they failed to learn their Shorter Catechism— and forgot to come back for them. When Stewart learned that they escaped through a classroom window, he flogged all of them until the strap was covered in blood.[53] Stewart would eventually find his way into one of George's novels, *Alec Forbes of Howglen*, as the cruel schoolmaster Murdoch Malison, who cripples for life one of his more frail pupils during a wrathful outburst.[54]

One of George's other brothers, John, fell victim to the same malady that forced the amputation of their father's leg: tuberculosis, or 'the family accident' as it came to be called.[55] The disease claimed both John and their mother Helen. In *Ranald Bannerman's Boyhood*, a book inspired by George's own boyhood, Ranald remembers his mother bending over a baby before

---

50 RAEP, pp. 21-22 (Raeper's brackets).
51 US, p. 284 (par. 26 in 'Abba Father!', second series).
52 See RAEP, p. 29. Situations like this were not uncommon in MacDonald's time.
53 See RAEP, p. 30.
54 See pp 163-164, 222 below
55 RAEP, p. 25.

falling asleep. After waking, Ranald sees that both mother and the cradle have disappeared. This probably describes George's last memories of his mother and brother. His mother, unlike his father, is someone MacDonald hardly ever mentions, at least explicitly, in his writing. The closest he gets, perhaps, is when he writes of Ranald remembering his mother holding his head to her bosom and the comfort she provided, as well as having to stay outside all day so his ailing mother could enjoy a quiet house.[56]

Whatever the effect of MacDonald's mother's death, it is most likely that his early acquaintance with death—his two brothers and mother, as well as the great funeral of a duke that he witnessed and counted as one of his first memories[57]—helped cultivate in young George's mind something of a preoccupation with death.[58] It is certainly a preoccupation of his fiction. One would be hard-pressed to find a more frequently recurring theme in all of MacDonald's writing. A predictable example can be found in *The Portent*, a spooky story full of uncanny images. As the hero Duncan Campbell remembers from his boyhood:

> so far from being terrified by these imaginings [of ghosts and coffins], I used to delight in them; and in the long winter evenings, when I did not happen to have any book that interested me sufficiently, I used even to look forward with expectation to the hour when, laying myself straight upon my back, as if my bed were my coffin, I could call up from underground all who had passed away, and see how they fared, yea, what progress they had made towards final dissolution of form.[59]

Morbid images, coffins in particular, show up nearly as much in his more realistic novels, as in *Annals of a Quiet Neighbourhood*. At one point a new parson in a parish makes his first visit to the carpentry shop of Thomas Weir. Their conversation quickly reveals Weir to be an atheist, and a brief discussion of the world's evils follows after Walton, the parson, takes notice of what the joiner happens to be working on at the moment: a coffin for his recently deceased sister. The conversation reveals how Walton the character and MacDonald the author both had empathy, even a measure of sympathy, with a certain kind of atheism. When the carpenter remarks that the world is not "'such a good job'",

---

56   See RAEP, p. 28; and George MacDonald, *Ranald Bannerman's Boyhood* (Whitehorn: Johannesen, 1993), pp. 16-19. *Bannerman* first published in 1871.

57   See RAEP, p. 25, for the funeral of Duke Gordon.

58   As indeed many of his time were, though 'preoccupation' may not be the right word since the inescapability of death was then much more a fact of daily living. We, in the age of improved medicine, hygiene and life-spans may in comparison be described as 'preoccupied' with avoiding the subject of death, since technology has made it possible to put it off for longer.

59   George MacDonald, *The Portent and Other Stories* (Whitehorn: Johannesen, 1994) pp. 8-9.

Walton responds by referring to the coffin Weir is working on: "'Neither is that coffin'".[60] When a puzzled Weir retorts that the coffin isn't finished yet, the parson explains his meaning: "'You thought I was hasty in my judgement of your coffin; whereas I only said of it knowingly what you said of the world thoughtlessly. How do you know that the world is finished anymore than your coffin? And how dare you then say that it is a bad job?'".[61]

This idea of the world as a work in progress, the trust that God works good out of tragedy, is something that MacDonald returns to again and again in his stories. But also characteristic is the honesty with which he treats the argument. The characters of Walton and Weir can indeed be seen as an allegorical representation of the argument that must have taken place in MacDonald's own mind, with Walton representing the MacDonald who trusts in spite of appearances to the contrary, and Weir representing the MacDonald whose deep acquaintance with grief made it all but impossible to trust in any overarching Goodness. This acknowledgement of two sides of the argument is seen plainly when Weir responds to Walton's comparison of the world to his unfinished coffin: "'That's supposing [...] that the Lord did make the world. For my part, I am half of a mind that the Lord didn't make it at all'".[62] Instead of arguing further with Weir about whether God made the world, Walton, perhaps reflecting MacDonald's own divided mind, responds thus: "'I am very glad to hear you say so'".[63] And after a bewildered pause from Weir, he explains:

> "Of course it seems to me better that you should not believe God had done a thing, than that you should believe He had not done it well!"
>
> "Ah! I see, sir. Then you will allow there is some room for doubting whether He made the world at all?"
>
> "Yes; for I do not think an honest man, as you seem to me to be, would be able to doubt without any room whatever. That would be only for a fool. But it is just possible, as we are not perfectly good ourselves [...] it's just possible that things may be too good for us to do them the justice of believing in them."
>
> "But there are things, you must allow, so plainly wrong!"
>
> "So much so, both in the world and in myself, that it would be to me torturing despair to believe that God did not make the world; for then, how would it ever be put right? Therefore I prefer the theory that He has not done making it yet."[64]

MacDonald, like his character Walton, continued throughout his life,

60   George MacDonald, *Annals of a Quiet Neighbourhood* (Whitehorn: Johannesen, 1995) p. 44. *Annals* first published in 1867.

61   AQN, p. 44.

62   AQN, p. 45.

63   AQN, p. 45.

64   AQN, pp. 45–46.

or at least throughout the entirety of his writing, to prefer the idea of a good God who would right wrongs to the idea of no God at all. If at first glance the wrong things made him question the existence of a good God, a second thought seemed to demand a good God to purge from the world things "'so plainly wrong'".

Early Troubles for Lewis

Things wrong with the world reminds us of Lewis's atheism, which, once achieved, lasted until he was thirty years old.[65] As we have learned, his own early experience with death and other ill fortune, along with his intellectual consideration of the state of the universe, led him to disbelieve in a good God. Like MacDonald, Lewis witnessed much cruelty during his school days, first at Wynyard School in Hertfordshire where he was sent in 1908 after the death of his mother.[66] He speaks of it in his autobiography in the chapter entitled 'Concentration Camp'. The school's headmaster, the Reverend Robert Capron, had a history of brutality toward his students and was most likely going mad during Lewis's time at Wynyard.[67] He was in fact certified insane and died two years after the school folded in 1910. Lewis remembered one 'dear, honest, hard-working, friendly, healthily pious' classmate of his being 'flogged incessantly' by "'Oldie'" simply because he was the son of a dentist and, to Oldie's ear, had a vulgar accent: 'I have seen Oldie make that child bend down at one end of the schoolroom and then take a run of the room's length at each stroke'.[68]

But despite Oldie's cruelty and mind-numbing, substandard education (with the exception of geometry), Lewis thought that Wynyard ultimately did him little harm. 'We had many pleasant hours alone together, we five remaining boarders', he writes.[69] Life at a swiftly declining boarding school, like life at home with his brother after their mother's death, still had its bright spots. He and his fellows banded together under the shadow of their schoolmaster, going for long walks and enjoying good conversation whenever they could: 'At home, the bad times had drawn my brother and me closer together; here, where times were always bad, the fear and hatred of Oldie had something of the same effect upon us all [...] We stood foursquare against the common enemy'.[70]

---

65 Lewis converted to theism in the Trinity Term of 1929, and to Christianity in September of 1931. See SBJ, chs 14 and 15; and CSL, chp. 4.
66 See CSL, p. 27.
67 From 1908-1910. See CSL, p. 26.
68 SBJ, p. 27.
69 SBJ, p. 31.
70 SBJ, p. 32.

It was during his time at Wynyard, in fact, that Lewis became, for a brief time, a practising believer. His move to atheism would be delayed by a fear he developed while attending the Anglo-Catholic church at Wynyard. According to Lewis, he at that age had developed no real skepticism, in spite of the general feeling of his that everything would work opposite to how one wanted it to. As we have learned, it was only the God that granted one's every wish that Lewis had lost belief in after his mother's death. What Lewis was exposed to at the high Anglican church at Wynyard was a different sort of God, one who had power over the destiny of his soul. By hearing 'the doctrines of Christianity taught by men who obviously believed them', Lewis remembers having a belief brought to life in him that, with no developed skepticism, he would have already admitted: that there was a hell and that his soul needed saving.[71] As he recalls, 'I feared for my soul; especially on certain blazing moonlit nights in that curtainless dormitory—how the sound of other boys breathing in their sleep comes back! The effect, so far as I can judge, was entirely good. I began seriously to pray and to read my Bible and to attempt to obey my conscience'.[72]

Lewis's situation, and his devotion, began to change after his father sent him to Cherbourg, a preparatory school at Malvern College near Worcester.[73] It was here that he remembers 'ceasing to become a Christian'.[74] One 'conscious cause' which Lewis linked to his growing apostasy was the matron of Cherbourg, Miss G.E. Cowie, who unintentionally contributed with her interest in several varieties of the 'Anglo-American Occultist tradition'.[75] Though Lewis had always been interested in reading about strange creatures and other worlds, he had never, before meeting Miss Cowie, actually believed in any kinds of spirits other than God and men.[76] But with Cowie's mere introduction of the subject, he began to think how 'there might be real marvels all about us, that the visible world might be only a curtain to conceal huge realms uncharted by my very simple theology'.[77] This new thinking, Lewis remembered, 'started in me something with which, on and off, I have had plenty of trouble since—the desire for the preternatural, simply as such, the passion for the Occult'.[78] And quite apart from the mere preoccupation with the preternatural, it was the speculative nature of the newly introduced Occultism that helped lead Lewis away from his former belief:

---

71 SBJ, p. 33.
72 SBJ, p. 34.
73 See CSL, p. 29.
74 SBJ, p. 58.
75 SBJ, p. 59 (Lewis mentions Theosophy, Resicrucianism and Spiritualism).
76 See SBJ, p. 59.
77 SBJ, p. 60.
78 SBJ, p. 60.

I was soon (in the famous words) "altering 'I believe' to 'one does feel'". And oh, the relief of it! Those moonlit nights in the dormitory at [Wynyard] faded far away. From the tyrannous noon of revelation I passed into the cool evening of Higher Thought, where there was nothing to be obeyed, and nothing to be believed except what was either comforting or exciting.[79]

Lewis remembers that he was at this point in his life very anxious to escape his religion anyway, and writes how Miss Cowie's introduction of the Occult provided a release that he unconsciously, but desperately, welcomed. It was a release not only from obedience and religious belief, but also from his own hyper-active conscience, or what Lewis himself called 'the false conscience'.[80] For Lewis it meant a constant and excruciating self-examination during and after prayer. The faith that came to Lewis at Wynyard had become a burden of forced feeling: 'It had [...] brought me to such a pass that the nightly torment projected its gloom over the whole evening, and I dreaded bedtime as if I were a chronic sufferer from insomnia. Had I pursued the same road much further I think I should have gone mad'.[81]

Instead of going mad, Lewis became an atheist. By the time he left Cherbourg in the summer of 1913 his faith was in ruins. It would remain so for the next fifteen years. During these years Lewis saw in suffering, his and others', a continuing basis for disbelief in a good and powerful God. As he put it in the *Problem of Pain*, 'If God were good, He would wish to make His creatures perfectly happy, and if God were almighty, He would be able to do what He wished. But the creatures are not happy. Therefore God either lacks goodness, or power, or both'.[82]

Lewis left public schools altogether when he was handed over to William T. Kirkpatrick, a former headmaster of Lewis's father who was now a private tutor. The two and a half years that Lewis was to spend with Kirkpatrick in Great Bookham, Surrey, were perhaps the most peaceful he ever enjoyed. Lewis would thrive under 'The Great Knock', a man who hated small talk and loved argument. If George MacDonald can be said to have had the greatest impact on Lewis's imagination, Kirkpatrick served as the greatest influence on his mind. 'If ever a man came near to being a purely logical entity, that man was Kirk', Lewis wrote of his teacher: 'The idea that human beings should exercise their vocal organs for any purpose except that of communicating or discovering truth was to him preposterous. The most casual remark was taken as a summon to disputation'.[83]

---

79   SBJ, p. 60.
80   SBJ, p. 61. Compare to the 'prattler' of George Herbert's poem 'Conscience' in *The Temple*.
81   SBJ, pp. 61-62.
82   PP, p. 26.
83   SBJ, pp. 135-136.

Like young Lewis, Kirkpatrick was an atheist who could explain exactly why he was an atheist. A '"Rationalist" of the old, high and dry nineteenth-century type',[84] Kirkpatrick subscribed to the anthropological and pessimistic atheism found in Frazer's *The Golden Bough*[85] and the writings of Schopenhauer. Although the two never argued about religion directly, 'The Great Knock' did help deepen Lewis's atheism, or at least his ability to articulate it: 'What I got there was merely fresh ammunition for the defence of a position already chosen', Lewis remembered. 'Even this I got indirectly from the tone of his mind or independently from reading his books. He never attacked religion in my presence'.[86]

At the same time that Lewis's mind was being sharpened by Kirkpatrick, his imagination was first exposed to George MacDonald—through that copy of *Phantastes* he picked up in October 1915 at the Leatherhead train station in Surrey.[87] Lewis's taste for romantic fantasy had never waned, even as his mind was increasingly filled with doubts about God. At Cherbourg Miss Cowie's interest in the preternatural had first introduced Lewis to the notion that various spirits could actually exist around him. But Lewis's taste for the fantastic had began much earlier. Even his love of nature had always been highly romantic. As a boy, and later as an adult, Lewis's instinctive interest was always for those features in nature that astonished: 'I attended almost entirely to what I thought awe-inspiring, or wild, or eerie, and above all to distance. Hence mountains and clouds were my special delight; the sky was, and still is, to me one of the principal elements in my landscape'.[88] Even when his gaze could be drawn down to earth, it was still only the romantic that caught his eye, as the views from the Holywood Hills just outside Belfast attracted him as a young boy.[89] Only after he met Arthur Greeves, just months before being sent to Kirkpatrick in 1914, did Lewis begin to appreciate the 'Homely' in nature or in literature.[90] What he and Arthur liked best was when the homely and the romantic 'met in sharp juxtaposition':

> if a little kitchen garden ran steeply up a narrowing enclave of fertile ground surrounded by outcroppings and furze, or some shivering quarry pool under a moonrise could be seen on our left, and on our right the smoking chimney and lamp-lit window of a cottage that was just settling down for the night.[91]

---

84 SBJ, p. 139.
85 Sir James George Frazer, *The Golden Bough: A Study in Magic and Religion* (1922).
86 SBJ, p. 140.
87 See p. 1, above.
88 SBJ, p. 152.
89 See SBJ, pp. 152-157.
90 SBJ, p. 158.
91 SBJ, p. 158.

But this was Lewis and Greeves together.[92] Alone, Lewis's tastes were utterly romantic. Only when he came across the world of *Phantastes* did Lewis, according to his own recollection, find the homely and the romantic fully combined, not simply juxtaposed. It was not merely the romantic in contrast to the ordinary that Lewis encountered in MacDonald. For the first time Lewis found that ordinary things themselves became romantic:

> For the first time the song of the sirens sounded like the voice of my mother or my nurse. Here were old wives' tales; there was nothing to be proud of in enjoying them. It was as though the voice which had called to me from the world's end was now speaking at my side. It was with me in the room, or in my own body, or behind me. If it had once eluded me by its distance, it now eluded me by proximity—something too near to see, too plain to be understood, on this side of knowledge.[93]

To tell more of what Lewis found in *Phantastes* would be to describe his idea of 'Joy'—the Joy he yearned for after his mother's death but only received in occasional fits or 'stabs'.[94] More will be said in a later chapter about this joy, and how it relates to MacDonald's influence.[95] For now it will be enough to say that the Joy Lewis found in *Phantastes* was unlike any Joy he remembered encountering in all his previous reading. This new quality of Joy is described by Lewis in *Surprised by Joy* as a 'bright shadow' and identified as 'Holiness'.[96] If Lewis's memory, and interpretation of that memory, can be trusted, it seems that his imagination was seized at this time by what his conscious mind rejected: the goodness of God. 'My imagination was, in a certain sense, baptized', he writes, 'the rest of me, not unnaturally, took longer'.[97]

The rest of Lewis would soon find itself on the front lines in the First World War, finding little evidence, it would seem, of any bright shadow. He had begun his first term at University College, Oxford, in April of 1917. He was immediately enchanted and at home amid the towers, spires, libraries and book shops of Oxford, but all this was soon interrupted by the war. After four months of training Lewis arrived in France, on the front lines in the Somme Valley, on 29 November 1917, his nineteenth birthday.[98] Lewis fell ill with trench fever, or Pyrexia, in February of 1918 and was sent for three weeks to recover at a hospital at Le Treport.[99] He returned to the trenches three weeks

---

92 Lewis and Greeves would remain friends and correspondents until Lewis's death in 1963.

93 SBJ, pp. 179-180.

94 SBJ, p. 21. See p. 5, above.

95 See below, chp. 6.

96 SBJ, p. 181.

97 SBJ, p. 181.

98 See CSL, p. 53.

99 During which time he became acquainted with the writing of G.K. Chesterton,

before Germany launched its great offensive on 21 March. Lewis was at or near the front line when the Germans attacked a second time, from 9 to 25 April.[100] Lewis was wounded on 15 April, on Mount Berenchow, when an errant English shell exploded near him, striking him in the arm and chest. He spent most of the remaining months of the war recuperating, returning to duty only a few weeks before the 11 November armistice. He would return to study at Oxford in January of 1919.[101]

In his autobiography Lewis downplays his war experience, claiming that it had little or nothing to do with the story he was trying to tell in that book.[102] Lewis, indeed, may have had good reasons to downplay it. *Surprised by Joy* is largely the story of his coming to find God, or as Lewis might put it, God's coming to find him. His war experience (apart from the reading he did while convalescing) may have had relatively little bearing on this story. Another reason for not over-emphasising the war was that so many more men experienced so much more of it than he did.[103]

But he did say something of it. He does not present his days in the trenches as uninterrupted gloom; he goes into some detail about the camaraderie and friendship that developed between his fellow soldiers, as well as a new respect and admiration for the 'ordinary' men that served alongside more publicly educated soldiers like himself.[104] As for the war itself, what remained most distinct in his memory was not so much the actual fighting, but the waiting to fight: 'Through the winter, weariness and water were our chief enemies. I have gone to sleep marching and woken again and found myself marching still. One walked in the trenches in thigh gum boots with water above the knee; one remembers the icy stream welling up inside the boot when you punctured it on concealed barbed wire'.[105] The horrors of fighting itself Lewis found more difficult to recall:

> the frights, the cold, the smell of H.E. [High Explosive], the horribly smashed men still moving like half-crushed beetles, the sitting or standing corpses, the landscape of sheer earth without a blade of grass, the boots worn day and night till they seemed to grow to your feet—all this shows rarely and faintly in memory. It is too cut off from the rest of my experience and often seems to have happened to someone else.[106]

---

another Christian author who would come to affect him greatly. See SBJ, p. 190.

100 See CSL, p. 54.

101 See CSL, p. 55.

102 See SBJ, p. 197.

103 'The war itself has been so often described by those who saw more of it than I that I shall here say little of it' (SBJ, p. 195).

104 See SBJ, pp. 191-196.

105 SBJ, p. 195.

106 SBJ, p. 196.

A Spirit in Bondage

Lewis's war experience, however much of it may have faded from his memory by the time he wrote *Surprised by Joy*, did show up in his first published work. He was, in fact, a war poet. A poem from that first work, *Spirits in Bondage*, was included in a quarterly for disabled soldiers called *Reveille*. The February 1919 edition in which Lewis's 'Death in Battle' appeared also included work from other soldier-poets: Siegfried Sassoon and Robert Graves. But one would be mistaken to call Lewis at this time a 'war poet' in the same sense as Sassoon or Graves, for *Spirits in Bondage* is not primarily war poetry. Lewis's war experience may have indeed had a significant influence on the work: in its themes and as source material for some of its imagery. But only two of the forty poems in the work[107] are specifically about war. And Lewis, in fact, began writing the poems in 1915 while on Easter holiday in Belfast, soon to go back to Kirkpatrick's tutoring.[108] The last poems were written by Lewis in 1918 to replace earlier poems that the publisher, William Heinemann, had wanted to omit.[109] As Lewis said at the time, the poems may have had some 'indirect bearing' on the war,[110] but they represent far more than a soldier's reaction to the First World War, or any war.

What *Spirits in Bondage* represents is the state of Lewis's thinking and imagination from the years 1915 to 1918. If it is a war poem at all, it is a poem that reflects the war within Lewis himself: between his thinking and his imagination. His reason, sharpened by Kirkpatrick, at this time in his life was telling him, as we have seen, that a good God could not have created a world with so much pain, suffering and unhappiness in it. His experience of the war in many ways probably cemented this in his mind, as Kirkpatrick and his books had done at Great Bookham. But his imagination, which had been romantic for his entire life and which had recently come into contact with George MacDonald's books, somehow kept longing and hoping, even if his reason told him it was all in vain. And so we see in *Spirits in Bondage* moments of impassioned blasphemy against the evil maker of an evil world. But at least as strong are the images of beauty and sublimity that Lewis creates—images that stand as a reaction to, or an escape from, the things his reason told him were true.

The first poem of the work, 'Satan Speaks', quickly identifies malevolent Nature as the inescapable and cruel villain who lords over all who dare imagine a better world:

> I am Nature, the Mighty Mother,
> I am the law: ye have none other.

107 'French Nocturne' (II), and 'Death in Battle' (XL).
108 See CLET, p. 115.
109 See CLET, p. 397.
110 CLET, p. 406.

I am the flower and the dewdrop fresh,
I am the lust in your itching flesh.

I am the battle's filth and strain,
I am the widow's empty pain.

I am the sea to smother your breath,
I am the bomb, the falling death.[111]

And in the fifth set of couplets, satanic Nature declares which side she takes, or which side she is, in the conflict between reason and imagination:

I am the fact and crushing reason
To thwart your fantasy's new-born treason.[112]

It may very well be that the phrase 'your fantasy's new-born treason' refers directly to the challenge that George MacDonald's *Phantastes* presented to Lewis's reasoned atheism. If some read Lewis's later recollections of the impact of *Phantastes* with suspicion, thinking that he overemphasised the effect of MacDonald's book in light of his conversion to Christianity, here is, perhaps, evidence to the contrary. Lewis, after all, first read *Phantastes* in 1916, during the same period of time in which he was composing the poems that would become *Spirits in Bondage*. In this sense the effect of *Phantastes* on Lewis would be 'new-born'. And the images and tone of MacDonald's book, the 'bright shadow' that Lewis found there, would by any reading present a sort of 'treason' (if only an imaginary challenge) to Lewis's atheism. Even if Lewis didn't recognise at the time that his imagination had been 'baptised', it seems likely, by the example of *Spirits in Bondage*, that he was acutely aware of a new tension presented by the faery world of *Phantastes*. Even if Lewis's 'crushing reason' still made an atheist of him, it was an atheism made much less comfortable by what may have indeed been his *Phantastes*'s 'new-born treason'.

The proof of MacDonald's influence on *Spirits in Bondage*, however, need not be limited to just one phrase. Indeed, it is the development of the poems as a whole work that suggests such an interpretation of such a phrase, for the poems ultimately go far beyond mere blasphemy. There are the first twenty-one poems which make up Part I, 'The Prison House', which most clearly depicts the struggle between longing spirit and evil nature. Then comes a brief moment of 'Hesitation' in the three poems that make up the middle section. The last sixteen poems make up Part III, 'The Escape', which, as we shall see, represent a thoroughly romantic escape into spirit, as far away as possible from the tension introduced in Part I. This, of course, doesn't mean that Lewis believed in a world of peace and harmony that one could actually escape into.

---

111 C.S. Lewis, *Spirits in Bondage: A Cycle of Lyrics* (San Diego: Harcourt Brace and Company, 1984), p. 3 (I). First published in 1919 under the pseudonym of Clive Hamilton (his own Christian name combined with his mother's maiden name).
112 SIB, p. 3 (I).

But it may indeed mean that Lewis wanted escape from what his reason told him was true. If he could not do so in fact, he would write a collection of poems that did.

Lewis's original title for the poems, 'Spirits in Prison',[113] reflects this yearning for escape. It is probably an allusion to 1 Peter (3.19) of the New Testament where Christ, after his death and resurrection, is described as preaching 'unto the spirits in prison', or as in the common interpretation, to spirits in hell.[114] Lewis's prologue makes it clear that he intends to do something similar by preaching to prisoners of a hellish earth. Likening himself to Phoenicians of old who sing of legends and lore on their voyage to the Tin Isles,[115] Lewis explains his poems thus:

> So in mighty deeps alone on the chainless breezes blown
> In my coracle of verses I will sing of lands unknown,
> Flying from the scarlet city where a Lord that knows no pity
> Mocks the broken people praying round his iron throne,
> —Sing about the Hidden Country fresh and full of quiet green.
> Sailing over seas uncharted to a port that none has seen.[116]

This 'Hidden Country' was in part inspired by a passage from Andrew Lang,[117] which Lewis quotes before the prologue:

> The land where I shall never be
> The love that I shall never see.[118]

It is this hidden or unknown country to which Lewis's poem attempts to escape, even if Lewis the poet didn't actually believe in it. He would still do for his readers, and for himself, what the Phoenician singers did for the 'rowers down below' who toil 'at the stroke and feather through the wet and weary weather'.[119] He would sing of the 'quiet green' of the 'Hidden Country' until his listeners 'forgot their burden in the measure of a song'.[120]

But before the escape comes the strife of Part I, 'The Prison House', in which dreams of other worlds come in sharp conflict with a hostile reality. In

113 The proposed title was deemed too close to *A Spirit in Prison* (1908) by Robert Hichens. See CSL, pp. 58-59; CLET, pp. 399-400 (18 Sept. 1918).
114 See also Milton, *Paradise Lost*, 1.658.
115 The ancient Phoenician and Roman name for the British Isles, named so for Cornwall's rich deposits of tin ore. See Herodotus's *History* (3.115).
116 SIB, pp. xli-xlii.
117 Lewis quotes from memory the following lines from Lang's *History of English Literature* (1912): 'The love whom I shall never meet / The land where I shall never be'. See CLET, pp. 283-284; and CSL, p. 48.
118 SIB, p. ix.
119 SIB, p. xli.
120 SIB, pp. xli-xlii.

'French Nocturne (Monchy-Le Preux)',[121] for example, the narrator looks out over a battle ground, but not only a battle ground. Just as *Spirits in Bondage* is not primarily a poem about war, so 'French Nocturne' is not content to describe the trenches or the ruined villages. Added to the picture of war on the ground is the sky of hope and dreaming. In this one poem we see Lewis's imagination and his reason coming into bloody conflict along the line of the visible horizon. Below are the 'long leagues' of trenches 'on either hand', the facts of earth that Lewis's reason interpreted as proof of no good God.[122] But above is the sky with its moon that had always transfixed Lewis's yearning eyes. And so the 'gross line' of trenches 'drinks in' from the sky 'the frosty silences divine', with 'the pale, green moon [...] riding overhead'.[123] The earth, however, is not content to drink from the sky. It must also eat:

> The jaws of a sacked village, stark and grim,
> Out on the ridge have swallowed up the sun,
> And in one angry streak his blood has run
> To left and right along the horizon dim.[124]

But even with a wounded sky, the narrator does not give up hope. He suddenly sees a 'buzzing plane' flying, it seems, 'straight into the moon'.[125] Perhaps someone has escaped the world's ugly facts by flying to the moon:

> Lo! Where he steers
> Across the pallid globe and surely nears
> In that white land some harbour of dear dreams![126]

But no. A moment's thought on his situation brings the narrator back down to earth. The brutality in and around him are too much:

> False mocking fancy! Once I too could dream,
> Who now can only see with vulgar eye
> That he's no nearer to the moon than I
> And she's a stone that catches the sun's beam.
>
> What call have I to dream of anything?
> I am a wolf. Back to the world again,
> And speech of fellow-brutes that once were men
> Our throats can bark for slaughter: cannot sing.[127]

This is, however, only the first of many battles that make up the war in the first part of *Spirits in Bondage*. Lewis's imaginative yearning, however

---

121 Lewis, if he did not write the poem in Monchy-Le-Preux, certainly wrote about the place. He was stationed there for a time in 1917. See CLET, p. 346.
122 SIB, p. 4 (II).
123 SIB, p. 4 (II).
124 SIB, p. 4 (II).
125 SIB, p. 4 (II).
126 SIB, p. 4 (II).
127 SIB, p. 4 (II).

seriously beaten, never quite dies. Or if it does die, rises again, as in 'Victory', which opens with a proclamation that best-loved legends have died. Roland, Cuchulain, Triton, 'Helen's eyes', 'Iseult's lips', faerie people, dryads and King Arthur are all declared missing.[128] 'The ancient songs', says the narrator, have all withered 'as the grass' and 'waste as doth a garment waxen old'.[129] 'All poets have been fools', he says, 'who thought to mould / A monument more durable than brass'.[130] But the death of so many legends does not therefore kill the longing of man's spirit:

> For these [legends] decay: but not for that decays
> The yearning, high, rebellious spirit of man
> That never rested yet since life began
> From striving with red Nature and her ways.[131]

And so the yearning imagination of man's spirit—Lewis's Prometheus—continues to war with the cruel facts of Nature and reason:

> Though often bruised, oft broken by the rod,
> Yet, like the phoenix, from each fiery bed
> Higher the stricken spirit lifts its head
> And higher—till the beast become a god.[132]

But a few poems later, in 'Apology', the poet turns from the nobleness of man's yearning spirit back to the sort of pessimism that shuns day-dreaming. Here Desponia answers men who ask why she speaks of 'nothing glad nor noble' to 'lighten hearts beneath this present curse' and 'build a heaven of dreams' in 'real hell'.[133] In short, Lewis brings into question the original purpose of the poems as stated in the prologue, with 'Apology' acting as a brief argument against all romantic literature. Desponia's answer against romantic wistfulness begins with noting the torture that such yearning brings upon earth-bound creatures:

> "There were no greater grief than to recall,
> Down in the rotting grave where the lithe worms crawl,
> Green fields above that smiled so sweet to us."[134]

All the songs of heroes past are vain because they disappoint. The glory of the tales does not square with the reality we know. The romance of our imaginations does not square with the reason by which we view a cruel world. Far better, says Desponia, to get used to the real world rather than to keep

---

128 SIB, p. 7 (IV).
129 SIB, p. 7 (IV).
130 SIB, p. 7 (IV).
131 SIB, p. 7 (IV). See Tennyson, *In Memoriam A.H.H.*, 56.15.
132 SIB, p. 8 (IV).
133 SIB, p. 12 (VII).
134 SIB, p. 12 (VII).

singing when there's nothing to sing about:

> All these were rosy visions of the night,
> The loveliness and wisdom feigned of old.
> But now we wake. The East is pale and cold,
> No hope is in the dawn, and no delight.[135]

This pessimism continues in the bitterly blasphemous 'Ode for New Year's Day' in which 'sons of pain' are encouraged to curse the hour of their birth, 'For sorrow on sorrow is coming wherein all flesh has part'. In no other place, perhaps, does Lewis's atheism more fully manifest itself than here. If there is a God who created the universe, he cares nothing about what humans call goodness and deserves only our curse:

> It's truth they tell, Desponia, none hears the heart's complaining
> For Nature will not pity, nor the red God lend an ear.
> Yet I too have been mad in the hour of bitter paining
> And lifted up my voice to God, thinking that he could hear
> The curse wherewith I cursed Him because the Good was dead.
> But Lo! I am grown wiser, knowing that our own hearts
> Have made a phantom called the Good, while a few years have sped
> Over a little planet.[136]

The only thing left for inhabitants of such a universe is to imagine the impossible:

> Ah, sweet, if a man could cheat him! If you could flee away
> Into some other country beyond the rosy West,
> To hide in the deep forests and be for ever at rest
> From the rankling hate of God and the outworn world's decay![137]

Even if there is a God of goodness, the god of this world tells us in a second poem entitled 'Satan Speaks' that he will never come. All creatures living in his world will remain in tortured darkness, hearing only stories of a light that they will never see:

> But far away
> He walks the airy fields of endless day,
> And my rebellious sons have called Him long
> And vainly called. My order still is strong
> And like to me nor second none I know.[138]

The God of goodness and light, Satan declares, will always be 'Dreams dreamed in vain, a never-filled desire'.[139]

---

135 SIB, p. 12 (VII).
136 SIB, pp. 14-15 (VIII).
137 SIB, p. 15 (VIII).
138 SIB, p. 22 (XIII).
139 SIB, p. 22 (XIII).

But however true Satan's words may be, he is heard from less and less throughout the rest of Lewis's work. The second time that 'Satan Speaks' is indeed the last time that we hear directly from him. Even in the remaining eight poems of the first section, we hear less of the strain between the dark prison of fact and the dreams of light and goodness. Lewis, before the third section of 'Escape', is already beginning to turn his back on what Satan and the facts say, as he clearly does in the poem entitled 'The Philosopher'. Here the poet asks who shall lead the escape from the facts of known reality. It is certainly not the old man of reason shut up in his tower of books, blind to any delight and joy that could be. Such a one as this, a philosopher imprisoned by the bare facts, is surely not the one to lead an escape into something better. The only one who can lead to the unknown country of joy and delight is one who has not lost his imagination. As he has done throughout the first section of *Spirits in Bondage*, Lewis makes a sharp contrast between reason and romance. It is now reason that is described as the traitor and enemy, as 'fantasy' was identified earlier as traitor to reason:

> But let our seer be young and kind
> And fresh and beautiful of show,
> And taken ere the lustyhead
> And rapture of his youth be dead,
> Ere the gnawing, peasant reason
> School him over-deep in treason[140]

As spirit and nature were wholly opposed to each other in the earlier poems, so here is no reconciliation between reason and romance ever attempted. One must choose: reason or romance, the darkness of fact or the light of imagination. Much of the rest of *Spirits in Bondage* may be described best as the poet becoming drunk with an abundance of romantic imagery. He is very tipsy indeed by the end of the first section, which ends with 'The Autumn Morning'. There is 'ghostly mist' hanging from tree to tree during a 'pale autumn dawn'. There are 'wizard things' and 'magic dances dread' drifting through the 'middle air' over the poet's head.[141] Dryads, elves, fauns and leprechauns all make an appearance as the poet walks alone at the seashore, in the 'haunted fen' or through the 'mountain glen'.[142]

There is, of course, the middle section of three poems—'Hesitation'—during which the poet wavers. But Lewis's desire for the Other cannot be put to rest. However much he envies those who lack such a desire,[143] his imagination must go on with its yearning, despite the facts. In the last third of *Spirits in Bondage*, all hesitation is over. 'The Escape' is on. In the first poem of

140 SIB, p. 28 (XVI).
141 SIB, p. 34 (XXI).
142 SIB, pp. 34-35 (XXI).
143 See 'In Praise of Common People' (XXIV).

the section, a group of pilgrims, despite present hardships and losing several members to death, sing of how they have no rest and cannot turn 'Back to the world and all her fruitless pain'.[144] The pilgrims seek a haven of peace and tranquillity where there dwells, amidst 'flowery copses' and 'crooning' birds, 'ever living queens that grow not old' and 'poets wise in robes of faerie gold'.[145] To gardens of sweet whispering the pilgrims must go to 'sleep and play / For ever and for ever and a day'.[146]

And so the escape continues throughout the remainder of *Spirits*. There is the 'happy isle, / Where eternal meadows smile' in the poem entitled 'Song'.[147] Or the Yeats-like[148] 'Night' in which the escape is achieved by the spell of 'the windy folk' who dwell in the 'scented gloom divine' of a Druid wood.[149] Even when Lewis draws from his own personal experience, as in 'Oxford', the theme is still escape, as in these lines:

> It is well that there are places of peace
> And discipline and dreaming and desire,
> Lest we forget our heritage and cease
> The Spirit's work—to hunger and aspire[150]

In 'Hymn', boys' voices sing of a Manichean retaliation against matter:

> All the wizardries of God—
> Slaying matter with a nod,
> Charming spirits with his rod[151]

Dreamy talk of the horizon and of things above or beyond it is found in poems entitled 'The Roads', 'Hesperus' and 'The Star Bath'.[152]

But in 'World's Desire',[153] the penultimate poem of *Spirits*, a tension returns. A castle tower is situated on the other side of a forest and a 'barren, sharp' ravine that echoes 'to the crushing roar and thunder of a mighty river / Ringing down a cataract'.[154] The sound of the great river in the rugged ravine frightens the grey wolves and drowns out the call of birds. So, too, is 'the

---

144 SIB, p. 47 (XXV).
145 SIB, p. 48 (XXV).
146 SIB, p. 48 (XXV). Compare Tennyson's 'The Lotos-eaters'.
147 SIB, p. 50 (XXVI).
148 Early Yeats, that is.
149 SIB, p. 55 (XXIX).
150 SIB, p. 57 (XXX).
151 SIB, p. 58 (XXXI).
152 See SIB, pp. 63-67.
153 Lewis's title is inspired by *The World's Desire* (1890), by H. Rider Haggard and Andrew Lang, an early favourite of Lewis's. See CSL, p. 264; and CLET, pp. 309, 434-435.
154 SIB, p. 72 (XXXIX).

thought and speech of man' drowned 'in the boiling water's sound'.[155] The sound and fury of the river resembles the sound and fury of real life. But as ever with Lewis, there is something else, something above and beyond the world's troubles. Here that something is symbolised by the castle towers. The towers are, to be sure, 'slanted all away' by the trouble of the earth: 'Because the driving Northern wind will not rest by night or day'.[156] But the towers, indeed ivory towers, are in no danger of being blown over by the facts of the earth:

> Nothing is can trouble it, hate of the gods nor man's endeavour,
> And it shall be a resting-place, dear heart, for you and me.[157]

A faerie maiden is seen wandering through the 'sorrow laden' forest on this side of the castle towers:

> Through the thistle and the brier, through the tangles of the thorn,
> Till her eyes be dim with weeping and her homeless feet are torn.[158]

She looks up to the castle gate 'with vain endeavour', for 'her soulless loveliness to the castle winneth never'.[159] For some reason the faerie maiden cannot get in. She cannot escape the sorrowful forest. Yet still the poet goes on about what might be inside:

> But within the sacred court, hidden high upon the mountain,
> Wandering in the castle gardens lovely enough folk there be,
> Breathing in another air, drinking of a purer fountain
> And among that folk, beloved, there's a place for you and me.[160]

In the last poem of *Spirits in Bondage*, 'Death in Battle', the speaker, like the faerie maiden of the previous poem, is trying to get in:

> Open the gates for me,
> Open the gates of the peaceful castle, rosy in the West,
> In the sweet dim Isle of Apples over the wide sea's breast,
> Open the gates for me![161]

He, like the faerie maiden, longs to escape the world's darkness. He wants to get out, or away from, the facts of the earth—to a place where

> I shall not see
> The brutal, crowded faces around me, that in their toil have grown
> Into the faces of devils—, yea, even as my own—[162]

---

155 SIB, p. 72 (XXXIX).
156 SIB, p. 72 (XXXIX).
157 SIB, p. 73 (XXXIX).
158 SIB, p. 73 (XXXIX).
159 SIB, p. 73 (XXXIX).
160 SIB, p. 73 (XXXIX).
161 SIB, p. 74 (XL).
162 SIB, p. 75 (XL).

And he wants to get into a place he's never known but always desired: the 'Hidden Country' of the prologue or the 'Country of Dreams' here in the last poem of the cycle.[163]

More Troubles for MacDonald

Both Lewis and MacDonald, as young men, shared the same literary aspiration: to become, first and foremost, a poet.[164] MacDonald's first published book, like Lewis's, was a book of poetry: a long blank verse drama in five parts entitled *Within and Without*. Like *Spirits in Bondage*, *Within and Without* is filled with the conflict between the imagination of the spirit and the experience of real life. The troubles of life were uppermost in both men's minds as they wrote.

MacDonald had lived for ten more years than Lewis had when his first book was published in 1855.[165] MacDonald had not fought in a war by this time, but he had plenty of time to suffer some of the more commonly felt pains of life. His continuing poor health and frustration at not finding a steady source of income with which to support his family[166] were quite enough to acquaint him with the world's troubles. And like Lewis, MacDonald's imagination was exceedingly romantic when he wrote his first work.

When George Sr. could not afford fees for MacDonald to attend the 1842-43 session at King's College, Aberdeen, the younger MacDonald spent a year cataloguing a library in a nobleman's mansion somewhere in the far north of Scotland. It is likely that the mansion in question was Thurso Castle, owned by Sir George Sinclair, a scholar of German who was also well-versed in ancient and modern languages. His large library, full of romantic poetry and German literature, was to have a profound impact on MacDonald.[167] It was here, perhaps, that MacDonald mastered German and here, also, where he first encountered the mystical romances of Novalis.[168] 'Novalis' was the literary pseudonym of Friedrich von Hardenburg (1772-1801). He was a member of an early group of Romantic writers active in Jena between 1795 and 1801. His

---

163 SIB, p. 75 (XL).

164 See RAEP, p. 125; David S. Robb, *George MacDonald* (Edinburgh: Scottish Academic Press, 1987), pp. 18-19; Robert Lee Wolff, *The Golden Key, A Study of the Fiction of George MacDonald* (New Haven: Yale University Press, 1961), p. 266; C. Walsh, *The Literary Legacy of C.S. Lewis* (New York: Harcourt Brace Jovanovich, 1979), pp. 35, 55-58; and CLET, pp. 925, 927, 928-931.

165 MacDonald was thirty; Lewis was twenty in 1919 when *Spirits in Bondage* was published.

166 He and his wife had three children by 1855.

167 See RAEP, pp. 48-49.

168 As well as Jacob Boehme (1575-1624), Emanuel Swedenborg (1688-1772) and E.T.A. Hoffman (1776-1822).

work[169] may be best described as a literary and imaginative rebellion against the rationalism and deism of the Enlightenment. As Richard Littlejohns has written, Novalis was held up for over 150 years after his death to be 'the most Romantic of all Romantics in a popular and trivialising sense: the unworldly dreamer who sentimentally longed for a flower of unspeakable beauty, the poet whose mysterious devotion to his dead child fiancee led him into a cult of death'.[170] Novalis's work was to exercise an influence on a wide range of Romantics: from French Symbolists like Maurice Maeterlinck (1862-1949) to neo-Romantic mystic Herman Hesse (1877-1962).

Novalis certainly had a profound effect upon MacDonald, an effect comparable to the effect that MacDonald had on Lewis. What Lewis said about his 'master' can also be applied to Novalis in relation to MacDonald: there is perhaps no book MacDonald wrote in which Novalis's influence is not obvious. There is much of Novalis, for example, to be found in the book that affected Lewis's imagination most: *Phantastes*. Before the story begins, MacDonald quotes some of Novalis's notions on fairy stories. For example, "'The world of the fairy-story is that world which is opposed throughout to the world of rational truth, and precisely for that reason it is so thoroughly an analogue to it, as Chaos is an analogue to the finished Creation'".[171] MacDonald goes on in *Phantastes* attempting to follow Novalis's advice, it might be said, with a dreamy, chaotic plot. Novalis is directly quoted before two other chapters, including the last one where MacDonald quotes a passage that he could not keep out of a number of his books: *'Unser Leben ist kein Traum, aber es soll und wird vielleicht einer werden'*. Or as MacDonald translated it, "'Our life is no dream; but it ought to become one, and perhaps will'".[172] And throughout *Phantastes*, as throughout all of MacDonald's work, we see themes, especially 'good death', that can be traced back to Novalis. Later chapters will consider these themes more closely. For now it will be enough to say that the already romantic MacDonald was likely made more romantic by reading Novalis in a large castle library. And so the teenaged MacDonald in this respect was very much like the teenaged Lewis.

And like Lewis, MacDonald was struggling with doubts about God and his goodness, even if there is no evidence that he actually became an atheist. During his time at King's College, MacDonald was at strife with the Calvinist teaching that he found in the local Blackfriars Street Church. His friend Robert Troup remembered how MacDonald used to brood, after Sunday meals, over the things that were said in church:

---

169 Most notably, *Hymnen an die Nacht* (1800), *Heinrich von Ofterdingen* (1802), and *Geistkiche Lieder* (1802).

170 Richard Littlejohns, 'Novalis', in Matthias Konzett (ed.), *Encyclopedia of German Literature, Vol. 2* (London: Fitzroy Dearborn, 2000), p. 771.

171 PHA, p. 3.

172 PHA, p. 182.

At the time he was, I think, in spiritual difficulty caused by the doctrine of everlasting punishment and generally by the Calvinist teaching then all but universal in Scotland—sat by himself after the meal was over—silent and thoughtful and sometimes reading while others talked. His elder friends were anxious about his spiritual state.[173]

The church's minister at this time, John Kennedy, taught and practised a strict Calvinism. There was much talk of 'the elect', or those chosen by God before all time to be saved, and there was the banishing of sinners from the fellowship with little chance for their repenting. At one point Kennedy decided to energetically protect his church from a perceived heresy associated with James Morison. Morison was a minister who had been thrown out of the Secession Church[174] in 1841 because of his refusal to distance himself from the belief that Christ had died for all men, not only 'the elect'. Kennedy openly criticised the new movement from the pulpit and dismissed Sunday school teachers who displayed Morisonian leanings. MacDonald was one of those dismissed. Such an incident may have caused other men to lash out at Kennedy, even against all organised religion. It did not have this effect on MacDonald. As William Raeper has written, 'It is characteristic of MacDonald that although he did not approve of the doctrine [of the elect], he stuck with the man'.[175] Kennedy's actions caused a mass exodus from Blackfriars, but MacDonald stayed. He even continued correspondence with Kennedy after he had left university.

But to the Calvinist doctrine of God intending to save only a few, MacDonald was always hostile.[176] Whereas Lewis's early crisis of faith sprung from his disbelief in a good God, MacDonald's early struggles sprung from his seemingly unbreakable belief in nothing less than a completely good God. If the early judgement from Lewis was something like 'This world is much too bad a place for there to be a good God', MacDonald's would have been 'God is much too good a God to be Calvinist'. Lewis would come to change his mind; MacDonald would not. But his trust in a good God would certainly be tested by his experience—which did not always seem as good as the God he hoped in.

---

173 RAEP, p. 50.

174 The ironically named United Secession Church was formed when the New Licht Burghers and New-Licht Anti-Burghers reunited in 1820. Both groups were descendents of groups that had broken away from the Church of Scotland, mainly over the issue of church-state establishment.

175 RAEP, p. 52.

176 For how MacDonald's rejection of much of Calvinist doctrine did not include a total rejection of all of his religious inheritance, see ROBB, pp. 5-8. Robb explains how MacDonald remained dedicated to much of what he was exposed to in the evangelical Missionar church in Huntly, including 'fervent outreach to all men' and a 'sense of the ideal Christian community' that looked back to the Church's early days (ROBB, p. 7).

Some of the first examples of MacDonald's brooding over life came while at Aberdeen. Quite apart from his experience with Kennedy's Calvinistic God were the more general problems presented by the haphazard or even hostile state of the world. As already mentioned, MacDonald had been acquainted with the fact of death and disease from early on, as were so many in the nineteenth century. The harsh windy weather of north-east Scotland, not always conducive to good health, seemed at times to personify for MacDonald all the world's adversity. The Rev. J. Maconachie found this out when he was invited by young George one wild and stormy night to go for a walk along the seashore near Aberdeen. When Maconachie returned home from the walk, he told his sister, with a distressed and anxious look on his face, 'I hope George MacDonald is not going out of his mind'.[177] When his sister asked why, Maconachie replied, 'Well, when he got to the shore he walked backwards and forwards on the sands amid the howling wind and spray and with the waves coming up to our feet and all the time went about addressing the sea and the waves in the most extraordinary manner. I was really frightened at him'.[178]

MacDonald's cousin, Helen MacKay, whom he grew close to during his time at Aberdeen, remembered how she was able to help him 'when he was puzzled and undecided as to what life was fit for'.[179] Perhaps the trials of life and the Calvinist idea of God combined to cause young MacDonald to question the answers that religion provided, or at least the answers that much Scottish religion of the time provided. A loathing of *religiosity* is certainly something that colours most of the novels he would come to write. But even in the midst of his perplexity, MacDonald's hope in a good God never seemed to wane. Indeed, the troubles during his days at university, by his own account, increased his hope. His application to a theological college displays both the honesty and the hope that would come to pervade his books:

> for a long time I did not seem to make any progress ... By and by I became more in earnest ... But I could feel little or no abiding joy in religion. I looked to myself and not to the atonement [of Christ]. All I had been taught in my youth I required to learn over again. In my distress I could only cry to God to help me, and often in the midst of it felt assured he helped me [...] I read my bible and continued to cry to God. My unhappiness compelled me to it.[180]

After graduating from university in 1845, MacDonald soon left Scotland to begin looking for work in London. He eventually entered Highbury Theological College in the autumn of 1848 to begin training as a congregational minister.[181]

177 RAEP, p. 52.
178 RAEP, pp. 52-53.
179 RAEP, p. 53.
180 RAEP, p. 53.
181 See RAEP, p. 62.

It was during this time that MacDonald met and became engaged to Louisa Powell.[182] George and Louisa were a good match. They would enjoy by all accounts a long and deeply affectionate partnership that would span more than five decades. As William Raeper writes, their engagement in 1848 would begin a relationship that was uniquely suited to burden-bearing:

> if Louisa felt herself weak in intellect and in need of MacDonald's support, then he was often weak in body and in need of her nursing. In this way the one could not do without the other, and during their haphazard life together it was often Louisa's determination that carried them through.[183]

It would not take long for the burden-bearing to begin. In the summer of 1849, while George was gaining ministry experience by filling a vacant pulpit in Cork, Ireland, Louisa's family suffered two deaths in one day. And George was laid up again with bronchitis. She was relieved when he returned to Highbury after the summer, but they would soon receive news that his cousin, Charles Edward, who had grown up in the same house as George, had died at age twenty-three.

MacDonald left Highbury College without taking a degree and began 1850 looking for a job with which to pay off some debts and support his future wife and family. The pressure to do so is evident in one of his father's letters:

> I hope you will by and by be in circumstance to pay off your small debts, and make conscience of never venturing on taking a wife before then. If you begin thinking lightly of such a case, depend upon it, the carelessness will increase until none but yourself and such as are in similar circumstances can paint the agony it will entail.[184]

MacDonald's unorthodox style of preaching was one obstacle to achieving such a stable circumstance. After being rejected by a congregation in Stebbing, MacDonald wrote dejectedly to his father how 'many say they can't understand me'.[185] He continued: 'I tried to be as simple as possible [...] but I fear many people think they understand phrases they are used to and not much more'.[186] While George was trying to find a church that would accept him, Louisa's mother's health took a turn for the worse. She died in June.

MacDonald's vocational frustration finally ended when the Independent Church of Arundel, near Brighton, accepted him as their pastor.[187] He accepted their invitation and finally felt confident enough in his future to set a

---

182 See RAEP, p. 59.
183 RAEP, p. 66.
184 RAEP, p. 74.
185 RAEP, p. 75.
186 RAEP, p. 75.
187 See RAEP, p. 76.

date to marry Louisa. They would marry in March of 1851. But just as things began looking brighter, MacDonald's health faltered again. In November of 1850 he suffered from one of the many severe lung haemorrhages that would plague him periodically throughout the rest of his life. MacDonald's doctor ordered him to quit preaching for up to eight weeks, and so his illness was also financially damaging. He had to pay a substitute preacher two pounds a week from his meagre £150 annual salary.[188]

He was sent to convalesce at his aunt's home at Newport on the Isle of Wight. It was during this time that MacDonald began writing *Within and Without*. It would be published four years later, MacDonald's first significant literary statement. Like Lewis's *Spirits in Bondage*, MacDonald's poem is filled with a tension between the world's troubles and the poet's own inward vision. Unlike Lewis's cycle, however, MacDonald's work more fully represents the author's lifelong thematic emphasis. In the pages of this first work one can see in germ all the major themes that MacDonald would explore in four decades' worth of novels, fantasy and fairy tales. Also condensed in *Within and Without* is MacDonald's literary reaction to pain and suffering. As we shall see, it was a reaction essentially different from the reaction of young Lewis.

Within and Without

Within and Without begins with Julian, the protagonist, doing what young MacDonald often did: brooding. He is a monk alone in a convent cell observing the sunset. The soliloquy that follows quickly sets the tone for the rest of the work. Julian, like Lewis in *Spirits in Bondage*, notices the contrast between light and darkness. But the associations MacDonald establishes in the first few lines are completely reversed from those of Lewis's work. Lewis clearly identified darkness with the outside world (or nature, as in 'Satan Speaks') and light with his own imagination (though his imagination could not help but borrow from nature to express its 'light'). These associations made it inevitable that Lewis's poems would develop into an escape: from the darkness of the outside world to the light of his own imagination. We see immediately how MacDonald's poem, while maintaining a struggle between light and darkness, will differ. He does not imagine the sunset as some dualistic, bloody battle between the earth and sky.[189] Instead, he sees 'clouds and shadings of the mimic heaven!'.[190] He imagines the sunset as a blushing bride 'with glowing arms outstretched' receiving home her husband the sun.[191] And when Julian laments the fading

---

188 See RAEP, p. 81.
189 See p. 25, above.
190 George MacDonald, *Within and Without: A Dramatic Poem* (London: Longman, Brown, Green, Longmans & Roberts, 1857), p. 3 (I.i). First published in 1855.
191 WW, p. 3 (I.i).

of the light from his cell, we see where the points of contention are reversed from those in *Spirits in Bondage*. Instead of placing the darkness in the world, MacDonald places it in Julian. If a spirit here is in bondage to the darkness, it is his own self that acts as jailer. It is the darkness within contrasted with the light without, or as Julian asks himself, 'what is light to me, while I am dark!'.[192]

When the light from the sunset is gone, Julian is left alone in the dark to contemplate his soul's essential loneliness and insufficiency. Julian, like Lewis in *Spirits in Bondage*, feels a great distance between himself and the Something he knows not:

> my soul is as a speck of life
> Cast on the deserts of Eternity;
> A hungering and a thirsting, nothing more.
> I am as a child new-born, its mother dead,
> Its father far away beyond the seas.[193]

And like the speakers in so many of Lewis's poems, Julian aches to close the distance:

> I cry to Him: as if I sprinkled ashes,
> My prayers fall back in dust upon my soul.[194]

Julian, like young Lewis, has sought escape. He's flown from the world to a monastery but is still unsatisfied.

Later Julian tells Robert, a brother monk, how the others in the community see him as unorthodox, or of being an atheist 'at the least'.[195] Perhaps here we see a literary reflection of MacDonald's own situation: how most of his religious friends, and perhaps the congregations who rejected him, didn't understand his brooding over the nature of God and the state of the world. Julian is not like his singing, jolly brother monks. The monks gossip amongst themselves about Julian. Perhaps he is a jilted lover who has come to knock at God's door after being turned away from a lady's. Whatever the truth regarding his flight from the world, Julian himself knows and declares one thing to be true: He cannot get *in* to God. Like the speaker in Lewis's 'Death in Battle'[196] who beats upon the gates of the 'peaceful castle',[197] Julian finds no answer from the other side. 'I knock at God's [door]', he says, but 'He has not yet been pleased to let me in'.[198]

---

192 WW, p. 3 (I.i).
193 WW, p. 4 (I.i).
194 WW, p. 4 (I.i).
195 WW, p. 5 (I.i).
196 See p. 30, above.
197 SIB, p. 74 (XL).
198 WW, p. 8 (I.i).

Robert, trying to cheer him, suggests that Julian come with him on the morrow to find what light and beauty there is in nature, but this is no consolation. Julian refuses to be content with the light of nature, finding it too impersonal and unsatisfying. He yearns to get in behind nature to the Source of Nature's light:

> not having seen Him yet,
> The light rests on me with a heaviness;
> All beauty seems to wear a doubtful look;
> A voice is in the wind I do not know;
> A meaning on the face of the high hills
> Whose utterance I cannot comprehend.
> A something is behind them: that is God.[199]

MacDonald, much influenced by the German and English Romantics,[200] is much less angry at nature than the young Lewis. Nature, we see, is not the enemy here. But a contrast between spirit and nature is still evident. It is not a contrast resulting from a conflict between enemies, as in Lewis's poems, but between something that will satisfy and something that does not. Nature, Julian admits, is God's language, but it is not enough for his spirit. He will be satisfied, he thinks, with nothing less than God himself. Only then, when he has got into the Father of nature, will nature become any kind of home to him:

> I have not yet been held close to his heart.
> Once in his inner room, and by his eyes
> Acknowledged, I shall find my home in these,
> 'Mid sights familiar as a mother's smiles.
> And sounds that never lose love's mystery.
> Then they will comfort me. Lead me to Him.[201]

He cannot get into God, and God has not got into him. He indicates a crucifix on the wall and states his belief that God is in Christ, but this knowledge is not enough. 'There standeth Manhood [that is, Christ]: and God is there', he admits, but God is 'not here, not here', he laments, pointing to his own bosom.[202] Julian's stay at the monastery has not led him to God. All his acts of self-torture and penance have led him no nearer God's light:

> They talk
> Of penance! Let them talk when they have tried,
> And find it has not even unbarred Heaven's gate,
> Let out one stray beam of its living light.[203]

And so Julian decides to leave the monastery to seek after God in the wide world.

---

199 WW, p. 9 (I.i).
200 See RAEP, pp. 107-111; GK, pp. 374-375, 272-273.
201 WW, p. 10 (I.i).
202 WW, p. 10 (I.i).
203 WW, p. 11 (I.i).

But before he goes he achieves a sort of peace, and it is here that we begin to see how MacDonald in *Within and Without* goes much further than Lewis ever went in *Spirits in Bondage*. Despite the imaginative escape of *Spirits*, in the end the poet is left standing outside the gates of the peaceful castle crying for someone to let him in.[204] Here, still in the third scene of the first part of *Within and Without*, MacDonald's main character gains a paradoxical sort of calm from his own painful longing. In a dream he speaks, or God speaks, through his heart:

> Thou mak'st me long, and therefore thou wilt give;
> My longing is thy promise, O my God.
> If, having sinned, I thus have lost the claim,
> Why doth the longing yet remain with me,
> And make me bold thus to besiege thy doors?[205]

God tells Julian in his dream how the sense of his absence, and subsequent hungering for his presence, is a blessing:

> Thou art not quite dead
> While this pain lies in thee. I bless thee with it.[206]

Julian takes the voice of God in the dream at its word. Unlike the speaker at the end of Lewis's cycle of poems, Julian has, within his darkened cell, gained a trusting patience. He no longer cries for the gates to God's heart to be opened immediately:

> I am content to wait.
> A voice within I cannot but believe,
> Oft calls aloud: God *will* reveal himself.[207]

But he does more than just wait; and unlike Lewis in *Spirits*, he does more than seek escape through imagination or contemplation alone. As already mentioned, he feels compelled to go out into the world:

> Thirsting desire
> Wakens within me, like a new child-heart,
> To be abroad on the mysterious Earth,
> Out with the moon in all the blowing winds.[208]

Part Two of *Within and Without* wastes no time immersing Julian in a flood of worldly action. He manages to kill a Count Nembroni while struggling to protect his old love, Lilia. He nurses her back to health, much as Louisa often nursed MacDonald. In the midst of such action, Julian has time to speak of how imagining the ideal, as he had done in the monastery and as Lewis did in *Spirits*, is not nearly enough:

---

204 See SIB, pp. 74-75; pp. 28-29, above.
205 WW, p. 17 (I.iii).
206 WW, p. 18 (I.iii).
207 WW, p. 18 (I.iii).
208 WW, p. 18 (I.iii).

The loftiest of them dreamers; and the best
Content with goodness such as needs no thought [that is, 'care']
It cannot be God's will I should be such.[209]

He goes further to say that the world is much more than a place to escape from. It is, in fact, the world with its troubles, not any introspective convent, that offers any hope for those longing for the ideal:

such ['houses of foolishness'] are not God's nurseries for his children
My very birth into a world of men
Shows me the school where he would have me learn;
Shows me the place of penance; shows the field
Where I must fight and be victorious,
Or fall and perish.[210]

MacDonald's greatest expression of this idea in the poem, however, comes in the third act, within the confines of a prose story that Julian reads. It is five years since he fled the monastery, and he is now living in London with Lilia, now his wife, and their young daughter Lily. Julian is sitting beside the sleeping child, reading in a low voice out of a book which contains a story entitled 'The Singer'. In this story within a poem, readers get their very first taste of what MacDonald would come to do so well: dreamlike, fantastical myth. It is a glimpse, in content and style, of the sort of writing that would captivate young Lewis in the pages of *Phantastes*, published only three years after *Within and Without*.

The story is the telling of a dream by an old man named Melchah, who stands looking upon the corpse of his son saying, 'He hath told his tale to the Immortals'.[211] When Melchah's friend Abdiel asks him what he means, the old man tells his dream. In the dream Melchah is lying near the foot of what seems like a cliff near the top of a great mountain. Beneath him are clouds; above, 'the heavens deep and dark'.[212] Hearing voices 'sweet and strong', he lifts up his eyes to see 'a hundred majestic forms' seated and reclining in and about the crags and recesses of a rocky slope.[213] The forms look 'as of men who had striven and conquered'. He hears one of them say 'What wouldst thou say unto us, young man?'. A young, trembling voice replies, 'A song which I have made for my singing'.[214] The youth is then led to a hole in the rock which has a narrow entrance but is deep and wide within. The youth enters into the hole and vanishes. Melchah, looking on in terror, sees the men in

209 WW, p. 56 (II.xvi).
210 WW, p. 56 (II.xvi).
211 WW, p. 73 (III.i).
212 WW, p. 73 (III.i).
213 WW, p. 74 (III.i).
214 WW, p. 74 (III.i).

the rock leaning forward with their heads to one side, 'as if listening to a far-off sound'.[215] Melchah, much nearer the hole than they, listens too but hears nothing. He does, however, see their faces change 'like waters in a windy and half-cloudy day'.[216] At different times it seems that one form or another is sighing, or praying, beside him. At one point he hears a 'clang of music triumphant in hope'.[217] He looks up to find that the music is actually the men in the rock standing on their feet and singing. They then cease their singing, sit down and begin listening again. When one of the forms approaches Melchah, he asks what the singing and listening can mean. The answer the form gives is that the youth wished to 'sing to the Immortals'.[218]

'It is a law with us,' he says, 'that no one shall sing a song who cannot be the hero of his tale—who cannot live the song that he sings'.[219] Again, we see the difference between the young MacDonald and the younger Lewis. With MacDonald the emphasis is never just on dreaming, or imagining, or as in Melchah's dream, not just singing. In this dream within a story within a poem, MacDonald paradoxically keeps a vigilant tone. The youth who wants to sing a song is not allowed to simply sing. By order of the Immortals, he must first *live* the song that he desires to sing. If the youth, like the young Lewis who yearns to escape in the poems of *Spirits in Bondage*, wants only to sing or imagine the ideal, he has come to the wrong dream. In Melchah's dream the youth must go to some world where he can become what he desires to sing about.

At one point the form tells Melchah that the sighs he heard were the youth's 'longings after his own Ideal' and that 'thou didst hear him praying for the truth he beheld, but could not reach'.[220] In this the youth is much like the faerie maiden of Lewis's 'World's Desire', who

> Often to the castle gate up she looks with vain endeavour,
> For her soulless loveliness to the castle winneth never.[221]

But MacDonald's youth is not as soulless as Lewis's faerie maiden. He isn't content to long and stare. He prays for the ideal of loveliness and then goes about doing something that might make his soul lovelier. As the form tells Melchah, 'We sang, because, in his first great battle, he strove well and overcame'.[222]

Julian, for one, learns the message of the dream. After putting the book down, he thinks of how his earlier impatient yearnings to hear from God were

---

215 WW, p. 74 (III.i).
216 WW, p. 74 (III.i).
217 WW, p. 74 (III.i).
218 WW, pp. 73-74 (III.i).
219 WW, p. 74 (III.i).
220 WW, p. 74 (III.i).
221 SIB, p. 73 (XXXIX). See pp. 29-30, above.
222 WW, p. 75 (III.i).

misguided. Julian, like Lewis's speakers in *Spirits*, was impatient to get into a light much too bright for the eyes of his youthful soul:

> My prayer arose from lonely wastes of soul;
> As if a world far-off in depths of space,
> Chaotic, had implored that it might shine
> Straightway in sunlight as the morning star.
> My soul must be more pure, ere it could hold
> With thee communion. 'Tis the pure in heart
> That shall see God.[223]

Instead of beating against the gates of the Ideal with his imagination, Julian is resolved to walk the long road with his faith and will:

> And though I am not yet come near to Him,
> I know I am more nigh; and am content
> To walk a long and weary road, to find
> My father's house once more [...]
> I am content, rejoicing to go on,
> Even when my home seems far away;
> And over grief, and aching emptiness,
> And fading hopes, a higher joy ariseth.[224]

On cue, the action of Part Three commences to test Julian. The church, having gobbled up all of Julian's and Lilia's wealth in Italy, has left the family in poverty.[225] An even deeper misery is brought on by disappointment in their marriage: both Julian and Lilia come to feel that the other doesn't really love them anymore. Julian is brooding again, 'often silent, sometimes moody, Drowned in much questioning'.[226] He wonders if anything can be done to bring life back to his marriage and muses over how all that once seemed sublime has now faded into a dreary commonness. Everything he knows, it seems, even his young daughter, has lost its magical glow:

> But now the gilt is nearly all rubbed off.
> Even she, the goddess of the wonder-world,
> Seems less mysterious and worshipful.[227]

He even goes so far as to question whether the wonder itself was an illusion from the beginning:

> Was love to the eyes as opium, making all things more beautiful
> than they were? [...]
> Is this [commonness] the real, the cold, undraperied truth; a skeleton
> admitted as a guest

---

223 WW, pp. 76-77 (III.i). See Mat. 5.8; Psalm 15.1-2.
224 WW, p. 77 (III.i).
225 See WW, pp. 80-81 (III.ii-iii).
226 WW, p. 92 (II.vi).
227 WW, p. 103 (III.ix).

At life's loud feast, wearing a life-like mask?[228]

This is perhaps as close as MacDonald gets to the low ebb Lewis achieved in the most despairing portions of *Spirits in Bondage*. His honesty about life's trouble and dreariness almost allows Julian to sink into a morass of despair.

But MacDonald's equally characteristic hope comes in time to lift him. MacDonald, in Julian, dares to go beyond both despair and imagination: to actually believing that the sublime is real and no mere opiate:

> No, no; my heart would die if I believed it [...]
> The Lovely is True. The Beautiful
> Is what God made.[229]

It is our selves, our eyes, not the wonders of the world, that have grown old. As Julian puts it, we are

> Men from whose narrow bosoms
> The great child-heart has withered, backward look
> To their first-love, and laugh, and call it folly.[230]

To all those who sneer and mock at child-like wonders and loves, to those who say 'I was so when a boy—look at me now', MacDonald and Julian turn their back:

> Youth, be not one of them, but love thy love.
> So with all worship of the high and good,
> And pure and beautiful.[231]

MacDonald's remedy for despair is a simple and direct call to courage. Through Julian he tells the reader that it is the death of this world, around us and in one's heart, that obscures the beautiful Truth. The wise child is one who believes in spite of appearances, who 'knows the hours will dissipate the mist'.[232] As Walton urges Weir the coffin-maker in *Annals*,[233] the virtue of patience is urged here:

> Time is God's, and all its miracles are his;
> And in the Future he o'ertakes the Past,
> Which was a prophecy of times to come.[234]

At this point MacDonald uses a variety of images to symbolise the coming glory. These images—flashing stars, the sun and the moon, daisies' joyful reaction to the warming sun of Spring, inward glory from the mirror of the soul— all involve light.

---

228 WW, p. 103 (III.ix). Compare to Ransom's fears in C.S. Lewis, *Perelandra: A Novel* (New York, MacMillan, 1986), pp. 160-170. See pp. 55-56, below. *Perelandra* first published in 1943.
229 WW, p. 104 (III.x).
230 WW, p. 104 (III.x).
231 WW, p. 104 (III.x).
232 WW, p. 104 (III.x).
233 See AQN, pp. 45-46; pp. 15, above.
234 WW, p. 105 (III.x).

But as usual, it is not simply thinking about the light, or one's Ideal, that will bring one into it. Real belief involves action in the here and now. This is illustrated later in the story after Julian's health, and especially his daughter's health, worsens. One night, while sitting up with the sick child, he falls asleep and then into a sort of trance. During the trance Julian is given a choice between his Ideal and Lilia. He first sees an overpowering vision of feminine beauty. At the foot of this form of perfection lies sleeping another woman-form, a sort of incarnation of the overwhelming vision of ideal womanhood:

> It is the same shape, line for line, as she
> That stands above it; only more like one
> That needs to lie on something.[235]

He then recognises the incarnation as his wife Lilia who

> Came down from off her statue-pedestal,
> And was a woman in a common house,
> Not beautied by fancy every day,
> And losing worship by her gifts to me.[236]

In this striking vision MacDonald uses feminine images to present a choice to be made. And in this choice we see the most important difference between *Within and Without* and *Spirits in Bondage*. In Lewis's first book a choice is also presented: the choice between an entirely desirable, but ultimately unattainable, Ideal on the one hand, and a wholly repugnant reality on the other. Lewis, with his imagination, attempts to escape from reality to the Ideal in *Spirits in Bondage*. The title of the work itself sums up what we read in the poems. It is spirits who are in bondage in the prison of this world. Lewis's imagination acts as a battering ram by which spirits attempt an impatient escape from the natural or 'real' world to the world of pure spirit. If the escape ultimately fails and he is left outside the gates of the Ideal, it is not for a lack of imaginative effort. Lewis, choosing the Ideal, went as far as his imagination could take him.

In *Within and Without*, the choice is portrayed differently. There is not as sharp a distinction between the Ideal and the real. There is, to be sure, a painful discrepancy between one's desire for the Ideal and the apparent fulfilment of this desire in this world. It is the difference between the God that Julian hungers for and the natural world that fails to satisfy that hunger, even as it increases or awakens such hunger. But from the beginning, the Ideal and the real world are more closely intertwined than in *Spirits in Bondage*. Reality, or nature, as Julian knows it, is not wholly malevolent, only inadequate to his deepest longings.[237]

---

235 WW, p. 169 (IV.xxxi).

236 WW, p. 169 (IV.xxi). Compare to Curdie's mother in George MacDonald, *The Princess and Curdie* (London: Penguin, 1994), pp. 82-83; pp. 254, below. *Curdie* first published in 1883.

237 See WW, pp. 9-10 (I.i); p. 38, above.

And in the incarnation of Lilia that lies beneath the form of the Ideal, we see another example of this intertwining of the Ideal with the ordinary, the sort of thing in MacDonald that Lewis would come to call 'bright shadow'.[238] The choice is between the absolute Ideal of feminine beauty that Julian could imagine and the incarnation of that beauty in his wife Lilia. It is not a choice between an imaginary heaven on one hand and a real hell on the other, as in *Spirits in Bondage*. In *Within and Without*, heaven, or the Ideal, has somehow come down into what one calls the real world and revealed itself, however inadequately, in nature, and here, in his wife. The choice before Julian is between the pure heaven of his imagination and the heaven, or bits of heaven, that already inhabit the real world of the present. Instead of having to choose between Romance and Reality, Julian must choose between mere imaginative Romance and the measure of real Romance available and attainable in this world. It is not that MacDonald, like more modern authors, sweeps away the Ideal and beckons Julian, and the reader, to get on with the real business of living, or reading, or moping, in an unromantic world. In *Within and Without* he urges Julian, and the reader, to get on with the real business of real romance, loving the truly lovely and becoming truly lovely, rather than sitting alone in a monastery cell contemplating abstract Beauty.[239]

So when Julian chooses his real wife over his imaginary Ideal, we see the difference in movement in the two works. The movement in MacDonald's drama is outward, away from mere imagination and imaginative escapism. There is escape, to be sure, but the escape is from mere dreaming. In the scene in question, Julian seeks to escape from his trance in order to get to his real wife. It is not enough, even, to choose his wife over the Ideal womanhood within the confines of the trance. He must get away from his trance. He must wake up into the real and escape escapism:

> I will not stay to choose, nor look again
> Upon the Beautiful—give me my wife,
> The woman of the old time on the Earth.[240]

He must get back to where he can do more than contemplate or imagine. As he declares to the vision of his wife, moments before waking up, he must get back to where he can act and love:

---

238 See SBJ, pp. 179-181.

239 Hooper and Green note in their biography how MacDonald's Curdie stories helped wake up Lewis to a similar truth: 'that imaginative people, such as himself, are likely to confuse the mere thinking about a duty with the actual doing it' (CSL, p. 109). They point to a passage in *The Princess and the Goblin* in which 'Curdie dreams that he has waked and then, upon really waking up, finds that he is still in bed' (CSL, p. 109). They note that Lewis, in a letter written to Arthur Greeves on 15 April 1930, acknowledged how this passage helped remind him how easy it is "'to confuse an aesthetic appreciation of the spiritual life with the life itself—to dream that you have waked, washed, and dressed and then to find yourself still in bed'" (CSL, p. 109).

240 WW, p. 170 (IV.xxi).

O woman-soul, fold not thy parted hands,
Nor let thy hair weep like a sunset-rain
From thy bent brows, shadowing thy snowy breasts!
If thou descend to Earth, and find no man
To love thee purely, strongly, in his *will*,
Even as he loves the Truth, because he will,
And when he cannot see it beautiful;
Then thou mayest weep, and I will help thee weep.[241]

MacDonald, through Julian, puts the emphasis as he sees it on something deeper than appearances, imaginings and feelings. He puts it, as we see plainly by MacDonald's italics, on one's will. It is not a vision of loveliness, imagined or otherwise, that matters most in this life. It is being or becoming lovely one's own self—by loving. As we shall see in later chapters, it is this loving, or becoming lovely, that helps bring heaven down to Earth in MacDonald's writing. It is closely related to the 'beauty of Holiness' or 'Goodness' or 'bright shadow' that Lewis describes as transforming the ordinary, as opposed to escaping the ordinary.[242] In MacDonald, Lewis first discovered fantasy that was not pure escapism. In MacDonald the young Lewis found a joy that was not limited to what one could imagine. As he wrote in *Surprised by Joy*, 'Up till [reading MacDonald] each visitation of Joy had left the common world momentarily a desert—"The first touch of the earth went nigh to kill"'.[243] As in the poems of *Spirits in Bondage*, 'when real clouds or trees had been the material of the vision, they had been so only by reminding me of another world; and I did not like the return to ours'.[244] Only after encountering MacDonald's stories did Lewis see 'the bright shadow coming out of the book into the real world and resting there, transforming all common things and yet itself unchanged'.[245]

This, of course, is Lewis remembering and interpreting his initial encounter with MacDonald by the light of his conversion to Christianity. But there are indications within the text of *Spirits in Bondage* that such a change had already begun to find its way into young Lewis's poetic expression. As has been said, *Spirits in Bondage* is about escaping the present real world. But even as young Lewis disbelieved in anything other than imaginative escape, there are a few curious passages that demonstrate how MacDonald's bright shadow may have already begun to influence a part of his mind.

In 'Dungeon Grates', for example, the speaker laments how the lonely soul of man 'shudders' before an uncaring, deterministic universe 'too merciless

---

241 WW, p. 170 (IV.xxi).
242 See SBJ, pp. 179-181; ANTH, pp. xxxiii-xxxiv.
243 SBJ, p. 181. For 'The first touch [...]', see Keats, *Endymion*, 4.618.
244 SBJ, p. 181.
245 SBJ, p. 181.

for hate, / The nightmare march of unrelenting fate'.[246] But he also speaks of the hope of joining some 'strange power of unsought Beauty' that can build a bridge of light out of the 'strife and storm' of an uncaring reality.[247] He has not gone as far as MacDonald here in admitting that the strife and storm of the world is itself the path that one must take. But the speaker does, like MacDonald, begin to speak of a beauty that's more than something to gaze upon. He begins to wonder whether there may need to be a beauty within as well as without:

> When of some beauty we are grown a part
> Till from its very glory's midmost heart
> Out leaps a sudden beam of larger light
> Into our souls.[248]

The light that lights up our souls, he says, is the same light that transforms what we once perceived as common:

> All things are seen aright
> Amid the blinding pillar of its gold,
> Seven times more true than what for truth we hold
> In vulgar hours.[249]

And in 'L' Apprenti Sorcier', the first poem in the short middle section entitled 'Hesitation', we see Lewis's imagination, perhaps, even contemplating a jump into the real world—not an escape from it—as the way forward. The speaker is situated on a 'weedy stone' above the roar and thunder of a tempestuous sea.[250] Numerous 'thin, elemental people' who live 'beyond our heavy sphere' call from this frightful sea for the speaker to join them.[251] These beings, calling from the distant Ideal, urge the speaker to join them, but only by jumping into a sea of real life:

> "Leap in! Leap in and take thy fill
> Of all the cosmic good and ill,
> Be as the Living ones that know
> Enormous joy, enormous woe"[252]

Only by jumping into such a sea of good and ill can the speaker hope to 'find the real life and be/ As are the children of the deep!'.[253] As Julian jumped into the seemingly haphazard life of the world from the isolation of his convent

---

246 SIB, p. 25 (XV).
247 SIB, p. 25 (XV).
248 SIB, p. 25 (XV).
249 SIB, pp. 25-26 (XV).
250 SIB, p. 39.
251 SIB, p. 40 (XXII).
252 SIB, p. 40 (XXII).
253 SIB, p. 40 (XXII).

cell, so the speaker is urged to

> "Be bold and dare the glorious leap,
> Or to thy shame, go, slink again
> Back to the narrow ways of men."[254]

It is even possible that the title, 'L' Apprenti Sorcier', is inspired by MacDonald, who to Lewis no doubt seemed very much like a sorcerer in the context of his atheistic doubts. The speaker of the poem is himself an apprentice who wishes to do what the characters in MacDonald's books do: jump into the world's mixed sea of good and ill. The poem ends, however, in indecision. The apprentice cannot yet do what his master urges. The speaker, like young Lewis, does not go as far as Julian. He does not take the plunge. He stands striving to wake from the vision 'because I feared the flood'.[255]

The greatest example of MacDonald's emerging influence on Lewis's young imagination, perhaps, comes in one of the last poems of *Spirits in Bondage*: 'Tu Ne Quaesieris',[256] a taut series of couplets that expresses both anguised despair and a new kind of hope. Despair and hope, as we have seen, are themes that run through most all of the poems of *Spirits*. But here both the despair and the hope are different, for both sentiments are, for the first and last time in *Spirits*, directed toward the speaker himself. All the rest of Lewis's poems are directed outward: the hope for the undiscovered country and the despair at not discovering it. Even when the poems speak of getting 'in', it is always about getting 'in' to the other world, the country of dreams, the peaceful castle.[257] Only here do we see Lewis writing a poem in which the speaker talks of getting something 'in' to his own self. It's as if he echoes Julian's words in the opening soliloquy of *Within and Without*: 'But what is light to me while I am dark!'.[258] Here and only here does Lewis's first work dwell on the difference between imagined Beauty and the lack of Beauty in one's own self.

Even if the speaker were to get into some far off country of dreams where all was well, what good would it be if he himself remained unwell?:

> Though it were sure and proven well
> That I shall prosper, as they tell,
> In fields beneath a different sun
> By shores where other oceans run,
> When this live body that was I

---

254 SIB, p. 40 (XXII).
255 SIB, p. 40 (XXII). A very similar scene occurs in PHA, pp. 125-126 (XVIII), in which Anodos does take such a plunge.
256 See Horace's *Odes*, 1.11.
257 Which, in a paradoxical sense, can be seen as inward, if these places are only in his imagination.
258 WW, p. 3 (I.i). See pp. 37, above.

> Lies hidden from the cheerful sky,
> Yet what were endless lives to me
> If still my narrow self I be
> And hope and fail and struggle still,
> And break my will against God's will,
> To play for stakes of pleasure and pain
> And hope and fail and hope again,
> Deluded, thwarted, striving elf
> That through the window of my self
> As through a dark glass scarce can see[259]
> A warped and masked reality?[260]

Like Julian, the speaker here seems to see that contemplation of the Ideal is not enough. As Melchah was told by the Immortals, 'It is a law with us that no one shall sing a song who cannot be the hero of his tale—who cannot live the song he sings; for what right hath he else to devise great things, and to take holy deeds in his mouth'.[261]

But the speaker of 'Tu Ne Quaesieris' despairs. The job seems too difficult. His own searching up till now has yielded only imaginative Beauty. He himself is still a 'narrow self' who hopes and fails and struggles against God's will, seeking nothing more than the presence of pleasure and absence of pain. The shadowy life of this world remains to him a painful mystery: a 'riddling earth' that no amount of imaginative lore can clarify. The speaker himself is too shadowy to see in the world anything other than 'a warped and masked reality'.

But the last five couplets of the poem declare a hope that is different than any other hope found in *Spirits in Bondage*. Elsewhere, the speakers only hope to see the light, to get to that region from where the light comes. Only here does the speaker hope to actually mingle *with* the Light, to have the Light come into him *while still in* the land of shadows. During the brief span of this poem, Lewis is not preoccupied with a quick escape to the light. He is content to submit to the light-in-shadow, submit to the trials of real life, and like all living things in the world, submit to a kind of good death that makes MacDonald's fiction much more than mere escapism:

> But when this searching thought of mine
> Is mingled in the large Divine,
> And laughter that was in my mouth
> Runs through the breezes of the South,
> When glory I have built in dreams
> Along some fiery sunset gleams,

---

259 See 1 Cor. 13.12.
260 SIB, p. 68 (XXXVII).
261 WW, p. 74 (III.i).

And my dead sin and foolishness
Grow one with Nature's whole distress,
To perfect being I shall win,
And where I end will Life begin.[262]

This is as close as Lewis gets in *Spirits in Bondage* to expressing the choice that Julian makes in *Within and Without*. It would take many more years and books and conversations with friends before Lewis would come to actually believe in and share MacDonald's Christian view of the world. And so we see that *Spirits in Bondage* remains, almost entirely, a group of poems about escaping from the world's troubles.

Most of the rest of the action in *Within and Without* is negligible for our purposes here. Julian, Lilia and Lily all die and are reunited in heaven, or as MacDonald describes it, 'a world not realized'.[263] And so, some might say, MacDonald's work ends in the same kind of escape as Lewis imagined in *Spirits in Bondage*.

There is certainly no doubt that the death and heaven that MacDonald presents here is a sort of escape. As Julian sings just before Lily dies:

Come Away! Above the storm
Ever shines the blue;
Come Away! Beyond the form
Ever lies the True.[264]

But it is a hard-fought escape that comes only at the end of a long and arduous earthly life. MacDonald, as always, is comforting. There *is* an undiscovered country to get to. But only after one's been purified and made beautiful in a world of troubles. MacDonald's comfort, unlike Lewis's anguished imaginings, is patient and vigilant. 'Work on', he writes immediately after having written comforting assurances that 'the primrose time will come again'.[265] His comfort is never without a call to courage and vigilance.

Neither the young Lewis nor the young MacDonald ignored the light of heaven. The difference is that the young MacDonald actually believed in it, and that there was a path to it, a way to get 'in'. He makes clear throughout *Within and Without* that the only path or way into the light of heaven is through the shadows and trials of earthly life. This is seen again in the final scene, when Julian and Lily see their wife and mother Lilia rising up through the clouds to meet them. The heavenly Lilia is obviously MacDonald's symbol for perfected Beauty, for she is described as 'a woman-form, a wonderful mingling of the

---

262 SIB, pp. 68-69 (XXXVII).
263 WW, p. 185 (V.i).
264 WW, p. 189 (V.ii).
265 WW, p. 183 (V).

earthly and the unearthly in its pure beauty'.[266] But the perfected Beauty, the getting 'in' to the light of heaven, as always with MacDonald, is not without its costs. As Julian says,

> So riseth up my lily from the sea
> Where human souls are tried in awful dreams.[267]

It remains to be seen, though, how Lewis came to share MacDonald's view of earthly life as a sort of purifying ordeal, how he came to reconcile pain and suffering with belief in a good God. It also remains for us to explore how these beliefs manifested themselves in the rest of MacDonald's and Lewis's work.

---

266 WW, p. 192 (V.iii).
267 WW, p. 193 (V.iii).

CHAPTER 2

SILVER THREADS

Only this much let me crave of Thee [...] that I am Thy creature, and by
Thy goodness (which is Thyself) that Thou wilt suffer some beam of Thy
majesty so to shine into my mind, that it may still depend confidently
on Thee.   —a prayer of Sir Philip Sidney[1]

And ever I had mind of you
The Land of Doubt when I rode through.
    —Sir Grime to the lady, in *History of Sir Eger,*
        Sir Gryme, and Sir Gray-Steel[2]

And the light shineth in the darkness.
    —John 1.5

Now that we have reviewed MacDonald's and Lewis's early experience and
knowledge of pain and suffering, and their first literary responses to it, it
remains to be seen how they responded to evil fortune in the rest of their
writings. And so we move to consider more fully the answers they gave to the
questions that the world's troubles present.

For MacDonald this will mean looking at variations on a theme that
can be found in the pages of *Within and Without*. As we have already learned,
this earliest book is written by someone already committed to belief in a good
God, despite life's adversities. In *Within and Without* MacDonald had already
begun to interpret pain and suffering in the light of this belief and begun to
fight spiritual ennui with it.

Lewis, on the other hand, would have to change his mind in order to
reach a belief comparable to MacDonald's. The baptism of his imagination
may have already begun after reading *Phantastes*, but the rest of him, namely
his reason, would remain unconvinced for some time. A decade would pass
after the publication of *Spirits in Bondage* before the rest of Lewis would begin
to catch up with the yearning of his imagination—before he would actually
come to believe in a good God and write books about him. He became a theist
in 1929[3] and a Christian in 1931 at the age of 32. His poem 'The Philosopher'
in *Spirits in Bondage* may have cast doubt on reason's ability to 'cross over for us
the bridge of fears [...] in to the country where the ancient Mothers dwell'.[4] But

---

1   Quoted in AQN, p. 515.
2   Quoted in ELSC, p. 69.
3   He 'admitted that God was God and knelt and prayed' (SBJ, p. 228).
4   SIB, p. 27 (XVI).

in an ironic twist, it is Lewis the philosopher, the pupil of W.T. Kirkpatrick, the reasoner, who would come to actually believe in the light that his poetry could only dream of.

In this respect Lewis, much more than MacDonald, would consciously defend the validity and importance of human reason. Lewis was always very romantic, but unlike MacDonald, he did not grow up in a literary age that was still busy reacting to eighteenth-century rationalism. All of MacDonald's books can be seen, in many respects, as following the lead of the English and German romantics, not to mention his fellow countrymen MacPherson, Burns and Scott, who revolted against certain enlightenment concepts, such as empiricism, and the idea of a mechanical, clock-work universe. Lewis's works are different. His very conversion, in fact, depended in part on a reconciliation between, or recognised compatibility of, romantic instinct and reason's light, as the title of his first post-conversion work of fiction makes clear: *The Pilgrim's Regress: An Allegorical Apology for Christianity, Reason and Romanticism.*[5]

This study will not tell the complete story of Lewis's conversion. Other books have already done this,[6] and it need not be done here. All this study need do is concentrate on those aspects of his conversion that directly concern his change from one who disbelieved in a good God due to the problem of pain and suffering, to one who somehow came to believe in a good God in spite of the world's troubles. Another reason we need not go into too much detail about the conversion of Lewis's mind is that this change had mostly to do with influences other than MacDonald. In other words, this is a study about how MacDonald and Lewis, master and disciple, dealt with evil and goodness in their writing. It is not a study about everything that could be said about either MacDonald or Lewis separately. But since the conversion of Lewis's mind is important to how he deals with evil and goodness in his literature, it will be important here to show how his mind answered such questions, even if MacDonald did not have nearly as great an influence on Lewis's intellect as he did on his imagination.

It may also be pointed out that one of the best ways to show how much one man influenced another is to show where the influence stopped, to show how the two men were not identical. One of the chief differences between these two men, as mentioned, is that Lewis took the 'long road' to faith. His mind had to walk, by rational argument, to the place that his imagination longed for. The journey was perhaps longer than some because of his training in logic and dedication to human reasoning. Such a valuation of reason, as we shall see, gives an intellectual sharpness to much of Lewis's fiction that

5   C.S. Lewis, *The Pilgrim's Regress: An Allegorical Apology for Christianity Reason and Romanticism* (Grand Rapids: Eerdmans, 1997). First published in 1933.
6   See SBJ, CSL, CLET, and David C. Downing, *The Most Reluctant Convert: C.S. Lewis's Journey to Faith* (Downer's Grove: Intervarsity Press, 2002).

MacDonald's stories lack.

This faith of the intellect in the teeth of distress, however, helped give Lewis and his fiction, something remarkably similar to the kind of courage that we find expressed in MacDonald's fiction. Once his intellect had reached belief in a good God, it was this type of faith, gained in part through reason, which seemed to hold firm in times of distress. Lewis achieves with the help of reason what MacDonald seems to achieve by sheer force of will. But only seems. This study will not suggest that MacDonald was without any reason in his courage, nor that Lewis's intellectual faith existed in a vacuum, free from other influences. It may be that much of what leads a man to faith, and encourages him to keep faith, is, in fact, reason—though the man himself does not recognize or openly acknowledge it as such. This study will argue that this is in fact what happens with MacDonald, though he is not nearly as interested in argument as Lewis, and though his stories do not have the explicitly rational quality that most of Lewis's possess.[7]

But more on this later. For now, it will be well to say that the differences between the two men may be best explained by simply pointing out what they each left behind. MacDonald, as part of a romantic revolt against mere rationalism, wrote many highly imaginative books, one of which, *Phantastes*, attracted Lewis, the young romantic. Young Lewis, as a result of reading this book, began to leave mere imagination behind, as we have seen in the previous chapter. In this way, ironically, a romantic helps lead a romantic past mere imaginative romance. We shall see in this chapter how reason leads Lewis the rest of the way, and how reason helped sustain MacDonald's faith more than one might imagine at first glance. The differences between the two men, regarding reason and theory, may be easy to point out, but this study claims that there were important similarities. The common thread of faith that they both came to hold onto was very similar indeed, as their fiction and other writings demonstrate. In this chapter we will see how both men, in their minds and their fiction, moved beyond their doubts about a shadowy world of pain and suffering. And we shall see how their paths through these doubts and shadows were more alike than different. Remaining chapters will be concerned with what these paths actually led them to.

Omnipotence, Freedom, and Possible Worlds

We begin with the change in Lewis's mind regarding a good God and evil fortune. Lewis, as we've noted, was much more willing than MacDonald to speak to his readers with extended and undisguised logical argument. Lewis may be best known for his seven *Narnia* books, his science fiction trilogy, and

---

7   For a compilation of quotations that demonstrates the element of reason in MacDonald's faith, see Barbara Amell (ed.), *George MacDonald on the Logic of Faith* (Portland: B. Amell, 2000).

his satirical *Screwtape Letters*, but among many readers he is just as well known, or nearly as well known, for his devotional and apologetic works. As these books give an invaluable insight into who Lewis came to be, and therefore what kind of fiction he came to write, we should not ignore them here.

Lewis's most comprehensive attempt to answer the questions that pain and suffering present are found in the pages of *The Problem of Pain* (1940), the first of Lewis's three major apologetic works.[8] After an introductory chapter, Lewis begins his attempt at answering the problem in the second chapter entitled 'Divine Omnipotence'. He begins by summing up the intellectual problem concerning pain by presenting this syllogism: 'If God were good, He would wish to make His creatures perfectly happy, and if God were almighty, He would be able to do what He wished. But the creatures are not happy. Therefore God lacks either goodness, or power, or both'.[9]

The next thing he does is to say that this argument is in fact unanswerable if one is limited to only the popular meanings that are usually attached to the words 'good', 'almighty' and perhaps 'happy'. He goes on in much of the rest of the book to argue that these terms are equivocal, that 'good', 'almighty', and 'happiness' may not always mean what is usually assumed in everyday conversation. He argues that somehow the happiness of creatures, and therefore the idea of a good and almighty Creator, is consistent with pain and suffering.

The first part of Lewis's argument shows how 'almighty' cannot mean what most people think when it is applied to God in relation to the natural order he created. The first point he makes is that God cannot do the intrinsically impossible. As Lewis puts it, 'you may attribute miracles to Him, but not nonsense'.[10] For example, just because one can produce a grammatically correct sentence that reads 'God can make a round square' or 'I can fly in the sea', does not suddenly make the sentence meaningful. Squares, by definition, are not round, and flying is something that, by definition, cannot be done in the sea. Lewis applies this logic to the statement '"God can give a creature free will and at the same time withhold free will from it"'.[11] As Lewis writes, 'It is no more possible for God than for the weakest of His creatures to carry out both of two mutually exclusive alternatives; not because His power meets an obstacle, but because nonsense remains nonsense even when we talk it about God'.[12] And so, Lewis argues, omnipotence must mean '"power to do all that is intrinsically possible"'.[13]

---

8   The other two are *Mere Christianity* (1943) and *Miracles* (1947). Another book, *The Abolition of Man* (1947), could be included as a fourth, but it is not here because it never goes so far as to argue in favour of a particular faith. Its purpose is to argue for objective value judgments and against subjective relativism in education.

9   PP, p. 26.

10   PP, p. 28.

11   PP, p. 28.

12   PP, p. 28.

13   PP, p. 28.

Lewis argues in this chapter that to create a world of free willed creatures with the assurance of no suffering would be intrinsically impossible. It would be a nonsense statement, and as such, no threat to God's omnipotence or goodness. According to Lewis, a relatively independent or 'inexorable' nature has to exist in order for free will to be truly free. Still, he admits that 'the inexorable "laws of Nature" which operate in defiance of human suffering or desert, which are not turned aside by prayer, seem at first sight to furnish a strong argument against the goodness and power of God'.[14]

Lewis conveys a sense of this distant, uncaring nature in *Perelandra*, the second book of his science fiction trilogy. Ransom, the hero, is a philologist who has journeyed to the planet Venus, or Perelandra, which he finds an unspoiled paradise. The crisis comes when Ransom takes up the task of defending the planet's queen, a beautiful green lady, against the potentially corrupting influences of Weston, another visitor from Earth. At one point in this defense Ransom is travelling across the sea in pursuit of Weston and has the time to contemplate his surroundings. It is important to note here that Perelandra, unlike Earth, is a place where no moral corruption has taken place. But yet the planet's natural surroundings still tempt Ransom's imagination to doubt and despair. It is an indifferent nature, not a hostile nature, that makes him begin to wonder. At the strange, wild cry of some swan-like birds, Ransom begins to brood in earnest:

> The crying of these birds was often audible, and it was the wildest sound that Ransom had ever heard, the loneliest, and the one that had least to do with Man [...] The sea-noises continuously filled his ear: the sea-smell, unmistakable and stirring as that of our Tellurian [Earth] oceans, but quite different in its warmth and golden sweetness, entered his brain. It also was wild and strange. It was not hostile: if it had been, its wildness and strangeness would have been the less, for hostility is a relation and an enemy is not a total stranger. It came into his head that he knew nothing at all about this world.[15]

Like MacDonald's brooding Julian in *Within and Without*, Ransom begins to realize how nature by itself seems to make a poor home for man.[16] It could possibly be made into a sort of home, or house rather, but in itself it is wholly oblivious to man and his concerns. Many of the animals and creatures in Lewis's stories talk, but not on this journey. Ransom comes across a group of sea-people feeding upon seaweed, but his contact with them only deepens his sense of loneliness.[17] After a day and a night of brooding loneliness, Ransom's

---

14   PP, p. 29.
15   PER, p. 160.
16   See WW, p. 10 (I.i). See pp. 38, above.
17   See PER, p. 162.

faith in Purpose seems to reach the breaking point.[18] He even begins to doubt the validity of morality.[19] The prohibitions he finds on Perelandra, like the prohibitions he knew of on Earth, seem now to prove only one thing: 'Need it prove anything more than that similar irrational *taboos* had accompanied the dawn of reason in two different worlds?'.[20] Such thinking, predictably, leads to doubts about goodness in general and about a God of goodness who cares:

> It was all very well to talk of Maleldil: but where was Maleldil now? If this illimitable ocean said anything, it said something very different. Like all solitudes it was, indeed, haunted: but not by an anthropomorphic Deity, rather by the wholly inscrutable to which man and his life remained eternally irrelevant. And beyond this ocean was space itself.[21]

Ransom's doubts and fears are intensified when Weston comes and talks to him of life itself as a brief aberration:

> "All the good things are now—a thin little rind of what we call life, put on for show, and then—the *real* universe for ever and ever [...] Homer knew—that all the dead have sunk down into the inner darkness: under the rind. All witless, all twittering, gibbering, decaying."[22]

These passages from *Perelandra* give us some idea of the depths to which Lewis's imagination could sink. The reason he and his fiction did not remain so submerged is due, in part, to just that: the light of reason. As mentioned above, Lewis, in the *Problem of Pain*, meets this sort of doubt with his reason. As to the uncaring nature of Nature, he submits that 'not even Omnipotence could create a society of free souls without at the same time creating a relatively independent and "inexorable" Nature'.[23]

He argues that some sort of environment or medium is intrinsically necessary for individuals to exist as conscious selves and to relate to other conscious selves. As he writes, 'There is no reason to suppose that self-consciousness, the recognition of a creature by itself as a "self," can exist except in contrast with an "other," a something which is not the self'.[24] And so, the need for an environment: 'It is against an environment, and preferably a social environment, an environment of other selves, that the awareness of Myself stands out'.[25]

---

18 See PER, pp. 163-164.
19 See PER, p. 164.
20 PER, p. 164.
21 PER, p. 164.
22 PER, pp. 167-168.
23 PP, p. 29.
24 PP, p. 29.
25 PP, p. 29.

Freedom, too, he says, demands an environment, for 'the freedom of a creature must mean freedom to choose: and choice implies the existence of things to choose between'.[26] A creature with no environment of otherness and other things would have no choices to make and no freedom, he writes. And this environment, for our choices to remain free, must be an independent environment in order for different creatures with free will to exist within it. It must have its own independent nature that cannot be altered at the whim of the creatures, or else the medium begins to crumble as a true environment, becoming a mere extension of the creatures' wills. It is not clear, Lewis argues, that one creature could even make himself known to another creature in a nature that was not neutral—'all the matter by which you attempted to make signs to me being already in my control and therefore not capable of being manipulated by you'.[27]

And so Lewis argues that there must be a neutral playing field for creatures with free will to interact with each other. The independent matter, or Nature, that separates us is the thing that allows us to make contact with each other and make choices. And thus we begin to see Lewis's first answer to the problem of evil fortune. Two of the greatest sources of evil fortune, an 'uncaring' nature and the free will of those who would hurt us, are met with one argument. As Lewis reasons, it is impossible to have free will to any significant degree unless Nature *is* 'uncaring', or independent. It could not have been otherwise. If one likes the idea of free will, or the good and caring acts that come from it, one has to be reconciled to the idea of an 'uncaring' nature that cannot be agreeable to everyone's will at once. As Lewis explains:

> If a man travelling in one direction is having a journey down hill, a man going in the opposite direction must be going up hill. If even a pebble lies where I want it to lie, it cannot, except by a coincidence, be where you want it to lie. And this is very far from being an evil: on the contrary, it furnishes occasion for all those acts of courtesy, respect, and unselfishness by which love and good humour and modesty express themselves.[28]

He does admit that this fixed state of nature is a double-edged sword. The same independent nature that allows for the performance of good acts also allows for the performance of evil acts. The independent nature itself may not be evil, but it does make evil acts possible: 'The permanent nature of wood which enables us to use it as a beam also enables us to use it for hitting our neighbour on the head. The permanent nature of matter in general means that when human beings fight, the victory ordinarily goes to those who have

---

26 PP, p. 29.
27 PP, p. 32.
28 PP, pp. 32-33.

superior weapons, skill, and numbers, even if their cause is unjust'.[29]

And it will do no good, Lewis argues, to conceive of a world in which all hurtful actions, all results of the abuse of free will, would be corrected at every moment by God, 'so that a wooden beam became soft as grass when it was used as a weapon, and the air refused to obey me if I attempted to set up in it the sound waves that carry lies or insults'.[30] Such a world, he writes, would be free of evil only because it is a place where truly free actions would be impossible. The lack of evil would not be due to the goodness of free wills; it would be due to the impossibility of free wills.[31]

So according to Lewis, the nature of this world, or of any world with free will creatures, must be independent, must seem not to care. A good God, in this sense, must not crowd out his creatures' free wills by interfering with this independent nature too much. His goodness, in a physical sense, stays away to give us room, or freedom, to be. As Lewis puts it, 'Perhaps this is not the "best of all possible" universes, but the only possible one'.[32] And so what one calls an 'uncaring' nature is often merely a neutral nature. To call it uncaring, according to Lewis's argument, is to be anthropomorphic. In this sense nature, whatever our emotions tell us, can be neither good nor evil in the sense that we attribute to humans. And in this sense 'evil fortune' would cease to be really evil in the sense that we attribute evil to humans. It would, according to Lewis's argument, be merely 'fortune' that is not always agreeable to every creature.[33]

The question can be asked, Lewis admits, whether or not it would have been better to leave the universe uncreated, given the inherent possibility of suffering that creation would mean for creatures. But the question, though it can be asked, may not mean very much, Lewis thinks: 'Some comparison between one state of being and another can be made, but the attempt to compare being and not being ends in mere words. "It would be better for me not to exist"—in what sense "for me"? How should I, if I did not exist, profit by not existing?'.[34]

And so Lewis leaves the question alone. He goes on, in the remainder of the book, to try to show 'how, perceiving a suffering world, and being assured, on quite different grounds [than the reality of suffering], that God is good, we are to conceive that goodness and that suffering without contradiction'. His first course of action, in the following chapter, is to discuss divine goodness and how it may be reconciled with the fact of suffering. In this discussion he

29   PP, p. 33.
30   PP, p. 33.
31   See PP, pp. 33-34.
32   PP, p. 35.
33   How important this distinction between evil fortune and evil men is in both Lewis's and MacDonald's fiction will be discussed in the following chapter.
34   PP, p. 36.

mentions the grounds which, he thinks, assure us that God is in fact good: the moral judgments that humans make, or the moral law as perceived by humans.

The Mistress of the Silver Moon

This internally perceived sense of morality is of the utmost importance in all that Lewis writes after his conversion. It is perhaps the single most important ground on which Lewis bases his faith in a good God, despite the world's troubles. But we need not keep to one chapter of *The Problem of Pain* to examine this ground for Lewis's confidence in God's goodness, for we find most of his books, fiction and non-fiction, replete with either a defense or depiction of human moral judgments. The validity of human moral judgments was essential to his conversion, and it is fundamental in all his stories. It is this light of human conscience that begins to show us important parallels between how Lewis found faith and how MacDonald kept it. An elucidation of these parallels will be easier, perhaps, if we begin with the use of the image of silver moonlight in MacDonald's fiction.

Silver moonlight figures prominently in two of MacDonald's most loved and influential books: two long fairy stories entitled *The Princess and the Goblin* and *The Princess and Curdie*. It is Queen Irene, the Mistress of the Silver Moon, and her dealings with the princess and Curdie that show us something of how MacDonald depicted the challenge of believing in a good God despite appearances to the contrary. We shall find that this image for belief provides an especially fitting metaphor when considering how Lewis came to believe in a good God, and how he and MacDonald kept their faith.

The silver lady's first appearance occurs in chapter three of the first book, just after Irene, a young princess, has gotten lost in her own castle. As in many of Lewis's stories, the action begins on a very wet day when one is forced to stay indoors.[35] With this rain, we already see a metaphor for the world's adversity. The world is not always as we would have it. The bad weather of the world forces us inward to the realization of greater things, perhaps, than weather. The imperfect weather of the world forces us to move beyond circumstance to something that might never be noticed if the weather were always 'perfect'. In Irene's case, she becomes miserable and decides to do a bit of indoor exploration. She finds a curious, old and ill-used stair and decides to see where it actually leads. After many twists and turns, she becomes lost among the lonely passageways of the castle's upper floors. After much weeping and travail, she at length comes across a narrow stairway that leads up to the mysterious silver lady's room. Here, indoors, Irene discovers someone who is both older and younger, and more profound, than mere circumstance.[36]

---

35   See *The Lion, the Witch, and the Wardrobe* (1950) and *The Magician's Nephew* (1955).
36   See George MacDonald, *The Princess and the Goblin* (London: Penguin, 1996), chp. 3. First published in 1872.

Irene pays a second visit to her silver-haired grandmother in chapter eleven, this time after having experienced sharp pain. The pain in her thumb, like the rain in chapter two, sends her wandering around indoors. She finds her way to the foot of the staircase leading up to the lady's chambers, noticing moonlight streaming down from the room. She follows the moonlight up the stairs and finds the lady again, noticing that the silver moonlight and the old lady herself are closely intermingled: 'There was the moonlight streaming in at the window, and in the middle of the moonlight sat the old lady in her black dress with the white lace, and her silvery hair mingling with the moonlight, so that you could not have told which was which'.[37]

When the old lady, known to Irene as her 'great grandmother', notices Irene's hurt thumb, she applies sweet smelling ointment from a mysterious silver casket to drive away the pain. After accepting her grandmother's invitation to stay and spend the night, Irene has to have her feet washed in a large silver basin before getting into bed. And just before going to sleep, Irene learns that a great silver moon-like lamp hanging in the middle of the room acts as a beacon for all of the lady's pigeons.

This emphasis on the moon and its light is one way MacDonald offers encouragement to his readers. As the old lady tells Irene, even '"in the darkest night"' the light of her moon '"never goes out, night or day"'. In other words, there are some things that one can trust in, even though the painful world and its troubles seem so untrustworthy. There are things, perhaps, like ointment from a silver casket, like washing in a silver basin or sleeping under a silvery moon, that will comfort and give courage. And there is, of course, the silver moon and the old lady herself. We shall see later how MacDonald developed this theme in other chapters and other books. Here it is enough to say that he proclaims in these books, in this way, that the good God has not utterly forsaken troubled men of a troubled world. As dark as the world sometimes becomes, there is still some light reflected from the moon. Men living too long in the land of shadows may have forgotten or stopped believing in daylight, but they are not left without any basis for hope.

The *Tao*

In Lewis's books we can find a similar sort of light—only moonlight, perhaps, but enough light, he would decide, to overcome his early doubts. In his case it was his reason, in response to the problem of pain and suffering, that stumbled across the light. He had always yearned for such light with his imagination, as we have already seen in the restless lines of *Spirits in Bondage*, but it was his reason that led him to actually believe in it. If he could not often meet God's goodness in the nature around him—in the broad daylight of an uncaring,

37 P&G, p. 86.

independent nature—then Lewis's reason led him inward to a more subtle light, as the princess was driven up into the inward and upper parts of her own castle by rain and pain. It is, indeed, the contrast between these two realities—an outer world seemingly unconcerned with justice and an inner world of conscience that is very much concerned with justice—that seems to have been one of the strongest factors in Lewis's conversion. The moonlight of human conscience is the thing that took Lewis beyond imagination to actual faith. And it is this faith that helped change his imagination and his fiction.

We see, for example, how Lewis appeals to the validity of conscience as a foundation for the most popular apologetic work he ever wrote: *Mere Christianity*, the printed version of a series of radio broadcasts he delivered during the Second World War. The book begins with a consideration of conscience. The title of this first section, 'Right and Wrong as a Clue to the Meaning of the Universe', suggests straight away that the human moral sense may be very important indeed. It may be the moonlight that suggests that there is more to reality than shadowy trouble and dark indifference.

The content of the section makes explicit what the title suggests. He spends the first three chapters, in fact, establishing and defending the validity of the moral law that most humans seem to know about. In the fourth and final chapter of the first section he argues that God is the Something that lies behind the moral code. In other words, this human sense of right and wrong is an unmistakable clue to meaning in the universe. It is the silver moonlight by which Lewis's intellect finds God, a clue that all is not dark and hopeless. As he writes in chapter five, if we looked only at the natural world outside us, we should have little reason to hope for a God who cares: 'If we used ['the universe He has made'] as our only clue, then I think we should have to conclude that He was a great artist (for the universe is a very beautiful place), but also that He is quite merciless and no friend to man (for the universe is a very dangerous and terrifying place)'.[38]

But when one looks inside, as MacDonald's princess Irene explored the inside of her own castle amidst outside rain and dreariness, one finds something more. Lewis himself calls this 'second bit of evidence' our 'inside information' and says it is better evidence: 'You find out more about God from the Moral Law than from the universe in general just as you find out more about a man by listening to his conversation than by looking at a house he has built'.[39] What the evidence tells us, he writes, is 'that the Being behind the universe is intensely interested in right conduct—in fair play, unselfishness, courage, good faith, honesty and truthfulness'.[40] And so, Lewis reasons, we should gather

---

38   C.S. Lewis, *Mere Christianity* (New York: Macmillan, 1984), p. 37. First published in 1952.
39   MC, p. 37.
40   MC, p. 37.

from the fact of the Moral Law that God is 'good', that there is an absolute Goodness who is interested in our goodness—not necessarily in what we call our 'happiness', but, at the least, in our being good.

His argument begins by pointing out common quarrels people have, such as "'How'd you like it if anyone did the same to you?'" or "'Leave him alone, he isn't doing you any harm'" or "'Come on, you promised.'" The interesting thing about all these disputes, he writes, is how everyone who has them is appealing to an objective standard of conduct and not, he emphasises, 'merely saying that the other man's behaviour does not happen to please him'[41]:

> He is appealing to some kind of standard of behaviour which he expects the other man to know about. And the other man very seldom replies: "To hell with your standard." Nearly always he tries to make out that what he has been doing does not really go against the standard, or that if it does there is some special excuse.[42]

From this fact about quarrelling over behaviour, Lewis argues for a real 'Law of Right and Wrong', or 'Law of Human Nature'.[43] Although there are exceptions to everyone knowing this Law—'just as you find a few people who are colour-blind or have no ear for a tune'—Lewis argues that the Law itself is universal to 'the race as a whole'.[44] If there is no real Law of 'Decent Behaviour' that is obvious to most, Lewis argues that we can blame no one for anything with any justification, even the Nazis:

> What was the sense in saying the enemy were in the wrong unless Right is a real thing which the Nazis at bottom knew as well as we did and ought to have practised? If they had no notion of what we mean by right, then, though we might still have had to fight them, we could no more blame them for that than for the colour of their hair.[45]

Lewis anticipates the objection that this Moral Law is unsound due to different civilizations having very different moralities. He counters it by asserting that it is simply not true that all civilizations we know of have had very dissimilar moralities. He explores this in some depth in his book *The Abolition of Man*, the whole of which is dedicated to defending the natural law, that is, a real Law of decent behaviour based on universals that are not simply a matter of individual taste or feeling. In *Abolition*, Lewis, following oriental tradition, refers to this objective code as the '*Tao*', the great or greatest thing: 'It is the way in which the universe goes on [...] It is also the Way which every man should tread in imitation of that cosmic or super cosmic progression,

---

41   MC, p. 17.
42   MC, p. 17.
43   MC, p. 18.
44   MC, p. 18.
45   MC, pp. 18-19.

conforming all activities to that great exemplar'.[46]

What is common to all civilizations' moral codes—whether oriental, Platonic, Aristotelian, Stoic or Christian—is this idea that these rules of conduct have a root in an objective reality, not a subjective or existential reality. As Lewis writes:

> It is the doctrine of objective value, the belief that certain attitudes are really true, and others really false, to the kind of thing the universe is and the kind of things we are. Those who know the *Tao* can hold that to call children delightful or old men venerable is not simply to record a psychological fact about our own parental or filial emotions at the moment, but to recognize a quality which *demands* a certain response from us whether we make it or not.[47]

And so, also, Lewis asserts, does our moral sense tell us something about reality outside us: namely, that there *is* courtesy, justice and unselfishness, whether or not we ourselves choose to admit these things, or choose to be courteous, just or unselfish. He goes into some detail in the appendix of *Abolition* attempting to show how all civilizations—from ancient Egyptian to old Norse to Australian Aboriginal—have, in fact, very similar ideas of objective morality. As he sums up in *Mere Christianity*:

> Men have differed as regards what people you ought to be unselfish to—whether it was only your own family, or your fellow countrymen, or everyone. But they have always agreed that you ought not to put yourself first. Selfishness has never been admired. Men have differed as to whether you should have one wife or four. But they have always agreed that you must not simply have any woman you liked.[48]

This doctrine of a real, objective moral code is important in the context of this study because it shows where Lewis believes that there is something other than an uncaring, haphazard nature: that there is Goodness, and even a God who cares, despite appearances to the contrary. The human sense of morality is a clue that tells us that there is something more than amoral chaos. According to Lewis, it is a beam of moonlight that suggests, or reflects, significance.

Dwarves and Other Skeptics

Lewis argues that the significance the moral law reflects is a God of Goodness who expects goodness from humans, but he knew that there were those who claimed to see no such significance. His portrayal of such skepticism is frequent

---

46   C.S. Lewis, *The Abolition of Man* (New York: Macmillan, 1986), p. 28. Lewis paraphrases here from A.B. Keith, 'Righteousness' (Hindu), in J. Hastings (ed.), *The Encyclopedia of Religion and Ethics*, Vol. X. (Edinburgh: T&T Clark, 1912). *Abolition* first published in 1947.

47   ABO, p. 29.

48   MC, p. 19.

in his fiction and closely resembles similar depictions in MacDonald's stories.

In *The Princess and the Goblin*, for example, the first person who doesn't believe in whom the moonlight leads to is Lootie, the child's nurse. Irene tells her that she's been 'a long way up and up' to see her great grandmother with silver hair who is so very beautiful though so very old.[49] The nurse tells Irene she's talking nonsense, but Irene persists. "'I'm not talking nonsense'", she says, rather offended. "I will tell you all about her. She's much taller than you, and much prettier'".[50] The nurse continues in unbelief, however, accusing Irene of making it up. Irene bursts into tears, and the nurse becomes vexed. Later, as Irene and her nurse are making peace, we see a hint, perhaps, as to why the nurse did not feel inclined to believe Irene. She doesn't like the idea of someone existing who makes her feel ugly:

> "And you won't say I'm ugly, any more—will you, princess?"
> "Nursie, I never said you were ugly. What can you mean?"
> "Well, if you didn't say it, you meant it."
> "Indeed, I never did."
> "You said I wasn't so pretty as that—"
> "As my beautiful grandmother—yes, I did say that; and I say it again, for it's quite true."
> "Then I *do* think you *are* unkind!" said the nurse, and put her handkerchief to her eyes again.
> "Nursie, dear, everybody can't be as beautiful as every other body, you know. You are *very* nice looking, but if you had been as beautiful as my grandmother—"
> "Bother your grandmother!" said the nurse.[51]

It is not difficult to imagine a similar reaction to what Lewis's moonlight brought him to: a perfectly good God who expects us to be good. The existence of anything higher or better than one's self may often produce such reactions in those of us who do not want to be reminded of our shortcomings. As Lewis writes about the existence of a real Goodness, the Source of meaning in the universe can also be, once It is believed to be real and conscious, the cause of great discomfort:

> [T]he trouble is that one part of you is on His side and really agrees with His disapproval of human greed and trickery and exploitation [...] On the other hand, we know that if there does exist an absolute goodness it must hate most of what we do [...] We cannot do without it, and we cannot do with it. God is the only comfort, He is also the supreme terror: the thing we most need and the thing we most want to hide from [...] Some people talk as if meeting the gaze of absolute goodness would be fun. They need to think again. [...] Goodness is

---

49   P&G, p. 19.
50   P&G, p. 20.
51   P&G, p. 23.

either the great safety or the great danger—according to the way you react to it.[52]

Irene's behaviour in MacDonald's tale, in trying to make peace with Lootie, is reflective of MacDonald, who was not in the habit of allowing himself or his characters to remain long estranged from those who did not see the truth as he did.[53] But it is also indicative of MacDonald and his characters in that they are happy about the truth and want others to be happy too. Irene makes peace but still would like Lootie to be able to believe in her great grandmother. Another one of his characters, North Wind in *At the Back of the North Wind*, puts it this way in her definition of a poet: "'A poet is a man who is glad of something, and tries to make other people glad of it too'".[54] And so Irene, the poet, before falling asleep, asks once more if her nurse will come and see her grandmother.[55]

Sometimes, though, even when people are persuaded to go and see her grandmother, they don't see what Irene sees. Such is the case with Curdie late in the story when Irene persuades him to go up with her to see her grandmother. Irene has just helped Curdie to escape the dark cave of the Goblins by following a magical silver thread tied to a ring, both of which were given to Irene by her grandmother. Throughout their escape Curdie cannot see the silver thread that Irene insists she is following. But grateful for help in escaping, Curdie accepts her offer to go see her grandmother, though he remains quite skeptical: "'I never doubted you believed what you said'", returned Curdie. "'I only thought you had some fancy in your head that was not correct'".[56]

After following Irene up the stair to her grandmother's room, he still can't see or hear what Irene can. Irene hears her grandmother's sweet voice beckon her into the room. She is taken up by her grandmother to sit in her lap. She and her grandmother discuss Curdie. But Curdie still cannot see the old, beautiful lady. He cannot see her or how fine her room is.[57] He sees only a big, bare garret room, a tub, a heap of musty straw, a withered apple, and a "'ray of sunlight coming through a hole in the middle of the roof and shining on your head, and making all the place look a curious dusky brown'".[58] Curdie takes Irene's descriptions of things he can't see or hear as an extravagant insult, and there is a subsequent increase in frustration on both sides.

---

52 MC, p. 38.
53 See, for example, RAEP, p. 52, concerning John Kennedy.
54 George MacDonald, *At the Back of the North Wind* (Ware: Wordsworth, 1994), p. 69. First published in 1871.
55 See P&G, p. 24.
56 P&G, p. 171.
57 See P&G, pp. 174-175.
58 P&G, p. 175.

Similar depictions of skepticism meet us in Lewis's fiction. The images are so similar that one cannot avoid attributing a direct influence to MacDonald's Curdie books. One example is *The Lion, the Witch, and the Wardrobe*, in which Peter, Susan and Edmund doubt Lucy about the wardrobe. As Curdie saw only an ordinary garret, the three children doubt Lucy's story about the wardrobe leading to a snowy world, a faun and a witch. They even go and open up the wardrobe to humour her. But when Susan puts her head inside and pulls the fur coats apart, she sees only a common piece of furniture that leads to nowhere.[59] Even Lucy herself, this time, sees only a wardrobe. Like Irene with Curdie, and later in the story when her silver thread seems to lead to nowhere, Lucy becomes frustrated and distressed.[60] In *Prince Caspian* it is Lucy again who, like Irene, sees when others can't. It is she who tells the group that she sees Aslan and that he wants them to follow him. No one else, at first, can see him; they look at her in 'puzzled silence', much like Curdie looked at Irene when she took him to her grandmother's room.[61]

Trumpkin, a dwarf, plays the part of skeptic in *Prince Caspian* as Curdie did in *The Princess and the Goblin*. This choice by Lewis plays upon the fact that dwarves are traditionally portrayed as no-nonsense creatures strongly attached to the earth and earthly things. In J.R.R. Tolkien's books, for example, dwarves are renown for their craftsmanship and their desire for precious metals and gems. They build great cities under the earth. They possess a fine practical wit and sense of honour. But they are slow to acknowledge beauty that they cannot dig up or hammer, or unearthly truths that they cannot easily grasp or chew. In Tolkien's books this dwarfish disposition is seen in the stark contrast between a dwarf named Gimli and his companion in battle, an elf named Legolas. MacDonald, before Tolkien or Lewis, did something similar in the contrast between Curdie, a miner boy, and Irene, a princess. And Lewis does it with Trumpkin the dwarf and Lucy, the most sensitive of Lewis's Narnia characters.[62] In *Prince Caspian*, Trumpkin offers a doubtful, watered-down interpretation of what Lucy said she saw. The lion Lucy saw was probably just an ordinary lion, he says, or else Aslan has grown ordinary himself.[63] Trumpkin's saying that Aslan may have gone wild and witless has much the same effect on Lucy as Lootie's words ('"Bother your grandmother!"') had on Irene: '"Lucy turned crimson and I think she would have flown at Trumpkin,

---

59   See C.S. Lewis, *The Lion, the Witch and the Wardrobe* (New York: Harper Collins, 1994), p. 26.

60   See LWW, p. 27.

61   PC, p, 132.

62   Compare Lewis's traditional dwarves with the *pfifltrigg* of Malacandra in his *Out of the Silent Planet* (New York: Macmillan, 1986), especially pp. 112-116.

63   See C.S. Lewis, *Prince Caspian* (New York: Harper Collins, 1994), p. 132. First published in 1951.

if Peter had not laid his hand on her arm'".[64]

Dwarves make a final appearance in Lewis's last Narnia book, *The Last Battle*, and they are at least as skeptical as Trumpkin is in *Prince Caspian*.[65] In a chapter entitled 'How the Dwarves Refused to be Taken In', we find a situation very much like that in the first Narnia book: a door has been made from one world into another, only this time the door is affixed to a stable, not a wardrobe, and the movement is from Narnia, not to it. The stable door leads to "'the country where everything is allowed'" and will offer us, in a later chapter of this study, a glimpse of Lewis's literary vision of heaven.[66] But in this chapter it will give us a glimpse of how the dwarf-like can doubt the heavenly, even when it's right under their noses.[67]

Eleven dwarves[68] have traveled through the door but are oblivious to the wonders around them. Instead of walking about enjoying themselves, or lying down and resting, they are seated very close together in a circle facing each other and seem to notice nothing. They do not even notice the approach of Queen Lucy and King Tirian until they get close enough to touch them. It so happens that they can hear, but they cannot see all that's to be seen. All the dwarves insist that they are sitting in a "'pitch-black, poky, smelly little hole of a stable'".[69]

Again it is Lucy, like Irene before her, who tries to convince that there is much more than darkness: "'But it isn't dark, you poor stupid Dwarfs," said Lucy. "Can't you see? Look up! Look round! Can't you see the sky and the trees and the flowers? Can't you see *me*?'".[70] A dwarf named Diggle[71] insists, as Curdie insisted to Irene, that there's not much there, though Diggle sees even less, and is more rude, than Curdie: "'How in the name of all Humbug can I see what ain't there? And how can I see you any more than you can see me in this pitch darkness?'".[72] Frustrated but persistent, Lucy tries to appeal to other senses by picking some wild violets for him to smell. The dwarf, though,

---

64   PC, p. 133; P&G, p. 23.

65   Trumpkin eventually comes to belief in Aslan. He is, indeed, playfully tossed about by the great Lion. The dwarves in *The Last Battle* (1956) never come to belief.

66   See chp. 6, below.

67   To be fair to these dwarves, it should be noted that they have been hoodwinked once already in the story, when they are persuaded to believe that a donkey dressed in a lion's skin is the real Aslan.

68   Eleven is also the number of Jesus's disciples immediately after the death of Judas, the betrayer. Dwarves in *The Last Battle* have betrayed Prince Tirian.

69   C.S. Lewis, *The Last Battle* (New York: Harper Collins, 1994), p. 181.

70   LB, p. 181.

71   No doubt a play on 'dig', another indication of the dwarfish preoccupation with the earth and things below the earth.

72   LB, p. 181.

thinks it's only 'filthy stable-litter' with a thistle in it.[73] Like Curdie, the dwarf fails to sense the sublime or the sweet. And here, sensing only stable-litter and painful thistles, he reminds us of how young Lewis once saw in the world little more than pain and dreariness. Diggle is unmoved by anything that Lucy or Tirian can say.

The dwarves will not be persuaded, even when Aslan himself appears. When he comes close to the dwarves and gives them a low growl that sets the air shaking, the dwarves take it to be a machine of some sort, used by the others to try and frighten them. Likewise, when Aslan lifts his head and shakes his mane to produce a glorious feast at the dwarves' knees, it is to no avail. They begin eating greedily, but they insist that the great feast is only hay, or the odd bit of old turnip or raw cabbage leaf. The rich red wine in golden goblets, to the dwarves' taste, is only '"dirty water out of a trough that a donkey's been at!"'.[74] The sublime feast is, in the end, turned into a ridiculous food fight, with every Dwarf beginning to suspect 'that every other Dwarf had found something nicer than he had'.[75] After their fight, when they sit back down with their black eyes and bleeding noses, they're all consoled by this thought: '"Well, at any rate there's no Humbug here. We haven't let anyone take us in. The Dwarfs are for the Dwarfs"'.[76]

So, seemingly contented with their own selves and their own limited perceptions, Aslan leaves them be: '"You see," said Aslan. "They will not let us help them. They have chosen cunning instead of belief. Their prison is only in their own minds, yet they are in that prison; and so afraid of being taken in that they cannot be taken out"'.[77]

The contrast between belief and unbelief is also at the heart of the last novel Lewis wrote, *Till We Have Faces*. Here, as in the Narnia books, he uses metaphors very similar to ones found in *The Princess and the Goblin* to express such a contrast.

Till We Have Faces is Lewis's retelling of the myth of Cupid and Psyche.[78] In the myth, Venus, jealous of Psyche's beauty, sends Cupid to cast a spell on Psyche that will cause her to fall in love with the worst, basest sort of men. Venus's plan backfires, however, when Cupid himself sees Psyche and is besmitten. He carries her off to a stately palace where he visits and loves her

---

73   LB, p. 182.
74   LB, p. 184.
75   LB, p. 185.
76   LB, p. 185.
77   LB, pp. 185-186.
78   The story first occurs in *The Golden Ass* (4.28–6.24), sometimes called *Metamorphoses*, of Lucius Apuleius Platonicus (born in A.D. 120s). See Lewis's own citation in *Till We have Faces: A Myth Retold* (San Diego: Harcourt Brace & Company, 1985), pp. 311-313. *Faces* first published in 1956.

by night but forbids her to see his face. When Psyche begs that she might be visited at the palace by her two sisters, Cupid reluctantly agrees. The sisters are much delighted with the lavish feasts and many splendours of the palace but are secretly envious because their own husbands and homes cannot compare to Cupid and his palace.

Lewis's telling of the myth is similar to Apuleius's version. Like it, his story involves a beautiful woman named Psyche and her two sisters. But Lewis's story is significantly different in that it is told from Orual's point of view. She, in Lewis's version, is Psyche's older and uglier half-sister. Her jealousy of Psyche's husband and his palace is an important element in the story that Lewis keeps, though it is not identical to the jealousy of Apuleius's sisters.[79] And in this respect Orual resembles MacDonald's Lootie, Irene's nurse who does not like the idea of Irene constantly talking of someone more beautiful than she is. But this element of jealousy in the Cupid-Psyche myth is transformed in Lewis's story when he follows MacDonald's lead by making the god's palace invisible to Orual. With this alteration Lewis adds another layer of meaning to the myth which allows him to explore the relationship between belief and unbelief. Orual follows Lootie and Curdie, and Lewis's own dwarves, as a character who shows us Lewis's idea of what unbelief is like (as Psyche, in comparison a more minor character, shows us what he thinks belief is like).[80]

Lewis, however, due to the kind of book *Faces* is, is able to say things with Orual that neither he nor MacDonald could in their fairy tales. *Faces* is a thoroughgoing character study as well as a story. The entire book is an account of events from Orual, but her account tells the reader much about Orual herself. She is by far the most carefully drawn character in all of Lewis's fiction. Part of her identity is a curious mixture of fear and skepticism. From the beginning she is skeptical of the local god, Ungit, and fearfully repelled at the worship of Ungit, as when the priest of Ungit visits their father, the king of Glome:

> I had a fear of that priest which was quite different from my fear of
> my father. I think that what frightened me (in those early days) was
> the holiness of the smell that hung about him—a temple-smell of

---

79 Apuleius's sisters envy Psyche for what she has and what they do not. Orual, in Lewis's version, is not preoccupied with what Psyche has; indeed, she often denies what Psyche says she has. Orual's preoccupation is with Psyche herself, and all of her thoughts and feelings about what Psyche has (her new husband and palace) spring from this preoccupation. In this respect the jealousy of Lewis's Orual is much more a kind of love than the jealousy of Apuleius's sisters.

80 For a detailed study of the tension between reason and imagination in *Faces*, and in the rest of Lewis's fiction, see Peter J. Schackel, *Reason and Imagination in C.S. Lewis: A Study of Till We Have Faces* (Grand Rapids: Eerdmans, 1984).

blood (mostly pigeons' blood, but he had sacrificed men, too) and burnt fat and singed hair and wine and stale incense. It is the Ungit smell. Perhaps I was afraid of his clothes too; all the skins they were made of, and the dried bladders, and the great mask shaped like a bird's head which hung on his chest. It looked as if there were a bird growing out of his body.[81]

And so when Psyche offers herself up as a sacrifice to the holy Shadowbrute (that is, Ungit or Ungit's son, the god of the mountain—or both), Orual, who claims a deep love for Psyche, is horrified. This horror is exacerbated and complicated by the fact of Psyche's own belief: she thinks that her sacrifice to the Shadowbrute (which the priest says is necessary to heal the barren, diseased land) is the same as marrying the Shadowbrute. Far from dreading the great sacrifice, she looks forward to it as the greatest fulfillment, calling the longing for it "'the sweetest thing in all my life'".[82] From Orual's reaction to this we learn that her unbelief, her horror at Ungit and the Shadowbrute, is mixed with more than a little wounded jealousy, much like Lootie's jealousy of Irene's grandmother[83]: "'And that was the sweetest? Oh, cruel, cruel. Your heart is not of iron—stone, rather'".[84] Psyche, not seeming to hear her sister, goes on about her sweet destiny.[85] Orual is exasperated at Psyche's going on and on about her lover, just as Lootie was exasperated at Irene going on and on about her grandmother. Lootie said this to Irene: "'Then I *do* think you *are* unkind! [...] Bother your grandmother!'".[86] In *Faces* we hear a near echo from Orual to Psyche: "'I only see that you have never loved me [...] It may well be you are going to the gods. You are becoming cruel like them'".[87]

And, as mentioned above, MacDonald's influence can be seen in Lewis's most significant change in the telling of the myth. When Orual, unable to prevent the sacrifice, journeys to the Grey Mountain to collect Psyche's bones (she thinks wild animals, or bad men, or starvation, have had their way with Psyche), she finds Psyche herself instead. Orual is joyfully surprised to see Psyche alive at all, much more because she, apart from her tattered clothes, seems healthy and unharmed. But the joy is soon turned to frustration and despair when Orual, like Curdie, begins to be told of things she can't see. Psyche sees a banquet of food fit for the gods; Orual sees cool, dark berries in a green leaf. Psyche sees a noble wine in the fairest of cups; Orual tastes a silvery trickle of mountain water gathered in Psyche's hands. Orual plays along with

---

81 FAC, p. 11. Compare to Tash in *The Last Battle*, especially chp. 12.
82 FAC, p. 75.
83 See P&G, chp. 4.
84 FAC, p. 75.
85 See FAC, p. 76.
86 P&G, p. 23.
87 FAC, p. 76.

Psyche at first, choosing to take her descriptions as hyperbole, as Curdie took Irene's words as a sort of "'game'".[88]

But she begins to see that Psyche is in earnest as she tells the story of her ordeal: of her own doubts while waiting alone, chained to a sacrificial tree; of a transformation which included her being caught up in the arms of the West-Wind; of her being taken to a great palace; and finally of her meeting the Bridegroom, the god himself. Psyche's account here reminds us of Irene's account of her great grandmother's beautiful room: "'Don't you see the lovely fire of roses [...] nor the blue bed? Nor the rose-coloured counterpane? Nor the beautiful light, like the moon, hanging from the roof?'".[89] It becomes clear that Orual cannot see the wonders described, no more than Curdie or the dwarves could. When Orual asks how far it is to the god's house, Psyche is astonished, informing Orual with white face and staring eyes that she is "'standing on the stairs of the great gate'".[90]

This scene leads to chapter eleven, the part of the book which Orual calls 'that part of my history on which my charge against the gods chiefly rests'.[91] Orual's complaint, according to her own account, springs from the separation between herself, who cannot see, and her sister, who can.

It is important to note here that belief and unbelief, in *Faces*, are not portrayed as things inhabiting wholly different and separate universes. Orual and Psyche, to be sure, are different in how much they see or believe, but the two are not simply opposites, as it may sometimes seem with characters in the Narnia or Curdie books. This has already been hinted at in chapter ten when Psyche herself tells of her own doubts while bound to the Tree. For a long time after everyone left the Tree, she recalls, nothing happened at all: "'And all I could do was to pray, pray, pray to the gods that whatever was going to happen to me might happen soon. But nothing happened, except that my tears made me thirstier'".[92] Cattle and a lynx-like creature come and pay her the animal attentions of mooing and sniffing, but Psyche, like Ransom in *Perelandra*,[93] eventually becomes lonely and doubtful: "'At first I was trying to cheer myself with all that old dream of my gold and amber palace on the Mountain... and the god...trying to believe it. But I couldn't believe in it at all. I couldn't understand how I ever had. All that, all my old longings, were clean gone'".[94]

And in chapter eleven, we see that Orual's disbelief is not without *its* doubts. After Psyche speaks of their standing at the palace gate, Orual's first

---

88   P&G, p. 175.
89   P&G, pp. 174-175.
90   FAC, p. 116.
91   FAC, p. 117.
92   FAC, p. 108.
93   See pp. 57-58, above.
94   FAC, p. 109.

thought is of madness, but not just of Psyche's madness: 'My whole heart leaped to shut the door against something monstrously amiss—not to be endured. And to keep it shut. Perhaps I was fighting not to be mad myself'.[95] Her words to her sister are that they must leave that '"terrible place"', but her thoughts show more than a simple disbelief in the wonders Psyche describes. They reveal a fear of being taken in, or losing control of one's reality:

> Was I believing in her invisible palace? A Greek will laugh at the thought. But it's different in Glome. There the gods are too close to us. Up in the Mountain, in the very heart of the Mountain, where Bardia had been afraid and even the priests don't go, anything was possible. No door could be shut. Yes, that was it; not plain belief, but infinite misgiving—the whole world (Psyche with it) slipping out of my hands.[96]

This is not the first time Orual has doubted her perception, or cynical interpretation, of the world. On the journey to collect Psyche's bones, she had wondered, while looking down from a high ridge across to the Mountain, whether reality was, in fact, troubles and sorrows merely:

> And my struggle was this. You may well believe that I had set out sad enough; I came on a sad errand. Now, flung at me like frolic or insolence, there came as if it were a voice—no words—but if you made it into words it would be, "Why should your heart not dance?" It's the measure of my folly that my heart almost answered, "Why not?" I had to tell myself over like a lesson the infinite reasons it had not to dance.[97]

The reasons she rehearses to herself to argue against any beneficence in the world are a catalogue of her personal troubles, past and present. But the beautiful prospect before her makes even this long catalogue, for the moment, difficult to attend to, much as the vast, lonely Perelandrean seascape made it difficult for Ransom to keep believing in Purpose[98]: 'The sight of the huge world put mad ideas into me [...] The freshness and wetness all about me (I had seen nothing but draught and withered things for many months before my sickness) made me feel that I had misjudged the world; it seemed kind, and laughing, as if its heart also danced'.[99] Even Orual's physical ugliness, a misfortune that runs as an important undercurrent throughout most of the novel, is temporarily put out of mind: 'Who can *feel* ugly when the heart meets delight? It is as if, somewhere inside, within the hideous face and bony limbs, one is soft, fresh, lissome and desirable'.[100]

---

95   FAC, p. 117.
96   FAC, pp. 117-118.
97   FAC, pp. 95-96.
98   See pp. 57-58, above.
99   FAC, p. 96.
100   FAC, p. 96.

But Orual struggles and prevails against all this strong sweetness with her sense of her own grief: 'Mere seemliness, if nothing else, called for [a 'struggle against this fool-happy mood']. I would not go laughing to Psyche's burial. If I did, how should I ever again believe that I had loved her? Reason called for it. I know the world too well to believe this sudden smiling'.[101] Even after Orual discovers that Psyche is not dead, she still struggles against belief. And against Psyche herself, literally. When Psyche cries for Orual to try and feel what she can't see ('"Touch it. Slap it. Beat your head against it."'), and grabs her hands in an effort to help her feel it, Orual wrenches free and attempts to thrust back the possibility of belief 'by brute force', falling on Psyche and shaking her like a child.[102]

Lewis's handling of the dialogue, after the sisters fall apart, leaves the reader free to doubt Orual's first account of what she actually tasted when she ate and sipped. Orual, in any case, records her close brush with belief after she tells Psyche that the wine was only water and the cup only Psyche's hands. In this account we see where Lewis, though following MacDonald, goes a bit further, at least in this passage. Curdie, when Irene first showed him grandmother's room, never admitted to seeing anything but a '"big, bare, garret-room"' with things common to such a place.[103] He never, upon his first introduction, sees Irene's grandmother or the wonders of her bedroom. His denial upon first introduction is simple. He simply cannot believe in what he cannot see. Orual's continued unbelief is not so clear cut.

For example, there is the utterly convincing dejection of Psyche at her sister's apparent blindness. It's as if Lewis were taking something from MacDonald's story—Irene's frustration and dejection at Curdie's blindness—and developing it in the action between Orual and Psyche, for after hearing her sister's despair at her blindness, Orual almost comes to believe that she may not be able to see all that might be there: 'I came almost to a full belief. She was shaking and stirring me a dozen different ways. But I had not shaken her at all [...] This valley was indeed a dreadful place; full of the divine, sacred, no place for mortals. There might be a hundred things in it that I could not see'.[104]

There is also Psyche's inability to see the god himself. When Orual demands for Psyche to show this master of the palace to her, and asks her what he's like, we see where Lewis keeps to the Cupid-Psyche myth as it is usually told, for Psyche says she has not yet seen him: '"He comes to me only in the holy darkness. He says I musn't—not yet—see his face or know his name.

---

101 FAC, pp. 96-97.
102 FAC, p. 118.
103 P&G, p. 175.
104 FAC, p. 120.

I'm forbidden to bring any light into his—our—chamber'".[105] This particular keeping of the myth, of course, shows us how Lewis does not, in *Faces*, merely paraphrase the passages from MacDonald, or merely reproduce, in slightly different garb, the Lucy/Dwarf passages from his Narnia books. Irene did see her grandmother and Lucy did see Aslan. But Psyche here admits that she has not seen, has indeed been forbidden to see, the god she believes in and loves. In this instance, perhaps, we see Lewis painting a picture more faithful to the nature of faith than either MacDonald or his own Narnia passages did, or could, paint. For surely faith includes not being able to see or experience all things. If faith is at all believing in what one cannot see, then Psyche's belief at this point in the story is closer to expressing the actual nature of faith, the faith that Lewis and MacDonald held, than when Irene sees her grandmother or Lucy sees Aslan. Psyche is utterly convinced of the god's existence and presence, not because she can see him or know him fully in the present, but because of everything else that she *can* see, or feel or hear.

The Light of Reason

We have proof from Lewis's non-fiction that this is just the sort of faith that he had. In an address to the Oxford Socratic Club entitled 'Is Theology Poetry', for example, Lewis said this about his faith: 'I believe in Christianity as I believe that the Sun has risen, not only because I see it, but because by it I see everything else'.[106] Or to use MacDonald's metaphor of the moon and its light, one can believe in the light of the sun even if the sun itself is not directly visible. According to MacDonald and Lewis, even when things on earth seem most meaningless and ungodly, it is possible for us to believe in a good God, for we find the light of God reflected from things around us, or, as mentioned above, from things inside us like conscience. A knowledge of right and wrong acts as the moon to 'reflect' God and his goodness to us. To Lewis, the human sense of morality, as we have already seen, was a clue, or a reason for belief in a good God. If Lewis could not always see God himself, he could very well see his palace and eat and drink of the palace's food.

Another reason for Lewis's belief was reason itself. Lewis thought human reason, like human conscience, was another clue: a bit of moonlight that led back to God. He argues such in his most ambitious apologetic work, *Miracles*, in which he attempts to show how we can do no confident thinking unless we admit that reason transcends nature, that it comes from God. It will be impossible, of course, to reproduce the whole of his argument here without reproducing the entire book. It is also unnecessary, for we need only say enough to show how he believed that reason, like the validity of conscience, acts as a

---

105 FAC, p. 123.
106 C.S. Lewis, *The Weight of Glory and Other Addresses* (New York: Simon and Schuster, 1996), p. 106.

clue that leads beyond an uncaring, haphazard nature.

In the opening sentences of the book, Lewis shows us how similar his subject is to the situation in *Till We Have Faces*. He writes that he has only met one person in all his life who claims to have seen a ghost. The interesting thing, he writes, 'is that that person disbelieved in the immortal soul before she saw the ghost and still disbelieves after seeing it'.[107] In *Faces* both Psyche and Orual were looking at the same valley, but each 'saw', or admitted, something different. What we read about are two different interpretations of the same valley, as there were two different interpretations of grandmother's room in *The Princess and the Goblin*, and of the inside of the stable in *The Last Battle*. One looks and sees only ordinary things; the other looks and sees the home of a god. Or, as in the ghost sighting mentioned here in *Miracles*, one actually does see what looks like a ghost, but interprets it as an illusion or trick of the nerves.

This example of interpretation in *Miracles* is even more like Orual's interpretation than the discussion of *Faces* above reveals, for we have not yet noted that Orual does in fact remember getting a glimpse of the palace, even of its god. After parting from Psyche, she drinks from the river that flows from the valley of the god's palace. As the ice-cold drink steadies her mind, she looks back through a fog from where she'd come and gazes at the following scene: 'There stood the palace, grey—as all things were grey in that hour and place— but solid and motionless, wall within wall, pillar and arch and architrave, acres of it, a labyrinthine beauty. As [Psyche] had said, it was like no house ever seen in our land or age'.[108]

Orual, however, chooses to interpret this sight—for her own reasons— differently than Psyche. Throughout most of the rest of the book she disbelieves in the good and beautiful god that Psyche speaks of. And so do many people interpret things differently in actual life, writes Lewis in *Miracles*, as in the woman's seeing a ghost but interpreting it as probably a trick of the nerves. 'And obviously', Lewis writes, 'she may be right. Seeing is not believing'.[109]

With this observation Lewis begins his book, which in large measure is an argument against the sort of empiricism encouraged by Hume's famous essay 'Of Miracles'.[110] This empiricism, which effectually limits what one can believe as true to what can be predicted from past experience, has been used to discredit many forms of *a priori* knowledge, from metaphysics to belief in the supernatural, to religious faith.[111] It is an interpretation of reality that

---

107 C.S. Lewis, *Miracles: A Preliminary Study* (New York: Macmillan, 1978), p. 3.

108 FAC, p. 132.

109 MIR, p. 3.

110 Published in *Enquiry Concerning Human Understanding* (1748).

111 For a concise and lucid example of this thinking, see A.J. Ayer, *Language, Truth and Logic, Second ed.*, (London: Gollancz, 1946), especially chs 1 to 4. In the preface Ayer states that his treatise, which argues against metaphysical philosophy, is derived

excludes the supernatural from the realm of all possible knowledge because the supernatural, apparently, cannot be observed. Hume's empiricism, to speak metaphorically, looks at grandmother's room and sees only a garret with ordinary furniture. It is the tongue of the dwarf that tastes dirty donkey's water instead of rich red wine, or the mind of Orual that admits, for its own reasons, only an ordinary valley where some eyes (even her own) had seen a god's palace. In our own non-fictional world it admits only the natural.[112]

Lewis himself once admitted only the natural. He changed his mind, in part, because he came to believe that there was something behind, and indeed mixed up with, nature. The Naturalist argument against the supernatural (or subnatural) is no good, Lewis argues in *Miracles*, because it is an argument that says all arguments are based on, in a logical sense, nothing. If all reason is a product of nature, which itself is a product of mindless, non-rational chance, Lewis argues, then we have little reason to suppose it to be anything other than a feeling or a response. And we should, therefore, trust the logical statement 'A=B & B=C, therefore C=A' as little as we trust a taste or a prejudice, or wishful thinking, to tell us something definitely true. All of these things, say the Naturalist, arise from an essentially mindless Nature and therefore, according to Lewis's view of their argument, we have no reason to trust any argument as reasonable.

If the Naturalist, or anyone else, wants to make a rational argument about anything, he must accept human reasoning as something more than a natural feeling in his head. As Lewis argues:

> If the feeling of certainty which we express by words like *must be* and *therefore* and *since* is a real perception of how things outside our own minds really "must" be, well and good. But if this certainty is merely a feeling *in* our own minds and not a genuine insight into realities beyond them—if it merely represents the way our minds happen to work—then we can have no knowledge.[113]

---

from the doctrines of Bertrand Russell [*The Principles of Mathematics* (1903), *The Problems of Philosophy* (1912), *The Analysis of Matter* (1927)] and Ludwig Wittgenstein [*Tractatus Logico-Philosophicus* (1961), *Philosophical Investigations* (1963), *On Certainty* (1979)], and the empiricism of George Berkeley [*Essay Toward a New Theory of Vision* (1709), *Treatise Concerning Human Knowledge* (1710), *Dialogues between Hylas and Philanous* (1713)] and David Hume [*Treatise of Human Nature* (1739), *Philosophical Essays* (1748), *Enquiry Concerning Principles of Morals* (1751)]. It should also be noted here that both Lewis and MacDonald were very clear that the essence of truly religious faith is not simply belief in the supernatural, though it must include it. See chs 4 and 5, below.

112 See *Miracles*, especially chp. 13.

113 MIR, p. 14.

As he argued in *Mere Christianity*[114] that a wholly naturalistic explanation of morals would invalidate any moral judgement, so he argues in *Miracles* that all rational statements and arguments are invalidated once they can be identified wholly as a product of nature. As he summed up such an argument elsewhere:

> Every particular thought (whether it is a judgement of fact or a judgement of value) is always and by all men discounted the moment they believe that it can be explained, without remainder, as the result of irrational causes. Whenever you know what the other man is saying is wholly due to his complexes or to a bit of bone pressing on his brain, you cease to attach any importance to it. But if naturalism were true then all thoughts whatever would be wholly the result of irrational causes. Therefore, all thoughts would be equally worthless. Therefore, naturalism is worthless. If it is true, then we can know no truths. It cuts its own throat.[115]

This distinction (not to be confused with total separation) between things natural and supernatural is important in the context of this chapter, of course, because it is important in the context of Lewis's fiction. Or rather, it *is* the context of Lewis's fiction. Even if no supernatural God of Goodness actually exists to mix with the world we know, the worlds of Lewis's books, like MacDonald's, are without doubt shot through with the supernatural, with Goodness, and with God. And it would not have been so if Lewis had not come to think that certain facts were actually clues that lead us beyond nature to the Something or Someone who, unlike irrational and amoral nature, really does care about humans and human goodness. Both Lewis and MacDonald believed strongly in this distinction between the natural and the supernatural, and both saw it as a clue that there is, in fact, a good God: or in other words, that the supernatural element in man was a sort of living connection, a silver thread if you will, leading to the eternal God of goodness.

Lewis, for example, describes human reason as 'the little tell-tale rift in Nature which shows that there is something beyond or behind her'.[116] He uses the analogy of a pond surface covered with scum, floating vegetation and a few water lilies to illustrate his idea:

> The Naturalist thinks that the pond (Nature—the great event in space and time) is of an indefinite depth—that there is nothing but water however far you go down. My claim is that some of the things on the surface (i.e. in our experience) show the contrary. These things (rational minds) reveal, on inspection, that they at least are not floating but

---

114 And in *Miracles*, chs 5 and 6.
115 C.S. Lewis, *God in the Dock: Essays on Theology and Ethics* (Grand Rapids: Eerdmans, 1993), p. 137. From 'Religion without Dogma?', a paper originally read to the Oxford Socratic Club on 20 May 1946.
116 MIR, p. 29.

attached by stalks at the bottom. Therefore the pond has a bottom. It is not pond, pond for ever.[117]

And so, according to Lewis's thinking, reality is not nature for ever. Here and there we see or know things that cannot be explained away as mere nature, things that act as pinholes of moonlight in the relative darkness of an irrational, uncaring Nature. Lewis, in all of his apologetic books, worked hard with his mind and pen to try and persuade that these distinctions were undeniable, as Princess Irene, Lucy and Psyche tried hard to get others to see, or feel or taste, the wonders they knew.

This effort is particularly evident in chapters like the second of *Mere Christianity*, entitled 'Some Objections'. Some of the letters Lewis received from people were those that expressed unbelief similar to that of Curdie, the dwarves, and Orual. These correspondents, like Lewis, had experienced the reality of what Lewis called the Moral Law, but they didn't see what he did. Lewis opens the door of conscience, looks inside and sees a law of morality that transcends nature and points to a God of Goodness. Others look into that same door and see only the herd instinct, an instinct developed from nature just like all our other instincts.

One of the ways Lewis responds to such an interpretation shows us how he seeks to highlight a real distinction between nature and the supernatural. If the Moral Law is simply one of our natural instincts, what is it, Lewis asks, that chooses between two or more conflicting instincts? If our minds are nothing but a jumble of instincts, he argues, then 'obviously the stronger of the two [conflicting instincts] must win'.[118] But how, then, he asks, does this account for the times when we are 'most conscious of the Moral Law', when 'it usually seems to be telling us to side with the weaker of the two impulses'?[119] As he puts it, 'You probably *want* to be safe much more than you want to help the man who is drowning: but the Moral Law tells you to help him all the same'.[120]

It also does no good, Lewis argues, to attempt to explain away the Moral Law as merely a social convention. As Lewis writes, 'The people who ask that question are usually taking it for granted that if we have learned a thing from our parents or teachers, then that thing must be merely a human invention'.[121] One is reminded here of those who accuse Irene, Lucy and Psyche of making up stories. As these stories—according to Curdie, the dwarves, or Orual—were simply 'made up', so is the Moral Law, to some, merely something 'made up' by society. Those parents and teachers who tell their children and students

---

117 MIR, p. 30.
118 MC, p. 22.
119 MC, p. 22.
120 MC, p. 22.
121 MC, p. 24.

about a real right and wrong are merely passing down a sort of made-up fable that possesses no truth in itself: a fable told for the purposes of social control or some reason other than the truth in the 'story' itself. Lewis disagreed:

> But, of course, that is not so. We all learned the multiplication table at school. A child who grew up alone on a desert island would not know it. But surely it does not follow that the multiplication table is simply a human convention, something human beings have made up for themselves and might have made different if they had liked?[122]

And so Lewis maintains that the Moral Law, like mathematics, reveals truths that are beyond nature and, also, not simply invented by social convention.

The *Tao* in Fiction

As mentioned above, MacDonald spilled little ink attempting to convince non-fiction readers of his reasons for believing in a good God. He never wrote a chapter attempting to answer logical misgivings by setting out carefully reasoned arguments. As said above, he was more concerned with writing about truths than defending truths. It does not follow, of course, that he did not believe in truth, or truths, and it does not follow that we cannot find some reasons for believing in his writing if we look closely enough. When we actually do, we find that MacDonald's reasons for believing in a good God closely resemble Lewis's.

The distinction between nature and the supernatural, for example, lies hidden in the plot of *The Princess and the Goblin*. Another way of putting it may be to say he depicts the distinction between the human and the beastly or, more specifically, the distinction between humans and the goblins. The goblins live deep underground and have plans to overthrow the human kingdom above them. Quite literally it is the creatures of the dark—who by their long dwelling underground with beasts have become more beastly[123]— who threaten the 'sun-people'.[124] One of their stratagems against the humans involves the breaking of a long-standing barrier between themselves and the humans. The part of the mountain hollowed by the human miners had always been shut off from the part inhabited by the goblins, but as MacDonald writes, 'now that a passage was broken through, [...] it was clear to Curdie that the mine could be destroyed in an hour'.[125] The goblins plan to flood the humans. The way to guard against the plan, Curdie thinks, is to try to block the new

---

122 MC, p. 24.
123 Compare to Gollum in J.R.R. Tolkien's *The Lord of the Rings*.
124 P&G, p. 142.
125 P&G, p. 71.

passageway with stone and clay, or lime—in other words, to try and fortify the old wall, or distinction, between the goblins and the humans.

This strengthening of the distinction between supernatural man and natural beast is just what MacDonald, in his own way like Lewis, attempts to do in his stories. Lewis did it, as we have seen, more obviously in non-fiction passages about human conscience and reason. MacDonald, more often than not, mixed these distinctions into the action and tone of his stories, as in *The Princess and the Goblin*, and it is in these distinctions that we see some of his reasons for believing in a God of Goodness. It's important to note here that MacDonald's age was one that was in fresh and sometimes deep doubt concerning the distinction between men and beasts, with Darwin's *Origin of Species* having been published in 1859, just three years after MacDonald published his first book. John Ruskin, a friend of MacDonald's, is just one example of such doubt.[126] But MacDonald himself kept vigilant, insisting again and again that the distinction between man and beast was one of kind, not just degree. Theories of evolution and geological discoveries never rocked MacDonald's belief in the distinction between man and beast, or indeed, between man and all of Nature.

This distinction was proof, as it was to Lewis, that there was something other than an uncaring, competitive Nature. It was not as if men had nothing in common with the beasts, or with Nature, or that man should hate or despise the natural or animal part of himself. In all of Curdie's dealings with the goblins, he never tries to kill, or even unnecessarily hurt, any of them.[127] It is only when they attempt to take over the human king's house that any violence must be attempted (much of it accomplished by stamping upon the goblins' feet). The goblins, 'beast and man so mixty',[128] must not be allowed to supplant human rule, and the reason for this is obvious: the goblins have lost, or nearly lost, their souls—the thing that distinguishes them from nature.[129]

The goblins with no souls must be kept from overrunning the king's house. And the worst of the goblins is the part-human goblin queen who denies her own humanity and, instead of settling for the death or torture of

---

126 See RAEP, p. 217. See also T. Hilton, *John Ruskin, The Early Years, 1819-1859* (London: Yale University Press, 1985), p. 167; and T. Hilton, *John Ruskin, The Later Years* (London: Yale University Press, 2000), pp. 169-170.

127 See P&G, p. 139.

128 P&G, p. 138.

129 This is seen clearly in a comic ditty that MacDonald puts into the mouth of Curdie, whose pun on the words 'sole' and 'soul' indicate the soul-lessness of the goblins. See P&G, pp. 145-146.

Curdie alone, suggests a grand scheme to eliminate all humans whatsoever.[130] Far from wanting to actually live in the broad daylight, the queen covets the humans' kingdom for use as "'a sort of outhouse'" and grazing land for livestock.[131] Hunger seems to be the queen's chief concern. She does not want to become human, does not even want to step out into the light for very long. Her conquest over humanity is simply a conquest of the beastly over the human. She only wants to eat and use what the humans have to eat more. It is this unbridled animal hunger that denies and disregards conscience and all things human[132] that Curdie and the King's men labour to defeat.

In the second Curdie book, published ten years later,[133] the same danger rears its head in a different way. In the beginning of the story, Curdie, who still has never seen Irene's grandmother, is still working as a miner and growing older and more stupid in the miners' company. If there is any doubt that Lewis's dwarves are influenced by MacDonald's miners, a passage in the second chapter of *The Princess and Curdie* should lay it to rest. Here we are told that the miners of Curdie's association are a mixed lot, but that they all seem to know 'very little about the upper world, and what might or might not take place there'.[134] They are very wise indeed about things underground, 'with their lanterns and their hands searching after this or that sign of ore, or for some mark to guide their way into the hollows of the earth', but when it comes to believing in things above their heads, they show almost as much mocking contempt as the goblins in the first book: 'as to great-great-grandmothers, they would have mocked Curdie all the rest of his life for the absurdity of not being absolutely certain that the solemn belief of his father and mother was nothing but ridiculous nonsense. Why, to them the very word "great-grandmother" would have been a week's laughter!'.[135]

Under their influence Curdie himself has become more and more a creature of the dark, growing fast in body but not in mind, believing 'less and less in things he had never seen'.[136] One could say that he was forgetting, in himself, the distinction he had fought against in the first book: the distinction between man and beast. Or as MacDonald puts it here, the distinction between the child-like man[137] and the 'common-place man': 'he was becoming

---

130 See P&G, p. 144.
131 P&G, p. 145.
132 Toes included. The queen hides them, evidence of her own humanity, under cover of shoes.
133 1872, 1882.
134 P&C, p. 11.
135 P&C, p. 11.
136 P&C, p. 12.
137 'Child-like' here should not be confused with childish. For more on this, see chp. 5, below.

more and more a miner, and less and less a man of the upper world where the wind blew. On his way to and from the mine he took less and less notice of bees and butterflies, moths and dragonflies, the flowers and the brooks and the clouds'.[138]

The narrator's discussion of Curdie's character gives MacDonald the opportunity to identify the chief difference between the two kinds of men: one is concerned with truth and belief; the other is so afraid of belief that his only truth and only concern becomes eating, just like the goblin queen in the first book:

> One of the latter sort comes at length to know at once whether a thing is true the moment it comes before him; one of the former class grows more and more afraid of being taken in, so afraid of it that he takes himself in altogether, and comes at length to believe in nothing but his dinner: to be sure of a thing with him is to have it between his teeth.[139]

It is not too difficult, after reading this passage, to see how Lewis's dwarves in the Narnia books are an elaboration of MacDonald's miners, and that the chapter entitled 'How the Dwarfs Refused to Be Taken In' in the last Narnia book—in which the dwarves get into a jealous food fight on the outskirts of a Heaven they won't see—is inspired by the passage quoted above.[140]

But Curdie is not allowed to linger in dark unbelief forever. In the same chapter that tells how Curdie is becoming more like the miners, Curdie is starkly reminded of the difference between man and beast. The difference that pricks his heart and understanding is his conscience, which leads to his first sighting of Irene's great-grandmother, much as human conscience in Lewis's non-fiction and fiction always leads to a good God who's interested in goodness.

After first admiring a snow-white pigeon, and even imagining what it would be like to be the bird, he shoots it for no good reason with his bow and arrow.[141] The bleeding creature, not quite dead, looks up into Curdie's face, 'asking what was the matter, and where the red sun had gone, and the clouds, and the wind of its flight'.[142] The boy, in response, begins to struggle with what he's done: 'Curdie's heart began to grow very large in his bosom. What could it mean? It was nothing but a pigeon, and why should he not kill a pigeon?'.[143] The bird opens and closes its eyes a couple of times, fixing its gaze upon Curdie whenever they're open, before finally closing them, its throbbing at an end. This last look somehow reminds Curdie of Princess Irene and how

---

138 P&C, p. 12.
139 P&C, p. 12.
140 See pp. 69-70, above.
141 See P&C, p. 14.
142 P&C, p. 15.
143 P&C, p. 15.

she and he were 'saviours of each other'.[144] The distinction between this kind of behaviour and the behaviour he had just exhibited immediately lays hold of his mind. In his own way, MacDonald is highlighting here what Lewis, in *Mere Christianity*, refers to as the Law of 'Human Nature',[145] a Law that Curdie is no longer able to ignore: 'He had stopped saving, and had begun killing! What had he been sent into the world for? Surely not to be a death to its joy and loveliness. He had done the thing that was contrary to gladness; he was a destroyer! He was not the Curdie he had been meant to be!'.[146]

At this point the whole world around him seems to break out in upheaval.[147] In the growing darkness an 'evil something' begins to move in his heart, and he is on the verge of throwing the bird from him and whistling. '"What a fool I am!", he says to himself.[148] But before he can begin disregarding his conscience in earnest, a great brightness shines down all around him. He looks up and sees a light like 'silver at the hottest heat' radiating from above the roof of the castle where the princess claimed to see her great-grandmother.[149] He feels the bird flutter and runs towards the light in hopes that it may not be quite dead. After many twists and turns and climbings inside the house, Curdie finds the Mistress of the Silver Moon, who sorrowfully takes the pigeon and begins to restore it.

He discovers more of what he has become when the old lady asks him to tell her what other bad things, besides hurting the white bird, he has done today. MacDonald's description here of Curdie's thoughts is a picture of one struggling against, but finally giving into, the truth of God-given conscience. He sinks into a reverie in which he can scarcely tell the difference between the sound of the lady's voice and the sound of 'his own heart'.[150] At first he's inclined to 'consider himself a very good fellow on the whole' but at the same time he cannot 'honestly feel that he was worth standing up for'.[151]

A sudden light, then, breaks upon his mind, and he awakes out of his reverie to see the withered old lady with her spinning wheel 'singing on' in the middle of the moonlight. Curdie then acknowledges what the lady had spun into him with her moonlit spinning wheel:

> "Thank you, ma'am, for spinning it into me with your wheel. I see now that I have been doing wrong the whole day, and such a many days besides! Indeed, I don't know when I ever did right, and yet it seems as

---

144 P&C, p. 15.
145 MC, p. 18.
146 P&C, p. 15.
147 Compare to the fall of man in Genesis chp. 3.
148 P&C, p. 16.
149 P&C, p. 17.
150 P&C, p. 26.
151 P&C, p. 26.

if I had done right some time and had forgotten how. When I killed your bird I did not know I was doing wrong, just because I was always doing wrong, and the wrong had soaked all through me."[152]

We see here how MacDonald, in a few lines of fairy tale dialogue, stresses the same point that Lewis does by arguing logically for (as in *Mere Christianity* and *Miracles*), or by giving historical examples of (as in the appendix to *Abolition of Man*): the reality of an objective moral code and the human failure to live up to it; indeed, how it is broken so often that humans become insensitive to their own badness and thus to the reality of the objective moral code. Lewis, in *Mere Christianity*, says it like this: 'We know that if there does exist an absolute goodness it must hate most of what we do'.[153] Or in *The Problem of Pain* like this:

> Everyone *feels* benevolent if nothing happens to be annoying him at the moment. Thus a man easily comes to console himself for all his other vices by a conviction that "his heart's in the right place" and "he wouldn't hurt a fly," though in fact he has never made the slightest sacrifice for a fellow creature. We think we are kind when we are only happy.[154]

Or like this:

> If, being cowardly, conceited and slothful, you have never yet done a fellow creature great mischief, that is only because your neighbour's welfare has not yet happened to conflict with your safety, self-approval, or ease.[155]

MacDonald says much the same in a different way, as we read in Curdie's response to the old lady:

> I was doing the wrong of never wanting or trying to be better. And now I see that I have been letting things go as they would for a long time. Whatever came into my head I did, and whatever didn't come into my head I didn't do. I never sent anything away, and never looked out for anything to come. I haven't been attending to my mother—or my father either. And now I think of it, I know I have often seen them looking troubled, and I have never asked them what was the matter. And now I see, too, that I did not ask because I suspected it had something to do with me and my behaviour, and didn't want to hear the truth. And I know I have been grumbling at my work, and doing a hundred other things that are wrong.[156]

---

152 P&C, pp. 26-27.
153 MC, p. 38.
154 PP, p. 56.
155 PP, p. 65.
156 P&C, p. 27.

These passages, from both writers, begin to reveal their conceptions of what goodness, or love, is. The nature of goodness, as these two men thought and wrote about it, will be discussed in a later chapter.[157] Here we merely note that the rock solid fact of goodness, as they saw it, is one of the reasons why MacDonald, and Lewis, continued to believe in a good God. It was the silver light that told them that all was not dark, and that men ought not to become beasts (or miners or dwarves) by ignoring the light of conscience. Lewis pointed to this sort of danger by arguing in *The Abolition of Man* that education in Britain at the time was leading students astray by leading them away from objective value judgements, or by asserting in an essay entitled 'The Poison of Subjectivism' that the Moral Law is much more than a matter of individual perception or arbitrary environmental conditioning.[158] Lewis thought human morality was evidence of something eternal and enduring. Any effort to treat it as a subjective sentiment, or complex, or attitude that could differ completely from person to person, or culture to culture, was to Lewis the beginning of the end of man as man: 'Out of this apparently innocent idea comes the disease that will certainly end our species (and, in my view, damn our souls) if it is not crushed; the fatal superstition that men can create values, that a community can choose its 'ideology' as men choose their clothes'.[159]

We can see in MacDonald's writing the same thinking, the same reasoning, though we almost always look to the plot and dialogue of a story to find it.[160] In *The Princess and Curdie*, for example, Curdie meets his great-grandmother, who gives him a mission to accomplish and a special power to help him accomplish it. The following dialogue between the lady and Curdie helps him understand what his new power is:

> "Have you ever heard what some philosophers say—that men were all animals once?" [asked the lady]
>
> "No, ma'am."
>
> "It is of no consequence. But there is another thing that is of the greatest consequence—this: that all men, if they do not take care, go down the hill to the animals' country; that many men are actually, all their lives, going to be beasts. People knew it once, but it is long since they forgot it."[161]

The emphasis here is on beastly actions. The men who are becoming beasts do not know they are becoming beasts because they have been doing beastly things for so long and not, as in the passages of Lewis quoted above, because they

---

157 See chp. 5, below.
158 See C.S. Lewis, *Christian Reflections* (London: Harper Collins, 1991).
159 CHR, p. 99.
160 With the exception of his sermons, of course.
161 P&C, pp. 71-72.

had begun believing in a subjective theory of morality. But both MacDonald and Lewis are obviously working from the same principle: the objective Moral Law. It is objective goodness that the beastly ignore, whether in theory or in action. And the deeper the beastly descend into beastliness, the more they are ignorant of the descent, as Curdie is told: "'a beast does not know that he is a beast, and the nearer a man gets to being a beast the less he knows it'".[162]

This ignorance of beastliness in the beastly obviously implies a growing ignorance of one's conscience and the objective truth which it reveals—a danger which both writers warn against in their books. A descent into beastliness, for them, is a move away from objectivity. Curdie's power, it turns out, is the power of perceiving what a creature is growing to be (a man or a beast) when his hand comes into contact with its hand (or paw, or hoof, etc.). It is the power of perceiving objective truth. And just before sending Curdie out on his mission, the Lady of the Silver Moon reminds Curdie about following an objective truth that will be revealed to him, and which is far superior to his own subjective feelings:

> "You have orders enough to start with, and you will find, as you go on, and as you need to know, what you have to do. But I warn you perhaps that it will not look the least like what you may have been fancying I require of you. I have one idea of you and your work, and you have another. I do not blame you for that—you cannot help it yet; but you must be ready to let my idea, which sets you working, set your idea right."[163]

It is not suggested here that MacDonald's conscious purpose in this passage, or previous passages, was to stress the reality of the objective moral code and objective goodness, as Lewis consciously tried to do with his non-fiction books and essays. I only argue that his reasons for believing in a good God are apparent. These passages could only have been written by a man who believed that human conscience was a real insight into real goodness and that this goodness comes from outside ourselves—that is, from God. It is the same as when a man composing and writing a grammatically coherent sentence tells us that he believes in grammar, even if it is not his express purpose to write a sentence expressing his belief in grammar. These passages from MacDonald's stories show us that he and Lewis believed in the goodness of God for very similar reasons. The particular reason we have been discussing, the fact of something other than the rule of the jungle, can be found in every sort of book that MacDonald wrote.

In one of his Scottish novels, *Sir Gibbie*, for example, Gibbie, a poor dumb waif who finds himself wandering about in the Scottish countryside, alerts a

---

162 P&C, p. 73.
163 P&C, pp. 78-79.

rabbit of the approach of a hungry spaniel. At Gibbie's shriek, the rabbit speeds off into a wood, and the dog gives chase. Gibbie, turning away 'sad at heart', makes the first generalisation of his young life, saying to himself, "'Ilka cratur 'at can [...] ates ilka cratur 'at canna!'".[164] But not many years after, the narrator tells us, Gibbie supplements this with a conclusion: "'But the man 'at wad be a man, he maunna'".[165] MacDonald thus sums up the difference between man and beast in a couple of lines of thought from a speechless orphan. And in so doing, provides us with more evidence that proves he believed that competitive nature is not all there is in the world, especially not all there is to man.

Lewis was apt to point out the same distinction in non-fiction prose, as these concluding words to an essay show:

> We are strangers here. We come from somewhere else. Nature is not the only thing that exists [...] If we "belonged here" we should feel at home here. All that we say about "Nature red in tooth and claw",[166] about death and time and mutability, all our half-amused, half-bashful attitude to our own bodies, is quite inexplicable on the theory that we are simply natural creatures. If this world is the only world, how did we come to find its laws either so dreadful or so comic? If there is no straight line elsewhere, how did we discover that Nature's line is crooked?[167]

Lewis goes on to say, in refined and concise English, what Gibbie thought to himself in broad, but even more concise, Scotch vernacular: that men are more than natural and should therefore know more than hunger and do more than eat:

> [Nature] has nothing to teach us. It is our business to live by our own law not by hers: to follow, in private or in public life, the law of love and temperance even when they seem to be suicidal, and not the law of competition and grab, even when they seem to be necessary to our survival [...] We must resolutely train ourselves to feel that the survival of Man on this Earth, much more of our own nation or culture or class, is not worth having unless it can be had by honourable and merciful means.[168]

In Lewis's fiction the reality of the Moral Law is sometimes implicit, sometimes explicit, but always present. There is, for example, the first story Lewis wrote after his conversion, *The Pilgrim's Regress, An Allegorical Apology for Christianity, Reason and Romanticism*. The book begins with a chapter

---

164 GIB, p. 74. Every creature that can eats every creature that can't.
165 GIB, p. 74. But the man that would be a man, he must not.
166 See Tennyson, *In Memoriam A.H.H.*, 61.15.
167 C.S. Lewis, *Compelling Reason: Essays on Ethics and Theology* (London: Harper Collins, 1996), p. 120. From 'On Living in the Atomic Age' (1948).
168 CR, p. 121.

entitled 'The Rules', which turns out to be very much like the chapter in *The Princess and Curdie* in which Curdie shoots the white pigeon. John, the main character in *Regress*, discovers the Law in nearly the same way: in the garden one morning, he makes ready with his sling to take a shot at a bird sitting on a branch. The cook, before he can accomplish the deed, comes running and smacks him soundly, telling him that 'he must never kill any of the birds in the garden'.[169] When John asks why, the cook tells him that the Steward would be very angry. The Steward is 'the man who makes rules for all the country round here' because the Landlord, who owns all the country, tells him to do it.[170] The Landlord here is obviously Lewis's symbol for God, or at least for as much of God as the religion of Lewis's early experience let through: the joyless God, much like the Calvinistic God of MacDonald's youth, who seems to be concerned with only the rules. We read later in *Regress* how God is more than this, but in the opening pages John learns morality from the Steward of Puritania who, when he slips on an awful mask with a long white beard, tells John the hard and terrible truth that the Landlord is very much concerned with rules of behaviour. He also tells John of very serious consequences indeed if the rules are broken.[171]

At this point one is reminded of Lewis's fearful moonlit nights at Wynyard School,[172] or of the following remark in *A Grief Observed*: 'What do people mean when they say, "I am not afraid of God because I know He is good?" Have they never even been to a dentist?'.[173] John, in *Pilgrim's Regress*, inspired by such fear of such Goodness, is persuaded by Mr. Enlightenment to drop his religion. John does so and, for the moment, is relieved. Life is much easier without the rules or the Landlord behind the rules.

Another character content with his unbelief is Uncle Andrew, the magician in *The Magician's Nephew* who patronises young Polly and Digory for their belief in good and evil. He is like Lewis's dwarves and MacDonald's miners in unbelief, but rather than seeming to be below the *Tao*,[174] Andrew pretends to be above or beyond it, as he tells Digory:

> "Oh, I see. You mean that little boys ought to keep their promises [...]
> But of course you must understand that rules of that sort, however
> excellent they may be for little boys—and servants—and women—and
> even people in general, can't possibly be expected to apply to profound
> students and great thinkers and sages."[175]

---

169 REG, p. 3 (I.i).
170 REG, pp. 3-4 (I.i).
171 See REG, pp. 4-5 (I.i).
172 See SBJ, pp. 33-34; p. 17, above.
173 C.S. Lewis, *A Grief Observed* (New York: Bantam, 1976), pp. 50-51.
174 See pp. 65-70, above.
175 C.S. Lewis, *The Magician's Nephew* (New York: Harper Collins, 1994) p. 20.

And later, when Jadis, Queen of Charn, tells of how she killed all living things except herself by uttering the Deplorable Word, she defends her killing of the innocent women, children and animals of Charn in much the same way as Uncle Andrew defends himself. Both, we see, try to exempt themselves from the universality of the *Tao* and establish a sort of individual morality, or amorality, for themselves:

> "I had forgotten that you [Digory] are only a common boy. How should you understand reasons of State? You must learn, child, that what would be wrong for you or for any of the common people is not wrong in a great Queen such as I. The weight of the world is on our shoulders. We must be freed from all rules. Ours is a high and lonely destiny."[176]

Lewis, of course, is depending upon the reader here to realise that the actions of both Uncle Andrew and Jadis are actually deplorable, that any one in any world who did such things would be breaking a real Code of Goodness. In his non-fiction books and essays, he gives reasons arguing for the validity of the moral code. In his stories, like MacDonald before him, he is appealing to the reader's conscience, so that the evil of Andrew's or Jadis's actions will be real to the reader in so far as the reader takes his or her own conscience seriously. For the reader to agree that Jadis is actually a deplorable person, or has actually done a deplorable thing, is to agree that there is a real, objective Goodness in the universe and that anyone who does such things as these is wrong in going against it. In this way Lewis establishes a sort of cooperative interaction between the text and the reader. The reader who came to the text without such an awareness or belief in the objective validity of conscience would be unable to interact with the text in such a way, and thus much of the action and meaning of the story would be unintelligible, as it would be unintelligible to a chimp (or perhaps a dwarf) who had somehow learned to read, or a Nietzschean Superman who, like Jadis, had somehow moved 'beyond' good and evil.[177]

And so we see how, in different ways, MacDonald and Lewis portrayed and defended the reality of reason and morality, and how these distinctively human things, for both writers, led back to a God of goodness, as the silver moonlight in MacDonald's stories led to one's great-great-grandmother.

It should be noted, however, that this belief was not always easy for either man. They both knew very well how dark the world seemed (to others and to themselves) and how difficult it was, in such darkness, to believe in enduring light. We have already considered the experiences that, in their youth, excited doubt or perplexity and influenced their literary depictions of both doubt and

---

176 MN, p. 71.
177 See Nietzsche, *Thus Spoke Zarathustra* (1883-1885) and *Beyond Good and Evil* (1886).

belief. A brief summary of their later experiences, and their literary responses to them, will help complete our picture of how they came to depict pain, suffering, and belief in Goodness as they did.

More Troubles

The story of Lewis's greatest loss in later life is well known to many through a teleplay, stage play and film entitled *Shadowlands*.[178] After living most of his life as a bachelor, he met, became friends with and later married Joy Davidman, an American poet, novelist, and mother of two.[179] According to Lewis's own recollection, they lived several intensely happy years together before her death to cancer in 1960. Lewis's grief was great, and according to some his faith began to crumble completely.[180] His own record of his grief certainly reveals moments of sharp bitterness:

> go to [God] when your need is desperate, when all other help is in vain, and what do you find? A door slammed in your face, and a sound of bolting and double bolting on the inside. After that, silence. You may as well turn away. The longer you wait, the more emphatic the silence will become. There are no lights in the windows. It might be an empty house. Was it ever inhabited? [...] Cancer, and cancer, and cancer. My mother, my father, my wife. I wonder who is next in the queue.[181]

MacDonald, on the other hand, did not in adult life experience any one thing that could be considered his one great loss. But this is only because he suffered a series of great pains and losses. As mentioned above, MacDonald himself was plagued with respiratory ailments throughout his life, coming very near to death on a couple of occasions. One winter (1871-72), in an effort to boost his family's finances (which were perpetually low and often inadequate), MacDonald embarked upon a lecture tour of the northeastern United States with Louisa and their eldest son Greville. Louisa wrote later of how, after one particularly cold train journey (the carriage stoves had failed to heat properly), MacDonald's asthma flared up:

> He stood gasping in the street holding on to Greville's arm, tears rolling down his cheeks as if he would die then and there—and could not move for minutes, though it was only across the road he had to go to get to our inn. But the thermometer was five degrees below zero, and he said afterwords the air felt like strong acid cutting up his lungs.[182]

---

178 All three—teleplay (1985), stage play (1989) and film (1993)—have scripts written by William Nicholson.

179 Her works include *Letter to a Comrade* (1938), *Anya* (1940), *Weeping Bay* (1950), and *Smoke on the Mountain* (1955).

180 See C. Walsh, in afterword of GOB, p. 149.

181 GOB, pp. 4-5, 12.

182 RAEP, p. 296.

Even when he attempted to escape to healthier climates, the climates themselves seemed to catch a cold, as if the harsh Scottish weather he loved to contend with obliged him by following him around the globe. In the winter of 1856-57, when he fled to Algiers, he, Louisa and their daughter Mary encountered the worst weather there for thirty years. 'Thunder, hail, rain, wind and strong seas' aggravated his bronchitis, and he began spitting up blood.[183] And Louisa contracted an eye disease that lasted several months. Anyone who has read much about MacDonald's life will know that it was filled with such instances: coughing up blood, convalescing for months, moving from one place to another to make ends meet or to escape winter weather.

But MacDonald's greatest sorrows, with little doubt, were the deaths of his children. Four of his children died before he did. At the funeral of the eldest, Lilia, his son Greville remembered how his father could hardly leave the gravesite: 'he came back twice after all the others had left, and it was with difficulty he was at last led away'.[184]

Judging from the trouble they suffered, one might have cause to wonder whether or not the two men lost their faith in a good God who cared. The bitterness of Lewis's words quoted above (there are many such words in *A Grief Observed*) may even lead one to think it probable, as might the following description of MacDonald in old age, after his strength began failing him for the last time, and his mind began failing him for the first time:

> The eczema became alarming, so gravely did it interfere with sleep. It was a constant torture [...] and my father's sadness increased. He realized that his brain sometimes would not respond to his imagination, though he set himself a course of reading as if to discipline his fatigue into some renewal of life. Then even this became difficult [...] My father's dejection was akin to Job's; and if at his worst, just before his deliverance from the evil thing came [that is, a stroke in 1898], he even echoed the words of his Master that God had forsaken him [...][185]

But saying they lost their faith in a good God, after having read all their other words, would be a mistake. They could, of course, have lost their faith and cursed God to themselves without writing it down or telling anyone. But this is a literary study which will not make guesses about losses of faith that were never observed or recorded. There is absolutely no doubt that both men saw and felt the world to be very dark at times. There is no doubting their moments of pain, despair, dark emotion, perplexity, even anger. Their words and others' words confirm this. But the facts of pain, despair, dark emotion and perplexity do not necessarily add up to a loss of faith and hope in a good

183 RAEP, p. 140.
184 RAEP, p. 32.
185 RAEP, p. 388. See Greville MacDonald, *George MacDonald and His Wife* (London: Allen and Unwin, 1924), p. 558.

God. There is quite enough literary evidence to prove that they in fact held on to the end, as many of the characters in their books do.

We will begin to understand this if we follow the quote from MacDonald's son above to its end. MacDonald did not just ask why God had forsaken him. After this, Greville tells us, 'his spirit was thereupon commended to God'.[186] Here, near the end of his life, before the stroke that would silence him for his last seven years, MacDonald exhibits the trust in the midst of pain and perplexity that characterises so many of his literary exhortations.

He seems to be sharing in the 'pain' and 'infinite perplexity' of Job which he wrote of over a decade before in a sermon entitled 'The Voice of Job': 'Job is nothing of a Stoic, but bemoans himself like a child—a brave child who seems to himself to suffer wrong, and recoils with horror-struck bewilderment from the unreason of the thing'.[187] He does not look for a logical reason in his misery, for 'misery is rarely logical; it is itself a discord'.[188] For him, 'No answer will do [...] but the answer that God only can give; for who but God can justify God's ways to his creature?'[189] Until he gets such an answer, he gets on with the business of trusting: 'The true child, the righteous man, will trust absolutely, against all appearances, the God who has created in him the love of righteousness'.[190] It is the sufferer's knowledge of and love for Goodness that keeps him trusting.

Even if the sufferer should actually begin to doubt the existence of God, this could not mean, according to MacDonald's sermon, what is usually meant by the words 'loss of faith', for even the doubts themselves point to more than doubt, as he says of Job's doubt:

> there must in the chaos have mingled some element of doubt as to the existence of God. Let not such doubt be supposed a yet further stage of unbelief. To deny the existence of God may, paradoxical as the statement will at first seem to some, involve less unbelief than the smallest yielding to doubt of his goodness.[191]

MacDonald emphasises here the vital difference, as he sees it, between doubting God's existence and denying his goodness. The smallest yielding to doubt of his goodness is, MacDonald writes, far more serious than the fullest denial of his existence.[192] But he also makes a distinction between doubting God's Goodness and *yielding* to these doubts: 'I say *yielding*; for a man may be haunted with doubts, and only grow thereby in Faith. Doubts are the

186 RAEP, p. 338; GMW, p. 558.
187 US, p. 329 (par. 1 in 'The Voice of Job', third series). See p. 10-11, above.
188 US, p. 332 (par. 4 in the same sermon).
189 US, p. 332 (last quarter of par. 3 in the same).
190 US, p. 353 (par. 23 in the same sermon).
191 US, p. 354 (first quarter of par. 26 in the same).
192 See pp. 15, above.

messengers of the Living One to rouse the honest. They are the first knock at our door of things that are not yet, but have to be, understood [...] Doubt must precede every deeper assurance'.[193]

One thing this study argues is that neither MacDonald nor Lewis *yielded*. No one, perhaps, except themselves and God, if he exists, can know for sure. But there is no real evidence to suggest that they did yield, and overwhelming evidence to suggest that they did not. The last years and moments of MacDonald's waking life exhibit everything he had always practiced, preached and written about before. Pain and sorrow were not new to him when the last trials came, and his last days seemed to be filled with the same sort of courage that we find throughout all of his days. And Lewis, too, it can be shown, did not yield, having learned courage from MacDonald's books, or as much courage as can be learned from reading a man's writing.[194]

Encouragement

One way they responded to suffering in their books was to try and give reasons why it may be compatible with God's good will. Lewis, we know, wrote quite a few books and essays attempting to use logical argument to answer intellectual problems. *The Problem of Pain* is, of course, one of these books. His attempt to reconcile the fact of pain and suffering with the fact of God's goodness lies in explaining, as we have already seen, how our natural environment is morally neutral, how it had to be neutral in order for creatures to lead any kind of free existence. Another argument he uses is that our true happiness includes being made more lovable or loving, which according to Lewis's reasoning, would be impossible for fallen, defective creatures who live in a world where pain and suffering were impossible. His argument is to try and show that 'the old Christian doctrine of being made "perfect through suffering" is not incredible'.[195] He argues that men who are not yet good can only become good by learning to be good when they do not always feel like it, and that this cannot be done without a world of contingency and possible pain. Our goodness, he argues, cannot be perfect, cannot be real, if it is a mere coincidence of doing what we happen to like doing in a continually pleasant environment.

As Lewis writes, our goodness, 'to be perfect, must be done from the pure will to obey, in the absence, or in the teeth, of inclination'.[196] God, the eternal Goodness, being completely good himself, will settle for nothing less in his creatures, for anything less than a creature being perfectly good according to its capacity would be settling for less than complete happiness. So long as the

---

193 US, pp. 354-355 (first quarter of par. 26 in the same).
194 Lewis also read Greville's biography of his father. See ANTH, p. xxi.
195 PP, p. 105.
196 PP, p. 99.

incompleteness lasts, it will separate one from knowing God 'face to face',[197] which according to Lewis's (and MacDonald's) view, is the only complete happiness a creature can have. As Lewis writes elsewhere, God himself has suffered and died to enable us to become loveable and perfectly happy, to become sons of God ourselves.[198] A hard-wrought goodness and a hard love, he admits, but so he believed and so he argued.

We see signs of this belief in his fiction, as in *The Screwtape Letters*, in which a demon, writing to a junior tempter, describes, to his own disgust, this sort of loyalty to God's goodness:

> [God] cannot "tempt" to virtue as we do to vice. He wants them to learn to walk and must therefore take away His hand; and if only the will to walk is really there He is pleased even with their stumbles. Do not be deceived, Wormwood. Our [that is, the demons'] cause is never more in danger than when a human, no longer desiring, but still intending, to do our Enemy's will, looks round upon a universe from which every trace of Him seems to have vanished, and asks why he has been forsaken, and still obeys.[199]

In this Lewis is following MacDonald himself, who wrote very much the same thing in another unspoken sermon entitled 'The Eloi':[200]

> God does not, by the instant gift of his Spirit, make us always feel right, desire good, love purity, aspire after him and his will [...] The truth is this: He wants to make us in his own image, *choosing* the good, *refusing* the evil. How should he effect this if he were *always* moving us from within, as he does at divine intervals, towards the beauty of holiness? God gives us room to *be*; does not oppress us with his will; "Stands away from us," that we may act from ourselves, that we may exercise the pure will for good.[201]

Later in the sermon we discover that the words Lewis put into Screwtape's pen are very near in spirit to words originally written by MacDonald: 'The highest condition of the Human Will, as distinct, not as separated from God,

---

197 See 1 Cor. 13.12.

198 See *Mere Christianity*, 2.4; and Aslan on the Stone Table in LWW, chp. 14. For 'sons of God', see John 1.12; Rom. 8.14, 19; Phil. 2.15; 1 John 3.1-2.

199 C.S. Lewis, *The Screwtape Letters* (New York: Macmillan, 1982), p. 39; Letter VIII.

200 The title of the sermon refers to some of Christ's last words from the cross. 'Eloi' refers to the repetitive call of Jesus to his Father in Aramaic: 'Eli, Eli'. See Mat. 27.46: 'And about the ninth hour Jesus cried with a loud voice, saying, Eli, Eli, lama sabachthani? that is to say, My God, my God, why hast thou forsaken me?'. These are the words, cited above, that Greville MacDonald heard his father echo in the days before his stroke. See p. 93, above.

201 US, p. 117 (first quarter of par. 12 in 'The Eloi', first series).

is when, not seeing God, not seeming to itself to grasp him at all, it yet holds him fast'.[202]

And so both MacDonald and Lewis argue that the perfection of the human will, without which men cannot be truly happy, can only be accomplished in a shadowy world full of pain and sorrow. But both also knew that reconciling the pain of men to the goodness of God, in words and argument, was not enough. They knew that courage, and encouraging others, would help in the actual bearing of pain more than any number of arguments could. Lewis admits as much from the very beginning, writing in the preface to *The Problem of Pain* that

> the only purpose of this book is to solve the intellectual problem raised by suffering; for the higher task of teaching of fortitude and patience I was never fool enough to suppose myself qualified, nor have I anything to offer my readers except my conviction that when pain is to be borne, a little courage helps more than much knowledge, a little human sympathy more than much courage, and the least tincture of the love of God more than all.[203]

In this he follows MacDonald, who stresses again and again in everything he writes that head knowledge is not nearly enough, as in his sermon 'Righteousness'. Here he shows his distaste for mere systems of thought, opposing them to the belief of a child: 'The wise and prudent must make a system and arrange things to his mind before he can say, *I believe*. The child sees, believes, obeys—and knows he must be perfect as his father in heaven is perfect'.[204]

This distaste for relying on systems of thought should not, of course, be confused with a disavowal of reason altogether, especially, as this paper has argued, if human reason is part of the 'seeing' that precedes belief. But MacDonald's words here, in relation to righteousness, will also show us how he must have known that courage, too, must be more than something written or thought: 'To teach your intellect what has to be learned by your whole being, what cannot be understood without the whole being, what it would do you no good to understand save you understand it in your whole being—if this be the province of any man, it is not mine'.[205]

But even if teaching righteousness and courage with the intellect was not MacDonald's 'province', his stories show that he did what he could with words to encourage. Princess Irene, for example, in the first book, saves Curdie from the 'utter darkness' of a cave by following the silver thread from her great

---

202 US, pp. 118-119 (the middle of par. 16 in the same sermon).
203 PP, p. 10.
204 US, p. 589.
205 US, p. 590.

grandmother.[206] The thread is too fine to see easily in the darkness, but Irene can feel it.[207] She was told by her grandmother when given it that it may lead her 'a very roundabout way indeed' but that Irene can be always sure of one thing: 'that while you hold it, I hold it too'.[208] In this way following the silver thread is very much like faith in a good God, as MacDonald and Lewis see it. Over the course of one's life, as in MacDonald's own life, it leads one in many uncertain directions, through much that is dark, adverse and confusing. But if one keeps hold to it, MacDonald and Lewis write, he will find the good God at the end.

Irene, when first following the thread, expects it to lead straight up the old stair and back to her grandmother. Instead, she finds that it leads in 'quite the opposite direction'.[209] It leads out of the house and into the open air, much as Julian in *Within and Without* felt led out into the wide world, and much as Lewis learned that getting to the Ideal, or to God, is more than a matter of imagination or aesthetic rapture. One's soul must be made lovely in a world full of people and circumstances that are not always agreeable. Before singing one's song before the Immortals, one must 'be the hero of his tale' and 'live the song that he sings' in this world.[210] Following Christ's example, he must remain loyal to the Light in spite of pain, suffering and the rest of the world's darkness.

At one point Irene's thread leads down into a dark hole in a mountain. Irene becomes perplexed in the surrounding gloom, but she finds that she has reasons to go on following the thread:

> she kept thinking more and more about her grandmother, and all that she had said to her, and how kind she had been, and how beautiful she was, and all about her lovely room, and the fire of roses, and the great lamp that sent its light through stone walls. And she became more and more sure that the thread could not have gone there of itself, and that her grandmother must have sent it.[211]

Here we find something in MacDonald that runs, like a silver thread itself, throughout whatever sort of writing he attempted: the depiction of, or exhortation to, a courage characterised by trust in the best of what one *knows* despite the worst of present circumstance.

In a poem near the end of *Sir Gibbie*, for example, MacDonald has one of his characters, Donal Grant, a Burns-like farmer boy, produce a poem entitled 'The Laverock', or lark, which sums up some of the book's most important

206 P&G, p.141.
207 See P&G, p. 119.
208 P&G, p. 119.
209 P&G, p. 151.
210 WW, p. 74 (III.i).
211 P&G, p. 154.

themes. Gibbie, the story's speechless hero, endures poverty, the death of his alcoholic father, the brutal murder of a good man, wandering homeless in the countryside, a whipping across his bare back, a great flood, and other adversity, but he keeps faith in goodness by being and doing good. His joy, signified at times by his standing or hopping upon one foot, never seems to wane. And Donal, his friend, near the end of the book's action, writes a poem about a singing lark that exhibits similar faith and joy—a faith that can seem like lunacy to those who don't have it. The speaker who hears the bird singing begins the poem by asking why the bird makes music when things in the world seem so bad:

> Haith! ye're ower blythe:
> I see a great scythe
> Swing whaur yer nestie lies, doon i' the lythe (*shelter*)[212]
>   Liltin' laverock!
>
> Eh, sic a soon'!
> Birdie, come doon—
> Ye're fey to sing sic a merry tune, (*death-doomed*)[213]
>   Gowkit[214] laverock![215]

The man tells the 'menseless', or unmannerly, bird to come down, stop singing and attend to common bird duties: searching for worms and sheltering from the storm. After the bird refuses, the man concludes that the 'feathert priestie' and 'wee minor prophet' may actually know something that he doesn't:

> I'm nearhan' persuaudit
>   To gang to your schule!
>
> For, birdie, I'm thinkin'
>   Ye ken mair nor me—
> Gien[216] ye haena been drinkin',
>   An sing as ye see.[217]

The bird sees better because he doesn't let outer circumstances cloud what he sees, or knows, on the inside:

> Ye maun[218] hae a sicht 'at
>   Sees geyan[219] far ben;[220]
> An a hert for the micht o' 't

---

212 'Lythe', as shown here, is translated in the text by MacDonald.
213 'Fey', as shown here, is translated in the text by MacDonald.
214 silly
215 GIB, p. 445.
216 If
217 GIB, p. 446.
218 must
219 considerably
220 inwards

Wad sair[221] for nine men!

Somebody's been till[222]
Roun[223] to ye wha[224]
Said birdies war seen till
E'en whan they fa'![225]

Donal's reference in the last two lines to the words of Christ, that no sparrow falls to the ground without God's knowledge and care,[226] emphasizes the belief that even death is not as dark as it seems. The brave lark with the heart of ten men sees inside that God is all good, and so trusts that even death cannot be all bad. It must be within his good plan, and so he sings according to his inner sight, or knowledge, of God's goodness.

There is even the possibility that this sort of singing will eventually *change* circumstance, as we learn from a single line in *Phantastes*. Anodos finds and follows a stream in the desert, a bit like Irene following her thread through the dark. Anodos describes the stream thus: 'It was born in a desert; but it seemed to say to itself, "I will flow, and sing, and lave my banks, till I make my desert a paradise"'.[227] This means much more to MacDonald than making the best of a bad situation, and it certainly does not represent the sort of subjective warping of reality that we may find in modern and post-modern existentialism. What it certainly does mean is that something is *beginning* to be transformed by something else, and that even present circumstance, in the light of this transformation, cannot be as bad, ultimately, as it may seem to some.

Such is the case in *At the Back of the North Wind*, in which Diamond, a character much like Gibbie, transforms things by trusting in, or working out, the Light inside. Diamond, a young boy born into a poor family, meets North Wind, a good and beautiful goddess-like character who whisks him away on marvelous adventures. The interaction between these two characters, and the rest of Diamond's actions, compresses in parabolic fashion everything that MacDonald ever wrote about trust in the midst of calamity.

North Wind in many ways resembles Irene's silvery grandmother. She appears in many forms to Diamond throughout the story, and warns him of it in the first chapter. When Diamond promises to go with her because she is good and beautiful, North Wind warns him that she may not always look so: "'What if I should look ugly without being bad—look ugly myself because

---

221 serve
222 to
223 Whisper
224 who
225 Fall. GIB, p. 446.
226 See Mat. 10.29-31.
227 PHA, pp. 64-65.

I am making ugly things beautiful?'".[228] Diamond is confused and so North Wind explains to him that she will not always *appear* to him as she really is, and that he must hold on to what he *knows* her to be:

> "If you see me with my face all black, don't be frightened. If you see me flapping wings like a bat's, as big as the whole sky, don't be frightened [...] You must believe that I am doing my work. Nay, Diamond, if I change into a serpent or a tiger, you must not let go your hold of me, for my hand will never change in yours if you keep a good hold. If you keep hold, you will know who I am all the time, even when you look at me and can't see me the least like the North Wind. I may look something very awful."[229]

And so God must often appear to those who believe in his goodness, when so many frightful things are permitted to happen in the world. At times there appears to be no God at all, as when Diamond and North Wind are separated and the narrator observes, 'Now it is always a dreadful thing to think there is somebody and find nobody'.[230]

But even worse, as we find in chapter six, is the fear that God is not good, that he is uncaring, or even malevolent. North Wind does in fact change to appear as a wolf, causing difficulty for several characters. It is doubtful that the character of North Wind is meant to be a clear-cut symbol for an all-knowing or all-powerful God, for there are times when she is uncertain herself as to why, exactly, she's doing the things she's doing—as if she is taking orders, or forced by some unavoidable way of things. It is probable that North Wind, like many of the characters and situations in MacDonald's fantasy, symbolizes several things at once. North Wind may in fact be a combination of God and the world's troubles, in which case she would, according to MacDonald's actual belief, stand as a symbol for how the world really is: a mixture of good and bad, light and shadows. But whatever or whomever North Wind corresponds to, she always urges Diamond to hold on to the good that he knows, as in the following passage, just before North Wind sinks a ship full of people. Diamond, utterly confounded at this, tells North Wind that "'It's not like you'".[231]

> "How do you know that?" [replied North Wind]

> "Quite easily. Here you are taking care of a poor little boy with one arm, and there you are sinking a ship with the other. It can't be like you."[232]

---

228 NW, p. 22.
229 NW, p. 22.
230 NW, p. 24.
231 NW, p. 77.
232 NW, pp. 77-78.

Diamond cannot reconcile in his mind the goodness with the trouble. North Wind responds with a question and thus initiates a sort of Socratic dialogue which, in MacDonald's simple and compressed fairy tale style, gets to the root of the matter:

"Ah! but which is me? I can't be two mes, you know." [asked North Wind.]

"No. Nobody can be two mes."

"Well, which me is me?"

"Now I must think. There looks to be two."

"Yes. That's the very point.—You can't be knowing the thing you don't know, can you?"

"No."

"Which me do you know?"

"The kindest, goodest, best me in the world," answered Diamond, clinging to North Wind.[233]

With the fact of her goodness seemingly established, North Wind continues, asking Diamond about the motives for her goodness:

"Have you ever done anything for me?" [North Wind asked.]

"No."

"Then I must be good to you because I choose to be good to you."

"Yes."

"Why should I choose?"

"Because—because—because you like."

"Why should I like to be good to you?"

"I don't know, except it be because it's good to be good to me."

"That's just it; I am good to you because I like to be good."[234]

At this point, North Wind has established that she herself is inherently good: she is good to others who have never done good to her, simply because she's good. Her goodness is not a means to some other end, but goodness for its own sake—'"because I like to be good"'. But Diamond is not completely satisfied with this. The pain and suffering in the world do not seem to fit with this goodness, and so he asks, '"Then why shouldn't you be good to other people as well as to me?"'.[235] North Wind insists that she is good to everyone.

233 NW, p. 78.
234 NW, p. 78.
235 NW, p. 78.

When Diamond persists and says that "'It looks quite the other thing'",[236] North Wind does not spend time attempting to reconcile the dark appearance with the good truth. Instead, she urges Diamond to hold fast to what he does know beyond shadow of doubt:

> "Well, but listen to me, Diamond. You know the one me, you say, and that is good."
>
> "Yes."
>
> "Do you know the other *me* as well?"
>
> "No. I can't. I shouldn't like to."
>
> "There it is. You don't know the other me. You are sure of one of them?"
>
> "Yes."
>
> "And you are sure there can't be two mes?"
>
> "Yes."
>
> "Then the me you don't know must be the same as the me you do know,—else there would be two mes?"
>
> "Yes."
>
> "Then the other me you don't know must be as kind as the me you do know?"
>
> "Yes."
>
> "Besides, *I* tell you that it is so, only it doesn't look like it. That I confess freely."[237]

Diamond is satisfied at this point, but North Wind herself brings up the possibility that Lewis feared the most,[238] and the one that MacDonald viewed as the most serious: believing that the real me, the real God, was actually evil to the core: "'You might say that the me you know is like the other me, and that I am cruel all through'".[239] Diamond himself is quick to answer, saying that she can't be because she's so kind. But the kindness, North Wind proposes, may be "'only a pretence for the sake of being more cruel afterwards'".[240] This hastens the end of the discussion, with Diamond clinging to North Wind 'tighter than ever' and reconciled to the fact of calamity because he knows deep down that a cruel North Wind cannot explain the loving North Wind he knows, nor the love in his own heart:

---

236 NW, p. 79.
237 NW, p.79.
238 See GOB, p. 5.
239 NW, p.79.
240 NW, p.79.

"No, no, dear North Wind; I can't believe that. I don't believe it. I won't believe it. That would kill me. I love you, and you must love me, else how did I come to love you? How could you know how to put on such a beautiful face if you did not love me and the rest? No. You may sink as many ships as you like, and I won't say another word. I can't say I shall like to see it, you know."[241]

"'That's quite another thing'", North Wind replies, content for Diamond to trust the light he knows despite the darkness that he can neither explain nor like.[242]

Now MacDonald may not have called attention to this as an argument, but it is an argument nonetheless. To believe in a God of goodness because one's own sense and experience of real goodness and love could not have come from nowhere, and could never have come from a divine Fiend, to believe that goodness and love must be rooted in an eternal and independently good God who is at least as good as our best ideas of goodness: surely this is an argument. In his own style, with North Wind and Diamond, he gives reasons to believe and trust in a God of goodness.

We find almost identical reasons in Lewis's writing, as in *Mere Christianity* where he remembers his old argument against God, how 'the universe seemed so cruel and unjust'.[243] But his very reaction to injustice—the fact of his reaction—argues for something more than cruelty:

> But how had I got this idea of *just* and *unjust*? A man does not call a line crooked unless he has some idea of a straight line. What was I comparing this universe with when I called it unjust? If the whole show was bad and senseless from A to Z, so to speak, why did I, who was supposed to be part of the show, find myself in such violent reaction against it?[244]

Diamond did not see how the goodness, beauty and love that he knew could have come to exist if North Wind were essentially cruel. Lewis, in like manner, cannot see how he could have come to have any idea of goodness or justice if the whole universe was bad and senseless. Lewis could have abandoned his idea of goodness by 'saying it was nothing but a private idea of my own'.[245] But doing this, he argues, invalidates his original argument against a good God:

> for the argument depended on saying that the world was really unjust, not simply that it did not happen to please my private fancies. Thus in the very act of trying to prove that God did not exist—in other words,

241 NW, pp. 79-80.
242 NW, p. 80.
243 MC, p. 45.
244 MC, p. 45. Compare to Boethius's argument for the perfect good from the evidence of that which is imperfect: *The Consolation of Philosophy*, 3.10.1-6.
245 MC, p. 45.

that the whole of reality was senseless—I found I was forced to assume that one part of that reality—namely my idea of justice—was full of sense.[246]

This idea of justice—a belief in a real goodness—again, acts as one of the clues that lead MacDonald and Lewis back to God. Their very reaction to (or judgement of) the darkness around them initially causes doubt but turns out to be a silver thread itself. As MacDonald wrote sixty years previously, 'Doubts are the messengers of the Living One to rouse the honest'.[247] Or as Lewis wrote in response to an enquiry from the philosopher C.E.M. Joad[248] about a chapter in *The Problem of Pain*: 'The more Shelleyan, the more Promethean my revolt, the more surely it claims a divine sanction [...] God within us steals back at the moment of our condemning the apparent God without'.[249] If our hearts are at all correct in cursing the gods, in taking issue against the cruelty around us, then there must be a Great God of eternal, unalterable goodness, else all our judgements are themselves part of the nonsense and cruelty:

> Thus in Tennyson's poem the man who had become convinced that the God of his inherited creed was evil exclaimed: "If there be such a God, May the Great God curse him and bring him to nought."[250] For if there is no "Great God" behind the curse, who curses? Only a puppet of the little apparent "God". His very curse is poisoned at the root: it is just the same sort of event as the very cruelties he is condemning, part of the meaningless tragedy.[251]

So Lewis, like MacDonald, chooses to hold on to the thread, to believe that there is a God of goodness from whom the silver threads come, even the silver thread of honest doubt. And both men wrote their fiction accordingly. MacDonald, as we have seen, gives us the metaphor of the silver moonlight, and the goodness and beauty of great-grandmother and North Wind. Lewis, too, offered his readers reminders of God's goodness and, also like MacDonald, gave examples of characters' courage in keeping to such threads of light.

In *The Silver Chair*, for example, Jill, Eustace, Prince Rillian and Puddleglum find themselves prisoners underground, where the Queen of Underland attempts to convince them that there is no Aslan. Indeed, by burning enchanted, sweet-smelling incense and playing an entrancing tune,

---

246 MC, pp. 45-46.
247 US, p. 355 (second quarter of par. 26 in 'The Voice of Job', second series).
248 Joad (1891-1953), educated at Balliol College, Oxford, was famous in Britain for his involvement in the popular radio programme 'The Brain Trusts'. His works include *Introduction to Modern Philosophy* (1924), *Matter, Life and Value* (1929), *Guide to Philosophy* (1936), and *Guide to Philosophy and Morals* (1938).
249 GDK, p. 171.
250 See Tennyson, 'Despair', 19.106.
251 GDK, p. 171.

she attempts to convince them that there is nothing *other* than Underworld. No matter how much they protest, the witch begins to chant into their heads that Narnia and all of Overland are all a dream. Puddleglum, a perpetually glum swamp creature, is persistent in holding onto the light he knows, as persistent in his own way as Irene, Lucy or Psyche: "'I know I was there once. I've seen the sky full of stars. I've seen the sun coming up out of the sea of a morning and sinking behind the mountain at night, and I've seen him up in the midday sky when I couldn't look at him for brightness'".[252]

The witch, however, is not easily defeated. She strums her instrument some more, attempting to explain away the sun by saying it is merely an elaborate copy, in men's heads, of a lamp. And Aslan (the Christ-like lion, creator and redeemer of Narnia) is only a copy, in men's minds, of a cat. Everything other than her dark world, she chants, can be explained away. Just as everyone, even Puddleglum himself, begins to be taken in by the witch's spell, the marsh-wiggle gathers his strength and courage and, instead of engaging in more argument, does something very MacDonald-like: he *acts*. He stamps out the witch's fire with his bare feet and clears the air. He has had enough and tells the witch they are leaving. But before he does, he gives the witch a piece of his mind. These parting words constitute perhaps the most courageous speech Lewis ever put into the mouth of one of his characters, and it is important to note that it comes from his gloomiest character. Puddleglum invariably looks on the dim side of things, nearly always doubts, nearly always predicts the worst. In one sense he is the Narnian most like Lewis himself: the young Lucrecius-reading atheist who once described life as 'term, holidays, term, holidays, till we leave school, and then work, work, work till we die', but who later saw more meaning and light, even in his doubts. And so, too, Puddleglum, confronted with the enchanting argument against a sunlit world, tells the witch that he's holding on to the best truth he knows:

> "Suppose we *have* only dreamed, or made up, all those things—trees and grass and sun and moon and stars and Aslan himself. Suppose we have. Then all I can say is that, in that case, the made-up things seem a good deal more important than the real ones. Suppose this black pit of a kingdom of yours is the only world. Well, it strikes me as a pretty poor one. And that's a funny thing, when you come to think of it. We're just babies making up a game if you're right. But four babies playing a game can make a play-world which licks your real world hollow. That's why I'm going to stand by the play-world. I'm on Aslan's side even if there isn't any Aslan to lead it. I'm going to live as like a Narnian as I can even if there isn't any Narnia [...] we're leaving your court at once

---

252 C.S. Lewis, *The Silver Chair* (New York: Harper Collins, 1994), p. 185. First published in 1953.

and setting out in the dark to spend our lives looking for Overland."[253]

The truth of Underland cannot match the truth he has known, and so Puddleglum remains loyal to the idea of Aslan, the sun, and Overland. In this he is very much like MacDonald's princess Irene who followed her silver thread down deep into the mountain, eventually coming to what feels like an impassable heap of stones piled against a cavern wall:

> For one terrible moment she felt as if her grandmother had forsaken her. The thread which the spiders had spun far over the seas, which her grandmother had sat in the moonlight and spun again for her, which she had tempered in the rose-fire and tied to her opal ring, had left her—had gone where she could no longer follow it—had brought her into a horrible cavern, and there left her! She was forsaken indeed![254]

The princess, however, after a good cry, does something. She pulls away stone after stone to find that the thread does lead somewhere: to Curdie who's been trapped by the Goblins in a cave. Continuing to trust in her thread and where it came from, she leads Curdie up out of the cave. Curdie, who does not yet believe in Irene's grandmother, at least believes in Irene and trusts her. And so both trust, and find their way out into the world of the sun-people, as Puddleglum and company find their way back to Narnia.

This trust in the face of circumstance, or feeling, is a common theme in all of MacDonald's writing, and throughout what we know of his life. In his case, it is fittingly summed up in the word 'courage', for he made the word a sort of life motto. In 1875 he moved his family from London to Bournemouth in an effort to find a healthier climate for his daughter Mary who had contracted a severe case of scarlet fever.[255] He named the house they moved into *Corage*, which is taken from an anagram he made from his own name: 'Corage! God mend al!'[256] Later, in the early 1880s after the family had lost Mary and Maurice,[257] the family built a winter home in Bordighera, Italy. He named it *Casa Coraggio*.[258] The phrase 'Corage! God mend all!' also adorned MacDonald's book plate, which features Blake's illustration of Robert Blair's *The Grave*[259] which shows an old man leaning on a stick being driven into his

---

253 SC, pp. 190-191.

254 P&G, p. 155.

255 Mary Josephine was MacDonald's second eldest daughter, and first child of his to die, in 1878 at age 25. She had just become engaged to Ted Hughes, the son of Arthur Hughes who illustrated many of MacDonald's stories.

256 See RAEP, p. 336.

257 Maurice, youngest child of George and Louisa, died in 1879 at age fifteen, within a year of Mary's death.

258 See RAEP, p. 352.

259 Blair (1699-1746), a Scottish poet and clergyman, published *The Grave* in 1743. He was a member of the informal group of eighteenth-century 'graveyard poets'.

tomb, but reborn above it as a youth 'with head uplifted to the risen sun'.[260]

All of his life, in the midst of his own ailments, his family's nomadic poverty, and the death of his children, MacDonald wrote to others in their distresses offering comfort and encouragement. In June of 1881, for example, he wrote from *Casa Coraggio* to George Rolleston[261] who was near death:

> I write because I hear you are very ill. I know not a little about illness, and my heart is with you in yours. Be of good courage; there is a live heart at the center of the lovely order of the universe—a heart to which all the rest is but a clothing form [...] hope grows and grows with the years that lead me nearer to the end of my earthly life.[262]

Again and again MacDonald would have his readers trust in the live and lovely heart of reality despite the dark 'clothing form' of circumstance and our own moods. As he urged Rolleston, 'May he make you triumph over pain and doubt and dread'.[263]

As in his letters, so in his fiction. His call to courage is there, as we have seen, in his first book, *Within and Without*, and it is in one of his last, *Lilith*. Vane, after finding himself lost in a strange, fantastic world, tries to find his way home. Like Irene, he follows a path lit up by the light of the moon, which is made known to him first by 'a faint sense of light' awaking 'in me'.[264] Hideous creatures threaten him on all sides of his journey, but the light of the moon, though faint, thwarts all their efforts.[265] None of the strange beasts of Vane's circumstance can harm him so long as he keeps to the moon-lit path. It is significant that this sense of light comes to Vane 'the moment I was on my feet', for belief with MacDonald is ever an active thing. And so toward the end of *Lilith* does Adam tell Vane in response to a question, '"Be content for a while not to know surely"'.[266] The important thing is not that we should know everything in the present moment. '"The hour will come"', he explains, when '"thou shalt behold the very truth, and doubt will be for ever dead [...] Thou hast not yet looked Truth in the face, hast as yet at best but seen him through

---

Blake illustrated an 1808 edition of the poem.

260 RAEP, pp. 368-369.

261 Rolleston, the British anatomist (1829-1881), corresponded with a number of eminent Victorians, including Charles Darwin, Charles Kingsley, David Livingstone, Herbert Spencer and William Gladstone.

262 George MacDonald (G.E. Sadler, ed.), *An Expression of Character: The Letters of George MacDonald* (Grand Rapids: William B. Eerdmans, 1994), p. 305; 18 June 1881.

263 MLET, p. 305.

264 George MacDonald, *Lilith* (Whitehorn: Johannesen, 1998), pp. 75-76. First published in 1895.

265 See LIL, p. 78.

266 LIL, p. 370.

a cloud"'.[267] But until we do look Truth in the face, we know quite enough already to act on, to actively believe in, in spite of our circumstances, as Adam makes clear:

> "But to him who has once seen even a shadow only of the truth, and, even but hoping he has seen it when it is present no longer, tries to obey it—to him the real vision, the Truth himself, will come, and depart no more, but abide with him for ever [...] Trials yet await thee, heavy, of a nature thou knowest not now. Remember the things thou hast seen."[268]

In other words, one is to act on what he knows, to follow the silver moonlight of conscience and other divine knowledge until one is acquainted with the full, sun-like Truth and know It as It knows us—until we have faces and eyes that can see Him as He sees us.

This growing to have a face with which to see the truth of God and his goodness brings to mind once more Lewis's *Till We Have Faces*. The development of Orual's character, one will notice, is similar to what occurs with many of MacDonald's characters: Vane, Anodos, Julian, Robert Falconer, and Donal Grant for example. They all move from mere contemplation of, or wrestling with, a truth they do not fully know, to a realization that they must act on what they do know, must grow in knowledge of the good by doing and becoming good. Only when this is accomplished, in a purifying world of pain and sorrow, will they have faces to see the Truth as it really is. Only then will they have faces and eyes substantial enough to receive such a vision. At the end of Book One in *Faces*, for example, Orual suspects that the gods are silent to answer her complaint 'because they have no answer' to give.[269] But in Book Two, after she has learned more about herself and the gods, she changes her mind:

> [My] complaint was the answer. To have heard myself making it was to be answered [...] When the time comes to you at which you will be forced at last to utter the speech which has lain at the center of your soul for years, which you have, all that time, idiot-like, been saying over and over, you'll not talk about joy of words. I saw well why the gods do not speak to us openly, nor let us answer. Till that word can be dug out of us, why should they hear the babble that we think we mean? How can they meet us face to face till we have faces?[270]

Here, in Lewis's last novel, we hear a variation of a theme that can be found in MacDonald's first book, *Within and Without*, a sort of echo of what Melchah was told in his vision:

---

267 LIL, pp. 370-371. See 1 Cor. 13.12: 'For now we see through a glass darkly; but then face to face: now I know in part; but then shall I know even as also I am known'.
268 LIL, p. 371.
269 FAC, p. 250.
270 FAC, p. 294.

"The youth desired to sing to the Immortals. It is a law with us that no one can sing a song who cannot be the hero of his tale—who cannot live the song that he sings; for what right hath he else to devise great things, and to take holy deeds in his mouth. Therefore he enters the cavern where God weaveth the garments of souls; and there he lives in the forms of his own tale; for God giveth them being that he may be tried. The sighs which thou didst hear were his longings after his own Ideal; and thou didst hear him praying for the Truth he believed, but could not reach."[271]

In both these myths, the vision of Melchah and the account of Orual, we see common features which are perhaps the essence of the meaning that both myths attempt to covey. Realising the essence of the two myths may help us, more than anything else we could do, to understand how MacDonald and Lewis reconciled, in their fiction, the fact of a painful world with the goodness of God. In both stories the human characters are not allowed to experience closest contact with the gods until they have been made strong through trials. Orual is unable to see or hear from the gods face to face until she has found her essential self, for her self as it is in the first book is not her truest self: it does not have a face with which to see the eternal Goodness. And the youth, in Melchah's vision, cannot presume to sing in the presence of the Immortals until he has first lived out, or become, his song. In both instances, ultimate reality cannot be reached by merely wishing for it or thinking about it, especially in Orual's case where one's own perception of ultimate reality is so limited and skewed. The Ideal is something we cannot get into until we have first gotten it into ourselves. The Beatific Vision is not something one can view until he has become beautiful enough himself not to be scorched by the vision.[272] And so we must descend into the painful world of becoming[273] where we are able to become our songs, or acquire our faces. Only after this painful becoming will we understand, to the fullness of our capacities, the goodness of God or the need for a shadowy world of becoming.

The myth of Cupid and Psyche, which both Lewis and MacDonald knew, is helpful here. Many of their stories, or portions of their stories, may in fact be versions of this myth. The god Cupid comes to Psyche, but by night. She is allowed to know something of his love, but is not allowed to see his face. This is analogous to human experience as MacDonald and Lewis saw it: we are allowed to know something of God's goodness, something of his love, but not his full beauty. We are aware of his goodness, and in this sense we know

271 WW, pp. 74-75 (III.i).
272 Or as he puts it in *At the Back of the North Wind* concerning the wind in the country at the back of the North Wind, 'It all depends on how big our lungs are whether the wind is too strong for us or not'. NW, p. 123.
273 See Plato's parable of the cave in *The Republic*, book 7, especially 516B-519C.

something of his beautiful essence. But we do not know the full brightness of his gaze. The world is beautiful with many splendours; distant echoes of the divine Melody still reach our ears from time to time. But the world is also very ugly at times: a brutal cacophony or uncaring silence. Earth is not heaven and God, as it were, hides his face. Until we have faces, all we can get is a glimpse of his back, or the shadow of his back.[274]

In Lewis's version of the myth, Orual is, in the first book, much more concerned with her complaint against the gods' supposed cruelty and ugliness than she is honest about her own cruelty and inner ugliness (though her outer ugliness, part of her complaint, is never far from her mind). She tricks Psyche, by threatening to take her own life, into taking her to the Shadowbrute (or common outlaw, she suspects) and exposing his face with a lamp. Instead of seeing his ugliness, she sees a face of great beauty and briefly senses his brutally honest vision of her self. Calamity follows and both Orual and Psyche are sent out into the calamity, as a voice tells Orual: "'Now Psyche goes out in exile. Now she must hunger and thirst and tread hard roads. Those against whom I cannot fight must do their will upon her. You, woman, shall know yourself and your work. You also shall be Psyche'".[275]

In Lewis's telling of the myth, as well as MacDonald's parable of Melchah, someone is sent out to find out who he or she really is. There can be no finding of God's face, or singing to the Immortals, until one has found one's own face, or become one's own song. And the exile from ultimate reality is somehow a necessary part of this finding or becoming one's true self. One must *do* something, must be good in spite of circumstances, be forced to choose good for its own sake when all does not *feel* good or look good. As Fox, Orual's and Psyche's old Greek tutor, reveals to Orual: "'Psyche must go down into the deadlands to get beauty in a casket from the Queen of the Deadlands, from death herself; and bring it back to give it to Ungit[276] so that Ungit will become beautiful'".[277]

Both Lewis's myth and MacDonald's vision reveal that a time of trial—a world of pain and suffering—is necessary for human souls to become truly beautiful and happy. Psyche, the soul, must follow the goodness she knows, the silver moonlight, through a world of darkness. Psyche must trust in the light, become light herself, in spite of the darkness.[278]

---

274 See Ex. 33.21-23.
275 FAC, pp. 173-174.
276 Lewis's version of Venus: a jealous, cruel god in the myth.
277 FAC, p. 301. Compare to the story of Orpheus going down to hell to bring back his wife Euridice back from the dead, and to the story of Persephone, Demeter's daughter, who is allowed to rise up from her husband Hades and the underworld during springtime.
278 The story of Adam and Eve's fall and subsequent eviction from Eden points

And so Lewis and MacDonald urged courage amidst the present darkness, as MacDonald, for example, sought to encourage Ruskin after the death of Rose La Touche, in 1875:

> Now we are all but Psyches half awake, who see the universe in great measure only by reflection from the dull coffin-lid over us. But I hope, I hope. I hope infinitely. And ever the longer I live and try to live, and think, and long to love perfectly, I see the scheme of things grow more orderly and more intelligible, and more and more convinced that all is on the way to be well with a wellness to which there was no other road than just this whereon we are walking.[279]

MacDonald sent this letter to Ruskin enclosed in an inscribed copy of *Alec Forbes of Howglen*, which itself offers encouragement typical of MacDonald's literary efforts. One way he does it is to have the narrator say it directly, using the action of the story as a springboard from which to make an observation, or in the following case, to offer encouragement. Young Alec Forbes, a country boy, is on his way to town to compete for a bursary to university. Alec's excitement at the opportunity[280] gives the narrator the chance to say this about getting into the secret of the world:

> the door into life generally opens behind us, and a hand is put forth which draws us in backwards. The sole wisdom for a man or boy who is haunted with the hovering of *unseen wings*, with the scent of *unseen roses*, and the subtle enticements of "*melodies unheard*", is *work*. If he follow any of those, they will vanish. But if he work, they will come unsought, and, while they come, he will believe that there is a Fairy-Land, where poets find their dreams, and prophets are laid hold of their vision. The idle beat their heads against its walls, or mistake the entrance, and go down into the dark places of the earth.[281]

---

toward a similar truth, as we see in Milton's version with some of Michael's last words to Adam before they are banished from Paradise: 'only add / Deeds to thy knowledge answerable [that is, add concrete deeds that correspond to their present abstract knowledge of goodness], add faith, / Add virtue, patience, temperance, add love, / By name to come called charity, the soul / Of all the rest: then wilt thou not be loath / To leave this Paradise, but shalt possess / A paradise within thee' (*Paradise Lost*, 12.581-587).

279 MLET, p. 243; 30 May 1875.

280 Alec 'felt as if he had got to the borders of fairy-land, and something was going to happen. A door would open and admit him into the secret of the world'. George MacDonald, *Alec Forbes of Howglen* (Whitehorn: Johannesen, 1995), p. 147. First published in 1865.

281 AFH, p. 148. It is unclear whether MacDonald is quoting any particular author with 'unseen wings', 'unseen roses' and 'melodies unheard', but it is interesting to note that Thomas Heywood (ca. 1575 - ca. 1650) uses the phrase 'unseen wings' in his play *Loves mistresse* (1640) when Psyche (or 'Psiche') speaks of how she has been swept

This passage, by itself, is scarcely distinguishable from many passages in MacDonald's sermons, but what the narrator says here about Alec is the same thing that is illustrated by the journey of Anodos in *Phantastes*, as we shall see in a later chapter. Or as we shall discover now in a less didactic passage of the same book when Annie Anderson, the heroine of the story, must find her way through a dark room to find Thomas Crann, a severely pious stonemason. The young girl throws open the door to the dark room but doesn't take a step. Thomas speaks to her from 'out of the gloom':

> "Ye're no feared at the dark, are ye, Annie? Come in."
>
> "I dinna ken whaur I'm gaein."
>
> "Never min' that. Come straucht foret. I'm watchin' ye."[282]

Thomas, we are told, had been sitting in the dark till he could see in it.[283] Annie obeys the voice she hears and walks straight forward to it. Thomas is satisfied and seizes her arm with one hand and places his other hand 'horny and heavy' on her head.[284] We have enough here already to identify a metaphor for faith, but as he often does in his novels, MacDonald makes it explicit, as Thomas Crann's words show us:

> "Noo, my lass, ye'll ken what faith means. Whan God tells ye to gang into the mirk, gang!"
>
> "But I dinna like the mirk," said Annie.
>
> "No human sowl can," responded Thomas.[285]

Faith and Feelings

These two passages from *Alec Forbes* give us the opportunity to notice how MacDonald, in positive and negative instances, urges the *doing* of faith despite what one feels. When Alec—like the young, imaginative Lewis—imagines he is about to get into the heart of things, the narrator takes the opportunity to remind readers that faith is not idle fancy. One must do something and be tested. On the other hand MacDonald shows, in Annie's case, how faith involves fighting one's fear: doing something even when one does not feel like doing it.

---

away from the rock by Zephyrus (or 'Zephirus') the West Wind, to banquet with the invisible god Cupid: 'Where am I now? for through the cheerfull ayre / Hither I have been brought, on unseen wings;' (I.i). Lewis, of course, describes the same event in his version of the myth. See FAC, pp. 110-113.

282 AFH, p. 125.

283 The narrator adds that this seeing is 'not an invariable result' (AFH, p. 125).

284 AFH, p. 125.

285 AFH, p. 125.

These examples, and those already mentioned, also show us how some interpretations of MacDonald have erred by saying that MacDonald revolted against the intellect in favour of feeling. Robert Lee Wolff, for example, argued in *The Golden Key* that MacDonald championed the emotions over reason as Wordsworth, Hoffman and Novalis had done before him. Many of MacDonald's heroes are 'Wordsworthian idiots', he argues, and MacDonald always chooses to laud the emotions over the intellect.[286] 'The slower the faculties', writes Wolff, 'the deeper the feelings, the more akin the human being is to Nature, the closer he is to MacDonald's God'.[287] MacDonald is the only Victorian that Wolff knows 'who makes his own the pure romantic doctrine of the uses of the imagination, and makes the Wordsworthian linkage between the rejection of the intellect and the acceptance of death as the way to life'.[288]

But Wolff is only partly right. There is no doubt, of course, that MacDonald was highly influenced by Wordsworth and other Romantics. This is evident to anyone who has read even a little of both Wordsworth and MacDonald. And MacDonald's ideas concerning the imagination are similar in many respects to both Wordsworth's and Coleridge's ideas.[289] But identifying MacDonald as closely as he does with the Romantics is a mistake, as it is a mistake to say that the good death in MacDonald's books is a simple regurgitation of the Romantic choice of emotion and feeling over the intellect.

We will consider in other chapters exactly what MacDonald's good death does mean, but it is enough here to say that MacDonald is not out to kill any one thing in a man. And he is certainly not a champion of the emotions, or feeling. It is easy to see how one might misread MacDonald's intentions here. As we have seen, he *is* against intellectual knowledge by itself, as he makes explicit in one of his sermons: 'Your theory is not your faith, nor anything like it'.[290] But neither is faith one's emotions, as we have learned from the two passages from *Alec Forbes* quoted above. With MacDonald, faith is always about obedience. One must often ignore one's emotions or feelings, just as much as one's intellect, when they get in the way of obeying God's known will. As he makes explicit in 'The Eloi':

> Troubled soul, thou art not bound to feel, but thou art bound to arise.
> God loves thee whether thou feelest or not [...] Try not to feel good
> when thou art not good, but cry to Him who is good [...] bethink thee

286 GK, p. 378.
287 GK, p. 378.
288 GK, p. 378.
289 Compare, for example, Coleridge's ideas on poetry as epiphenomena, in his letters on Shakespeare, and similar ideas in MacDonald's essay 'The Imagination: Its Function and Its Culture' in *A Dish of Orts, Chiefly Papers on the Imagination, and on Shakespeare* (1891). See also ROBB, pp. 53-54.
290 US, p. 532 (first quarter of par. 57 in 'Justice', third series).

of something that thou oughtest to do, and go and do it, if it be but the sweeping of a room, or the preparing of a meal, or a visit to a friend. Heed not thy feelings: Do thy work.[291]

If one is going to choose any one thing in man that MacDonald champions, it would be much more accurate to choose his will. But even this is too simple, for MacDonald is very far away from what, say, Nietzsche says about the will.[292] But more on this later.[293] Now we need only highlight the fact of MacDonald's emphasis on active belief—that obeys the goodness one knows despite circumstances, whether these circumstances be feeling, lack of understanding, or pain and sorrow.

Lewis, in his own way, clearly follows MacDonald in urging this sort of courage. 'It is your senses and your imagination that are going to attack belief', he writes in an essay. 'Our faith in Christ wavers not so much when real arguments come against it as when it *looks* improbable—when the whole world takes on that desolate *look* which really tells us much more about the state of our passions and even our digestion than about reality'.[294] Like MacDonald, he urges readers not to depend upon their feelings or their fancy.

And while he writes that the virtue of Faith is not fighting against reason itself, he admits that imperfect humans will have to rely on more than their own reason at certain times:

> The intention of continuing to believe is required because, though Reason is divine, human reasoners are not. When once passion takes part in the game, the human reason, unassisted by Grace, has about as much chance of retaining its hold on truths already gained as a snowflake has of retaining its consistency in the mouth of a blast furnace.[295]

Lewis always, more than MacDonald, admits the value of the intellect. And as much as MacDonald, admits the value of the imagination. But he learned from MacDonald, as early as reading *Phantastes*, that following the light, if it is to be a real following, must with divine grace find its way to one's heart: the will. The most striking example of this is in the *Screwtape Letters*, where we witness the demon Screwtape encouraging junior tempter Wormwood to think of his man as 'a series of concentric circles, his will being the innermost, his intellect coming next, and finally his fantasy'.[296] He advises Wormwood to keep trying to shove all the virtues as far out as possible, to the circle of fantasy. 'It is only in so far as they reach the will and are there

---

291 US, pp. 119-120 (first quarter and last quarter of par. 14 in 'The Eloi', first series).
292 See *Zarathustra, Beyond Good and Evil, The Will to Power* (1901).
293 See chs 3 and 4, below.
294 CHR, p. 63.
295 CHR, p. 63.
296 SCL, p. 31 (Letter VI).

embodied in habits that the virtues are really fatal to us'.[297] Lewis's devils know just as well as MacDonald that faith and goodness, if it is merely imagined or contemplated, is not real: 'All sorts of virtues painted in the fantasy or approved by the intellect or even, in some measure, loved and admired, will not keep a man from Our Father's [that is, Satan's] house: indeed they make him more amusing when he gets there'.[298]

In this sense it is unlikely that a literary study such as this can prove whether or not MacDonald and Lewis, throughout their lives, kept their faith. One would have to produce a record of events that showed their habitual acts of love and goodness in both pleasant and trying times. Such evidence may, in fact, exist, as biographies and personal recollections of both men do suggest,[299] but this, again, is a literary study. The only question we need answer here is whether or not one can detect any clues for a loss of faith in their writing: whether their treatment of suffering, evil and goodness changed in any significant way. We have already seen that Lewis's writing did change. He came to faith in a good God in no small part due to reading MacDonald's books. This changed, as we have seen, his literary treatment of pain and suffering. But were there further changes? Did MacDonald or Lewis, buffeted by their own worst troubles, begin to change what they wrote about pain and suffering?

In an obvious sense, the answer is 'yes'. MacDonald's *Diary of an Old Soul* is a collection of poems that would certainly have been different, if written at all, had not MacDonald lost children and suffered much hardship beforehand. Several of the poems specifically mention the children. And *A Grief Observed*, of course, is a book that would never have been written had Lewis not had a grief of that magnitude to observe. It goes further than anything he wrote in the depth of feeling expressed.

But in neither case do we find evidence of a loss of faith in a good God, unless of course we take Wolff's line of argument and assume that a 'reiteration of the assurances' of MacDonald's faith in his works 'reveals the insecurity that underlay them'.[300] Wolff argues that the more MacDonald declares God's innocence and good will toward men, the more insecure about God's goodness he really is. For evidence Wolff points to what he thinks is a violent outburst against humanity from MacDonald in his later novels. These outbursts, Wolff argues, show how MacDonald had had enough of pain and suffering and was finally venting his true feelings about humanity. And thus, Wolff tells us, we have evidence for a loss of faith: 'It is almost as if God had let MacDonald

297 SCL, p. 31 (Letter VI).
298 SCL, p. 31 (Letter VI).
299 See, for example, CSL, RAEP, GMW, and J. T. Como (ed.), *C.S. Lewis at the Breakfast Table* (New York: Macmillan, 1979).
300 GK, p. 384.

down and made it impossible any longer to repress his true feelings about mankind'.[301]

In relation to a late loss of faith by MacDonald, it will be enough here to ask one question: If MacDonald's late 'reiteration of assurances' of the goodness of God is proof for MacDonald's insecurity in the matter, what are we to make of MacDonald's *earlier* reiterations and assurances? Are they also proof for insecurity? MacDonald reiterates, in every book he ever wrote, the goodness of God. If we are to take such reiteration as proof of insecurity, we must then, to be consistent, assume that MacDonald was insecure about God's goodness for all of his life. But then this would not fit as neatly into Wolff's formula, for he assumes that MacDonald's later troubles sent him over the edge.

If MacDonald's later novels seem darker, it is due to something other than a hatred for mankind or loss of confidence in God's goodness. The next two chapters will show why any of MacDonald's books, late or early, seem dark at times. But now, in this chapter on literary responses to pain and suffering, we need only say that the trust in God's goodness, despite circumstances, is there from the very beginning and is consistently reiterated throughout his literary career.

It is there in his early works, as in *Phantastes*, the book that began MacDonald's influence on Lewis. For example, in the bald words of Anodos's narration: 'Afterwards I learned, that the best way to manage some kinds of painful thoughts, is to dare them to do their worst; to let them lie and gnaw at your heart till they are tired; and you find you still have a residue of life they cannot kill'.[302]

How can one be repressing something when he challenges it to do its worst? One does not get the impression when reading MacDonald that painful emotions and doubts are something seething beneath the repressive surface until troubles in later life cause an eruption. Rather, they appear early and often in his work as something he readily admits and expresses: not the deepest thing in him waiting to get out but something that buffets him from time to time. Deeper than these painful thoughts (or as Lewis might say, the 'blast furnace'[303] of passionate reaction) seems to be a courage based on faith in God's goodness.

MacDonald expresses this courage and faith in *Phantastes* when Anodos meets the old woman with young eyes. The four doors leading out of her cottage, Anodos learns, lead to different kinds of trouble. Behind the first door, the door of tears, Anodos suffers the death of a favourite brother. He runs back into the old woman's cottage by following a distinct sign that she had shown him before he left. Anodos, as in 'a feverish dream of hopeless grief', throws

301 GK, p. 384.
302 PHA, p. 55.
303 CHR, p. 63.

himself upon her couch and listens to her sing a song that restores his courage:

> The great sun, benighted,
> May faint from the sky;
> But love, once uplighted,
> Will never more die.
>
> Form, with its brightness,
> From eyes will depart:
> It walketh, in whiteness,
> The halls of the heart.[304]

Here again, in *Phantastes*, we see the old woman doing what all of MacDonald's books do: encouraging by reminding of the truth of good love that remains constant. As with the silver moonlight and the silver thread, the bright beauty of goodness remains constant and trustworthy, despite the surrounding darkness.

The next two doors Anodos opens lead to dissapointment and dismay, respectively. After returning from beyond the fourth door, which she had prohibited him from entering,[305] he learns that he must leave her. Waters are coming to flood the cottage because of what occurred beyond the fourth door. The woman says that she will be safe, as long as she keeps her fire burning, but that Anodos must go. She says she knows he will come back to her some day, and then gives him one last exhortation before he leaves. In this exhortation we see MacDonald's own 'last word' on faith amidst calamity, a word that he repeated again and again in all his books, and which reveals the essential character of his own faith:

> "In whatever sorrow you may be, however inconsolable and irremediable it may appear, believe me that the old woman in the cottage, with the young eyes" (and she smiled), "knows something, though she must not always tell it, that would quite satisfy you about it, even in the worst moments of your distress."[306]

In other words, trust in the light of goodness you do know: 'the old woman in the cottage, with the young eyes', in spite of the darkness around you: 'the worst moments of your distress'. We can see that many of MacDonald's most memorable characters are variations of this old woman, as we have already begun to see by the examples of Irene's great-grandmother and North Wind.

---

304 PHA, p. 137.

305 The 'door of the Timeless'. Anodos can remember nothing that occurred behind this door when he returns. A good guess is that this door signifies sin, or moral evil, as Eve's eating of the prohibited fruit does in the Genesis story. As in the Genesis story, general calamity commences after the prohibition has been broken. And Anodos is banished, for a time at least, from the woman's cottage, as Adam and Eve are banished from Eden after their fall. See Gen. chp. 3.

306 PHA, p. 144.

These characters do not always look lovely. They often frighten with their looks or their actions. But something about them, the sound of their voices or the light in their eyes, convinces one that there is something deeper that is eternally young and good and lovely. In this way the characters themselves are expressing the same thing that the silver moonlight, or the eternally buring fire in the woman's cottage, or a silver thread, expresses: that deep beneath the decaying crust of reality there is an inner heart of light and life. Deep beneath the ancient, brown parchment-like face of the old woman ('there was not a spot in which a wrinkle could lie that a wrinkle lay not') lies a voice of incomparable sweetness and melody and clear, large eyes: 'the eyelids themselves were old, and heavy, and worn; but the eyes were very incarnations of soft light'.[307]

MacDonald does the same thing towards the end of another, less fantastic book, *Annals of a Quiet Neighbourhood*. The narrator of the story, a vicar recalling goings-on in a rural parish of his, is interrupted in his account by his wife Ethelwyn. In the preceding account the narrator has allowed us to become acquainted with the character of the young Ethelwyn, and to know how and why he fell in love with and married her. But in the final chapter of his account these events are interrupted by Ethelwyn herself. She has now grown old, but as the narrator, contemplating his wife's face, observes, she is still her essential lovely self, or perhaps even more so:

> while she reads [Ethelwyn is looking over his manuscript], I will tell those who will read, one of the good things that come of being married. It is, that there is one face upon which the changes come without your seeing them; or rather, there is one face which you can still see the same through all the shadows which years have gathered and heaped upon it. No, stay; I have got a better way of putting it still: there is one face whose final beauty you can see the more clearly as the bloom of youth departs, and the loveliness of wisdom and the beauty of holiness take its place; for in it you behold all that you loved before, veiled, it is true, but glowing with gathered brilliance under the veil [...] from which it will one day shine out like the moon from under a cloud, when a stream of the upper air floats it from off her face.[308]

And so we see how MacDonald continuously expresses throughout the whole of his fiction his belief in an essential Brightness at reality's core, his faith in a good God despite the tears, disappointment and dismay around him. Indeed, we see it in the last sentence of the last book he ever wrote, when the dismay of decay had grown darkest in him: "'But God is deeper in us than our own life; yea, God's life is the very center and creative cause of that which we call ours; therefore is the Life in us stronger than the Death, in as much as the

---

307 PHA, p. 129.
308 AQN, pp. 573-574.

creating God is stronger than the created Evil'".[309]

MacDonald never does deny the fact of darkness. As we have already seen, he is honest about calamity and other evils, but never does he admit that they are anywhere near the heart of things. And so Lewis must have been encouraged, and influenced, in reading such things again and again in MacDonald's books. The fear that Ransom feels in Perelandra, and hears from Weston, that light and life are only the thin crust of reality,[310] is always denied in MacDonald's books. As in *Adela Cathcart*, when John Smith contrasts Christian hope with pagan pessimism: "'Let the old heathens count Darkness the womb of all things. I count Light the older [...] Darkness exists but by the light, and for the light'.[311]

Lewis, in fact, says something very similar when he discusses the Christian hope of the Resurrection. He, like his character Ransom, may have sometimes feared that what the old pagans believed was true: that life was a fleeting exception to the rule of essential chaos. But he, like MacDonald, believed otherwise, though he goes to greater lengths than MacDonald ever did to give reasons to try and prove it. In *Miracles*, for example, he writes, 'entropy by its very character assures us that though it may be the universal rule in the Nature we know, it cannot be universal absolutely'.[312] He uses the analogy of Humpty Dumpty falling off the wall to represent the decay in Nature we see. The fact of the fall, he argues, is proof itself that there is more to Humpty Dumpty than falling, and more to reality than death and decay: 'A Nature which is "running down" cannot be the whole story. A clock can't run down unless it has been wound up. Humpty Dumpty can't fall off a wall which never existed. If a Nature which disintegrates order were the whole of reality, where would she find any order to disintegrate?'.[313]

Like MacDonald, Lewis believed there must be something deeper than decay, for the decay cannot explain itself. The very existence of decay argues for the existence of some sort of order that can decay, just as the fact of trousers argues for the existence of legs. As MacDonald wrote before Lewis in *Phantastes*, 'The very fact that anything can die, implies the existence of something that cannot die'.[314] There must be a positive Something else that preceded decay; or, according to Lewis and MacDonald, a Someone else who is essential goodness, life and order and who can re-order what has been disordered. As Lewis writes:

309 George MacDonald, *Salted with Fire* (Whitehorn: Johannesen, 1996), p. 325. First published in 1897.
310 See pp. 57-58, above.
311 George MacDonald, *Adela Cathcart* (Whitehorn: Johannesen, 1994), p. 6. First published in 1864.
312 MIR, p. 152.
313 MIR, p. 152.
314 PHA, p. 180.

Humpty Dumpty is going to be replaced on the wall—at least in the sense that what has died is going to recover life, probably in the sense that the inorganic universe is going to be re-ordered. Either Humpty Dumpty will never reach the ground (being caught in mid-fall by the everlasting arms) or else when he reaches it he will be put together again and replaced on a new and better wall.[315]

Even though scientific, empirical experience shows us no evidence for this re-ordering, Lewis remains hopeful, due to the silver moonlight of his reasoning. Dwarfish empiricism cannot be expected, as useful as it may be in its own sphere of knowledge, to put the resurrection between its teeth:

Admittedly, science discerns no "kings horses and men" who can "put Humpty Dumpty together again." But you would not expect her to. She is based on observation: and all our observations are observations of Humpty-Dumpty in mid-air. They do not reach either the wall above or the ground below—much less the King with his horses and men hastening towards the spot.[316]

Such reasoning, in the midst of his own worst grief, no doubt seemed like the snowflake at the mouth of a blast furnace that Lewis said it would be.[317] The first part of *A Grief Observed* is evidence of this.[318] But we find, as the observations continue, signs of a deep faith that endures. At one point, for example, he wonders if Christ himself had found out the terrible truth on the cross: that his Father, the heart of the universe, was actually a cruel Fiend:

Almost His last words may have a perfectly clear meaning. He had found that the Being He called Father was horribly and infinitely different from what He had supposed. The trap, so long and carefully prepared and so subtly baited, was at last sprung, on the cross. The vile practical joke had succeeded.[319]

This dark thought is followed by a dark memory, of how false hopes for Joy's recovery were forced by 'false diagnoses, by X-ray photographs, by strange remissions, by one temporary recovery that might have ranked as a miracle': 'Step by step we were "led up the garden path." Time after time, when He seemed most gracious He was really preparing the next torture'.[320]

This observation, near the end of Part Two, is at or near the nadir of *A Grief Observed*. Soon after, in the very next observation in fact, Lewis is more composed, writing that his previous entry was 'a yell rather than a thought'.[321]

---

315 MIR, p. 152.
316 MIR, p. 152.
317 See CHR, p. 63; p. 115, above.
318 See pp. 92, above.
319 GOB, p. 34.
320 GOB, pp. 34-35.
321 GOB, p. 35.

He asks himself if it is rational to believe in a God who is as bad as what he imagined the previous night: 'The Cosmic Sadist, the spiteful imbecile?'.[322] Here, in one of his last books, Lewis briefly contemplates possibilities that were expressed in his first book *Spirits in Bondage*. But he soon returns to belief in the kind of goodness he began to read about in the pages of *Phantastes*. The 'Cosmic Sadist' or 'spiteful imbecile' idea of God, he reflects, is 'too anthropomorphic'.[323] He remembers a cruel acquaintance he once knew and contemplates the incompatibility between that sort of person and the sort of God who created so many good things, so many beacons of silver moonlight:

> the picture I was building up last night is simply the picture of a man like S.C.—who used to sit next to me at dinner and tell me what he'd been doing to cats that afternoon. Now a being like S.C., however magnified, couldn't invent or create or govern anything. He would set traps and try to bait them. But he'd never have thought of baits like love, or laughter, or daffodils, or a frosty sunset. *He* make a universe? He couldn't make a joke, or a bow, or an apology, or a friend.[324]

In other words, cruelty, no more than disorder, can be at the heart of things. It could not have brought the best things we know into being. There is pain and suffering and sorrow, and these are hard to take, hard to explain. But we know too much beauty and goodness to think that reality is the regurgitation of eternal disorder, or the work of essential cruelty. Lewis is no less honest in the remainder of *A Grief Observed*, but he is less prone to confuse 'feeling' with 'thought',[325] and his book changes into something more than a record of his grief. It becomes exactly what the title says it is: his own grief observed. At first it is God who is in the dock. By the book's end, his own grief has been observed, and he finds that his love for Joy needs to resemble what his love for God should be. This love, as we have begun to see, and shall see more fully in a later chapter, is very much what MacDonald depicted it as: something that must penetrate deeper than either thought or feeling. As Lewis observed, 'In both cases [his love for Joy and for God] I must stretch out the arms and hands of love—its eyes cannot here be used—to the reality, through—across—all the changeful phantasmagoria of my thoughts, passions, and imaginings'.[326] As Lewis had begun to learn by reading *Phantastes*, as Julian learned in *Within and Without*, love of any good thing, be it God or a woman, must be more than a matter of contemplating, or imagining, or feeling an Ideal. As Lewis is still learning in *A Grief Observed*, 'I musn't sit down content with the

---

322 GOB, p. 35.
323 GOB, p. 35.
324 GOB, p. 36.
325 GOB, p. 38.
326 GOB, p. 77.

phantasmagoria itself and worship that for Him, or love that for her'.[327]

At the end of *Grief,* we observe Lewis encouraging himself and others the way MacDonald encouraged all his readers. He knows enough to know that God is good. Joy herself could not have come from Disorder or Cruelty. He is content not to know everything, echoing words he once put into the mouth of Orual:[328]

> When I lay these questions before God I get no answer. But a rather special sort of "No Answer." It is not the locked door. It is more like a silent, certainly not uncompassionate, gaze. As though He shook His head not in refusal but waiving the question. Like, "Peace, child; you don't understand."[329]

Thus, moving beyond emotional sorrow and intellectual uncertainty, he follows MacDonald's advice, seeing how he must believe in God and his goodness by *doing*: 'And now that I come to think of it, there's no practical problem before me at all. I know the two greatest commandments, and I'd better get on with them'.[330] And so, willing to do his work and hope in the resurrection,[331] Lewis ends his book on his own grief with his faith, so far as one can tell from words, intact.

The closest MacDonald ever came to writing something like *A Grief Observed* is *Diary of an Old Soul.* Originally published under the title *A Book of Strife, in the Form of the Diary of an Old Soul,*[332] MacDonald's 366 stanzas, one for each day of a leap year, is perhaps the most personal expression of his faith he ever published.[333] Like Lewis's *Grief* it does not attempt to repress pain, suffering or grief: it attempts to struggle with it openly. It is from beginning to end the diary of an *old* soul, a 'book of strife' from one who had suffered greatly himself and who had just lost two of his children within a year. The poet is a man worn out with pain and grief and doubt, a Christian who admits it, not a Stoic who denies it:

> There is a misty twilight of the soul,
> A sickly eclipse, low brooding o'er a man,
> When the poor brain is as an empty bowl,

---

327 GOB, p. 77.

328 See p. 109, above.

329 GOB, pp. 80-81.

330 GOB, p. 81. See Mat. 22.37-40: 'Thou shalt love the Lord thy God with all thy heart, and with all thy soul, and with all thy mind [...] Thou shalt love thy neighbor as thyself'. See also Mark 12.30, 33; Luke 10.27; Deut. 6.5; 10.12; 11.1, 13, 22; Lev. 19.18, 34.

331 See GOB, p. 89.

332 For Lewis's admiration of the book, see CLET, pp. 834 (10 Oct. 1929), 872 (26 Jan. 1930).

333 First published, privately, in 1880. See RAEP, p. 121.

> And the thought-spirit, weariful and wan,
> Turning from that which yet it loves the best,
> Sinks moveless, with life-poverty opprest:—[334]

But the last line of this stanza calls to God still, revealing that his soul has not lost all its light: 'Watch then, O Lord, thy feebly glimmering coal'.[335] If nothing else, MacDonald's changing moods, and his ability to recognize the changes, proves to him, as Lewis would also observe, that one's grief and sorrow are not everything:

> I know at least which is the better mood.
> When on a heap of cares I sit and brood, [...]
> I am not *all* mood—I can judge betwixt.[336]

As he recognises himself distinct from his moods, so can he recognise his conscience, which 'Boisterous wave-crest never shall o'erwhelm'.[337] His knowledge of a transcendent Goodness, though in painful moods seeming like 'sea-float bark', is as sturdy 'as field-borne rooted elm'.[338] Such things make up the silver threads of his faith, which he follows throughout his *Diary*. Or as he puts it in another stanza, he keeps an ear open to 'hints' and 'whispers' drifting to him from a distant land of life:

> Yet hints come to me from the realm unknown;
> Airs drift across the twilight border-land,
> Odoured with life; and as from some far strand
> Sea-murmured, whispers to my heart are blown
> That fill me with a joy I cannot speak,
> Yea, from whose shadow words drop faint and weak:
> Thee, God, I shadow in that region grand.[339]

In two other stanzas, MacDonald expresses his faith in ultimate light and life by using the image of a seed planted deep in the dark earth:

> If thou hadst closed my life in seed and husk,
> And cast me into soft, warm, damp, dark mould,
> All unaware of light come through the dusk,
> I yet should feel the split of each shelly fold,
> Should feel the growing of my prisoned heart,
> And dully dream of being slow unrolled,
> And in some other vagueness taking part.[340]

---

334 George MacDonald, *A Book of Strife in the Form of the Diary of an Old Soul: Daily Writings for Devotional Reflection* (London: Triangle, 2001), p. 19 (25 Feb).
335 DOS, p. 19.
336 DOS, p. 83 (2 Sept).
337 DOS, p. 6 (13 Jan).
338 DOS, p. 6 (13 Jan).
339 DOS, p. 50 (29 May).
340 DOS, p. 44 (7 May).

Deep underground, the seed knows little of the world of light, but by something happening within itself, it gains a dull idea still that there is something other than darkness. It is growing into or becoming something other than darkness. It has relatively scant knowledge of the sunlit world:

And little as the world I should foreknow
Up into which I was about to rise—
Its rains, its radiance, airs, and warmth, and skies,
How it would greet me, how its wind would blow—[341]

But this is no excuse for not growing up, and away, from mere darkness. In the last three lines of the stanza, MacDonald makes the comparison between the seed's lack of knowledge of the sunlit world with our own limited knowledge of goodness, and while doing so expresses a faith that hopes for better things to come:

As little, it may be, I do know the good
Which I for years half darkling have pursued—
The second birth for which my nature cries.[342]

And so MacDonald continues in hope of the light, growing into more and more knowledge of God's bright love by growing more and more lovely through loving. As Lewis's Puddleglum would be resolved to spend his days searching for the light,[343] so MacDonald knows enough of the Light to never yield to the darkness around him:

"Back," said I! Whither back? How to the dark?
From no dark came I, but the depths of light;
From the sun-heart I came, of love a spark:
What should I do but love with all my might?
To die of love severe and pure and stark,
Were scarcely loss; to lord a loveless height—
That were a living death, damnation's positive night.[344]

MacDonald illustrated this love and light and resurrection in his stories, setting an example that Lewis would follow. He, for example, brings *At the Back of the North Wind* to a close with the death of young Diamond. To the narrator and MacDonald, this is ultimately a happy ending because it is also a beginning. The narrator's description of the final scene, when he gets to visit Diamond, makes it clear that he has physically died, but the last three sentences of the book make clear, as previous scenes foreshadow,[345] that Diamond has gone *through* death, not *into* it forever: 'I saw at once how it was. They thought he was dead. I knew that he had gone to the back of the north

---

341 DOS, p. 44 (8 May).
342 DOS, p. 44 (8 May).
343 See pp. 106-107, above.
344 DOS, p. 26 (16 March).
345 See chp. 10, for example.

wind'.[346] Diamond, according to the narrator, had gone through death into ultimate reality—the sunlit land from which the silver light originates. One is reminded here of the Old Man of the Sea's words to Mossy in 'The Golden Key', perhaps the greatest of MacDonald's shorter fairy tales:

> "You have tasted of death now," said the Old Man. "Is it good?"
>
> "It is good," said Mossy. "It is better than life."
>
> "No," said the Old Man: "it is only more life."[347]

Both Mossy and Diamond, in MacDonald's tales, pass beyond the thin crust of the present shadowy life and enter into the good and bright heart of things.

Lewis follows MacDonald in this by ending the *Chronicles of Narnia* with the death of all the main characters. As Aslan softly tells them, "'There *was* a railway accident [...] Your father and mother and all of you are—as you used to call it in the Shadowlands—dead. The term is over: the holidays have begun. The dream is ended: this is the morning'".[348]

Throughout both men's literature, then, we see them following their silver threads despite their circumstances. They knew enough of goodness to try and keep to it until death and, as they believed to the end, the resurrection into the heart of reality. It will be remembered that those last painful words of MacDonald's recorded by his son Greville did not end by echoing Christ's fear of abandonment on the cross. They ended with an echo of Christ's very last words as recorded in Luke's gospel: 'Father, into thy hands I commend my spirit'.[349] These last words indicate trust.

And Lewis, near his own death, would hand the manuscript of his very last book[350] to Walter Hooper, his secretary, with these words: "'If anyone thinks I have in any way lost my faith in Christ's promises [...] will you point them to what I've said in *The Last Battle*?'"[351] These words, in chapters of *The Last Battle* entitled 'Further Up and Further In' and 'Farewell to the Shadowlands', as we have seen above, indicate a trust in a good God and hope in the resurrection. And they hint at Lewis's conception of Heaven, just as portions of MacDonald's stories had done.

This study will take a brief look at these depictions of ultimate reality later, but we must not move too soon to heaven, for we have seen thus far only a part of the two authors' concept of 'good death'. Chapters on the 'nature'

---

346 NW, p. 391.

347 George MacDonald, *The Complete Fairy Tales* (New York: Penguin, 1999), p. 142.

348 LB, p. 228.

349 Luke 23.46; RAEP, p. 388; GMW, p. 558. These are also the last words of MacDonald's sermon on Christ's suffering, and ours. See 'The Eloi', in US, p. 121 (last sentence of the sermon, first series).

350 C.S. Lewis, *Letters to Malcolm: Chiefly on Prayer* (New York: Harcourt Brace Jovanovich, 1988). First published, posthumously, in 1964.

351 CSL, p. 235.

of evil and the 'character' of hell will be necessary, for both MacDonald and Lewis stressed with all their might that there was something in between that kept men from God's heaven—something that needed to die. This chapter has made clear that both authors wrote their books believing that the fact of a good God could be reconciled with the fact of this world's 'evil' fortune: pain, suffering and other calamity. But any interpretation that attempts to show in their work a reconciliation between Goodness and moral evil is, we shall see, missing the mark by the widest of margins.

CHAPTER 3

DEATH AND DIVORCE

Trifles of trifles and very vanities which I had made my mistresses now held me back and plucked me by my carnal robe, whispering me, 'Will you turn us away? Shall the moment come when you must part from us for ever?'.

–St. Augustine, *Confessions*, 8.11[1]

Trample on Death and Hell in glorious glee.
–Jospeh Hall, 'For Christmas Day'[2]

God is light, and in him is no darkness at all.
–1 John 1.5[3]

Sometimes those in the habit of explaining things, or explaining things away, miss the most obvious things. As Lewis once wrote of certain theologians: 'These men ask me to believe they can read between the lines of the old texts; the evidence is their obvious inability to read (in any sense worth discussing) the lines themselves. They claim to see fern-seed and can't see an elephant ten yards away in broad daylight'.[4]

William Raeper, the first major MacDonald biographer since Greville MacDonad in 1924, fell into this kind of habit when he attempted to tie MacDonald's stories too closely to the psychological theories of Carl Jung, as Wolff attempted to explain too much with Freud's theories. A refutation of Raeper's claim here will allow us to gain a clearer understanding of what MacDonald, and Lewis, actually meant when they wrote of evil.

The problem with interpreting MacDonald's work by Jung's theories is that MacDonald's stories are not nearly as inclusive as Jung's theories. There is a great deal in Jung's theories about myth, archetypes, and 'individuation'[5] that

---

1   Quoted by Lewis in *The Allegory of Love: A Study in Medieval Tradition* (New York: Oxford University Press, 1973), p. 66. *Allegory* first published in 1936.
2   Quoted by MacDonald in *England's Antiphon* (Whitehorn: Johannesen, 1996), p. 127. *Antiphon* first published in 1874.
3   Quoted in US, p. 541 (first quotation beneath the title in 'Light', third series).
4   C.S. Lewis, *Fern-Seed and Elephants, and Other Essays on Christianity* (London: Harper Collins, 1998), p. 93.
5   See C.J. Jung, *Psychological Types. or The Psychology of Individuation* (1921). For a discussion of how Jung's theories treat good and evil, see Aniela Jaffe, *The Myth of Meaning in the Work of C.G. Jung* (Hull: Hodder and Stoughton, 1970), especially chp. 6 ('Individiation'), chp. 7, ('Good and Evil'), and chp. 8, ('Answer to Job', which discusses Jung's idea of a 'Quaternity' that adds Satan to the orthodox doctrine of the

seems to be relevant and unusually applicable in the case of MacDonald's use of symbols. But there is a certain dualistic inclusiveness in his individuation that MacDonald fought hard against in everything he wrote. The elephant standing in broad daylight that Raeper somehow fails to take account of, the one that cannot be squeezed into Jung's inclusive theory of individuation, is MacDonald's idea of moral evil. As we shall see, MacDonald saw this moral evil as something that could never be negotiated with, that could never be included in the wholeness of an individual or the wholeness of ultimate reality.

Raeper, in his discussion of the change that takes place in Anodos in *Phantastes*, reminds us of what Jung's individuation means: a move to wholeness in which the divided elements within our psyche, elements including good and evil, will be reconciled to each other. The symbols and archetypes found in fairy tales, according to Jung, show us that 'it is possible for a man to attain totality, to become whole, only with the co-operation of the spirit of darkness, indeed that the latter is actually a *causa instrumentalis* of redemption and individuation'.[6]

Raeper sees very little difference between this sort of individuation and what goes on in MacDonald's stories:

> Jung's view on the necessity of evil is hard to accept perhaps, but it accords to a large extent with MacDonald's. MacDonald believed that even the devil himself would be redeemed and so God must have some reason why he was still allowed to run around the world causing harm. In MacDonald's eyes, harm is only a result of seeing in the wrong way. Turn harm inside out and there is a blessing lurking there.[7]

Raeper then quotes the penultimate sentence from *Phantastes* to help make his point: 'What we call evil, is the only and best shape, which, for the person and his condition at the time, could be assumed by the best good'.[8] He then concludes that 'Therefore even evil contributes towards redemption'.[9]

In the few paragraphs that remain in his chapter on *Phantastes*, Reaper sums up Anodos's adventures in fairy land and shows how all things come into a more harmonious relation toward the book's end: 'all the images of the mother—the earth, the beech tree and the wise woman—blend harmoniously as Anodos realises that evil is simply one shape of good'.[10] Many things that seem

Trinity).
6   Jung, in RAEP, p. 151. Raeper quotes from C.G. Jung, *The Archetypes and the Collective Unconsciousness* (New York: Pantheon Books, 1959).
7   RAEP, p. 152.
8   PHA, p. 185; in RAEP, p. 151. Unless using an edition I'm unaware of, Raeper misquotes the last phrase as 'could be assumed *to be* the best good' (RAEP, p. 151). Italics mine.
9   RAEP, p. 152.
10   RAEP, p. 153.

contradictory, Raeper argues, become simultaneously valid in MacDonald's poetic assembly of symbols: naturalism and Platonism; the erotic, or sexual, and the spiritual; and as already mentioned, good and evil.[11] He speaks of MacDonald's belief in a level of reality in which the distinction between these things, as that between the spiritual and the sexual, no longer exists.[12]

Now there is no doubt that MacDonald is fond of keeping seemingly contradictory things in a sort of poetic tension where both are valid. More will be said of this later regarding MacDonald's and Lewis's views regarding the character of God.[13] Here we need only say that, yes, quite a lot of seemingly contradictory things can be included in MacDonald's view of reality. The previous chapters of this study concerning pain, suffering and other forms of evil fortune have shown how MacDonald thought that enormous amounts of adversity could be consistent with God's goodness and his good purposes. He would not have had North Wind sink a boat full of people if he did not so believe, just as Lewis would not have written his book *The Problem of Pain* in a logical attempt to explain how pain and troubles in the world could be reconciled with God's goodness. As the narrator of *Sir Gibbie* admits: 'The will of the Brooding Spirit must be a grand one, indeed, to enclose so much of what cannot be its will, and turn all to its purpose of eternal good!'.[14]

But one will get a grossly distorted picture of MacDonald's and Lewis's views of evil if they fail to see how sharp a line they both draw between evil fortune on the one hand and moral evil on the other. Raeper, by not drawing attention to such a distinction in his discussion of MacDonald's symbols and Jung's individuation, greatly misleads. There may be some truth in applying to MacDonald's writing Jung's notion that personal totality can be achieved only with 'the co-operation of the spirit of darkness', especially if we identify this 'spirit of darkness' as simply something negative: death, the *via negativa*, fear, evil fortune or violence. One only needs to read a few of MacDonald's fairy tales to see that he is not one who portrays only peace and light. His tales and stories are filled with dangers, battles, and fearful things hidden in dark places. His fairy tale 'The Giant's Heart', for example, ends quite violently when a boy stabs a giant's heart to death: 'He sprang to the heart, and buried his knife into it, up to the hilt. A fountain of blood spouted from it; and with a dreadful groan the giant fell dead at the feet of little Tricksey-Wee'.[15] In this story, as in much of MacDonald's writing, there are frightful things and dreadful acts: wicked giants who eat children and the messy business of stabbing a giant's

11   See RAEP, pp. 153-154.
12   See RAEP, p. 154.
13   See chp. 5, below.
14   GIB, p. 20.
15   AC, p. 337.

heart to death. MacDonald, in fact, anticipated those who'd object to such stories. 'The Giant's Heart' originally appeared as one of many tales told by characters in the novel *Adela Cathcart*. The reading of the tale provokes the following reactions from some of the listeners: "'What a horrid story! [...] I don't think it at all a nice story for supper, with those horrid spiders, too'".[16] But yet MacDonald kept writing such stories, with such dreadful elements, for the rest of his life.

Another tale of MacDonald's, 'The Shadows', involves, literally, a host of shadows that in one way or another frighten people into realising urgent truths, or into some sort of action. One of these shadows, in a conversation with the chief human character of the tale, Ralph Rinkelmann, indicates why MacDonald may have included so much darkness in his stories: "'It is only in the twilight of the fire, or when one man or woman is alone with a single candle, or when any number of people are all feeling the same thing at once, making them one, that we see ourselves, and the truth of things'".[17] When Rinkelmann asks whether that which "'loves the night'" can be true, the shadow replies that "'The darkness is the nurse of light'".[18] This answer, it would seem, is very much in support of Raeper's claim that the dark things in MacDonald's stories contribute to the sort of overall wholeness associated with Jung's psychological theories. The shadow goes even further along these lines in his address to Rinkelmann when it laments the tendency of the modern world to try to evict all traces of anything that might alarm, frighten or disgust:

> "Sire, [...] our very existence is in danger. The various sorts of artificial light, both in houses and in men, women, and children, threaten to end our being. The use and the disposition of gaslights, especially high in the centres, blind the eyes by which alone we can be perceived. We are all but banished from towns. We are driven into villages and lonely houses, chiefly old farm-houses, out of which, even, our friends the fairies are fast disappearing. We therefore petition our king, by the power of his art, to restore us to our rights in the house itself, and in the hearts of its inhabitants."[19]

It is certain that MacDonald kept a place for such shadows in his books, and that he maintained that a recognition of these dark things was absolutely necessary in a progression to a more truthful wholeness. In this respect Raeper's associating MacDonald's fantasy with Jung's individuation is very appropriate indeed.

---

16   AC, p. 337.
17   AC, p. 195.
18   AC, p. 195.
19   AC, p. 196.

But again, Raeper's failure to distinguish shadows in general from the shadow of moral evil in MacDonald's writing is an oversight that is difficult to overstate. MacDonald never simply lumped moral evil in with all other things called 'evil', never wrote as if all these things must be accommodated by one attempting to reach greater wholeness. He certainly did not ignore the existence of moral evil when writing his tales. His symbols for such evil contribute greatly to the darkness of his works, and he evidently thought it good not to ignore such darkness. But it is simply untrue to suggest or claim that MacDonald thought moral evil to be something that ought to be included in one's growth toward wholeness. It is one thing to draw a picture of a monster, but quite another to say that we ought to *be* monsters—ought to reconcile ourselves to that part of us which is monstrous. The artist's picture of a monster may in fact be his way of saying we ought *not* to be monsters. This is in fact what MacDonald did in everything he wrote. He does indeed encourage a move to totality and wholeness, but only by killing the monster within—a monster which, to MacDonald's thinking, has no legitimate place there. A muddying of the waters concerning evil fortune and moral evil in one's interpretation and explanation of MacDonald's symbols does everything to obscure, and little to help us understand, his trumpet-like clarity on the issue.

Losing One's Shadow

The only difficulty in proving this lies in the choice of which books of MacDonald's to cite. There is simply not enough space here to cite them all, and any of them could serve the purpose—much as any random collection of elephants might help prove that the animals do, as a rule, possess trunks. A good place to start, however, might be the book upon which Raeper bases most of his argument: *Phantastes*. One will remember that he quotes the penultimate sentence of the book in an effort to link MacDonald with Jungian individuation. The sentence reads thus: 'What we call evil, is the only and best shape, which, for the person and his condition at the time, could be assumed by the best good'.[20] And Raeper argues thus: 'Therefore even evil contributes towards redemption'.[21] The only way that Raeper's claim can be anywhere near to accurately describing MacDonald's own idea is if he really only means 'evil fortune' when he speaks of 'evil' contributing toward redemption, but it is clear that he does not. A few paragraphs earlier we see him including the moral evils of blasphemy and incest in his definition of the 'evil' that he thinks MacDonald's stories accommodate.

---

20   PHA, p. 185.
21   RAEP, pp. 151-152.

Raeper's point is that MacDonald's stories are examples of the subconscious psyche allowing good and evil things, including morally good and evil things, to exist side by side in a harmony unachievable in one's conscious life. As he writes after mentioning blasphemy and incest: "'Man's worst sin,' wrote Jung, "is unconsciousness." MacDonald exposes the psyche and plunges us into a world that we have to come out of—changed".[22]

The truth here is that Raeper plunges us into a world of folly. He forgets that MacDonald's unconsciousness, however influential it may have been in suggesting symbols, did not write the book. No one's unaided unconsciousness—Jung's and Raeper's included—has ever written a book. Books are written by conscious minds, some of which are influenced by conscience and reason which do not recognise moral evil as 'contributing towards redemption'.[23] There can be no mistaking that MacDonald's mind was one of these. To his mind evil contributed nothing to one's wholeness or redemption. To him moral evil was the very thing that made one *un*-whole-some. It could never contribute towards one's redemption, to his mind, for to his mind redemption meant the utter destruction of moral evil, not an acceptance of it into a harmony of ongoing individuation. MacDonald, as we shall see, thought of moral evil as a cancer. Insofar as evil fortune, or other non-moral shadows, enable us to realise and take action against such a cancer, evil can indeed be seen as contributing towards redemption and wholeness. But speaking of moral evil contributing towards redemption would be to MacDonald's mind like saying cancer contributes towards the patient's physical health. And any interpretation that fails to take MacDonald's mind into account is, at best, unbalanced.

Raeper's interpretation of *Phantastes* fails to point out that Anodos does *not* approach wholeness by accepting his own shadow as one of many elements of reality. He does not achieve redemption by co-operating with his shadow. He has to lose it by going through a sort of death. In this way Anodos's own shadow in *Phantastes* is essentially different, in what it symbolises, than most of the shadows that confront Ralph Rinkelmann in 'The Shadows'. While the shadows that Rinkelmann encounters awake people to the ugly truth of their own moral evil, and other ugly things, Anodos's shadow does nothing of the kind. It is an obviously wicked influence. MacDonald gives us a clue to this in the chapter in which Anodos is first burdened with his shadow. Before the chapter begins, he quotes Mephistopheles from Goethe's *Faust*: "'I am a part of the part, which at first was the whole'".[24] As the chapter and story progresses, we see how this quotation foreshadows a move *away* from wholeness.

---

22 RAEP, p. 150.
23 RAEP, p. 152.
24 PHA, p. 55. MacDonald's translation of *Faust*, 1.1349.

The shadow attaches itself to Anodos in the strange cottage of an ogress. Its influence on everything it comes in contact with is destructive, not at all tending towards wholeness. When, for example, Anodos gets up from lying on a bed of wildflowers, he sees the flowers where he had lain rise again and 'rejoice in the sun and air'.[25] Not so with the place where his shadow had lain: 'The very outline of it could be traced in the withered lifeless grass, and the scorched and shrivelled flowers which stood there, dead, and hopeless of any resurrection'.[26] At another point this 'evil demon', of its own accord, moves around in front of Anodos and turns into a sort of pulsating shadow sun, sending out 'rays of gloom' that bring 'void' and 'desert' to everything it touches.[27] One of the rays from this 'black sun' reaches up to the actual sun in the sky and smites it on the face, causing it to wither and darken.[28] All the wonders of Fairy Land that Anodos's shadow comes in contact with are either destroyed or diminished.

Things get even worse when Anodos begins to feel satisfied with the shadow's presence and becomes proud that the shadow should be destroying so much wonder and beauty.[29] At one point he meets a maiden carrying a mysterious globe of magic crystal. Anodos becomes increasingly curious about the maiden's globe and becomes possessive of it, holding it to make it tremble, quiver and emit flashes of coloured flame. The maiden's prayerful and tearful entreaties for him to let go of the globe are ignored. He keeps hold of it, and the intensity of its music and throbbing increases until the globe bursts in their hands. A black vapour breaks upwards out of it, and the maiden runs crying into the forest with the remnants. Her cry comes back for many nights to haunt Anodos's memory just before sleep: '"You have broken my globe; my globe is broken; ah, my globe!"'.[30]

MacDonald's symbolism can, as he himself admitted,[31] mean several things at once, but it is certain here that Anodos's behaviour towards the maiden and her globe is not presented as something that contributes to anyone's totality or wholeness. After some time under the evil influence of the shadow, Anodos has done something wicked, something that in important aspects resembles the act of rape. In a fit of violent curiosity and passion, he has trampled upon the wishes and possessions of another, just as the shadow had previously brought destruction to wildflowers and the sun itself. Influenced by

25 PHA, p. 59.
26 PHA, p. 59.
27 PHA, p. 59.
28 PHA, p. 59.
29 See PHA, p. 61.
30 PHA, p. 62.
31 See 'The Fantastic Imagination' in CFT, pp. 8-9. This essay first appeared in *A Dish of Orts* (1893).

the shadow, he has destroyed a thing of beauty and wonder, and made a girl cry.[32]

32   It is true that the young maiden appears near the end of the story and actually thanks Anodos for breaking her globe: "'You broke my globe. Yet I thank you. Perhaps I owe you many thanks for breaking it'" (PHA, p. 164). She speaks of how she has "'something so much better'" than her globe: the fact that she can sing to others and deliver them without relying upon her globe to play for her. It is surprising that Raeper does not mention this, as it seems to support his Jungian and inclusive characterisation of MacDonald's view of evil. Anodos's wrong deed has apparently contributed, paradoxically, to the maiden's ultimate joy. This passage is indeed difficult, given its apparent inconsistency with the hard line that MacDonald takes against moral evil in all else that he writes. How can one who takes such an uncompromising position against moral evil, as the rest of this chapter shows, seem to admit here in *Phantastes* that a morally evil act has actually contributed to the maiden's blessedness, that she in the end has "'nothing to forgive'" Anodos for, seeing that his evil deed served as the opportunity for her being uplifted in her own 'sorrow and well-doing' (PHA, p. 165)?

     It may be helpful here to jump to a distinction stressed later in this chapter: the difference between evil 'fortune' and moral evil. It is important to distinguish in *Phantastes* between the moral evil done to the maiden by Anodos and the corresponding misfortune of sorrow felt by the maiden. This chapter shows below how MacDonald often spoke of all misfortune as potentially working for the best good, and so in this respect MacDonald would be consistent: the moral evil willed by Anodos does not transfer evil to the maiden's will. His evil act causes pain and sorrow, proving how closely pain and sorrow are sometimes connected to evil acts, but his evil act is not the same thing as her pain and sorrow. Though she knows more about moral evil from having felt the sorrow it causes, there is no indication that her will is itself corrupted by his act. Though the close connection between evil actions and the misfortune it causes allows for confusion here, I propose that the maiden is not thanking Anodos for his evil will in the end. She thanks him for the misfortune. Or her thanking him for his act is MacDonald's mythical expression of the paradoxical good of misfortune, and even the good of the close connection between moral evil and evil fortune. There is no evidence to suggest that she is thanking anyone in any way for moral evil itself.

     In essence, she is thankful for what Boethius has referred to as the 'striking miracle' of God exploiting evil 'to draw out of [evil things] an element of good' (Boethius, *The Consolation of Philosophy*, 4.6.50-53, P.G. Walsh, tr. [Oxford: Oxford University Press, 1999], p. 92) [Compare to Ransom's speech to the Un-man in PER, pp. 121. See p. 150, below]. The morally evil will in Anodos, symbolised by a shadow, must be put to death, as the rest of the story shows; but so long as it does last, God can still take advantage and make good out of its consequences. God has so arranged things that morally evil actions, though he never desires that men should commit them, are forced into the service of the good. As Boethius puts it, 'If something forsakes the planned order assigned to it, it slips back into some alternative pattern, admittedly different but none the less a due order' (4.6.53; p. 92). It is this 'element of good' (4.6.52; p. 92) or 'alternative pattern' (4.6.53; p. 92) that the maiden's thankfulness is likely pointing to at the end of *Phantastes*: the uplifting 'by sorrow and well-doing'

It is curious that Raeper did not mention such things when discussing MacDonald's idea of evil and Jung's more inclusive individuation. It is also curious how he leaves out Anodos's resolve, later in the story, to lose his shadow. This resolution shows us fairly clearly that evil is not treated as something that one must be reconciled to in order to achieve wholeness. On the contrary, it is that which keeps one from being one's true, whole self. As Anodos indicates in his own speech to his shadow, it is that which oppresses and keeps one from his potential totality, the thing which divides a whole man in two: "'Shadow of me!' I said; "which are not me, but which representest thyself to me as me; here I may find a shadow of light[33] which will devour thee, the shadow of darkness! Here I may find a blessing which will fall on thee as a curse, and damn thee to the blackness whence thou hast emerged unbidden'".[34]

Soon after this address Anodos stays several days in a fairy palace, washing daily in a fairy bath. From this point onward Anodos' shadow grows dimmer and dimmer, losing more and more of its influence as Anodos becomes more

---

that both MacDonald and Lewis thought necessary for the perfection of fallen creatures (PHA, p. 165). What is certain is that the maiden never gives thanks for the evil of anyone's will. She does not thank Anodos's evil shadow. A few paragraphs later, in fact, Anodos, encouraged by the maiden's example, humbles himself and loses his shadow. It is not something, as Raeper claims, that can be kept as a valid part of reality.

Such thinking is clear in MacDonald's narration of *Guild Court, A London Story* (Whitehorn: Johannesen, 1999; first published in 1868). Speaking of the protagonist's redemption near the end of the story, MacDonald speaks of how Thomas Worboise could 'give God thanks for the shame' of his sin, since 'sin gives birth to shame, and in this child-bearing is cleansed' (GC, p. 372). As MacDonald explains, there may be good things that God can bring out of evil, though the evil itself is no good at all: 'Verily there is One, I repeat, who bringeth light out of darkness, good out of evil. It comes not of the evil, but out of the evil, because He is stronger than the evil; and He, not evil, is at the heart of the universe' (GC, p. 372).

Still, even if MacDonald is consistent, this passage may serve to highlight a likely difference between MacDonald and Lewis regarding the relative good of innocence in contrast to the good of redemption. Lewis makes it clear that, although God will make good of whatever his creatures do, something great has been 'lost forever' when evil is committed (PER, p. 121; see p. 150 below). MacDonald, by contrast, has written that innocence may be but 'a bauble' in comparison to repentance (in *Thomas Wingfold, Curate*; quoted in B. Amell, *George MacDonald and the Logic of Faith* [Portland: B. Amell, 2000], p. 170). It is difficult to imagine Lewis ever suggesting in any context that moral innocence might be only a bauble, however much he valued repentance and reconciliation. All of the strength of the protagonist in *Perelandra*, for example, is directed against such a loss of innocence.

33   See Lewis's mention of a 'bright shadow' appearing in *Phantastes*: SBJ, p.181; p. 20, above.

34   PHA, p. 72.

and more of a person through trial, action and trust. He finally does lose his shadow after going through a sort of death himself. It is only after this death and loss of his shadow that Anodos awakes to the sort of harmony that Raeper cites. The harmony begins only after the shadow has been destroyed. The 'great good' that is coming to Anodos[35] does not come because Anodos has learned to accept moral evil as just another element of his psyche to be reconciled with other elements. And so it is quite obvious that the penultimate sentence of *Phantastes* that speaks of 'what we call evil' as being 'the only and best shape [...] assumed by the best good' cannot include moral evil. To suggest, as Raeper does, that it does ignores the story's central theme, and perhaps the greatest theme in all of MacDonald's writing: the need for good death. The most important part of this good death is the need to kill the morally evil false self. It is the death here that MacDonald considered good, not the evil shadow itself. When MacDonald speaks of 'what we call evil' being the best shape assumed by the best good, he means the evil *fortune* that somehow contributes toward redemption. Troubles, pain and suffering, while not good in themselves, can indeed help people to lose their false selves, MacDonald believed, just as troubles, pain and suffering help Anodos to lose his shadow in the story.

Such things are explicitly summarised in the last chapter of *Phantastes* as Anodos meditates on the significance of his journey through Fairy Land. He rejoices that he has lost his shadow. He thinks of the old woman in her cottage of four doors, three of which lead to Tears, Disappointment and Dismay. He thinks of the words of encouragement she told him to remember when 'oppressed by any sorrow or real perplexity'.[36] Surely it is sorrow, tears, disappointment and dismay that MacDonald speaks of when he speaks of the 'evil' that 'is the only and best shape, which, for the person and his condition at the time, could be assumed by the best good'.[37] As already mentioned, both MacDonald and Lewis came to believe that the troubles of this world are somehow necessary for the redemption of souls who are not already all good. Some of these troubles may indeed be caused by moral evil from individuals, and both authors believed that the temporary existence of all these things together is consistent with God's goodness and his good plan. But this is a far cry from the sort of individuation that allows moral evil a place in ultimate reality. In every book that MacDonald wrote, there is a stark difference between evil fortune and moral evil. Evil fortune is often the thing in his stories that leads the characters to realise, and combat, moral evil. But in all his books, MacDonald takes great pains to distinguish between these two things called 'evil'. When it cannot—or should not—be avoided, evil fortune

---

35   PHA, p. 185; RAEP, p. 153.
36   PHA, p. 184. For these encouraging words, see PHA, p. 144.
37   PHA, p, 185.

is to be accepted as within God's good will, but moral evil is to be rejected at every opportunity.

Evil Fortune

A few examples here will show how MacDonald achieves this distinction, and how Lewis followed suit in his stories. In MacDonald's last great fantasy, *Lilith*, for example, we find both kinds of evil, along with a clear indication of which is which. A conversation between Mr. Raven and Vane in the third chapter of the story clearly displays MacDonald's belief that bad fortune, like unpleasant weather, can have salutary effects. It is raining, and Vane tells Raven what "'fine weather'" it is "'for the worms'".[38] Raven agrees: "'Yes [...] the ground will be nice for them to get out and in!—It must be a grand time on the steppes of Uranus! [...] I believe it is raining there too'".[39] When Vane asks why rain on Uranus should be grand, Raven answers that all the animals there are burrowers, and will be for some time. After many ages and much more rain, he says, the earth will give a great heave and produce a beast that moves on land. Many rainy days are apparently needed to produce such a birth.[40]

Later in the story, Vane remarks how everything in the strange, fantastic world he has entered is chaotic. He has seen the moon go down and then, just a few hours later, rise to shine in all its glory. "'Everything is uncertain here'", he says to himself, "'—even the motions of the heavenly bodies!'".[41] But in the next paragraph he explains how seeming chaos is actually part of an order that he was unacquainted with: 'I learned afterward that there were several moons in the service of this world, but the laws that ruled their times and different orbits I failed to discover'.[42] Again, that which seems chaotic actually falls into a harmonious plan for good. Such is the case again when several children called 'the Little Ones' are interrupted in attempting to comfort two fighting leopards. One of the leopards, a great white cat, sends them running for the trees with a 'hideous yell'.[43] The reader finds out later how the white leopardess is actually a heroine of the story. Both her violence against the spotted leopard and the fright she gives the Little Ones turn out to be actions for good. After the leopardess's identity and good intentions are revealed, we see how "'A friend is one who gives us what we need, and the princess is sorely in need of a terrible scratching'".[44] The spotted leopardess with which Lona, the white

---

38 LIL, p. 29.
39 LIL, p. 29.
40 LIL, p. 29. Compare to a similar mode of birth in chp. 8 of *The Magician's Nephew* when Aslan causes the ground to spew forth plants and animals during his creation of Narnia. See also *Paradise Lost*, 7.449-504.
41 LIL, p. 124.
42 LIL, p. 124.
43 LIL, p. 269.
44 LIL, p. 307.

leopardess, was fighting turns out to be Lilith, princess of Bulika, the book's title character and chief villain.

Lewis does much the same thing in *The Horse and His Boy*. Like MacDonald he uses the fear of a great cat to bring characters to where they need to be. At one point the horse, Bree, and the boy, Shasta, are travelling through the desert at night when they are startled by a voice in the darkness ahead: 'a long snarling roar, melancholy and utterly savage'.[45] As a result Bree swerves to change his course away from the lion or lions. In this way he meets up with Aravis and her horse Hwin, who have been similarly thrown off course by their fear of a lion's growl.[46] At another point in the story the same snarling roar causes the two horses to break into a full gallop. This time the lion appears in broad daylight and seems to attack Aravis, getting close enough with its claws to give her a scratch across her back.[47] In a later chapter, when Shasta is brooding over his own misfortune, a 'Large Voice' comes to him from out of the darkness and reveals that it was he, Aslan, who caused Shasta, Bree, Aravis and Hwin these troubles, and who at several points in Shasta's present adventure and previous life has intervened with what can be seen as either good or evil fortune:

> "I was the lion who forced you to join with Aravis. I was the cat who comforted you among the houses of the dead. I was the lion who drove the jackals from you while you slept. I was the lion who gave the Horses the new strength of fear for the last mile so that you should reach King Lune in time. And I was the lion you do not remember who pushed the boat in which you lay, a child near death, so that it came to shore where a man sat, wakeful at midnight, to receive you."[48]

It was he, too, who wounded Aravis with his claws, he tells Shasta. And while he does not reveal to Shasta why he wounded her, the reason is revealed to the haughty and loveless Aravis later in the story: "'The scratches on your back, tear for tear, throb for throb, blood for blood, were equal to the stripes laid on the back of your stepmother's slave because of the drugged sleep you cast upon her. You needed to know what it felt like'".[49]

The entire plot of *The Horse and His Boy*, in fact, shows how events and adventures surrounding Shasta and Aravis lead to the best good for both of them. Shasta is the unfortunate orphan boy who learns through these events and adventures that he is actually much more than an unfortunate orphan

---

45 C.S. Lewis, *The Horse and His Boy* (New York: Harper Collins, 1994), p. 27. First published in 1954.

46 See HB, pp. 27-30.

47 See HB, pp. 151-154.

48 HB, pp. 175-176.

49 HB, p. 216.

boy. And Aravis learns, through events and adventures, something of her own arrogance and how it must be changed, much as Orual learns in *Till We Have Faces*. Events and adventures, like Anodos's and Vane's and Julian's adventures, help change them for the better. In *The Horse*, the hermit, whom they meet just after Aravis has been scratched by the lion's claws, hints at this redemptive function of 'fortune' as he is considering her wounds:

> "your wounds are washed and dressed and though they smart they are no more serious than if they had been the cuts of a whip.[50] It must have been a very strange lion; for instead of catching you out of the saddle and getting his teeth into you, he has only drawn his claws across your back. Ten scratches: sore, but not deep or dangerous."[51]

When Aravis responds that she has indeed had good luck, the hermit responds in a very MacDonald-like fashion:

> "Daughter [...] I have now lived a hundred and nine winters in this world and have never yet met any such thing as Luck. There is something about all this that I do not understand: but if ever we need to know it, you may be sure that we shall."[52]

These words of the hermit to Aravis, it will be noticed, resemble the words of the old woman to Anodos, in the cottage whose doors lead out to various kinds of evil fortune: "'In whatever sorrow you may be, however inconsolable and irremediable it may appear, believe that the old woman in the cottage, with the young eyes [...] knows something, though she must not always tell it, that would quite satisfy you about it'".[53]

And the hermit resembles the old woman in *Phantastes*, and so many other old women in MacDonald's stories, in more than just his words about luck. He, like them, lives in a simple, cottage-like building: 'a little low house of stone roofed with deep and ancient thatch'.[54] He, like them, is surrounded

---

50 Christ, of course, was whipped before his crucifixion. And so the hermit's remarks here are very much in keeping with MacDonald's saying that 'The Son of God suffered unto death, not that men might not suffer, but that their suffering might be like his' (US, p. 27 [last half of par. 17 in 'The Consuming Fire', first series]), especially when we remember that Aslan, the Christ figure of Lewis's Narnia tales, suffers himself in several instances, most notably upon the Stone Table in LWW. In this way Aravis's wounds are like what Aslan himself experienced, except that Aslan is not represented as in any way deserving his wounds or needing moral redemption. Lewis quotes this phrase from MacDonald's *Unspoken Sermons* at the beginning of his book *The Problem of Pain*.

51 HB, p. 158.

52 HB, p. 158.

53 PHA, p. 144.

54 HB, p. 155.

with simple, homely things: the sound of bleating and the sight of goats.[55] Aravis awakes in his house to find herself lying on a bed made of heather. She is given goat's milk to drink from a wooden bowl, and porridge and cream to eat.[56] As this setting resembles many of MacDonald's settings, so does the 'fortune' of the story, both 'good' and 'evil', lead to the best good for all of the characters. The 'evil fortune' in *The Horse and His Boy* is identical to the 'evil' MacDonald speaks of at the end of *Phantastes*: 'What we call evil, is the only and best shape, which, for the person and his condition at the time, could be assumed by the best good'.[57] Aslan, the great and good Lion of Narnia, in *The Horse and His Boy*—like North Wind in *At the Back of the North Wind*, or Irene's grandmother in the Curdie books, or the shadows in 'The Shadows'— assumes different shapes at different times to ensure the best good for all, even though these shapes be frightening, painful or otherwise troublesome. We see clearly here how Lewis closely follows MacDonald by illustrating a belief in the utility of 'evil' fortune to bring about good results, or to act as opportunities for specific acts of bravery and love which in themselves can be seen as good results. In this sense all 'evil fortune' can be seen as part of God's good plan. Instances of tribulation, it is made clear, are better for the characters than uninterrupted pleasantness.

We see this in every sort of writing that MacDonald attempted. He often presents misfortune as if it were really good fortune. Tibbie Dyster, in *Alec Forbes of Howglen*, for example, speaks of her blindness as a gift on par with other people's sight.[58] Later, she jokes about how poorly crafted her body seems to be: "'This body's nothing but a wheen[59] claes[60] to my sowl; and no verra weel made either, for the holes for my een[61] war forgotten i' the makin'".[62] But she immediately makes it clear to young Annie Anderson that she's content with what a good God gave her: "'I'm bit jokin', lassie; for it was the Lord's han' that made and mismade my claes; and I'm weel willin' to wear them as lang's he likes'".[63] In the same book the narrator speaks of the courage which enables a man to 'reap, against his liking, the benefits that spring from every fate steadfastly encountered'.[64]

---

55 See HB, p. 155.
56 See HB, p. 159.
57 PHA, p. 185.
58 See AFH, p. 228.
59 Few
60 Clothes
61 Eyes
62 AFH, p. 263.
63 AFH, p. 263.
64 AFH, p. 259.

In another of his Scottish novels, *Robert Falconer*, young Robert Falconer reaps such hard benefits after a particularly trying time. He has recently been exposed to the sublime delights of a beautiful lady, Mary St. John, and her piano playing, as well as learning to play music himself on a fiddle he comes to call his 'bonny leddy'. But in a flurry of misfortune he is separated from these things. His stern grandmother has thrown his bonny leddy into the fire, and the passageway that led from his own house to Mary St. John's room has been boarded up. He has gone to God in prayer but it does not seem to work. His feelings are of 'waste, misery, forsaken loneliness'.[65] But yet somehow even this 'taste of damnation' in Robert works for the good.[66] As the narrator tells us, 'there is no better discipline than an occasional descent from what we count well-being, to a former despised or less happy condition'.[67] One of the good results of Robert's descent is his reunion with his fiddle tutor, the town cobbler whom Robert had deserted. His own grief makes him think of the soutar's grief, and so he goes to see him the very next night.

It is, indeed, the very rich and constantly wealthy in MacDonald's books who are, to him, truly disadvantaged. In *David Elginbrod*, for example, Elginbrod tells young Hugh Sutherland, quite bluntly, how property and riches are no proof at all of good breeding: '"ye ken it's no riches 'at 'ill mak' a guid breed—'cep it be o' maggots. The richer cheese the mair maggots, ye ken"'.[68] And later in *Robert Falconer*, Robert, grown into manhood, has taken to working with the poor in London while looking for his long lost father. In a conversation with the narrator of the story, Archie Gordon, Falconer speaks of poverty being a blessing '"when it makes a man look up"' and trust in God.[69] In response to Gordon's query as to how often poverty is a blessing, Falconer responds that there are many things he is unsure of, but that a simple taking away of all adversity would not be the best thing for the poor: '"I cannot determine when, where, and how much; but I am sure it does [act as a blessing]. And I am confident that to free those hearts from it by any deed of yours would be to do them the greatest injury you could"'.[70]

This theme of poverty and troubles somehow being good for us runs throughout all of MacDonald's stories and sermons. There are simply too many instances to quote them all here. But they might all be summed up in a single sentence from the narrator of *Adela Cathcart*, who tells his readers 'We

---

65   George MacDonald, *Robert Falconer* (Whitehorn: Johannesen, 1995), p. 170. First published in 1868.
66   RF, p. 170.
67   RF, pp. 170-171.
68   George MacDonald, *David Elginbrod* (Whitehorn: Johannesen, 1995), pp. 69-70. First published in 1863.
69   RF, p. 352.
70   RF, pp. 352-353.

shall all have to thank God for the whip of scorpions which, if needful, will do its part to drive us into the kingdom of heaven'.[71]

Outside and Inside Evil

Such statements will no doubt seem cruel, especially when read outside the context of MacDonald's stories, his own painful life and his view of reality, just as the following statement of Lewis's is sometimes heard out of context: 'God whispers to us in our pleasures, speaks in our conscience, but shouts in our pains: it is His megaphone to rouse a deaf world'.[72] This sentence, or part of this sentence, is often used to sum up his thinking on pain and suffering, most notably in *Shadowlands*, the play and film about Lewis, his wife Joy, and the impact of her life and death.[73] Not many of the other sentences in the 157-page book are mentioned. We cannot quote them all here, of course, but we may be able to add a bit more context. It can be noted, for example, that Lewis goes out of his way to let his readers know it is not an easy truth to say, believe, or experience. As he says a little later in *The Problem of Pain*, 'How can I say with sufficient tenderness what here needs to be said?'.[74] But yet he forges ahead and attempts to say it anyway. Even those who are not remarkably cruel or evil need a descent from contentedness, he says, if they are to get anywhere near what will, ultimately, be best for them. Everyone is perplexed, he writes, 'to see misfortune falling upon decent, inoffensive, worthy people—on capable, hardworking mothers of families or diligent, thrifty little trades-people, on those who have worked so hard, and so honestly, for their modest stock of happiness and now seem to be entering on the enjoyment of it with the fullest right'.[75] But still, he attempts to persuade his readers, as MacDonald did, that mere happiness, as it is ordinarily understood, is not the highest potential reality for humans: 'Let me implore the reader to try to believe, if only for the moment, that God, who made these deserving people, may really be right when He thinks that their modest prosperity and the happiness of their children are not enough to make them blessed; that all this must fall from them in the end,

---

71   AC, p. 454.
72   PP, p. 93. Compare this to the narrator's words in MacDonald's *Guild Court*, p. 38 : 'all the discords we hear in the universe around us, are God's trumpets sounding a *réveillé* to the sleeping human will, which once working harmoniously with his, will soon bring all things into a pure and healthy rectitude of operation. Till a man has learned to be happy without the sunshine, and therein becomes capable of enjoying it perfectly, it is well that the shine and the shadow should be mingled, so as God only knows how to mingle them'.
73   See above, p. 89.
74   PP, p. 96.
75   PP, p. 96.

and that if they have not learned to know Him they will be wretched'.[76] Or, as he writes elsewhere, 'This avoidance of suffering, this self-preservation, is not what life is really about'.[77]

As we have seen in a previous chapter, much of what life is about, according to MacDonald and Lewis, is beginning to know something of God—beginning to get some of his goodness into ourselves. As Melchah, in MacDonald's parable, was told by one of the Immortals, '"It is a law with us that no one can sing a song who cannot be the hero of his tale—who cannot live the song that he sings"'.[78] No heaven, no deepest happiness or ultimate reality, can be granted to those who have not begun to get some of heaven— God and his goodness—into themselves. And apparently, this getting him and his goodness into creatures that are not yet wholly good is something that cannot occur when a fallen creature is wholly satisfied with his surroundings. As Lewis says in *The Problem of Pain*, one will never attend to what is unwell within himself so long as all seems well outside himself: 'While what we call "our own life" remains agreeable we will not surrender it to Him. What then can God do in our interests but make "our own life" less agreeable to us, and take away the plausible sources of false happiness?'.[79]

Or as MacDonald said before Lewis through Mr. Cupples, a character in *Alec Forbes*, who says the following to Alec's mother concerning her son's repentance: '"Ye see, mem, it's a pairt o' the education o' the human individual, frae the time o' Adam and Eve doonwith, to learn to refuse the evil and chowse the guid. This doesna aye come o' eatin' butter and honey, but whiles o' eatin' aise (ashes) and dirt"'.[80]

This was the hard truth that MacDonald believed in, and that Lewis came to believe in, and that both men attempted to explain and portray in their books: that sometimes 'evil fortune' is necessary in order for people to realise how they should refuse the moral evil and choose God's goodness. Each reader, of course, can make up his own mind as to how convincingly they do this, but what no reader needs to worry about is whether or not they believed in the necessity to refuse moral evil. Neither MacDonald nor Lewis believed that moral evil was a part of ultimate reality, or that it was a substantial good that we must accept as part of ourselves and reality if we are to approach wholeness and true happiness. Nothing could be more opposed to MacDonald's thinking, or Lewis's.

---

76   PP, p. 97.
77   FSE, p. 91.
78   WW, p. 74 (III.i).
79   PP, p. 96.
80   AFH, p. 359.

One way to see this more clearly with MacDonald is to look specifically at his more realistic works and his sermons, which contain less pure symbolism and more explicit explanation and comment from the narrator. In *Robert Falconer*, for example, Robert's grandmother is at one point consoled that her son, Robert's father, may still be alive. The evidence that consoles her suggests that her son has recently stolen a deed that was once in her possession. But even so, he may still be alive and free from hellfire, she thinks. It is obvious from the narrator's comment on this that MacDonald considered evil fortune, even the evil fortune of hell, to be of much less importance than one's moral evil: 'Terrible consolation! Terrible creed which made the hope that he was still on this side of the grave working wickedness, light up the face of his mother, and open her hand in kindness. Is it suffering, or is it wickedness, that is the awful thing?'.[81]

It is quite obvious that MacDonald thought wickedness the truly awful thing, the thing that does not belong and must be got rid of. Past wrongs may be forgiven, but all of the wickedness in a person must be killed. In *Annals of a Quiet Neighbourhood*, for example, Walton, the local vicar, gives a sermon in which he says that pain and hunger are evils indeed, but evils that can be turned to good: "'if faith in God swallows them up, do they not so turn into good? I say they do"'.[82] Moral evil, on the other hand, quite apart from the suffering it might cause, is treated as another thing altogether. The wise man of the story, Old Rogers, is a retired, weather-beaten fisherman who, like MacDonald himself, has had much experience with ill fortune. In a chat with Walton, he reveals MacDonald's essential belief and message on the certain difference between evil fortune and moral evil. When the vicar says that he, Walton, ought to be better for some recent troubles he's been through, Rogers re-assures him: "'You *will* be the better for it [...] I believe I've allus been the better for any trouble as ever I had to go through with. I couldn't quite say the same for every bit of good luck I had; leastways, I consider trouble the best luck a man can have"'.[83]

When Walton asks Rogers that he certainly can't mean that it would be good for us to have bad luck at all times, Rogers answers, "'sartinly not"'.[84] And when Walton presses him on why one can then call bad luck the best luck, Rogers in his own way tells how troubles, in themselves, are not good, but can be turned to good when God allows it and man trusts God through it. But the important point to note here, in the context of moral evil and Raeper's argument, is how Rogers, toward the end of his answer, tells Walton that the

---

81   RF, p. 154.
82   AQN, p. 204.
83   AQN, pp. 561-562.
84   AQN, p. 562.

only thing really bad—the one thing that can never be good—is the moral wickedness that comes from men themselves. In this one answer we get the essentials of MacDonald's view of both kinds of evil: "'I mean the bad luck that comes to us [can be good luck]—not the bad luck that doesn't come. But you're right, sir. Good luck or bad luck's both best when *He* sends 'em, as He allus does. In fac', sir, there is no bad luck but what comes out o' the man hisself. The rest's all good'".[85]

In other words, what evil there is that is called 'evil fortune' or 'bad luck', along with 'good fortune' and 'good luck', only exists because it is the best possible state for imperfect men to be in. The message from MacDonald, as we can see here with Old Rogers, is to entrust the 'outside' evil and circumstances that one cannot control, nor fully understand, to God, while at the same time joining with him in a fight against 'inside', or moral, evil. There is a clear distinction made between the two.

If one needs further evidence of this distinction, he need only turn to some of his written sermons. In a sermon entitled 'Salvation from Sin', in the last collection of sermons MacDonald published,[86] MacDonald is quite clear and unequivocal about the nature of moral evil and its relation to evil fortune. In the opening paragraphs he lists a number of different causes of human discomfort and notes that the 'greater part of the energy of this world's life' is spent in an effort to destroy such discomfort.[87] He notes how all such efforts, however successful, do not usually attack the ultimate '*cause* of their misery', which he identifies as moral evil:

> the cause of every man's discomfort is evil, moral evil [...] No special [that is, particular] sin may be recognizable as having caused this or that special physical discomfort—which may have indeed originated with some ancestor; but evil in ourselves is the cause of its continuance, the source of its necessity, and the preventative of that patience which would soon take from it, or at least blunt its sting.[88]

Both moral evil and the suffering that it causes are '*essentially* unnecessary' to God's reality of perfection and wholeness, he writes.[89] God does permit the possibility and actuality of moral evil, temporarily, so that free moral agents may be given the chance at redemption—a chance to have a pure free will developed in them, as MacDonald puts it. But as long as moral evil does last, MacDonald writes, 'suffering, whether consequent or merely concomitant, is absolutely necessary': 'Foolish is the man, and there are many such men', he writes, 'who would rid himself or his fellows of discomfort by setting the world

---

85   AQN, p. 562.
86   *The Hope of the Gospel*. First published in 1892.
87   HG, p. 10.
88   HG, p. 11.
89   HG, p. 11.

right, by waging war on the evils around him, while he neglects that integral part of the world where lies his business, his first business—namely, his own character and conduct'.[90]

Even if it were possible that the world *could* be righted from the outside ('an absurd supposition')[91], MacDonald declares how it would be impossible for the man who contributed to this outward healing to ever enjoy the fruit of his labours in the deepest sense: 'himself not in tune with the organ he had tuned, he must imagine it still a distracted, jarring instrument'.[92] One is reminded here of Julian's remark in *Within and Without*: 'What is light to me, while I am dark!',[93] or the development of Robert Falconer's will, which is likened in the novel to learning to play a fiddle. Robert, in fact, is unable to play the music he wants until he has himself lived the song that he wanted to play.

The entire plot of *Robert Falconer* is devoted to showing how Robert's life becomes the song he wanted to play as a boy, as the Immortals in *Within and Without* told the youth in the parable he must do.[94] In the beginning of the novel young Falconer struggles to play 'The Flowers of the Forest', an old Scotch song.[95] By the end of the novel, after his soul has been tried, after he has got more of God's goodness into him through suffering and self-sacrifice, he is much better at music, in more than one way. In the opening paragraphs of the second third of the novel, entitled 'His Youth', MacDonald hints at what will happen by comparing Robert's personal development to how his fiddle came to be an instrument of beautiful music. He compares the sycamore and pine wood of the violin to the 'living wood' of a human soul which must undergo a similar process of becoming.[96] One is invited to imagine the parallels as MacDonald describes how the wood must be 'chosen, separated, individualized, tortured into strange, almost vital shape, after a law to us nearly unknown, strung with strings from animal organizations, and put into the hands of man to utter the

---

90   HG, p. 11.
91   HG, p. 11.
92   HG, p. 12.
93   WW, p. 3 (I.i).
94   See WW, p. 74 (III.i). See p. 41, above.
95   The song referred to in *Robert Falconer* was written by Jane (Jean) Elliott (1727-1805) and published anonymously c. 1755. It is a lament for Scottish soldiers who died at the Battle of Flodden in 1513, when forces under Henry VIII routed the army of James IV. Between 5,000 to 10,000 Scots were killed, including James IV. Elliott's lament, once thought traditional, uses images of the 'hairst', or harvest, to help express the loss of so many soldiers. See M.B. Foster (ed.), *Songs of Scotland, the Royal Edition, vol. II* (London: Boosey and Co., 1877). MacDonald, in the novel, plays upon these harvest images to express something of his idea of 'good death'.
96   RF, p. 165.

feelings of a soul that has passed through a like history'.[97] Robert, though, at this point of the novel, cannot even think of such a process. He 'had to grow able to think it by being himself made an instrument of God's music'.[98]

And so all of those who wish to achieve real wholeness must be refined, as MacDonald says in his sermon. Harmony within, impossible without moral peace, must be achieved before harmony without: peace of circumstance. Until inner harmony is achieved, one's circumstances must not be entirely peaceful, else no peace at all can exist for man. The inner and the outer must one day be congruent, and so the outer, for a time, is allowed to be adverse to help drive out what disrupts all peace: moral evil. As MacDonald writes, 'The one cure for any organism, is to be set right—to have all its parts brought into harmony with each other [...] Rightness alone is cure. The return of the organism to its true self, is its only possible ease'.[99] This return to the true self, MacDonald makes very clear, has nothing to do with accepting moral evil as a legitimate part of the whole: 'the health at the root of man's being, his rightness, is to be free from wrongness, that is, from sin. A man is right when there is no wrong in him'.[100] Later in the sermon, he makes this point even more clear. All past sin will be forgiven, he writes, but man must resolve to come out of his wickedness. He must lose his shadow. A choice has to be made: 'The sin he dwells in, the sin he will not come out of, is the sole ruin of a man'.[101]

In the very next sermon in this collection, MacDonald speaks of how ridding one's self of one's own wickedness is impossible by one's own efforts, but that this is no reason at all for any compromise: '[the multitudes asking Jesus what they must do] could not rid themselves of their sins, but they could set about sending them away; they could quarrel with them, and proceed to turn them out of the house: the Lord was on his way to do his part in their final banishment'.[102] We see most clearly here how MacDonald's idea of inner harmony and Jung's idea of individuation are very different indeed. Later in the same sermon, MacDonald holds back nothing in an attempt to show to what degree Christ and his followers are opposed to moral evil: 'His whole work was and is to send away sin—to banish it from the earth, yea, to cast into the abyss of non-existence behind the back of God. His was the holy war; he came carrying it [the holy war, that is] into our world; he resisted unto blood; the soldiers that followed him he taught and trained to resist also unto

---

97   RF, p. 165.
98   RF, p. 165.
99   HG, pp. 12-13.
100   HG, p. 13.
101   HG, p. 16.
102   HG, pp. 32-33.

blood'.[103]

MacDonald's picture of holy war here is surely a very different thing from the muddy picture Raeper paints in his biography. To discover why, exactly, Raeper's picture is so muddy and inaccurate, is outside the purposes of this study, but it can be stated that a more careful reading of MacDonald's stories, and even a casual reading of his sermons, would keep anyone from such an error. With MacDonald there is no compromise at all to be had with the shadow of moral evil. It does not belong; it has to go.

A virtually identical view of evil is expressed, one will find, in Lewis's books. As we have already noted,[104] Lewis's most ambitious non-fiction book on the subject, *The Problem of Pain*, begins with a direct quote from MacDonald's *Unspoken Sermons*. So does *The Great Divorce, A Dream*, in which Lewis attempts to portray, in fiction, what the choice between evil and goodness is like. It is clear from the quote what sort of stand MacDonald took on evil, and what stand Lewis's story will take: '"No, there is no escape. There is no heaven with a little of hell in it—no plan to retain this or that of the devil in our hearts or our pockets. Out Satan must go, every hair and feather'".[105] This quote is included in Lewis's anthology of MacDonald's works,[106] and is marked by hand in Lewis's personal copy of the sermon. Another portion of the sermon that Lewis marked in his own copy, and included in the anthology, are these lines: 'Whoever will live must cease to be a slave and become a child of God. There is no half-way house of rest, where ungodliness may be dallied with'.[107] Lewis, while marking all of these lines with a simple vertical line in the margin, took additional time to underline these words: 'There is no half-way house of rest'.

All of this points toward the reason why Lewis wrote *The Great Divorce*:[108] to show how something *must* be refused. Both men's concepts of heaven, like their concepts of God, did not allow for any evil. Neither MacDonald nor Lewis held morally dualistic or Jungian beliefs about God and ultimate reality.

---

103 HG, p. 38.
104 See note 50, on p. 140.
105 C.S. Lewis, *The Great Divorce: A Dream* (London: Harper Collins, 1997), p. iii; US, pp. 263-264 (first quarter of par. 6 in 'The Last Farthing', second series). *Great Divorce* first published in 1945.
106 ANTH, p. 50 (reading 112).
107 US, p. 274 (last half of the last paragraph in 'The Last Farthing', second series).
108 Lewis acknowledged different reasons people have for writing books: artistic and non-artistic reasons. See chp. 1 of *A Preface to Paradise Lost*, his essay 'Christianity and literature' in *Christian Reflections*, chp. 8 of *An Experiment in Criticism*, and his essay 'Sometimes fairy stories may say best what's to be said' in *Of This and Other Worlds*. The 'reason' I mention here concerns the chief non-artistic reason why Lewis wrote *The Great Divorce*.

Lewis, as he explains in the preface of *The Great Divorce*, is writing against what can be taken as the meaning of Blake's famous work: 'Blake wrote the Marriage of Heaven and Hell[109]. If I have written of their Divorce, this is not because I think myself a fit antagonist for such a genius, nor even because I feel at all sure that I know what he meant. But in some sense or other the attempt to make that marriage is perennial'.[110]

We can see from what Lewis writes here that the 'attempt' he is writing against is the very attempt that Raeper accuses MacDonald of:

> The attempt is based on the belief that reality never presents us with an absolutely unavoidable "either-or"; that, granted skill and patience and (above all) time enough, some way of embracing both alternatives can always be found; that mere development or adjustment or refinement [or 'individuation', as Raeper, following Jung, phrased it] will somehow turn evil into good without our being called on for a final and total rejection of anything we should like to retain.[111]

As Lewis makes clear, he thinks this belief to be a 'disastrous error': 'I do not think that all who choose wrong roads perish; but their rescue consists in being put back on the right road [...] Evil can be undone, but it cannot "develop" into good'.[112] Paraphrasing MacDonald, he writes, 'if we accept Heaven we shall not be able to retain even the smallest and most intimate souvenirs of Hell'.[113]

All of the images of good death that we see in MacDonald, as in Anodos losing his shadow, find their counterparts in Lewis's depiction of divorce, in this book and others. It is that which is not of God—evil hell—which we must divorce ourselves from if we are to get into where, or what, God is—heaven. And as Ransom tells the demon-possessed Weston in *Perelandra*, it does no good to try to argue that God would not have been able to accomplish specific goods, like the good of Christ's incarnation, without some moral evil having first been accomplished, so that good is in some way dependent upon, or an equal partner with, evil:

> Of course good came of [man's evil fall on earth]. Is Maleldil [that is, God] a beast that we can stop His path, or a leaf that we can twist His shape? Whatever you do, He will make good of it. But not the good He had prepared for you if you had obeyed Him. That is lost for ever. The first King and first Mother of our world did the forbidden thing; and He brought good of it in the end. But what they did was not good; and what they lost we have not seen.[114]

---

109 *Marriage of Heaven and Hell* (1790).
110 GD, p. vii.
111 GD, p. vii.
112 GD, p. vii.
113 GD, p. viii.
114 PER, p. 121.

God, in other words, does not need hell to accomplish his highest heaven. According to Lewis, his goodness will prevail in spite of moral evil, not *because* of it. In *The Problem of Pain*, Lewis speaks of perhaps the only victory that evil can accomplish: the consignment of a soul to damnation. But even this 'victory', negative as it may be, is still dependent upon something created by a good God, as evil always is:

> it is objected that the ultimate loss of a single soul means the defeat of omnipotence. And so it does. In creating beings with free will, omnipotence from the outset submits to the possibility of such defeat. What you call defeat, I call miracle: for to make beings which are not Itself, and thus to become, in a sense, capable of being resisted by its own handiwork, is the most astonishing and unimaginable of all the feats we attribute to the Deity.[115]

In short, evil never really accomplishes or contributes anything. The illusion that it does accomplish or contribute would not be possible without the Good.

But we will examine the nature of evil more thoroughly in the following chapter. Here it is simply shown how MacDonald and Lewis thought that the evil of hell must be rejected. The reason Lewis and MacDonald are very clear on this is because they obviously believed very strongly in a God who was all good himself. We will see later how this does not mean that they believed God is *only* what is called moral goodness. Both believed that God is much more than a moral entity. But the point here is neither MacDonald nor Lewis believed that God was anything *less* than perfect goodness and that he works to fill humans with as much of this goodness as our capacities allow—while necessarily putting death to, or divorcing our true selves from, all that is evil. Death, or divorce, as MacDonald and Lewis believed, must occur if one is to get in to him and his goodness.

Choosing Goodness

A brief review of their belief in, and portrayal of, the fact of God's unalloyed goodness will serve to substantiate this and close out this chapter. In *Robert Falconer*, for example, the narrator takes the time to describe and discuss Robert's move away from the stern, strongly Calvinistic faith that his grandmother had taught him—the same sort of faith MacDonald himself was acquainted with as a youth. In this discussion the narrator writes with conviction: 'it is of far more consequence what kind of God, than whether a God or no. Let not my reader suppose I think it possible there could be other than a perfect God—

---

115 PP, p. 127. It will be mentioned in the next chapter how Lewis disagreed with MacDonald on the probability of a soul's damnation ever becoming an actual defeat for God. It will be enough to say here that the disagreement does not turn upon their views on the nature of God's goodness, or of evil.

perfect—even to the vision of his creatures, the faith that supplies the lack of vision being yet faithful to that vision'.[116]

MacDonald's point here is that God is perfectly good, and that God has let us know enough about himself to see that he can only be perfectly good. To MacDonald's mind, believing in no God at all would be better than believing in a God who was not all good. As in *Robert Falconer*, so in a sermon of his entitled 'Light', in which MacDonald warns his readers never to believe ill of God no matter how many apparently evil actions or statements are clumsily attributed to him. 'Let no one persuade thee', he writes, 'that there is in him a little darkness, because of something he has said which his creature interprets into darkness'.[117] One sentence later he urges his reader never to believe apparent evil of God, never to believe that what God does is good merely because it is done by a God: 'Say either the thing is not what it seems, or God never said or did it. But, of all evils, to misinterpret what God does, and then say the thing as interpreted must be right because God does it, is of the devil'.[118]

As we can see later in *Robert Falconer*, this belief about God's goodness is consistent with MacDonald's belief about Christ and his mission. At one point, Robert, grown into manhood, reverts to his native Scots while talking to his grandmother. On the subject of what Christ came to do, he tells her this:

> "He cam to lift the weicht o' the sins that God had curst aff o' the shoothers[119] o' them 'at did them, by makin' them turn agen[120] them, an' be for God an' no for sin. And there isna a word o' reconceelin God till's[121] in a' the Testament, for there was no need o' that: it was us that needed to be reconcilet to him."[122]

His grandmother, just before these words of Robert's, had told him how she believed that Christ had suffered on the cross to take the punishment 'due to oor sins' and 'to turn aside his [that is, God's] wrath an' curse; to reconcile him to us'.[123] Robert in his reply attempts to show her that she's erring in a number of ways. The error most important for us to note here is her belief about the reconciliation that Christ's death on the cross makes possible. Robert attempts to show her how Christ's work on the cross was *not* to reconcile God to us and our sin. It was not a case of God doing something to Christ in order to satisfy

---

116 RF, p. 166.
117 US, p. 549 (middle of par. 7 in 'Light', third series).
118 US, p. 549 (last half par. 7 in the same sermon). Lewis marks these words in his copy of the sermon, includes it in his anthology and comes to similar conclusions in *The Problem of Pain*. See ANTH, reading 216; PP, p. 100.
119 Shoulders
120 Against
121 To us
122 RF, p. 328.
123 RF, p. 328.

some legal requirement of punishment, so that He could then be reconciled to our sinning going on, perhaps forever. To Robert's understanding, Christ's work is the thing that reconciles *us* to *God*—by taking our sins away in more than a legal sense: "'he took them awa'—they're vanishin' even noo frae the earth, though it doesna luik like it in Rag-fair or Petticoat-lane'".[124] If God is perfect goodness, Falconer reasons, we can only be reconciled to Him by the eventual destruction of all sin.

MacDonald, it is clear, is not simply playing devil's advocate through Robert's speech here. Robert's understanding is his understanding. Many such words in many novels and stories exist to help prove this. His sermons, though, confirm it beyond all doubt. In 'The Consuming Fire', for example, he writes this of the goodness and love that God is: 'love loves unto purity. Love has ever in view the absolute loveliness of that which it beholds'.[125] A few sentences later we find the following words underlined in Lewis's copy of the sermon: 'Therefore all that is not beautiful in the beloved, all that comes between and is not of love's kind, must be destroyed'.[126] In other words, because God is perfect love, he always hates all that is not love. Since he loves us, he must somehow destroy that in us which is un-loving. All hateful evil must be destroyed by God's purifying love, which MacDonald, following Scripture,[127] describes as 'a consuming fire'.[128]

And we have much more than Lewis's underlining of MacDonald's sermons to prove that Lewis came to believe the same thing of God and his goodness. In *Mere Christianity* he puts forward the view that only two beliefs really 'face all the facts' in the world.[129] One of these, Dualism, he describes as 'the belief that there are two equal and independent powers at the back of everything, one of them good and the other bad, and that this universe is the battlefield in which they fight out an endless war'.[130] While Lewis calls this 'the manliest and most sensible creed on the market' after Christianity, he ultimately rejects it for several reasons.[131] Some of these reasons we will explore further in the following chapter on the nature of evil. Here we need only say that Lewis did indeed reject it, favouring instead the Christian view that says Goodness alone is independent and original, and that evil is an unoriginal, derivative perversion, or twisting, of something already good. God, he believed, being the original Good Power who created the universe, would one

---

124 RF, p. 328.
125 US, p. 18 (par. 2 in 'The Consuming Fire', first series).
126 US, pp. 18-19 (par. 3 in the same sermon).
127 See Deut. 4.24, Heb. 12.29.
128 US, p. 19 (par. 4 in 'The Comsuming Fire', first series).
129 MC, p. 48.
130 MC, p. 48.
131 MC, p. 48.

day triumph over evil and burn it away into nothingness. Even if it could be imagined that God, the Good Power, should somehow lose out to an evil force that somehow became more powerful, Lewis himself imagined that he ought to side with the perfect Goodness against the triumphant evil power. As he writes to a fictional correspondent in *Letters to Malcolm: Chiefly on Prayer*:

> You know my history. You know why my withers are quite unwrung by the fear that I was bribed—that I was lured into Christianity by the hope of everlasting life. I believed in God before I believed in Heaven. And even now, even if—let's make an impossible supposition—His voice, unmistakably His, said to me, "They have misled you. I can do nothing of that sort for you. My long struggle with the blind forces is nearly over. I die, children. The story is ending," would that be a moment for changing sides? Would not you and I take the Viking way: "The Giants and Trolls win. Let us die on the right side, with Father Odin."[132]

As MacDonald believed, so did Lewis come to believe. To both men it was much more important what kind of God one followed than that one followed a God. Both men quite obviously thought it right to follow God because he is good, not simply because he is powerful. They thought it good to side with him against moral evil, come what may. To them there was no question of negotiating a truce with such evil, even if that moral evil could somehow supply us with endless good fortune. What Raeper largely ignores in his biography is in fact what MacDonald and Lewis constantly attempt to do in all their stories. They attempt to go beyond the realm of 'fortune' and lead the reader to a higher, or deeper, reality. Both believed that life was much more than a pain-pleasure calculus. They believed that evil fortune itself could help us realise, in our minds and in our experience, something more profound than a preoccupation with fortune. This something, they believed, was the goodness of God. They encouraged their readers to follow it, whatever 'fortune' could do to them.

Both authors' stories are so full of instances that symbolise and illustrate this belief, it is difficult to understand how anyone could fail to see it.[133] We can finish this chapter with a few typically striking examples.

In *Alec Forbes*, as in *Sir Gibbie*, a flood provides the opportunity for the title character to accomplish self-sacrificing good for others. But whereas Gibbie rushes to the task (he seems as sinless as Diamond in *At the Back of the North Wind*), Alec hesitates. The hesitation allows MacDonald, in the

---

132 LM, p. 120 (letter XXII).
133 Raeper does admit MacDonald's belief in God's sternness towards sin in his chapter on MacDonald's theology (see RAEP p. 153), which makes the absence of any such mention in the chapter on *Phantastes* all the more curious.

dialogue between Alec and Thomas Crann, to make the distinction between self-sacrificial goodness and fortune-seeking even more clear. When Thomas and Alec hear that Annie Anderson and Tibbie Dyster are in danger of being drowned by an overflowing river, Thomas notices Alec's boat and shouts to him. Alec makes no reply; he is looking at the terrible water down below him and noticing how small his boat is. Thomas, agitated, calls to Alec again but still gets no answer. The narrator then lets the reader know what's passing through Alec's mind: 'The terrors of the night had returned upon Alec. Would the boat live? Was there more than a chance? And if she went down was he not damned forever? He made no reply. He was afraid'.[134]

After Thomas shouts for Alec once again, asking '"Will ye lat the women droon?"', Alec responds, showing his own preoccupation with his own good fortune: '"Thomas," answered Alec, weakly, trembling from head to foot, "gin I gang to the boddom, I gang to hell"'.[135] Thomas, in his retort, shows us how far MacDonald goes in his loyalty to self-sacrificing goodness: '"Better be damned, doin' the will o' God, than saved doin' noathing!"'.[136] Even eternal salvation, if it is conceived of merely in terms of personal fortune, is to be shunned the moment it keeps us from the self-sacrificing goodness of God.

Lewis stresses the same point, in a negative way, in *The Screwtape Letters*. In one of demon Screwtape's letters to his nephew Wormwood, he discusses how a human war affects their work of luring as many men to hell as possible. He admits, on the one hand, that the war is entertaining to demons. But he wonders about the permanent good it does them in their efforts to bring souls to their ruin. 'Certain tendencies' about this instance of human misfortune, he says, are not in the demons' favour: 'We may hope for a good deal of cruelty and uncharity. But, if we are not careful, we shall see thousands turning in this tribulation to the Enemy, while tens of thousands who do not go so far as that will nevertheless have their attention diverted from themselves to values and causes which they believe to be higher than the self'.[137]

In his very next letter to Wormwood, Screwtape writes how God 'wants men to be concerned with what they do' while the demons' business is 'to keep them thinking about what will happen to them'.[138] In another letter he argues for a subdued approach to tempting: anything they can do, or keep from doing, to keep their man satisfied and numb of heart. Young tempters may want to rock the boat a bit in order to be able to report 'spectacular wickedness', but Screwtape notes how uninterrupted good fortune, shallow contentedness,

---

134 AFH, pp. 285-286.
135 AFH, p. 286.
136 AFH, p. 286.
137 SCL, p. 26 (Letter V).
138 SCL, p. 28 (VI).

or even simple distraction with things that are not necessarily enjoyable, are usually more reliable in the demons' quest to edge the man 'away from the Light and out into the Nothing'.[139] 'Indeed', Screwtape writes, 'the safest road to Hell is the gradual one—the gentle slope, soft underfoot, without sudden turnings, without milestones, without signposts'.[140]

And Lewis is not afraid to bring up the distinction between fortune and morality in his Narnia books. In *The Magician's Nephew*, for example, young Digory has promised to go fetch an apple of youth and bring it back to Aslan untasted, so that the great Lion can use it to help protect Narnia. He is cruelly tempted on his quest by Jadis, queen of Charn.[141] First she tempts him to eat the apple himself and share it with her, promising that he and she will then live forever. He refuses, saying he'd rather just live a normal life. So then Jadis begins to speak of his mother's health. She knows that Digory's mother is very ill and suggests that they return to earth, share the apple with his mother, and see her recover to full health. This suggestion cuts Digory to the quick. It is worse than choosing between one's own good fortune and doing something one knows to be wrong; it is the choice between another's good fortune, his mother's, and doing something he knows to be wrong. His experience of Aslan and his goodness lets him know that Aslan is all good and that he cares for his mother. Indeed, after mentioning his mother to Aslan before, he had looked into the Lion's great eyes and seen such sorrow that 'for a moment he felt as if the Lion must really be sorrier about his Mother than [Digory] was himself'.[142] But still, the Witch's proposal of full health for his mother, even if it goes against Aslan's good orders, is tempting.

As he stammers and hesitates, the cruel witch begins to accuse Digory of cruelty. Digory interrupts, miserably telling her that he sees the possibilities, but that he made a promise. "'Mother herself'", says Digory, "'wouldn't like it—awfully strict about keeping promises—and not stealing—and all that sort of thing. *She'd* tell me not to do it—as quick as anything—if she was here'".[143]

The witch soon makes her mistake by suggesting that no one need know about the way he got the apple. He could leave his friend Polly behind in Narnia, and no one on earth would ever know, she suggests. This meanness convinces Digory that the witch is not to be trusted. Aslan, the great and good Lion who cares for his mother and who gave him the command, can be trusted. And so Digory chooses to obey his conscience rather than ensure

---

139 SCL, p. 56 (XII).
140 SCL, p. 56 (XII).
141 Later the White Witch of Narnia in LWW, and the Queen of Underland in *The Silver Chair*.
142 MN, p. 168.
143 MN, p. 194.

good health by doing wrong.[144] As the chapter ends he's very sad and not quite sure if he's done the right thing, though 'whenever he remembered the shining tears in Aslan's eyes he became sure'.[145]

In the following chapter we learn that the fruit, if Digory had done as the witch had suggested, would have cured his mother. But as Aslan makes clear to Digory, it would not have brought true joy: "'it would have healed her; but not to your joy or hers. The day would have come when both you and she would have looked back and said it would have been better to die in that illness'".[146] Digory, after hearing this, begins to cry, giving up 'all hopes of saving his mother's life; but at the same time he knew that the Lion knew what would have happened, and that there might be things more terrible even than losing someone you love by death'.[147]

Lewis, as much as anyone, must have known how difficult it was to write, read, or believe such severe words about such a situation. He, like MacDonald, it will be remembered, lost his mother as a young boy. Yet he, like MacDonald, believed and wrote such words. But this is really not surprising. Both men were Christians. Their words are no more severe than the words and life of the suffering Christ whom they both called Lord, the Christ who was the inspiration behind the character Aslan. This Christ, as we shall see in a later chapter, inspires their distinctive illustrations of God and his goodness. All of the severe and tender goodness that one finds in Aslan, in the rusty knight of MacDonald's *Phantastes*, in the older Robert Falconer, in Queen Irene,[148] Ransom and other of their characters, springs from both authors' recognition of these qualities in the person of Christ, and in what they felt to be his influence.

In this chapter it has been shown how MacDonald and Lewis thought loyalty to such goodness a worthy undertaking: an undertaking distinct from simply following after fortune, and most certainly an undertaking that involves setting one's self against the evil that distorts one's true self. Before going on to look more closely at this distinctive goodness, however, we will need to devote some space to identifying more clearly what they believed to be man's chief obstacle to wholeness.

---

144 See MN, pp. 194-195.
145 MN, p. 196.
146 MN, pp. 208-209.
147 MN, p. 209.
148 Princess Irene's great-great grandmother in the Curdie books.

CHAPTER 4

THE PHILOSOPHY OF HELL

Richard loves Richard; that is, I am I.
–Shakespeare, *Richard III*, 5.5[1]

Such a number of looking-glasses! oh Lord! There was no
getting away from oneself.
–Jane Austen, *Persuasion*, Chapter 13[2]

It is mine. I tell you. My own. My precious. Yes, my
precious.
–J.R.R. Tolkien, *The Lord of the Rings*, 1.1[3]

We must now go to hell and see what is there. Any deep understanding of
MacDonald's and Lewis's fiction requires an understanding of what they
thought moral evil is and what it may lead to if it is not put to death.

One way to do this is to identify what the villains in their stories have in
common. Two characters in particular will help: the demon-possessed Weston
of *Perelandra*, one of Lewis's most obviously odious characters, and Angus
MacPholp, a relatively minor character of MacDonald's found in *Sir Gibbie*.
MacDonald's probable influence upon Lewis can be quickly established here
by looking at what these two characters are called. In *Perelandra*, once it is
firmly established that Weston's body is inhabited and at times controlled by
a demonic force, the narrator begins to refer to him, or it, as 'the Un-man'.[4]
In *Sir Gibbie* MacDonald does something similar with MacPholp, a brutal
lackey of the story's chief villain, Laird Thomas Galbraith. After MacPholp,
under orders from the laird, has inflicted bloody wounds to Gibbie's waist and
back with his whip, the narrator refers to him as 'the unman'.[5] Comparing
MacPholp to Gibbie a few paragraphs later, the narrator explains the
gamekeeper's character with a simple statement: 'Angus was and was not a
man!'.[6] And if one needs further proof that Lewis's demonic Un-man was
partially inspired by MacPholp, he need only read a few chapters further when
Ginevra Galbraith, the laird's daughter, comes across a lonely hollow in a
hillside. The swampy hollow with a peat-bog at the bottom reminds her 'of
how she always felt when she came unexpectedly upon Angus MacPholp'.[7]

1 Quoted in PP, p. 118.
2 Admiral Croft on Sir Walter Elliot's dressing room.
3 Bilbo to Gandalf on the One Ring that he, like Gollum, calls his own.
4 PER, p. 122.
5 GIB, p. 134.
6 GIB, p. 135.
7 GIB, p. 198.

She thinks that 'it must have been just in such places that the people possessed with devils [...] *demons*—ran about!'.[8] That Lewis came to write of his own unman possessed by a devil or demons is surely no coincidence.

And it is from the name 'Un-man' or 'unman' that we can begin to discern perhaps the single most important thing about MacDonald's and Lewis's ideas of moral evil. To them evil was real as a condition but not real as an original 'substance' of its own. As MacDonald wrote of MacPholp, it both is and is not. As 'cold' is a word indicating the absence of heat, so is 'evil', to MacDonald's and Lewis's understandings, a word that indicates a lack, or a perversion, of an original good. To whatever degree a man is evil is the degree to which he is less of a man, as we see with MacPholp and Lewis's Un-man.

This belief is clearly on display in many of MacDonald's sermons, as in 'Justice' where he makes the point that 'evil exists only by the life of good, and has no life of its own, being in itself death'.[9] In so far as it is anything, moral evil, according to MacDonald, is a parasite. It is neither original nor, as we learned in the previous chapter, tending towards wholeness. To MacDonald evil is the opposite of good, not as 'left' is the opposite of 'right'—that is, an equally valid alternative—but as 'lack' can be conceived of as the opposite of 'fullness', or as an arrow missing its target can be conceived of as the opposite of one striking home. This last comparison, of course, accords with the Christian idea of 'sin'. The New Testament word most often used to indicate 'sin', *hamartia* (ἁμαρτία), was in fact originally used to indicate the missing of a target or a road.[10]

Lewis, like MacDonald, expresses such a belief in his non-fiction, as in *Mere Christianity* when he explains why he is a Christian and not a dualist. A dualist, he writes, is one who believes that 'there are two equal and independent powers at the back of everything, one of them good and the other bad, and that this universe is the battlefield in which they fight out an endless war'.[11] While acknowledging dualism to be a 'manly and sensible' creed, he ultimately rejects it in favour of the Christian explanation which 'agrees with Dualism that this universe is at war' but 'does not think this is a war between independent powers'.[12] Characteristically, Lewis goes much further than MacDonald in attempting to prove that this is the case. As he summed up in an article for *The Spectator*,[13] one of his objections has to do with a metaphysical difficulty. 'The two Powers [of Dualism], the good and the evil, do not explain each other',

---

8   GIB, p. 198.
9   US, p. 512 (second quarter of par. 31 in 'Justice', third series).
10   See, for example, George Arthur Buttrick (ed.), *The Interpreter's Dictionary of the Bible, Volume 4*, (Nashville: Abingdon Press, 1962), p. 371.
11   MC, p. 48.
12   MC, pp. 50-51.
13   In response to C.E.M. Joad's article 'Evil and God', *The Spectator*, vol. CLXVI (31 Jan. 1941), pp. 112-113.

he writes.[14] 'More ultimate than either of them is the inexplicable fact of their being there together. Neither of them chose this *tête-à-tête*'.[15] The two powers, he argues, cannot really be independent of each other, finding themselves somehow in the same reality which neither power created: 'Each of them [...] finds himself willy-nilly in a situation; and either that situation itself, or some unknown force which produced that situation, is the real Ultimate'.[16] As Lewis reasoned, two equal and independent powers 'has not yet reached the ground of being':

> You cannot accept two conditioned and mutually independent beings as the self-grounded, self-comprehending Absolute. On the level of picture-thinking this difficulty is symbolised by our inability to think of Ormuzd and Ahriman[17] without smuggling in the idea of a common *space* in which they can be together and thus confessing that we are not yet dealing with the source of the universe but only with two members contained in it.[18]

The other difficulty Lewis claims to find in dualism is that it requires that the evil power be 'a being who likes badness for its own sake'.[19] Reality, Lewis argues, contradicts this claim: 'We have no experience of anyone liking badness just because it is bad'.[20] Even those who are cruel, he argues, are not cruel for the sake of cruelty itself. They do it, he says, 'because they have a sexual perversion which makes cruelty a cause of sensual pleasure to them', or because they are getting something else out of it: 'money, or power, or safety'.[21] As pleasure, money, power and safety are in themselves good things, Lewis says that the evil or 'badness' of cruelty consists in seeking these good things 'by the wrong method, or in the wrong way, or too much'.[22] And so it is with any sort of evil, Lewis writes:

> wickedness, when you examine it, turns out to be the pursuit of some good in the wrong way. You can be good for the mere sake of goodness: you cannot be bad for the mere sake of badness. You can do a kind action when you are not feeling kind and when it gives you no pleasure, simply because kindness is right; but no one ever did a cruel action simply because cruelty is wrong—only because cruelty was pleasant or

14 GDK, p. 22.
15 GDK, p. 22.
16 GDK, p. 22.
17 The Good Power and Evil Power, respectively, of the Avestic or Zoroastrian religion.
18 GDK, p. 22. See also MIR, p. 31.
19 MC, p. 49.
20 MC, p. 49.
21 MC, p. 49.
22 MC, p. 49.

useful to him.[23]

Evil, then, is not one of two grand, eternal and equal alternatives. The devil, whatever he is, is not on equal footing with God and his goodness, MacDonald and Lewis believed. As Lewis wrote of the 'Bad Power' of dualism, his very ability to pervert goodness is derived from good things: 'To be bad, he must exist and have intelligence and will. But existence, intelligence and will are in themselves good. Therefore he must be getting them from the Good Power: even to be bad he must borrow or steal from his opponent'.[24]

The devil, then, though still an evil power, is not as important in determining the 'nature' of evil as God is in determining the nature of goodness. To MacDonald and Lewis, Satan is a created being who has perverted good things, as many human creatures have. That MacDonald believed the devil to be redeemable is proof enough of this. Raeper makes note of this possibility of redemption in his biography, but somehow manages to draw the wrong conclusions from it. As he puts it, God allowing 'even the devil himself' to run around causing harm until he is redeemed, is proof that moral evil must have some positive value of its own.[25] This mistake of Raeper's has two likely causes. The first is his associating the nature of evil too closely with the character of the devil, as if he were the great Power who is Evil and who radiates evil in the same way that God is Goodness who radiates goodness. It is like saying a defective mirror is the equal and opposite counterpart to the sun. Hence Raeper's use of the grand phrase 'even the devil himself', which likely springs from the habit of thinking of the devil too exclusively as a symbol for evil in MacDonald's fiction, when MacDonald in fact believed in Satan as an actual created being—who like any other fallen being needed redeeming. The reason MacDonald, and Lewis, believed God allowed Satan to continue existing and causing harm is not because they thought his evil sin contributes anything towards the wellbeing of the universe. He has been allowed to exist and keep doing harm, they believed, for the same reasons God allows fallen humans to exist and keep doing harm: because he and we have been redeemable and because his and our evil ways will not ultimately frustrate God's good plans.

The second likely cause of Raeper's mistake is a simple failure to realise, or apply, what redemption must involve. It means, to MacDonald and Lewis especially, being saved from one's sin: being put right or made better. This meaning argues against any positive, original meaning that dualists, Jung or Raeper may want to give to the word 'evil' or the word 'devil'. If the devil can be redeemed, or made right, then he cannot be an independent, self-sufficient, original power on par with God and his goodness. If he is that kind of power,

23   MC, p. 49.
24   MC, p. 50.
25   RAEP, p. 151.

he can no more be redeemed than the primary colour red can be redeemed into the primary colour yellow. A thing insufficiently red can be redeemed: it can be made more purely red. But it is intrinsically impossible to redeem red into yellow. If Red went to Yellow to be redeemed, the reply would surely be, 'Sorry, don't know how; never been red myself'. It might be possible, if colours had such powers, for yellow to destroy all trace of red (and all other colours) so that there would be only yellow, but destruction is not redemption, with either colours or independent, original powers. Having an independent, self-sufficient, original power saying 'I'm sorry' and being made better is simply a silly way of saying the power in question is not actually independent, original or self-sufficient. Such a power has no one else to go to in order to make him more of what he should be. Such a power, by definition, is independently and originally everything it needs to be.

And so while MacDonald and Lewis always present the battle between evil and goodness as a real and significant battle, they never present it as a battle between equals. It is a battle between the Great Someone and those who would be nothing, or between a man and that 'shadow of me [...] which art not me, but which representest thyself to me as me'.[26]

It is important to keep this is mind when noticing MacDonald's frequent use of some form of doppelgänger in his stories, a practice especially common among Scottish authors, it seems.[27] In *Phantastes* MacDonald achieves this by personifying a shadow, though he makes it quite clear that Anodos's shadow is not his equal, his opposite, his true self, or any real person at all.

In his more realistic novels he accomplishes this doppelgänger effect in a number of ways. In *Sir Gibbie*, for example, he gives the name of 'umnan' to a cruel but redeemable gamekeeper after directly comparing his character, or lack thereof, to the Christ-like Gibbie.[28] In *Robert Falconer* Dooble Sanny, the town drummer and cobbler, and Robert's fiddle tutor, battles against another self, as his name implies. As Anodos struggled against the influence of his shadow, Dooble Sanny finds his true self oppressed by that which is less true: 'That which was fine in him was constantly checked and held down by the gross; the merely animal over-powered the spiritual; and it was only upon occasion that his heavenly companion, the violin, could raise him a few feet above the mire and the clay'.[29] In the same story MacDonald uses two separate characters to do something similar: the young rogue Lord Rothie, also named

---

26 PHA, p. 72. See pp. 136, above.
27 James Hogg's *The Private Memoirs and Confessions of a Justified Sinner* (1824) and R.L. Stevenson's *The Strange Case of Dr. Jekyll and Mr. Hyde* (1886) being the most famous examples.
28 See GIB, p. 135.
29 RF, pp. 66-67.

Sandy, turns out to be the half-brother of Shargar, Robert's chief companion in the novel. Shargar, the illegitimate son of the elder Lord Rothie and a gypsy woman, is in the beginning of the story an uncivilized, roaming waif. Much like Gibbie or Diamond, Shargar's lack of worldly sophistication serves to accentuate his genuine and virtuous character. MacDonald's story encourages the reader to consider this genuineness and virtue of Shargar's, even after the boy grows up and becomes refined (but not corrupted) by civilisation. In stark contrast to Shargar stands the false, devouring and truly illegitimate character of his half-brother Lord Rothie.

Another example of this double effect in MacDonald's more realistic novels concerns Murdoch Malison, the cruel schoolmaster of Alec Forbes's boyhood. Malison is a brutal despot in the classroom. The reader learns that Malison is leading somewhat of a double life: he is autocratic and violent in the classroom but shy and retiring outside school amongst the pupils' parents. Much of this, the narrator tells us, is because he does in class what his conscience outside of class, in 'a more open atmosphere', blushes at.[30] At one point two poor, frail orphans join his classroom. Malison, in one particularly ruthless incident, cripples one of the twins, Andrew Truffey. When the boy, on crutches, finally returns to school, Malison's heart is broken by the thought of what he's done. He begins to mellow in his treatment of his students, and Truffey begins to haunt Malison with his presence, much as Anodos's shadow haunted him. Truffey's presence here reminds Malison of his own false self, and helps him to lose it:

> the marvel was to see how Andrew Truffey haunted and dogged the master. He was as it were a conscious shadow of him [...] And the haunting of little Truffey worked so on his conscience, that, if the better nature of him had not asserted itself in love to the child, he would have been compelled to leave the place. For think of having a visible sin of your own, in the shape of a lame-legged boy, peeping at you round every other corner![31]

Malison does indeed begin to repent and love the child, eventually giving his life trying to save Truffey from a flood. Here we can see MacDonald's moral 'good death' symbolised by the death of Malison and Truffey. Malison's self-sacrificial death, out of love for Truffey, shows that he has lost his false self and found his true self. And it will be remembered that Truffey was a twin. After Malison crippled the boy, this twin follows Malison around reminding the schoolmaster of his own false self: his own evil twin, so to speak. And the circumstances of Malison's and Truffey's deaths can easily be read as symbolic. A raging torrent sweeps away half of a bridge along with Malison and Truffey,

30   AFH, p. 107.
31   AFH, p. 133.

just as Malison has lost his own evil half, or twin. Malison, like Anodos, has undergone self-sacrificial death: on the bridge and in his own heart. The action and setting of *Alec Forbes* may be more realistic than that of *Phantastes*, but the development, growth, and death of Malison's character seems no less full of symbolic meaning.[32]

The One Principle of Hell

But what, specifically, do these doppelgängers, and other literary devices and methods, reveal of the defining characteristics of moral evil, as MacDonald understood them? What do his villains and evil shadows have in common that show us his idea of what wickedness is, or is like? Do we find similar things in Lewis's fiction? One way that helps us to answer such questions, as we have already seen, is to turn to their non-fiction.

One of MacDonald's sermons, 'Kingship', contains a remarkable paragraph which sums up what he believed to be the root of all evil. The fact that he uses the pronouns 'I', 'my', or 'myself' thirty-seven times in the space of a dozen sentences gives a clue as to the nature of this root. And the fact that Lewis marked and underlined the first sentence of the twelve in his copy of the sermon, and that he included it in his anthology of MacDonald's works,[33] confirms that he took special notice of the passage. The sentence he marks and underlines reads thus: 'For the one principle of hell is—"I am my own".[34] Here MacDonald claims that the root of all evil is the tendency of a self to pretend that it is all that there is—to pretend or act as if one's self has no context at all, or at least no context to which it should yield. The eleven sentences that follow amount to MacDonald's conception of a sort of creed of self-worship. It is worth quoting here in full to gain a clearer understanding of what MacDonald meant by this one principle of hell:

> I am my own king and my own subject. I am the centre from which go out my thoughts; I am the object and end of my thoughts; back upon me as the alpha and omega[35] of life, my thoughts return. My own glory is, and ought to be, my chief care; my ambition, to gather the regards of men to the one centre, myself. My pleasure is my pleasure. My kingdom is—as many as I can bring to acknowledge my greatness over them. My judgement is the faultless rule of things. My right is—what I desire. The more I am all in all to myself, the greater I am. The less I acknowledge debt or obligation to another; the more I close my eyes

---

32   It might also be noted here, regarding symbols of good death, that the name 'Truffey' is very close to the Scots word 'truff' which can refer to the turf over a grave, or the grave itself.
33   See ANTH, p. 88 (reading 203).
34   US, p. 495 (first quarter of par. 3 in 'Kingship', third series).
35   For Alpha and Omega, see Rev. 1.8; 21.6; 22.13.

to the fact that I did not make myself; the more self-sufficing I feel or imagine myself—the greater I am. I will be free with the freedom that consists in doing whatever I am inclined to do, from whatever quarter may come the inclination. To do my own will so long as I feel anything to be my will, is to be free, is to live.[36]

If anyone is doubtful as to what MacDonald's morally evil shadows are all about, or as to why portions of his books seem 'dark',[37] these sentences should help to clarify. The thing that must suffer good death, he thought, was the self out-of-context: the self that sees itself as its own. This self-worship, one will notice, is consistent with what we have already learned about MacDonald's and Lewis's ideas of evil: that it must borrow from, or twist, the good in order to be what it is. A self is a good thing created by God, but yet it can go wrong when it perceives itself in the wrong way. Perceiving itself as the center of the universe is of course something it could not do without something good: the self that God created. The evil is in the self thinking and acting as if it were not created by God—acting as if it were in fact its own God.

And we have additional evidence, other than underlining and inclusion in an anthology, that this view of evil took root in Lewis's mind. It comes out in his fiction, as we can see in an outburst from Weston in *Perelandra* before he becomes wholly dominated by a devil. At one point he is attempting to convince Ransom that what he calls the devil is actually "the Life-Force",[38] a forward-reaching "dynamism"[39] that is just as valid a part of reality as what Ransom calls God. As Weston puts it: 'The people like me, who do the reaching forward, are always martyrs. You revile us, and by us come to your goal'.[40] He attempts to keep Ransom from 'relapsing on to the popular level' and calling certain actions 'diabolical'.[41] Good and evil, he insists, 'are only moments in the single, unique reality'.[42] 'The world', he argues, 'leaps forward through great men and greatness always transcends mere moralism'.[43]

Then Ransom asks Weston how far his allegiance to such a Life-Force goes. "Would you still obey the Life-Force if you find it prompting you to murder me?", he asks.[44] Weston simply replies, "Yes".[45] He would murder Ransom,

36   US, p. 495 (first three quarters of par. 3 in 'Kingship', third series).
37   A question that deserves more consideration than this study can give, but which ought to be noted, is why there seems to be more darkness in MacDonald's later work than in his earlier fiction. For discussions on this, see ROBB, pp. 33-34, 69-75; and U.C. Knoepflmacher in CFT, p. 187.
38   PER, p. 93.
39   PER, p. 95.
40   PER, p. 95.
41   PER, p. 95.
42   PER, p.95.
43   PER, p. 95. Compare to Uncle Andrew and Jadis. See pp. 90-91, above.
44   PER, p. 95.
45   PER, p. 95.

sell England to the Nazis, and print lies as serious research in a scientific journal if the Life-Force prompted him to. Ransom expresses exasperation at this, but then attempts to find common ground with Weston, saying that his apparent "'total commitment'" to the Life-Force may be a "'point of contact between your morality and mine'".[46] As Ransom presses upon Weston the fact of their mutual obligation to something outside themselves, he is interrupted by Weston's outburst, an outburst identical in spirit to MacDonald's creed of hell quoted above:

> "Idiot," said Weston. His voice was almost a howl and he had risen to his feet. "Idiot," he repeated. "Can you understand nothing? Will you always try to press everything back into the miserable framework of your old jargon about self and self-sacrifice? That is the old accursed dualism in another form. There is no possible distinction in concrete thought between me and the universe. In so far as I am the conductor of the central forward pressure of the universe, I am it. Do you see, you timid, scruple-mongering fool? I *am* the Universe. I, Weston, am your God and your Devil. I call that Force into me completely..."[47]

It is at this point that Weston, the self-proclaimed universe, is inhabited and dominated by a devil. The resultant being, called 'the Un-man', goes on in the story to mutilate frogs for fun, tempt the sinless Lady of Perelandra to self-worship, and torture Ransom with a number of perverse, baboonish antics. In keeping with MacDonald's and his own idea of evil as something petty and insubstantial, Lewis's Un-man is everything his name implies:

> For temptation, for blasphemy, for a whole battery of horrors, [Ransom] was in some sort prepared: but hardly for this petty, indefatigable nagging as of a nasty little boy at a preparatory school [...] On the surface, great designs and antagonism to Heaven which involved the fate of worlds: but deep within, when every veil had been pierced, was there, after all, nothing but a black puerility, an aimless empty spitefulness content to sate itself with the tiniest cruelties, as love does not disdain the smallest kindness?[48]

In Ransom's daily and exhausting efforts to protect the Lady and other inhabitants of Perelandra from the Un-man, he discovers more and more how unbearable it is to live so long with a devil. He is disgusted by the Un-man's obscenity and silliness; alarmed at its hateful destruction of animals and vegetation, and terrified by having to live with what seems like 'a ghost or a mechanised corpse'.[49] But Ransom is never impressed by any grandeur or

---

46   PER, p. 96.
47   PER, p. 96.
48   PER, p. 123.
49   PER, p. 129.

sophistication from this demon. The Un-man can use Weston's reason when it needs to, as when tempting the Lady, but it is clear that this intelligence of Weston's in no way indicates anything admirable in the devil's character. Reason, intelligence, speech, Weston's body and mind, the Lady and her purity, the plant and animal life of Perelandra: they are all either tools or toys to the Un-man, never appreciated in their own right. They are simply dropped after they have been used or played with. Lewis's devil here, as the narrator tells us, is nothing at all like what Goethe or Milton have given us:

> [Ransom] had full opportunity to learn the falsity of the maxim that the Prince of Darkness is a gentleman. Again and again he felt that a suave and subtle Mephistopheles with red cloak and rapier and a feather in his cap, or even a sombre tragic Satan out of *Paradise Lost*, would have been a welcome release from the thing he was actually doomed to watch. It was not like dealing with a wicked politician at all: it was much more like being set to guard an imbecile or a monkey or a very nasty child.[50]

Lewis makes this point about the characterisation of Satan in at least two other places. One is a work of criticism, his *Preface to Paradise Lost*.[51] The other is in the preface to his own most famous work on evil, *The Screwtape Letters*, where he agrees with Ruskin[52] that Dante's devils, not Milton's, are more true to reality 'in their rage, spite, and obscenity'.[53] 'Milton's devils', he writes, 'by their grandeur and high poetry, have done great harm'.[54] Even worse, though, is Goethe's Mephistopheles, Lewis writes: 'It is Faust, not he, who really exhibits the ruthless, sleepless, unsmiling concentration upon self which is the mark of Hell. The humorous, civilised, sensible, adaptable Mephistopheles has helped to strengthen the illusion that evil is liberating'.[55]

That evil is not liberating is something that Lewis learned in part from MacDonald. Anyone who insists on his own way, MacDonald thought, is cutting himself off from the only thing that could supply real liberty. A prideful insistence upon one's own way, he thought, was a move away from abundant life into the prison of mere self. As he wrote in a sermon entitled 'Freedom', 'the liberty of the God that would have his creature free, is in contest with the slavery of the creature who would cut his own stem from his root that he might call it his own and love it; who rejoices in his own consciousness, instead of the life of that consciousness; who poises himself on the tottering wall of

---

50   PER, p. 128.
51   See C.S. Lewis, *A Preface to Paradise Lost* (London: Oxford University Press, 1944), pp. 92–93. First published in 1942.
52   See 'Grotesque Renaissance' in *The Stones of Venice, vol. II*.
53   SCL, p. ix.
54   SCL, p. ix.
55   SCL, p. ix.

his own being, instead of the rock on which that being is built'.[56] A self who did not create what he calls his self attempting to be his self by himself was to MacDonald a confining and delusional undertaking:

> Such a one regards his own dominion over himself—the rule of the greater by the less, inasmuch as the conscious self is less than the self—as a freedom infinitely greater than the range of the universe of God's being [...] To live without the eternal creative life is an impossibility; freedom from God can only mean an incapacity for seeing the facts of existence[57]

Such a one who calls one's own way better than God's way, MacDonald writes, does not even know of what he speaks when he says 'my way':

> "I answer [to such a one], You do not know what is your way and what is not. You know nothing of whence your impulses, your desires, your tendencies, your likings come. They may spring now from some chance, as of nerves diseased; now from some roar of a wandering bodiless devil; now from some infant hate in your heart; now from the greed or lawlessness of some ancestor you would be ashamed of if you knew him; or it may be now from some far-piercing chord of a heavenly orchestra: the moment it comes up into your consciousness, you call it your own way, and glory in it!"[58]

Such a person is locking himself outside the glory and heart of reality, MacDonald writes. Seemingly oblivious to the 'relation of creative and created',[59] the person is taking a limited consciousness of his self, mixing it with whatever desires, moods and feelings happen to be bubbling over at the time, and treating it as God. He is taking what he calls 'my own way',[60] fancying it as some sort of heaven, and stepping inside. MacDonald did not deny that an attempt at such a step could be made. He did not even deny that one could in some sense succeed in the attempt. He only denied that it would be any kind of heaven. He clearly thought that the degree to which one succeeded in climbing into 'his own self' and 'his own way' was the degree to which he confined himself to hell. We see here how MacDonald considered the one principle of hell—'I am my own'—to be the very substance of hell. Wanting

---

56   US, p. 486 (second quarter of par. 5 in 'Freedom', third series). Lewis marks all of this in his copy of the sermon and underlines 'in his own consciousness, instead of the life of that consciousness'.

57   US, pp. 486-487 (middle of par. 5 in the same sermon). In his copy Lewis marks the portion before the ellipsis and underlines: 'his own dominion over himself–the rule of the greater by the less, inasmuch as the conscious self is less than the self'.

58   US, p. 487 (third quarter of par. 5 in the same). Lewis marks all of this, and underlines 'the moment it comes up into your consciousness, you call it your own way, and glory in it!'.

59   US, p. 487 (third quarter of par. 5 in the same).

60   US, p. 487 (third quarter of par. 5 in the same).

one's 'own way' apart from God and his goodness is not only the way to hell. It *is* hell. As Lewis wrote in *The Problem of Pain*, '[The damned] enjoy forever [in hell] the horrible freedom they have demanded, and are therefore self-enslaved just as the blessed, forever submitting to obedience, become through all eternity more and more free'.[61]

Purgatory

It is now that we can begin to explore their understandings and literary pictures of what hell is like. Both men, it must first be said, believed in a purgatory, or purgatorial hell, that helps bring souls to a realisation of their own wickedness. MacDonald, especially, stresses how this is never punishment for punishment's sake. A realisation of the loathsome self lurking within, they both believed, was the ugly truth that (in this life or beyond) was to play a part in bringing one closer to God and his goodness. In his sermon 'The Fear of God', for example, MacDonald claims that not all fears are damaging: 'Until love, which is the truth towards God, is able to cast out fear, it is well that fear should hold; it is a bond, however poor, between that which is and that which creates [...] Verily, God must be terrible to those that are far from him'.[62] This kind of fear, MacDonald writes, so long as one remains unloving and self-worshiping, is 'the only true relation between' him and God.[63] The creature who is not yet fully loving will by nature be afraid of that Love which it is not. Only to the degree that it becomes fully loving itself will it cease to fear Love Himself, and only then, MacDonald maintains, will the creature be safe without any fear. And because God is Love and wishes to make his creatures love-ly, these creatures, if they insist on their own way, must be made to see what their own un-lovely, un-Godly way is really like. Their own evil must be exposed and rejected in order for the soul to get any closer to the One who is Goodness.

In the same sermon MacDonald compares the love of God to a raging fire, but with one important difference: 'The fire of God, which is his essential being, his love, his creative power, is a fire unlike its earthly symbol in this, that it is only at a distance that it burns—that the farther from him, it burns the worse, and that when we turn and begin to approach him, the burning begins to change to comfort'.[64] The soul, by yielding 'his self and all that self's low

---

61   PP, pp. 127-128.

62   US, pp. 315-316 (middle of par. 3 in 'The Fear of God', second series). Lewis marks all of this.

63   US, p. 317 (second quarter of par. 4 in the same sermon). Lewis marks and underlines.

64   US, pp. 318-319 (first quarter of par. 5 in the same). Lewis marks most of this sentence in his copy with two vertical lines, as opposed to the usual one line, in the margin.

world' and returning 'to his lord and God', contributes toward the purification in which all self-centred evil, 'the corrupt and deadly', is burned away by God and his goodness, that 'shining' 'essence of life and its joy'.[65]

It is clear that Lewis believed in this same sort of purification, or purgation, as an absolutely necessary and unavoidable step on the road that leads away from mere self to heaven. As he writes to his fictional correspondent in *Letters to Malcolm*:

> Our souls demand Purgatory, don't they? Would it not break the heart if God said to us, "It is true, my son, that your breath smells and your rags drip with mud and slime, but we are charitable here and no one will upbraid you with these things, nor draw away from you. Enter into the joy"? Should we not reply, "With submission, sir, and if there is no objection, I'd rather be cleaned first." "It may hurt, you know"—"Even so, sir."[66]

His favourite image of purgatory, he tells Malcolm, is of a dentist giving him something to rinse with after having pulled a diseased tooth:

> I hope that when the tooth of life is drawn and I am "coming round," a voice will say, "Rinse your mouth out with this." This will be Purgatory. The rinsing my take longer than I can now imagine. The taste of this may be more fiery and astringent than my present sensibility could endure. But More and Fisher[67] shall not persuade me that it will be disgusting and unhallowed.[68]

The disgusting thing, according to Lewis and MacDonald, is not the purgation but the deathly self-centredness that the purgation gets rid of.

Another way Lewis expresses this, in *The Great Divorce*, is when ghost-like beings on the farthest outskirts of heaven[69] are asked by 'Bright' or 'Solid People' whether or not they want to be freed from evil things that dominate them. These wraiths of Lewis's, out on a holiday excursion from hell, are

---

65   US, p. 319 (portions of the first half of par. 5 in 'The Fear of God', second series).

66   LM, pp. 108-109 (Letter XX).

67   See ELSC for Lewis's discussion of St. Thomas More's (1478-1535) and John Fisher's (ca. 1459-1535) depictions of purgatory. To Lewis their purgatories seem 'merely retributive' rather than 'genuinely purgative', as in Dante's *Purgatorio* (ELSC, p. 164). Given the accuracy of this characterisation, we can see in ELSC and LM that Lewis sides with Dante, Tyndale and MacDonald against More and Fisher. He quotes Tyndale in ELSC: 'To punish a man that has forsaken sin of his own accord is not to purge him but to satisfy the lust of a tyrant' (ELSC, p. 164). For More's depiction of purgatory, see *The Supplication of Souls* (1529), Bk. II. For Fisher's, see *This trestise concernyng the fruytfull saynges of Dauyd in the seven penytenciall psalms* (1508), in particular his sermon on Psalm 6.

68   LM, p. 109 (Letter XX).

69   '"Not Deep Heaven, ye understand"', says MacDonald, Lewis's guide in the story. GD, p. 53.

similar to MacDonald's doppelgängers. Just as MacDonald's characters are dominated by a shadow or false self, so these ghosts are controlled and kept ghostly by something that they call their own and refuse to let go of. One ghost, for example, is represented as a dwarf chained to a melodramatic actor called 'the Tragedian'. The interaction between this creature and his wife, who has come from deeper heaven to try and help him, reveals how he, or it, is a soul mutilated by its own self-centredness. The lady speaks to the dwarf and not the actor, revealing the actor to be the soul's false self, and the dwarf to be what little remains of the man.

Most of the time the dwarf lets the tragedian speak for him, but at one point Lewis the character is shocked to see both talking to each other in unison while contemplating a question asked of it by the lady. Here the narrator refers explicitly to what Lewis's literary symbol is meant to express: 'I realised then that they were one person, or rather that both were remains of what had once been a person'.[70] The dwarf, as it keeps refusing to let go of its self-centredness, becomes smaller and smaller until Lewis cannot tell the difference between it and the chain that binds him to the tragedian. In the end both dwarf and chain disappear: 'At the same moment [the tragedian] gathered up the chain which had now for some time been swinging uselessly at his side, and somehow disposed of it. I am not quite sure, but I think he swallowed it'.[71]

Final Damnation?

Now is a good time to discuss the implications of what MacDonald and Lewis thought and wrote concerning final damnation, for this picture of the dwarf and chain being swallowed by the tragedian is one of Lewis's pictures of what he believed must happen to one who refuses to be divorced from the evil which enslaves him. We shall find that MacDonald and Lewis clearly disagree as to whether there could ever be a final hell, but we shall also see how this disagreement is less important than it may seem at first glance.

The final hell, in Lewis's view, is the point at which a soul ceases to be a real person. Having refused to yield one's self as something that is not one's own, the damned self is reduced to that which it would 'be' without God.[72] It is abandoned to 'its own way', which, in keeping with his and MacDonald's view of moral evil, is more of a lack than anything else. It is a state of un-being in which the former person is, according to Lewis, necessarily locked out of God's good reality. If the soul will not loose its grip on itself to reach out toward Goodness, there is no other alternative, he believed. It must be

---

70   GD, p. 93.
71   GD, p. 100.
72   Quotes are used around 'be' since Lewis believed a soul could not have been at all without God creating it.

consigned to, or become, the nothingness it chooses. It will be left outside of any reality worth being in.

This sense of abandonment to a chosen nothingness is reflected in the dwarf-tragedian incident from *The Great Divorce*. What little there is left of a person, the dwarf, shrivels up smaller and smaller so long as he refuses to be rid of his false self, the tragedian. This shrinking continues until the person, once called Frank, cannot be distinguished from a chain that symbolises his choice to keep hold of what he calls himself. He becomes his choice and then, so far as can be seen, nothing at all. All that is left is the actor who is not recognised as Frank by Frank's wife: "'Where is Frank? [...] And who are you, Sir? I never knew you'".[73] When the increasingly invisible tragedian accuses Frank's wife of not loving him, in a 'thin bat-like voice', she responds: "'I cannot love a lie [...] I cannot love the thing which is not'".[74]

Lewis expresses much the same thing in non-fiction prose when he discusses the nature of hell in *The Problem of Pain*. Citing Scripture and Friedrich Von Hügel,[75] Lewis writes how it is possible to think of a soul's perdition 'not as a sentence imposed on him but as the mere fact of being what he is', or, as we have already seen, what he is not.[76] Such an 'egoist', having attempted to 'turn everything he meets into a province or appendage of the self', eventually gets just what he wants: 'He has his wish—to live wholly in the self and to make the best of what he finds there'.[77]

This, Lewis says, is hell. It is not, in his view, a place in which material flames torture a soul in a never-ending succession of time moments. Eternity, as he thinks of it, is not a line of time moments that extends forever; it is more like a 'plane or even a solid', the 'base-line' of which is drawn by 'human free will' in 'earthly life'.[78] The eternal form of one's soul, if misdrawn by a selfish will that will not yield to Goodness, will be a very ugly thing indeed, Lewis writes, if the result can be called a thing at all. Though God, he writes, will give every soul every real chance to yield or repent,[79] he believed that a soul

---

73 Compare Jesus's words concerning judgement and damnation in Mat. 7.22-23: 'in that day [...] then will I profess unto them, *I never knew you*: depart from me, ye that work iniquity' [italics mine]. See also his parable in Mat. 25.12, in which the bridegroom says to the five foolish virgins: 'Verily, I say unto you, I know you not'.
74 GD, p. 100.
75 John 3.19, 12.48; and 'What do we mean by Heaven? And what do we mean by Hell?' in Baron Friedrich Von Hügel, *Essays and Addresses on the Philosophy of Religion* (London: J.M. Dent and Sons, 1921).
76 PP, p. 123.
77 PP, p. 123.
78 PP, p. 123.
79 'I believe that if a million chances were likely to do good, they would be given' (PP, p. 124).

could freely choose this hell and get it.

In response to objections concerning the 'frightful intensity of the pains of Hell' as suggested by medieval art and Scripture, Lewis refers to Von Hügel again in warning readers not to confuse the 'doctrine itself' with 'the *imagery* by which it may be conveyed'.[80] Lewis refers to symbols used by Christ—'punishment'; 'destruction'; and 'privation, exclusion, or banishment into "the darkness outside"'[81]—in an effort to describe hell. The 'prevalent image of fire' is important in this regard, he says, since it 'combines the ideas of torment and destruction'.[82] While he rejects any idea of hell as anything other than something 'unspeakably horrible', he writes how it is not necessary to 'concentrate on the images of torture to the exclusion of those suggesting destruction and privation'.[83] What Lewis suggests is a state in which all three ideas are equally true. And since he doubts the intrinsic possibility of the utter annihilation of a soul, he suggests an image that symbolises next to nothing:

> In all our experience [...] the destruction of one thing means the emergence of something else. Burn a log, and you have gases, heat and ash. To have been a log means now being those three things. If soul can be destroyed, must there not be a state of having been a human soul? [...] What is cast (or casts itself) into hell is not a man: it is "remains". To be a complete man means to have the passions obedient to the will and the will offered to God: to have been a man—to be an ex-man or "damned ghost"—would presumably mean to consist of a will utterly centered in its self and passions utterly uncontrolled by the will.[84]

All un-men who do not yield to Goodness, then, must necessarily become ex-men. This idea is apparent in Lewis's *The Great Divorce* where inhabitants of hell are ghosts, and hell itself, infinite and empty to the inhabitants, can in reality fit down the tiniest crack in the floor of outer heaven. As MacDonald tells Lewis in the story, hell is a wasteland of unimaginable insignificance: "'All Hell is smaller than one pebble of your earthly world: but it is smaller than one atom of *this* world, the Real World [that is, heaven]. Look at yon butterfly. If it swallowed all Hell, Hell would not be big enough to do it any harm or to have any taste"'.[85]

MacDonald the author, however, never did come to believe in the finality of hell, so far as we can tell from his writing. From his first published word to his last, MacDonald displayed a belief that God's mercy would find a way to

---

80 PP, p. 124.
81 See, for example, Mat. 25.46 for punishment; Mat. 7.13 for destruction; and Mat. 24. 51, Mat. 25.10-12, Mat. 25. 30, and Luke 13.27-28 for banishment.
82 PP, p. 125.
83 PP, p. 125.
84 PP, pp. 125-126.
85 GD, pp. 103-104.

save even the worst soul from its false self. One can see this in the first edition of *Unspoken Sermons*, published in the early stages of his literary career. To wit, in 'The Consuming Fire':

> For then [when God casts 'Death and Hell' itself into 'the lake of Fire'] our poor brothers and sisters, every one—O God, we trust in thee, the Consuming Fire—shall have been burnt clean [that is, purified] and brought home [...] Shall, of all his glories, his mercy alone not be infinite?[86]

And we can see it in the last edition of *Unspoken Sermons*, published over twenty years later near the end of his literary career. In a sermon of this edition entitled 'Justice', MacDonald asserts how the 'absolute destruction of sin'[87] from reality is God's inexorable will and how God, if it is required, will 'spare nothing' that purgatorial suffering can do to deliver all of his children[88] from the 'Death' of sin.[89]

If such purgation was insufficient in separating the sinner from his sin, MacDonald writes how 'we need look for no more hell, but for the destruction of sin by the destruction of the sinner'.[90] And so we see how MacDonald only recognises a purgatorial hell, never a final hell as Lewis describes in *The Problem of Pain*. If a soul *would* not repent, MacDonald reasoned, then there would be no reason to keep him alive in a hell that could not cure him. In this he is consistent with Lewis: the only thing for such a soul is something akin to destruction. The difference between the two is that MacDonald refused to believe that God would ever let it get to that point. He never could imagine that God would be 'defeated' in this way:

> those who believe that God will be defeated by many souls, must surely be of those who do not believe he cares enough to do his very best for them. He is their Father; he had power to make them out of himself, separate from himself, and capable of being one with him: surely he will somehow save and keep them! Not the power of sin itself can close all the channels between creating and created.[91]

As we've already mentioned, Lewis did admit that such a 'defeat of omnipotence' was possible, and that it would indeed happen if a soul would not repent and be redeemed.[92]

---

86   US, p. 32 (second and third quarters of the penultimate paragraph of 'The Consuming Fire', first series).
87   US, p. 511 (first quarter of par. 31 in 'Justice', third series).
88   Unlike some Calvinists of his day, MacDonald believed everyone created was God's child, though he or she may not have begun to realise, accept or cooperate with such a fact. See, for example, his sermon 'Abba, Father!', US, pp. 275-295.
89   US, pp. 515-516 (par. 36 of 'Justice', third series).
90   US, p. 516 (same paragraph of the same sermon).
91   US, p. 516 (par. 37 of the same).
92   PP, p. 127. See p. 151, above.

There are a few places where this difference shows up in their fiction. In *Robert Falconer*, for example, Robert speaks of the pains of hell interrupting the pleasures of heaven: "'it'll be some sair upo' them to sit there [in Heaven] aitin' an' drinkin' an' talkin' awa', an' enjoyin' themsel's, whan ilka noo an' than there'll come a sough o' wailin' up frae the ill place, an' a smell o' burnin' ill to bide'".[93] Robert's concern for those in hell is not less after hearing his grandmother say that hell is not near enough to heaven for the redeemed to hear or smell the damned: "'Weel, but, grannie, they'll ken't a' the same, whether they smell't or no. An' I canna help thinkin' that the farrer awa' I thoucht they war, the waur[94] I wad like to think upo' them. 'Deed it wad be waur'".[95]

It must be remembered here that Robert, and MacDonald, are not speaking of the hell of '*having been*' that Lewis wrote of in *The Problem of Pain* or *The Great Divorce*. He is reacting against the hell of eternal, literal flames, the punishment for punishment's sake envisioned by Scotch Calvinists of his day. But still, Lewis never includes such passages in his books, perhaps because what the Scotch Calvinist hell has in common with the one he envisioned is that they can both be *final* damnation. Through Falconer, MacDonald reacts, in part, against this finality. The same sort of thing can be seen in his fantasy, as in *Lilith*, the darkest of his fantastical books. As Vane is told near the end of the story, everyone will have to come to repentance some time: "'Every creature must one night yield himself and lie down [...] he was made for liberty, and must not be left a slave!'".[96] The yielding and the lying down refer specifically in the story to submitting to sleep in the House of Death: MacDonald's symbol for things that include repentant self-surrender of a soul to its Maker. This yielding is most starkly illustrated when the chief villain, Lilith, is given the opportunity to 'Open thy hand, and let that which is in it to go'.[97] When she finds herself unable to open her clinched fist, Adam takes the sword of an angel and cuts the hand off. A new hand begins growing from where 'the dead deformity clung' and Lilith is enabled to sleep the necessary sleep.[98] As MacDonald wrote in his sermons, so he writes in his stories: whatever must be done to save all creatures from hell *will* be done.

But we should not make too much of the difference between MacDonald and Lewis on hell, for in all essentials they are agreed. What they differ on is simply how likely a final hell is. MacDonald could not believe in the final separation of a creature from its Maker because he did not believe any creature

---

93   RF, p. 81.
94   worse
95   RF, p. 81.
96   LIL, p. 361.
97   LIL, p. 323.
98   See LIL, pp. 345-346.

would choose the hell of mere self once they were shown what this hell is really like. Lewis did believe in the possibility of finality because he thought that free will necessarily means that the hell of mere self *can* be chosen. As he writes in *The Problem of Pain*:

> If a game is played, it must be possible to lose it. If the happiness of a creature lies in self-surrender, no one can make that surrender but himself (though many can help him to make it) and he may refuse. I would pay any price to be able to say truthfully "All will be saved." But my reason retorts, "Without their will, or with it?" If I say "Without their will" I at once perceive a contradiction; how can the supreme voluntary act of self-surrender be involuntary? If I say "With their will," my reason replies "How if they will not give in?"[99]

But apart from an occasional mention of the possibility, or improbability, of the finality of hell, there is no other important difference in the way these two writers depict it in their fiction. Both agreed as to what was hellish and what would keep one from hell. Lewis agreed that God would do all that could be done to free everyone from such a fate; MacDonald agreed that no escape from hell was possible without the willful self-surrender of an individual soul.

In the passage from *Lilith* just mentioned, for example, Lilith does not give up her clenched fist unwillingly. It is she, in fact, who specifically asks Adam to "'cut me off this hand that I may sleep'".[100] In this Lilith is no different from the ghosts in Lewis's *Divorce* who are asked if they will allow something to be removed or killed in order to stay in heaven. One such ghost is dominated by his lust that he will not give up, symbolised by a little red lizard that sits upon the ghost's shoulder whispering into its ear.[101] When an angel asks the ghost if it will let him kill the lizard, the ghost eventually asks why the angel did not just kill it without asking permission. The angel replies: "'I cannot kill it against your will. It is impossible'".[102] This situation, we can see, is very much like Lilith's. Adam, like the angel, does not perform his act until Lilith, like the ghost, gives permission. Both Lilith and the ghost are not able by their own efforts to kill that which dominates them, but their consent, the cooperation of their will, is nevertheless needed.

We can also see the importance MacDonald placed upon free will later in *Robert Falconer*, when Robert is discussing with his grandmother how far God can go in attempting to save a soul. Mrs. Falconer tells Robert how "'It winna do to meddle wi' fowk's free wull'".[103] "'To gar [that is, 'make' or 'force'] fowk

---

99   PP, pp. 118-119.
100 LIL, p. 345. Compare Mat. 18.8 and Mk. 9.43.
101 See GD, p. 82.
102 GD, p. 84.
103 RF, p. 330.

be gude wad be nae gudeness,'" she says.[104] Robert agrees with her on this. He only doubts that those commonly believed to have been damned have seen a true picture of their evil, and a true picture of God, and still chosen their own evil. In this particular response of Falconer's, we see how MacDonald did indeed see the implications and importance of free will: '"Gin I kent that a man had seen the trowth as I hae seen 't whiles, and had deleeberately turned his back upo' 't and said, 'I'll nane o' 't, than I doobt I wad be maist compelled to alloo that there was nae mair salvation for him, but a certain and fearfu' luikin' for o' judgment and fiery indignation'".[105] Falconer, and MacDonald, simply believe that God's ability to reveal '"the twoth"' would do much more to influence a person's salvation than many people imagined. And all this influence and truth-telling could be done, he thought, without '"meddlin' wi' the free wull"'.[106]

Any reader of MacDonald's sermons will find this to be the case. There are not many things expressed so often, or so strongly, as his belief that a man's will was an absolutely necessary part of his salvation. He consistently reacted against any theological doctrine which allowed no room for souls' individual free choice. As he writes in 'The Eloi': 'He wants to make us in his own image, *choosing* the good, *refusing* the evil. How should he effect this if he were *always* moving us from within [...]? God gives us room *to be*; does not oppress us with his will; "stands away from us," that we may act from ourselves, that we may exercise the pure will for good'.[107] In another sermon he speaks of a faith 'which is obedience', asking his rhetorical antagonist, '"How are you to believe he will do his part by you, while you are not such as to do your part by him?"'.[108] He asks how important beliefs about the mechanics of atonement matter, so long as 'you and God are not *at one*, do not atone together?'.[109] Myriad passages such as these, in his sermons and fiction, show that MacDonald, like Lewis, believed that the move away from hell had to involve an individual's free will choice.

The differences between the two authors regarding the finality of hell, then, are not as important as they may first seem. Because both agree upon the importance and implications of free will, and because both believed self-centredness to be the 'one principle of hell', their depictions of hell turn out to be very similar indeed. Lewis came to believe the same thing that MacDonald believed about human evil and what it led to. The 'substance' of hell, one might

---

104 RF, p. 330.
105 RF, pp. 330-331.
106 RF, p. 331.
107 US, p. 117 (second quarter of par. 12 in 'The Eloi', first series).
108 US, p. 397 (second quarter of par. 15 in 'The Truth in Jesus', second series).
109 US, p. 398 (third quarter of par. 15 in the same sermon).

say, is the same in both authors' works. Whether or not this substance could be finalised in reality is a relatively minor question when considering how they depict the quality of hell in their fiction, just as whether or not a particular food can be frozen forever tells one relatively little about the food in question. Much more important will be the taste, texture, smell, or nutritional value of the food itself.

The Substance of Hell

One reason the 'substance' of MacDonald's and Lewis's hells is so similar is that both men believed hell doesn't really have a substance. To them it is not so much a thing, or a place to go to, as it is one's sinking into his own dedication to self, something that can begin in the here and now. This is made clear in *The Great Divorce* when MacDonald the character tells Lewis the character: "'Hell is a state of mind—ye never said a truer word. And every state of mind, left to itself, every shutting up of the creature within the dungeon of its own mind—is, in the end, Hell'".110 Describing this state of mind, MacDonald tells Lewis:

> "There is always something they insist on keeping, even at the price of misery. There is always something they prefer to joy—that is, to reality. Ye see it easily enough in a spoiled child that would sooner miss its play and its supper than say it was sorry and be friends. Ye call it the Sulks. But in adult life it has a hundred fine names—Achilles' wrath and Coriolanus' grandeur, Revenge and Injured Merit and Self-Respect and Tragic Greatness and Proper Pride."111

We have already seen where MacDonald, the author, has symbolised such a state of mind with the character and clenched fist of Lilith. And we have seen it thoroughly described in his Creed of Self that follows from the 'one principle of hell'—'I am my own'—in the sermon 'Kingship'.112 Much of Lewis's writing on human evil and hell seems very much like echoes of these things. MacDonald's 'principle of hell' finds its near match, for example, in the 'philosophy of Hell' described in *The Screwtape Letters*. As Screwtape writes to his junior tempter Wormwood:

> The whole philosophy of Hell rests on recognition of the axiom that one thing is not another thing, and, specially, that one self is not another self. My good is my good, and your good is yours. What one gains another loses. Even an inanimate object is what it is by excluding all other objects from the space it occupies; if it expands, it does so

110 GD, p. 55.
111 GD, pp. 55-56.
112 See pp. 164-165, above.

by thrusting other objects aside or by absorbing them.[113] A self does the same. With beasts the absorption takes the form of eating; for us, it means the sucking of will and freedom out of a weaker self into a stronger. "To be" *means* "to be in competition."[114]

And so in the very next letter Screwtape writes of how all God's 'talk about Love' must be a 'disguise for something else'.[115] 'He must have some *real* motive for creating them and taking so much trouble about them', writes the demon.[116] The concept of Love to Screwtape and other devoted followers of the philosophy of hell is simply incomprehensible: 'We know that He cannot really love: nobody can; it doesn't make sense'.[117] The 'cock-and-bull story about disinterested Love', to those dedicated to themselves and to competition, must simply be a lie.[118] When he learns that Wormwood's man has fallen in love, he is livid, noting how the girl's 'family and whole circle' are infected with such impossible love: 'Could you not see that the very house she lives in is one that he ought never to have been entered? The whole place reeks of that deadly odour. The very gardener, though he has been there only five years, is beginning to acquire it [...] The dog and the cat are tainted with it'.[119]

The appearance of people being motivated by something other than selfish competition puts Screwtape into a confused rage: 'We are certain (it is a matter of first principles) that each member of the family must in some way be making capital out of the others—but we can't find out how. They guard as jealously as the Enemy Himself the secret of what really lies behind this pretence of disinterested love. The whole house and garden are one vast obscenity'.[120] Growing more and more furious, he compares the 'music and silence' of the girl's home of love with what he considers more true: the great Noise of Hell: 'Noise, the grand dynamism, the audible expression of all that is

---

113 Lewis, in his 1960 preface (p. xiii), acknowledges that the 'spiritual cannibalism' spoken of in *Screwtape* is inspired by scenes of beings absorbing each other in David Lindsay's (1878-1945) stark fantasy *A Voyage to Arcturus* (1920). See, for example, Moremaker's 'sorbing' in 'Panawe's Story' in chp. 7 and Crimtyphon's in chp. 9. Lindsay [*The Haunted Woman* (1922), *Sphinx* (1923)] admitted to being influenced by MacDonald, and there are undeniable thematic similarities in *Arcturus*, though Lindsay's story is more deeply grim, and metaphysically dualistic, than anything MacDonald wrote. See J. B. Pick's introduction in David Lindsay, *A Voyage to Arcturus* (Edinburgh: Cannongate, 1992).
114 SCL, p, 81 (Letter XVIII).
115 SCL, p. 86 (Letter XIX).
116 SCL, p. 86 (XIX).
117 SCL, p. 87 (XIX).
118 SCL, p. 86 (XIX).
119 SCL, p. 102 (XXII).
120 SCL, p. 102 (XXII).

exultant, ruthless, and virile—Noise which alone defends us from silly qualms, despairing scruples, and impossible desires. We will make the whole universe a noise in the end [...] The melodies and silences of Heaven will be shouted down in the end'.[121] Screwtape's rant against the idea of disinterested love, his undersecretary Toadpipe tells us though his dictation, becomes intense enough to change the demon into a large centipede.[122]

But Lewis's book is not primarily about the rage of demons. It, like much of the rest of his writing, is about human evil, as he makes clear in the 1960 preface: 'For of course [the book's] purpose was not to speculate about the diabolical life but to throw light from a new angle on the life of men'.[123] In keeping with this point, he goes on to note how he didn't have to look very far for the book's source material: 'Some have paid me an undeserved compliment by supposing that my *Letters* were the ripe fruit of many years' study in moral and ascetic theology. They forgot that there is an equally reliable, though less creditable, way of learning how temptation works. "My heart"—I need no other's—"showeth me the wickedness of the ungodly"'.[124]

Such is the case in everything Lewis wrote. His settings and characters may often be fantastic, but there are always strings attached to these kites, keeping both the author and the reader connected with present reality. It is the same kind of 'vigilance' that he remembers finding in MacDonald's books: romantic fantasy that maintains a morally realistic tone. Lewis speaks most often of the 'beauty of Holiness' in this regard,[125] but such realism can also be found in both authors' portrayals of wickedness.

Perelandra, for example, is a tale set on Venus, about a green woman and a demon-possessed scientist, but the evils the Un-man tempts the Lady to are familiar things: vanity and self-conscious pride. The Un-man makes a robe and a garland of feathers for her to wear and gives her a mirror to admire herself in. When the Lady, startled at the idea of considering and enjoying her own beauty, tells the Un-man that 'a fruit does not eat itself' and that 'a man cannot be together with himself', the Un-man persists in his attempts to teach her the familiar vice (familiar, that is, to Earth's inhabitants) of narcissism: "'A fruit cannot do that because it is only a fruit [...] But we can do it. We call this thing a mirror. A man can love himself, and be together with himself. That is what it means to be a man or a woman—to walk alongside oneself as if one

121 SCL, p. 103 (XXII).
122 See SCL, p. 103 (Letter XXII). As Screwtape's comments indicate, this transformation is inspired by a scene from *Paradise Lost* (10.504-547) where Satan and the demons of hell are changed into serpents and monsters after Satan returns from tempting Eve.
123 SCL, p. xii.
124 SCL, p. xiii. Lewis quotes from Psalm 36.1.
125 See ANTH, p. xxxiii.

were a second person and to delight in one's own beauty. Mirrors were made to teach this art'".[126]

Lewis does something very similar in *The Voyage of the Dawn Treader* when Lucy stumbles upon a magician's book of spells. One of the spells in the book, '*An infallible spell to make beautiful her that uttereth it beyond the lot of mortals*', features pictures of a girl reading a huge book, just as Lucy is doing as she is reading the spell.[127] On closer inspection Lucy sees that the girl in the picture *is* her. In the picture she is saying the spell and becoming dazzlingly beautiful. For a few minutes they look into each other's eyes, as happens in a mirror. The Lucy in the picture, who grows to look just as big as the real Lucy, is then shown seated on a throne surrounded by admirers. Kings fight each other because of her beauty, and all the nations of Narnia are laid waste as a result.

Having highlighted the familiar vice of competitive vanity in this fanciful way, Lewis immediately goes one step further in reminding his readers how very earthly and real such things can be. The next vision Lucy sees in the magic book is set on Earth. Lucy sees her older sister Susan, 'the beauty of the family', with a nasty expression on her face due to the fact that she is jealous of Lucy's new, dazzling beauty.[128] Susan's distress in the vision matters little, though, since 'no one cared anything about Susan now'.[129] The vision, of course, exposes Lucy's own envy, or possible envy: another familiar manifestation of the 'philosophy of Hell'. And so in a story full of magic spells, sea serpents, walking stars, talking mice, and one-legged imps called Dufflepuds, familiar evils are not ignored.

This pattern holds true for all of the Narnia stories: Uncle Andrew's cruelty and ambition in *The Magician's Nephew*, Edmund's greed and treachery in *The Lion, the Witch, and the Wardrobe*, Aravis's haughty arrogance in *The Horse and His Boy*, Nikabrik's clannish thirst for power in *Prince Caspian*, Eustace's selfish bullying in *The Dawn Treader*, the Dwarfs' selfish disloyalty and Shift's ruthless manipulation in *The Last Battle*, as well as Jadis's cruelty and pride in three books[130] and Susan's shallow vanity and conceit, revealed most notably in *The Last Battle*.[131]

---

126 PER, p. 137. Compare to Satan's flattery of Eve in *Paradise Lost*, Book 9.
127 C.S. Lewis, *The Voyage of the Dawn Treader* (New York: Harper Collins, 1994), p. 163. First published in 1952.
128 VDT, p. 164.
129 VDT, p. 165.
130 She appears as the White Witch in *The Lion, the Witch, and the Wardrobe*, as Jadis in *The Magician's Nephew*, and as Queen of Underland in *The Silver Chair*.
131 Phillip Pullman, a popular modern day writer of 'children's' fiction [*Northern Lights* (1996), *The Subtle Knife* (1997), *The Amber Spyglass* (2000)], has taken offense at Lewis's treatment of Susan, saying that she is 'sent to hell because she was

interested in clothes and boys'. Such, he claims, is evidence that the Narnia books are 'monumentally disparaging of girls and women' [See John Ezard, 'Narnia books attacked as racist and sexist: Phillip Pullman dismisses work of C.S. Lewis as blatant religious propaganda', in *The Guardian* (Monday, 3 June 2002)].

This criticism is unwarranted for a couple of reasons. First, his memory of events in Lewis's last Narnia book is simply inaccurate. Peter, Edmund, Lucy, Jill, Eustace, Digory, and Polly are involved in a railway accident that eventually sends all of them, by death, to Heaven (Jill and Eustace must first go to the aid of King Tirian in Narnia). These characters were meeting as friends of Narnia to reminisce about their old adventures, and also because Digory sensed that their help was needed in Narnia (See LB, chp. 5, 'How Help Came to the King' [pp. 56-59]). Susan, by her own choice, is not among these friends, and so is not involved in the meeting (see LB, chp. 13, 'Through the Stable Door' [LB, pp. 154-155]). She is not, therefore, killed in the railway accident along with the others. She is sent to neither Heaven nor hell because she does not die. The end of her story is never told. She simply does not show up in Heaven with the others after the railway accident—because she was not in the railway accident.

Pullman is right, however, in noticing that Lewis makes a distinct effort in the story to separate Susan from the others. But the reason for this is not what Pullman implies. Readers are told that she is 'no longer a friend of Narnia', that she no longer has time for the loveliness, goodness and wonders found there. Instead, she's interested only in 'nylons and lipstick and invitations' [See LB, p. 169].

Whatever Pullman makes of this, the characters in the book who hear and say these things have a different interpretation. It is not simply a matter of her wearing lipstick and liking boys. It is that she 'always was a jolly sight too keen on being grown-up' (LB, p. 169), a symptom of childish snobbery and conceit. The last picture of her in the Chronicles is of one who has succumbed to vanity, who is preoccupied with how she appears to others, or how she appears when compared with others. As MacDonald would put it, she is much more interested in seeming than being. This preoccupation with surfaces and appearances, it seems, keeps her from genuinely caring for other things or other people, or for what she ought to become. Lewis's words are few, but the implication is fairly obvious: Susan is too frivolous to want, or to be, anything of great value.

Lewis is not the only author, of course, who has depicted such a character in a bad light. If Pullman needs examples, he need only pick up a copy of one of Miss Austen's novels. All of the Bennet sisters in *Pride and Prejudice* (except Mary), for example, seem to be interested in members of the opposite sex. But only two of them, Kitty and Lydia, are frivolous. These two sisters, unsurprisingly, are the ones who 'like boys' most obviously and for the most frivolous reasons. Perhaps they only like the phenomenon of boys liking them. They, like Susan, are silly, and their liking or love for any particular boy will be easily recognised as a silly thing compared to the loves and likings of Elizabeth and Jane. Kitty and Lydia, like Susan, are necessarily condemned to a life of puerility if they will choose nothing else. Or as the narrator of *Persuasion* contrasts the attachments of Elizabeth Elliot with the more genuine attachments of her sister Anne: 'the origin of one all selfish vanity, of the other all

It is significant that the most obvious villains, like Jadis and Shift, are not the only ones who do villainous things, or who are tempted to do so. Lewis's writing makes clear that practitioners of the philosophy of Hell need not sport horns, a pitch fork or similar give-aways. As he writes in the 1960 preface to *Screwtape*:

> The greatest evil is not now done in those sordid "dens of crime" that Dickens loved to paint. It is not done even in concentration camps and labour camps. In those we see its final result. But it is conceived and ordered (moved, seconded, carried, and minuted) in clean, carpeted, warmed, and well-lighted offices, by quiet men with white collars and cut fingernails and smooth-shaven cheeks who do not need to raise their voice.[132]

Or as he writes in *The Problem of Pain*, concerning his chapter on hell:

> In order to rouse modern minds to an understanding of the issues, I ventured to introduce in this chapter a picture of the sort of bad man whom we must easily perceive to be truly bad. But when the picture has done that work, the sooner it is forgotten the better. In all discussions of hell we should keep steadily before our eyes the possible damnation, not of our enemies nor our friends (since both these disturb the reason) but of ourselves. This chapter is not about your wife or son, not about Nero or Judas Iscariot; it is about you and me.[133]

In bringing wickedness 'down to earth'—or, to put it metaphorically correct, 'up to earth'—Lewis follows his master. MacDonald's stories are full of devils, but nearly all of them would claim to be human.[134] His realistic novels allowed him to portray this everyday evil in realistic settings, something Lewis rarely did.

Sometimes the philosophy or principle of hell is expressed in a single line of dialogue, as when Herr von Funkelstein, the most obvious villain of MacDonald's first novel *David Elginbrod*, remarks to Hugh Sutherland, the protagonist, concerning the beauty of Euphra Cameron: "Well, I should say so [that Miss Cameron is very beautiful]; but beauty is not, that is not

---

generous attachment' [See Jane Austen, *Persuasion* (London: Penguin, 1985), p. 194]. And Austen, like Lewis, does not exclude men when painting such portraits (see the shallow vanity of Sir Walter in *Persuasion*, or Uncle Andrew in *The Magician's Nephew*, for example).

132 SCL, p. x.
133 PP, p. 128.
134 MacDonald would not claim that they were 'human' in the evil that they do and are; his sense of the word 'human' is too closely tied to God's idea of us, which excludes all evil. See US, p. 554, for example, where he speaks of evil being 'an intrusion upon' the truly human (penultimate paragraph in 'Light', third series).

beauty for us'".[135] In other words, her beauty exists to Funkelstein only insofar as Funkelstein can possess it. True to the philosophy of hell, Funkelstein recognises only that beauty or truth which *he* can get something out of. If he cannot use or control it, if it is in no way connected to him or his desires, it simply does not exist. The rest of the plot of *David Elginbrod* shows how he acts this philosophy out, employing his spiritualist tricks and influence to gain and keep control of Euphra's person.

Another way MacDonald depicts the philosophy of hell is in the growth of his characters from false to true. This happens in every novel he wrote, and his first novel sets the precedent in two ways. One is the growth of young Hugh Sutherland who, in the beginning, is too much concerned with *seeming*, as opposed to *being*. Because he is most concerned with the appearances of things, rather than the things themselves, he seeks after things that are false and is himself false. Hugh's ambition is set in contrast with the genuineness and self-forgetfulness of two other characters who appear in the novel: David Elginbrod and Robert Falconer. MacDonald does the same with Euphra Cameron who eventually overcomes the falsifying and mesmerising influences of Funkelstein. Her foil, the homely and humble Margaret Elginbrod (David's daughter), at one point in the story acts as Euphra's serving girl, helping to counteract Funkelstein's evil influences. Towards the end of the story the narrator tells of how, after 'terrible struggle', Euphra has become one true person, rather than the two she had been under Funkelstein's control.[136] This development from a sleep-walking, hypnotised minion of Funkelstein's to a real person runs parallel to Hugh's development in the same story, and to many other of MacDonald's characters: Anodos, Julian, Murdoch Malison, Dooble Sanny, Alec Forbes, Mr. Cupples, Donal Grant, and even Robert Falconer, all of whom lose their false shadows of self-regard and move to something more authentic.

MacDonald had other, more general ways of depicting evil in his realistic novels. One of his favourite methods is the portrayal of the pride common in certain 'respectable' circles of society. The greed of respectable merchants, the snobbery of respectable lairds and gentlefolk, and the hollow religiosity of respectable clergymen and church-goers illustrate MacDonald's view of hellish pride more thoroughly and more frequently than anything else in his realistic novels.

A good example of the respectable merchant is the grocer Robert Bruce of *Alec Forbes of Howglen*, who, as one character describes him, 'wadna fling a

---

135 DE, p. 204.
136 DE, p. 418.

bane[137] till a dog, afore he had ta'en a pyke[138] out of it himsel'.[139] He takes the orphan Annie Anderson, a distant relative, into his home, not because he cares for her or her well-being, but because it will likely be a boon to his financial interests. If she happens to die, her savings could come into his possession. Even if she remains healthy, he hopes to support her upon less than the interest that her savings will earn, pocketing the difference for himself. And she might just grow up and marry one of his sons, which would be another way of keeping her money at his disposal.[140] Bruce regards his grocery shop 'as his Bannockburn, where all his enemies, namely customers, were to be defeated, that he might be enriched with their spoils'.[141] He houses Annie in a wreck of a room haunted by rats. His wife, who spares no effort in giving her own sons the very best, will not even let Annie have a candle to help her find her way to her room.[142] She cuts off Annie's long beautiful hair to add a bit more profit to the till.[143] Mr. Bruce begins attending the local Missionar kirk on Sundays in order to keep another grocer who attends the church from winning the allegiance of a substantial bloc of customers.[144] Coming home from church, he holds the umbrella over himself rather than over Annie or even his own children because, as he reasons, 'his Sabbath clothes were more expensive than those of the children'.[145] Towards the end of the story, when he is threatening a poor widow (Alec's mother) as part of his plan to fleece an orphan (Annie), his defense of his actions exposes his motives and his undying loyalty to the 'one principle of hell': 'Fowk *maun* hae their ain. It's mine, an I maun hae 't'.[146]

The same sort of possessive evil can be found in the Baron of Rothie, who attempts to seduce young Mysie in *Robert Falconer* with his genteel but shallow charms. Mysie, much given to reading trashy novels, is overwhelmed when she meets Rothie. In the 'full strength and show of manhood', Rothie sports an elegant moustache and reminds Mysie of one of the heroes she reads about in her novels.[147] She blushes, drops her book, and is speechless before this gentleman of perfect appearances. He casts a spell over her with his 'slight, graceful, marrowless talk' and makes her tremble with a kiss of her hand.[148]

---

137 Bone
138 Nibble
139 AFH, p. 15.
140 See AFH, p. 15.
141 AFH, p. 22.
142 See AFH, p. 25.
143 See AFH, pp. 59-60.
144 See AFH, p. 162.
145 AFH, p. 279.
146 AFH, p. 426.
147 RF, p. 221.
148 RF, p. 221.

But as the narrator tells us in no uncertain terms, this man is no hero. His charm and kiss have little other than hell in them:

> She might well tremble. Even such contact was terrible. Why? Because there was no love in it. When the sense of beauty which God had given him that he might worship, awoke in Lord Rothie, he did not worship, but devoured, that he might, as he thought, possess! The poison of asps was under those lips. His kiss was as a kiss from the grave's mouth, for his throat was an open sepulchre.[149]

Later in the story a comment from Robert Falconer sums up how MacDonald sees, and presents, such dignified evil: "'There are good and bad men amongst them as in every class. But one thing is clear to me, that no indulgence of passion destroys the spiritual nature so much as respectable selfishness'".[150]

Falconer alludes to Pharisees in this passage, one of the respectable religious classes of Jesus's day. As anyone who reads his realistic novels cannot help but notice, MacDonald is at least as scathing towards the pride and falseness of religiosity as he is towards that found in lairds and ladies. Ministers and their congregations are often his most convincing sources of villainy, even when they do not act as the prime villain of the story's plot. MacDonald presents these manifestations of hell's pride in a particularly bad light, no doubt, because such people claim to be working on heaven's behalf. In *Sir Gibbie* MacDonald manages to squeeze three kinds of selfishness—commercial, social, and religious—into two characters: the Rev. Clement Sclater and his wife. Mrs. Sclater, formerly Mrs. Bonniman, is the widow of a wealthy merchant. She possesses good manners and good style but not much of a heart. Both her and her husband's care for people depend upon 'social distinctions' which both treat as belonging 'to existence itself'.[151]

That Mrs. Sclater's new husband may have married her for the money is revealed by the way he reacts to the disappearance of Gibbie from the town where he, Sclater, is a minister. He investigates the orphan's family and history, but finds no one willing to take on the responsibility of finding or caring for him. Sclater, having done his duty and found out that the boy 'was little better than an idiot, whose character, education, and manners had been picked up in the streets', ceases to care himself, leaving the boy to his predestined fate: 'Who was he, Clement Sclater, to intrude upon the divine prerogative and presume to act on the doctrine of election?'.[152] He ceases to care, that is, until he reads a newspaper article that reveals Gibbie to be the possible heir to £200,000 left

149 RF, p. 222. Compare Mat. 23.27-28.
150 RF, p. 357.
151 GIB, p. 296.
152 GIB, p. 271.

by a wealthy shipbuilder. Sclater immediately drops his untasted tea on the table and makes haste to his lawyer's office to investigate the possibilities and his possible gain from them.[153]

MacDonald most thoroughly illustrates the Sclaters' social pride and false religiosity in a chapter entitled 'The Sinner' when Mistress Croale, a down-and-out alcoholic, attempts to visit Gibbie at the Sclaters' home. Gibbie, eating his dinner with Mr. and Mrs. Sclater, puts down his spoon and rises to go when the maid announces that a woman is at the door to see him. But Sclater grabs Gibbie's arm and asks the maid "'What sort of woman'" it is.[154] When he is told it's a "'decent-lookin' workin'-like body'", the minister attempts to send the woman away.[155] Gibbie, though, disrupts these plans by dashing to the door to welcome Croale in. He attempts to pull her straight into the dining room but is checked by Rev. Sclater[156] who thinks it more proper to speak to Croale in the hall. But Gibbie keeps pulling Croale into the dining room until he is called over to Mrs. Sclater's side. In the following conference between Mrs. Sclater and Gibbie, and the actions that follow, MacDonald contrasts the evil of good-mannered religiosity with something more genuine:

> "Really, Gilbert, you must not," she said, rather loud for a whisper. "It won't do to turn things upside down this way. If you are to be a gentleman and an inmate of my house, you must behave like other people. I cannot have a woman like that sitting at my table. Do you know what sort of a person she is?"[157]

At this Gibbie raises his hands to ask a question. "'Is she a sinner?'", he signs to Mrs. Sclater with his fingers.[158] Mrs. Sclater nods, but doesn't get the response she hopes for from Gibbie. He immediately wheels round and springs into the hallway to where Rev. Sclater has exiled Croale. Sclater, who is attempting to smooth things over with Croale 'with an air of confidential condescension', is angered and shocked when he sees Gibbie rush up to Croale, throw his arms round her neck, and give her a 'great hug'.[159]

Sclater furiously orders Gibbie back into the dining room, and Gibbie goes, but when Sclater returns after seeing Croale out, he finds that Gibbie has gone after 'the sinner'. When their vexation subsides, Sclater and his wife joke

---

153 See GIB, p. 271.
154 GIB, p. 321.
155 GIB, p. 321.
156 Sclater had once told Croale that her soul was as precious to him as that of anyone else in his parish.
157 GIB, p. 322.
158 GIB, p. 323.
159 GIB, p. 323.

about their crude Gibbie taking the New Testament so seriously,[160] finish their dinner, and go to a church meeting. And again, MacDonald draws attention, this time in a single sentence dripping with irony, to the difference between Godly love and its sickly, shadowy counterfeit: 'Dinner over they went to a missionary meeting, where the one stood and made a speech and the other sat and listened, while Gibbie was having tea with Mistress Croale'.[161]

False Loves

These last three portrayals of 'respectable' evil in MacDonald's books show how evil may not at first glance seem like pure, unabashed egotism. It is mixed with, or masquerades as, something that is normally considered good. Bruce's greed, from a distance, could very well be seen as his good attempts to earn a living and provide for his family. It may have been only this before it was perverted. Rothie's kissing Mysie's hand, for one not acquainted with Rothie's heart, could be interpreted as an act of love or courtesy. Mrs. Sclater's refined manners may have at one point been a way of showing consideration to others, back before they became ends in themselves and therefore an obstacle to true love and consideration for others. And Mr. Sclater's religion, before it shriveled up into religiosity, may have had a stronger connection with the dispassionate love spoken of in the New Testament.

The phrase 'dispassionate love of the New Testament' is important, for MacDonald himself took the New Testament and its dispassionate love very seriously indeed. We will discuss more fully in the following chapter how MacDonald and Lewis understood and portrayed this love, but it will be necessary here to provide a working definition of it, for the most dangerous evils, according to both authors, are those things called love that will not be ruled by this sort of dispassionate love.

One of the most famous descriptions of it comes in Paul's first letter to the Corinthians where he places its value above prophecy, wisdom, faith and even acts of charity or self-sacrifice that do not spring from such love. This love or 'charity', as Paul's description makes clear, is all about actively considering others and their needs:

---

160 Mrs. Sclater to her husband: '"words which were of course quite suitable to the time when they were spoken, but which it is impossible to take literally nowadays"' (GIB, p. 325).
161 GIB, p. 325.

Charity suffereth long, and is kind; charity envieth not; charity vaunteth not itself,[162] is not puffed up,[163] Doth not behave itself unseemly,[164] seeketh not her own, is not easily provoked, thinketh no evil;[165] Rejoiceth not in iniquity,[166] but rejoiceth in the truth; Beareth all things, believeth all things, endureth all things.[167]

Using the word 'dispassionate' to describe this love is an effort in one word to show that it is not motivated by anything other than the enduring consideration of others that Paul describes. It does not mean that this active consideration of others and their needs is never combined with any emotion or strong feeling; it simply means that the active consideration will not stop if the emotions or feelings do. Love that is dispassionate, in the New Testament, does not depend upon anything else to be what it is. One who loves in this way does not love only because he feels like it or desires something. He loves everyone and everything,[168] not because it is *his*[169] or because he must possess it, or because he can get anything out of it (the thing loved or the loving itself). As MacDonald puts it, and as Lewis quotes him in his anthology, one loves this way not 'because he sees why, but because he loves'.[170] The act of dispassionate, unconditional love, while it may include and be mixed with other things, is never mercenary and never dependent upon anything less than itself. It gives without having to get.

A good example of this in MacDonald's fiction is Gibbie's love, whom we have just observed embracing an outcast sinner (though not the sin, as MacDonald would clarify). As MacDonald describes him and his love: 'Gibbie's was love simple, unselfish, undemanding—not merely asking for no return, but asking for no recognition, requiring not even that its existence

---

162 Or, 'is never boastful' [From *The New English Bible* (Oxford University Press, Cambridge University Press, 1961). The 1611 Authorised, or King James, Version was of course the most widely read version to English speakers in MacDonald's day, and the version he usually quotes from in his stories and sermons. MacDonald was familiar with all the major translations of his day, however, as well as the original Greek.]

163 or 'conceited' [NEB]

164 or 'is not rude' [NEB]

165 or 'keeps no score of wrongs' [NEB]

166 or 'does not gloat over other men's sins' [NEB]

167 1 Cor. 13.4-7 [AV]

168 See, for example, Christ's parable of the good Samaritan in Luke 10.25-37 and Mat. 22.39, as well as MacDonald's sermon 'Love Thy Neighbour', US, pp. 128-146.

169 See, for example, Mat. 5.43-48, and MacDonald's sermon 'Love Thine Enemy', US, pp. 147-156.

170 US, pp. 136-137 (third quarter of par. 25 in 'Love Thy Neighbour', first series). ANTH, reading 47.

should be known. He was a rare one, who did not make the common miserable blunder of taking the shadow cast by love—the desire, namely, to be loved—for love itself'.[171]

The narrator immediately goes on to say that the desire to be loved is not bad in itself—'neither wrong nor noble, anymore than hunger is either wrong or noble'—and that those who do not delight in being loved will come to be lost in an 'immeasurably deeper' and 'ruinous' evil of 'fiendish selfishness'.[172] But he makes clear that the hunger to be loved is not the same thing as Love, and that many who say they love someone are simply attempting to fill a hunger. He goes on in the paragraph to describe how someone who can only hunger or demand love is a very poor lover indeed.

Lewis was first exposed to this understanding of MacDonald's in *Phantastes*. At one point in the story Anodos, despite many warnings, is enchanted and nearly slain by an evil dryad. She, like Bruce or Rothie or the Sclaters, is respectable at first glance. She gives to Anodos, at first, 'the impression of intense loveliness'.[173] But in the midst of a sort of trance, Anodos learns her true nature. He sees a strange open coffin standing on its end, in the shape of a human. The coffin turns around to reveal the face and front of the Maiden of the Alder; only now in the morning light he sees that her eyes are dead and lustreless.[174] The 'hollow deformity'[175] is pulling long tresses of hair apart with its hands and laughing a low laugh 'full of scorn and derision'.[176] She invites another dryad, the less seductively evil Ash, into the cave to prey upon Anodos.

A couple of pages later we learn how the Alder Maiden is MacDonald's fantastic expression for hungry passion, or vanity, disguised as beautiful love. As Anodos is told:

> "the chief thing that makes her beautiful is this: that, although she loves no man, she loves the love of any man; and when she finds one in her power, her desire to bewitch him and gain his love (not for the sake of his love either, but that she may be conscious anew of her own beauty, through the admiration he manifests), makes her very lovely"[177]

This selfish facade of loveliness, Anodos is told, will eventually destroy all there ever could be of the Alder Maiden. Her self-centred false love, ironically,

---

171 GIB, p. 425. Lewis quotes part of this in his anthology. See ANTH, reading 332.
172 GIB, pp. 425-426.
173 PHA, p. 45.
174 Compare to Rothie, whose throat is an 'open sepulchre'. See p. 186, above.
175 PHA, p. 47.
176 PHA, p. 46.
177 PHA, p. 49.

will eat away her true self. It is "'constantly wearing her away within, till, at last, the decay will reach her face, and her whole front, when all the lovely mask of nothing will fall to pieces, and she be vanished forever'".[178]

Later in the book this kind of hunger is called a passion. In a fairy story found in the library of a fairy castle, Anodos reads of Cosmo, a man very much like himself, who becomes interested in a beautiful lady he observes in a magic mirror. His interest in her is described as blossoming into love, but then we are told how this love '*withered* into a passion'.[179] Becoming increasingly obsessed with having the lady, he turns to magic spells in an attempt to force her into his presence. One can see how love has withered into mere hunger in his own justification for his actions: "'If I do her wrong, let love be my excuse'".[180] Consideration and care for another's best good has been replaced by a desperate, possessive passion.

This passion of Cosmo and his struggle to kill it reflects in fine the most important struggle of the book: Anodos's struggle to lose his shadowy false self. In the penultimate chapter we are told what victory in such a struggle gets rid of, and what is gained. With his passions dead,[181] Anodos finds that he can 'love without needing to be loved again'.[182] Becoming his ideal rather than simply chasing it, he knows 'that it is by loving, and not by being loved, that one can come nearest the soul of another; yea, that, where two love, it is the loving of each other, and not the being beloved by each other, that originates and perfects and assures their blessedness'.[183] In so far as one attempts merely to use another, or use her love, to fulfill some mercenary craving of his own, is the degree to which the philosophy of hell has begun to stifle the love of heaven: 'in proportion as selfishness interferes, the love ceases, and the power which springs therefrom dies'.[184]

MacDonald makes this distinction between love and jealous, selfish, possessive craving in most everything he wrote. One example from *Alec Forbes* we have already mentioned: when Mrs. Bruce cares for her own children but neglects and even detests an orphan living under the same roof, simply because the orphan cannot be called *hers*. Her husband only does what he does for Annie because some of Annie's savings may thereby become *his*. This is made explicit early in the novel when the narrator speaks of Bruce having 'some animal affection' for his children and exhibiting 'an endless amount of

---

178 PHA, p. 49.
179 PHA, p. 94.
180 PHA, p. 97.
181 See PHA, p. 180.
182 PHA, p. 181.
183 PHA, p. 181.
184 PHA, p. 181. For the fulfillment of longings that are not mercenary, see chp. 6, below.

partisanship on their behalf' because of it, regardless of whether such affection or such partisanship does his children or anyone any good.[185] MacDonald then compares this relative lack of love to petty party politics: 'A man must learn to love his children, not because they are his, but because they are *children*, else his love will be scarcely a better thing at last than the party-spirit of the faithful politician. I doubt if it will prove even so good a thing'.[186]

Another way MacDonald illustrates the un-love-liness of things called love is his frequent critique of romantic love and lovers. We have already seen how he uses erotic passion in *Phantastes* to symbolise or allegorise all selfish passions, and how Mysie's and Rothie's love for each other, in *Robert Falconer*, is at best very weak, at worst a kind of hunting. Mysie, who gets her ideas of love from cheap novels, is easy prey for the ravenous Rothie. In *David Elginbrod* we know that Euphra Cameron and Hugh Sutherland have the capacity of being 'in love' with each other but are very much left in doubt as to their capacities for really loving each other. Margaret Elginbrod's love for Hugh, however, like her love for everyone else she comes in contact with, is never in doubt. She only smiles when the suggestion of her being in love with Sutherland is made.[187] Much the same is true in *Sir Gibbie*, in which Gibbie's best friend Donal Grant is obviously in love with Ginevra Galbraith. It is Gibbie, however, with his quieter and stronger love, who eventually gets the girl.

And in one of MacDonald's more obscure tales, *The Portent*, Duncan Campbell is tempted in much the same way as Cosmo is in *Phantastes*. In a chapter entitled 'Love and Power' he is possessed by a 'vehement desire' and compels by force of will the beautiful Lady Alice into his presence.[188] This continues until a later chapter when he begins to look on his own actions as shameful and less than loving: 'I could not now endure the thought of compelling the attendance of her unconscious form; of making her body, like a living cage, transport to my presence the unresisting soul. I shrank from it as a true man would shrink from kissing the lips of a sleeping woman whom he loved, not knowing that she loved him in return'.[189] In this Campbell is beginning to look upon Lady Alice as more than his personal play toy: a mere means by which he satisfies some craving of his.

In his *Unspoken Sermons*, MacDonald writes of this using rather than loving occurring in less dramatic and less alarming settings. In 'The Final Unmasking' he speaks of the possibility of a man sinking 'by such slow degrees' that 'long after he is a devil, he may go on being a good churchman or a

185 AFH, p. 40.
186 AFH, p. 40.
187 See DE, p. 392.
188 POR, p. 60.
189 POR, pp. 79-80.

good dissenter, and thinking himself a good Christian'.[190] The way such a man becomes such a devil, MacDonald writes, is his using people in supposedly loving relationships. In this regard he notes how Dante has reserved 'the lowest hell' to those 'who have been consciously false to their fellows; who, pretending friendship, have used their neighbour to their own ends; and especially those who, pretending friendship, have divided friends'.[191]

According to MacDonald, all of these kinds of hates, accomplished in the name of love, spring from a self's allegiance to the 'one principle of hell' that regards all relations and all reality as things that revolve around the centre of self. It is a subjective perspective that refuses to acknowledge objective facts and obligations that may impinge upon the self's cravings and allegiance to itself. It refuses to be ruled by objective love because it is ruled by subjective pride and desire. It gives only to get. And eats, uses, or attempts to possess whatever it supposedly loves, just as it attempts to possess its self.

As we have already begun to see in *Screwtape Letters* and the Narnia books, Lewis follows MacDonald in this very closely. And he is explicit in his non-fiction works, as MacDonald is in his sermons, about how possessive pride can twist good things and corrupt respectable folk. In a chapter of *Mere Christianity* entitled 'The Great Sin', he speaks of 'Pride' or 'Self-Conceit' being 'the essential vice' and 'utmost evil'.[192] Other sins, such as unchastity, anger, greed and drunkeness, he writes, are 'fleabites' in comparison to the Pride that sets men against each other and against God: 'it was through Pride that the devil became the devil: Pride leads to every other vice: it is the complete anti-God state of mind'.[193]

We can see how closely this resembles MacDonald's view if we remember how darkly MacDonald paints pride in his novels compared to how he treats other vices. In *Sir Gibbie*, for example, the drunkenness of Gibbie's father and Mistress Croale are not nearly as odious and spiritually destructive as the pride of more outwardly respectable characters: the Sclaters, minister Fergus Duff, and Ginevra's father Laird Galbraith. As the narrator makes clear, it is often much easier for goodness to find its way into drunken peddlar women (Croale)

---

190 US, p. 603 (par. 17 in 'The Final Unmasking', third series). Lewis marks this in his copy of the sermon and writes something similar in *The Screwtape Letters*: 'It does not matter how small the sins are, provided that their cumulative effect is to edge the man away from the Light and out into the Nothing [...] Indeed, the safest road to Hell is the gradual one—the gentle slope, soft underfoot, without sudden turnings, without milestones, without sign posts' (SCL, p. 56).

191 US, p. 602 (first quarter of par. 16 in the same sermon). See *Inferno*, Canto 32, where the pit of hell is filled with a frozen lake. Two inhabitants of this lowest cirlce are seen frozen together, gnawing upon each other's heads.

192 MC, p. 109.

193 MC, p. 109.

than into the hearts of the respectably self-satisfied: 'Deep are the depths of social degredation to which the clean, purifying light yet reaches, and lofty are the heights of social honour where yet the light is nothing but darkness'.[194]

Also, Lewis's characterisation of Pride as '*essentially* competitive'[195] echoes the distinction MacDonald constantly makes between proper aspiration and prideful ambition. In the same sermon in which he outlines the 'one principle of hell' and its implications, MacDonald calls ambition 'the dirt of the world's kingdoms' and necessarily opposed to Christ's kingdom 'in which no man seeks to be above another'.[196] Through the narrator of *Sir Gibbie*, in a discussion of the minister Fergus Duff's proud falseness, MacDonald distinguishes between proper aspiration to be and to enjoy, and ambition: the 'evil shadow of aspiration'.[197] While those who aspire attempt to 'be that which he is made most capable of desiring', those with ambition only desire to be *seen* doing things better than others.[198] That a thing is done well or enjoyed is not nearly as important, to the ambitious, as being recognised as doing it better than others, or enjoying the fact that they can enjoy or appreciate what others cannot. This is true of the ambitious Fergus, whose character is contrasted with that of Donal Grant. While Donal loves the lovely and turns 'toward it with desire to become like it', Fergus's appreciation of the lovely is 'spoiled by the paltry ambition of being distinguished'.[199] Fergus is not so concerned with fulfilling his potential as he is with being seen as better, or more thoughtful, or more eloquent, than his fellows. As Lewis describes such a preoccupation in *Mere Christianity*: 'Pride gets no pleasure out of having something, only out of having more of it than the next man. We say that people are proud of being rich, or clever, or good-looking, but they are not. They are proud of being richer, or cleverer, or better-looking than others. If every one else became equally rich, clever, or good-looking there would be nothing to be proud about'.[200]

Pictures of Hell

And so we see again how the one principle, or philosophy, of hell can twist or vitiate things that are originally good, according to MacDonald and Lewis. If the passion of Pride is not itself killed, they believed it will dilute, corrupt, and eventually kill all good loves and aspirations. We've already seen, in *Screwtape Letters* and the Narnia books, a few ways in which Lewis, following

---

194 GIB, p. 309.
195 MC, p. 109.
196 US, pp. 493-494 (second quarter of par. 2 in 'Kingship', third series).
197 GIB, p. 150.
198 GIB, p. 150.
199 GIB, pp. 150-151.
200 MC, pp. 109-110.

MacDonald, depicts this Pride in fiction. But there are three other works of his, *The Great Divorce*, *That Hideous Strength* and *Till We Have Faces*, that ought to be mentioned in connection with Pride. It is in *The Great Divorce* and *Till We Have Faces*, in particular, that we find Lewis's most striking and thorough illustrations of Pride.

The most striking pictures are found in *The Great Divorce*, the book in which Lewis writes himself and MacDonald in as characters who observe ghostly inhabitants of hell out on holiday. Lewis the author, in his crisp and condensed narrative and dialogue, reveals what keeps each ghost from leaving hell altogether and moving deeper into heaven. In each case, as mentioned above, the ghost is dominated by something that it will not give up. One of these ghosts, for example, is dominated by her own grumbling. Lewis, himself a ghost in the story, is told that the problem comes when the woman clings so tightly to her grumbling that it becomes a state of mind or state of being:

> "The question is whether she is a grumbler, or only a grumble. If there
> is a real woman—even the least trace of one—still there inside the
> grumbling, it can be brought to life again. If there's one wee spark
> under all those ashes, we'll blow it till the whole pile is red and clear.
> But if there's nothing but ashes we'll not go on blowing them in our
> own eyes forever. They must be swept up."[201]

The danger, as with the dwarf chained to the tragedian,[202] is the loss of personhood, of the person having become indistinguishable from the passion he will not be rid of. As MacDonald tells Lewis in the story:

> "ye'll have had experiences ... it begins with a grumbling mood, and
> yourself still distinct from it: perhaps criticising it. And yourself, in a
> dark hour, may will that mood, embrace it. Ye can repent and come out
> of it again. But there may come a day when you can do that no longer.
> Then there will be no you left to criticise the mood, nor even to enjoy it,
> but just grumble itself going on forever like a machine."[203]

The reader is not told whether there is enough woman left in the grumbler to make liberation and redemption a possibility, though her allowed presence on the outskirts of heaven would seem to argue for such a possibility. Another ghost, the man with the lizard of lust on his shoulder, does experience such liberation after letting an angel kill the lizard.

But these relatively undignified passions are not presented as either the most dangerous or most truly wicked. Lewis, following MacDonald's practice, shows how 'respectable' people doing 'good' things may be the most wicked of

---

201 GD, p. 60. Compare to Lewis's description of ash having been a log in his chapter on hell in *The Problem of Pain* (PP, p. 125; see p. 173, above).
202 See p. 171, above.
203 GD, p. 60.

all. There are many examples to choose from in the book, but the ghosts which are most difficult to cure are those whose loves have gone bad. Hell's greatest triumph, as depicted in *Divorce* and elsewhere, is when Pride poisons human loves: when the thing most divine in us, our concern for others' well-being, is twisted and pulverised into a mere means by which one uses another to satisfy some hunger or jealousy of his own. Lewis is just as clear as MacDonald on this point, as in *The Four Loves* when he speaks of sexual desire as something which, *by itself*, is unconcerned with the beloved or the beloved's good as ends in themselves: 'We use a most unfortunate idiom when we say, of a lustful man prowling the streets, that he "wants a woman." Strictly speaking, a woman is just what he does not want. He wants a pleasure for which a woman happens to be the necessary piece of apparatus'.[204] Lewis's main point in writing *The Four Loves*, though, is to warn his readers how things far nobler than simple sexual desire—family affection, friendship, and romantic love—can go wrong and cease to be real loves at all if they are not ruled by God's love: the sort of unconditional love that we have already mentioned and that we will discuss further in the following chapter.

The dangers of corrupted loves that Lewis explains in *The Four Loves* are memorably illustrated by three ghosts in *The Great Divorce*. One of these spectres we have already mentioned: the dwarf chained to the tragedian. Lewis makes clear through the extravagant words and actions of the tragedian that whatever love the man once had for his wife has dwindled into a self-pitying demand to be loved. Even his wife, now one of the most beautiful inhabitants of heaven, admits to him how both of their loves for each other were largely attempts to satisfy a personal need: '"There was little real love in it. But what we called love down there was mostly the craving to be loved. In the main I loved you for my own sake: because I needed you"'.[205] The reason he is still in hell is because his love, unlike hers, has never become anything other than a selfish craving. As she attempts to explain to him the nature of her new love, the tragedian goes on with his self-centred theatricals:

> "She needs me no more—no more. No more," he said in a choking voice to no one in particular [...] "Would to Gud[206] I had seen her lying dead at my feet before I heard those words. Lying dead at my feet. Lying dead at my feet."[207]

Not happy to see his wife enjoying the love and joys of heaven, or to join her in enjoying them, he keeps up his attempts to evoke, and indulge in, her pity for

204 C.S. Lewis, *The Four Loves* (San Diego: Harcourt Brace Jovanovich, 1991), p. 94. First published in 1960.
205 GD, p. 95.
206 His pronunciation of 'God'.
207 GD, p. 95.

him. It is revealed how most of his 'love' on earth had simply been an attempt to rouse and enjoy other people's pity for himself. It has all been about him.[208]

Another ghost is dominated by a 'love' which attempts to dominate her husband's life, as if she were also his mother and his God. Her husband exists, in her mind, as her own little project. That he should have interests and purposes unconnected with her ambitions is a claim she will not recognise. As her incessant chattering makes clear, her husband is simply something to be manipulated or used. The number of times she uses a first person pronoun shows just how much her love for Robert is really all about herself and her Pride:

> "The ingratitude! It was I who made a man of him! Sacrificed my whole life to him! [...] He was pottering along on about six hundred a year when I married him [...] It was I who had to drive him every step of the way. He hadn't a spark of ambition. It was like trying to lift a sack of coal. I had to positively nag him to take on that extra work in the other department [...] my day's work wasn't over when his was. I had to keep him going all evening [...] all the time I was working my fingers to the bone for him: and without the slightest appreciation [...] He had some silly idea of writing a book in those days ... as if he could. I cured him of that in the end [...] I knew from the first that those friends were doing him no good [...] They weren't quite at their ease, somehow, in my drawing-room: not at their best. I couldn't help laughing sometimes. [...] Every useful friend he ever made was due to me [...] I did my duty to the very end. I forced him to take exercise—that was really my chief reason for keeping a great Dane. I kept on giving parties. I took him for the most wonderful holidays. I saw that he didn't drink too much [...] How could I help it if he did have a nervous breakdown in the end? My conscience is clear. I've done my duty by him, if ever a woman has."[209]

In the name of love and duty, the woman has tortured her husband out of his wits. She has no remorse for having toyed with him thus, and even in heaven she turns down an opportunity to meet him if she cannot also control him and absorb his being into her own:

> "Put me in charge of him. He wants firm handling. I know him better than you do [...] Don't consult him: just give him to me. I'm his wife, aren't I? I was only beginning. There's lots, lots, lots of things I still want to do with him [...] I'm so miserable. I must have someone to—to do things to. It's simply frightful down there. No one minds about me at all. I can't alter them [...] Give him back to me. Why should he have everything his own way? It's not good for him."[210]

---

208 See GD, p. 99.
209 GD, pp. 69-72.
210 GD, p. 73.

And so forth and so on until the ghost shoots up like a dying candle flame and snaps. Lewis may not have achieved, poetically, quite what Milton has with his Satan, but this ghost surely conveys a sense of how unbearable a hellion may be to live with. This ghost's possessiveness reminds us, of course, of MacDonald's principle and creed of hell which is so ready to call so many things 'mine',[211] and of Lewis's own rendering of the philosophy of hell in *Screwtape*.[212] Readers will remember how Screwtape urges Wormwood to do all he can to encourage self-centred possessiveness: 'The sense of ownership in general is always to be encouraged. The humans are always putting up claims to ownership which sound equally funny in Heaven and in Hell, and we must keep them doing so'.[213] He advises Wormwood that they, through Pride and confusion, can eventually persuade the humans to possess their servants, wives, fathers and mothers in the same way that they possess their clothing:

> They can be taught to reduce all these senses [of 'my'] to that of "my boots," the "my" of ownership. Even in the nursery a child can be taught to mean by "my Teddy bear," not the old imagined recipient of affection to whom it stands in a special relation (for that is what the Enemy[214] will teach them to mean if we are not careful), but "the bear I can pull to pieces if I like."[215]

In *The Great Divorce* we see how Robert's wife, thinking she owns him, has spent her life pulling him to pieces. Because she cannot see and treat him as anything other than 'hers', she cannot survive in the objective and truly loving atmosphere of heaven.

Such is also the case with perhaps the most distressing of Lewis's illustrations of poisoned love in *Divorce*: a woman's ghost who refuses to enter heaven because her love for her son has become tyrannical. Here Lewis depicts even the best and seemingly 'holiest'[216] of natural loves, Mother-love, turning wicked. Like Robert's wife, this ghost thinks her 'love' for her son is all that could ever matter. She speaks fiercely of how she did her best to make Michael happy, how she gave up her whole life to do so. She insists how her love for him would not have gone bad had they lived together for a million years. She even boasts that she and her son would be 'perfectly happy' in hell, if only he were allowed to come live with her there.[217]

---

211 See pp. 164-165, above.
212 See pp. 178-179, above.
213 SCL, p. 97 (Letter XXI).
214 That is, God.
215 SCL, p. 98 (Letter XXI).
216 GD, p. 77.
217 GD, pp. 77-78.

She and her love for Michael, reminiscent of Mrs. Bruce's love for her sons in *Alec Forbes*, could never go wrong, though she readily admits how other mothers, sons, and loves do. Ten years after Michael dies, she keeps up the ritual of keeping his room exactly as he left it, keeps up anniversaries, and refuses to leave the old house even though her husband and daughter are 'wretched' there.[218] Her husband and daughter feel the loss of their son and brother just as sharply as she, but are forced to revolt 'against having their whole life dominated by the tyranny of the past: and not really even Michael's past, but your past'.[219] In heaven she demands to have Michael on her own terms: "'No one had a right to come between me and my son. Not even God. Tell Him that to His face. I want my boy, and I mean to have him. He is mine, do you understand? Mine, mine, mine, for ever and ever'".[220]

There are other examples in Lewis's fiction of jealous love growing into a kind of hate. The short length and fantastic nature of most of his books give him far fewer chances than MacDonald had to display the nature of such love over the span of several chapters, with particular characters in realistic settings. And so most of his depictions of Prideful love are limited to short and stark sentences, symbols, incidents, or bits of dialogue—as in *The Great Divorce*, *The Screwtape Letters*, or the Narnia books.[221] But there are a couple of exceptions.

One exception is the relationship of Mark and Jane Studdock in *That Hideous Strength*: a young, educated, upwardly mobile couple who've been married for six months but who have yet to learn to truly love each other. The narrator's account of Mark's and Jane's thoughts helps to reveal that each is, at the beginning of the story, still a self looking out primarily for its own interests and needs, rather than their spouse's interests and needs. Jane finds herself technically married but still struggles against the "'mutual society, help, and comfort'"[222] inherent in the idea of matrimony. As the narrator tells us at one point:

> To avoid entanglements and interferences had long been one of her first principles. Even when she had discovered that she was going to marry Mark if he asked her, the thought, "But I must still keep up my own life" had arisen at once and had never for more than a few minutes at a stretch been absent from her mind. Some resentment against love itself,

---

218 GD, p. 78.
219 GD, p. 78.
220 GD, p. 79.
221 Though there is the opportunity with the Narnia books to observe particular characters over several chapters, the actual space devoted to character development is still relatively small.
222 HS, p. 13.

and therefore against Mark, for thus invading her life, remained.[223]

This unformulated but potent fear of invasion and entanglement, we are told, 'was the deepest ground of her determination not to have a child—or not for a long time yet'.[224] She refuses or delays the realities of love because she holds on to a self she calls her own, much in keeping with MacDonald's one principle of hell: 'I am my own'. As Jane Studdock puts it in her thoughts, 'One had one's own life to live'.[225]

Mark Studdock, for his part, realises relatively late in the story how he has failed to take Jane's person seriously. He has been a clumsy 'lout and clown and clod-hopper' who, preoccupied with his own career and ambitions, has enjoyed the pleasures of marriage nonchalantly with far too little reverence for Jane herself.[226] He has been 'the coarse, male boor with horny hands and hobnailed shoes' who has blundered, sauntered, and stumped through the first few months of his marriage.[227] Only towards the end of the story does he gain a real respect for the sanctity of Jane's person: 'He was discovering the hedge after he had plucked the rose, and not only plucked it but torn it all to pieces and crumpled it with hot, thumb-like, greedy fingers. How had he dared? [...] The word *Lady* had made no part of his vocabulary save as a pure form or else

---

223 HS, p. 72.

224 HS, p. 73.

225 HS, p. 73. The fear of entanglement being presented as unloving here may seem to contradict Lewis's presenting the earthly relation between Robert and his wife as unloving in *The Great Divorce*. Both are marriages, and surely entanglement can't be loving and unloving at the same time? Why is Jane wrong to fear it, and Robert and his wife also wrong to have participated in it? Lewis's answer to such a complaint would likely be that one must distinguish between a fear of loving, in Jane's case, and the fact of tyranny, in the case of Robert being eaten alive by a wife who does not actually love him. Jane's fear of entanglement is not simply a fear of being abused in this way, though she may have come to feel that this is exactly what marriage and parenthood will mean for her. We are told, in fact, that Mark treats marriage too much like a meal, and so Jane's fears may in part be justified; but then this fear would be fear of un-love, not fear of the entanglements proper to marriage. In short, an entanglement between two people who love and respect each other is not the same as a relationship in which one simply abuses, eats or absorbs the other. To the degree that Jane fears being 'invaded' by the legitimate loves of her husband and future children is the degree to which she shares with Robert's wife a Pride that will not be ruled by true love. Jane's iciness and Robert's wife's despotism both spring from a Pride which refuses to be entangled. Jane fears entangling herself with Mark and their future children. Robert's wife refuses to entangle herself with the real Robert and the obligations that may flow from the realised fact that he is a person, not a toy or project. Both women will not yield to love, or a loving marriage.

226 HS, pp. 380-381.

227 HS, p. 381.

in mockery. He had laughed too soon'.[228]

Another character who finds out very late how false and hellish her loves have been is Orual in *Till We Have Faces*. The first part of the novel, twenty-one of the book's twenty-five chapters, consists of Orual's complaint against the monstrous gods for the injuries and troubles she has suffered in her life. It is not until the last four chapters, Part Two, that Orual realises that she herself has been the worst monster of the story.

"'I am Ungit'", she wails after having been forced to look upon her soul's ugliness unveiled.[229] "'Without question it was true. It was I who was Ungit. That ruinous face was mine. I was that Batta-thing, that all-devouring womblike, yet barren, thing. Glome was a web—I the swollen spider, squat at its center, gorged with men's stolen lives'".[230] Throughout the second part Orual painfully records what she has always been at pains to ignore: that she is the ugly thing that has set herself up as a god, consuming and absorbing men and lives with the jealousies, passions and cravings she has hitherto called 'love'. This second, more honest account admits, for example, how Orual increasingly neglected her eldest sister Redival. It is revealed how Redival used to say, "'First of all Orual loved me much; then the Fox came and she loved me little; then the baby came and she loved me not at all'".[231]

Not a hint of this loneliness of Redival's has been mentioned in Part One. Orual herself tells us why. Her own self-pity has blinded her to many things: 'I had never thought at all how it might be with her when I turned first to the Fox and then to Psyche. For it had been somehow settled in my mind from the very beginning that I was the pitiable and ill-used one. She had her gold curls, hadn't she?'.[232]

More of her selfishness is revealed when she meets Ansit, the widow of Bardia, Orual's loyal counselor and man-at-arms. Orual professes to have loved Bardia deeply, but her visit to the widow soon unmasks what sort of love it has been. The reasons for her going to visit the widow begin to give the reader hints. She goes out of duty and custom to the woman who, 'because he had loved her', she sees as an 'enemy'.[233] And she goes to *be* comforted, as if it were her husband who had died: 'yet who else in the whole world [but Ansit] could now talk to me?'.[234]

---

228 HS, p. 381. Compare to Anodos and the maiden's sphere in *Phantases*. See pp. 134-135, above.
229 FAC, p. 276.
230 FAC, p. 276.
231 FAC, p. 255.
232 FAC, p. 256.
233 FAC, p. 259.
234 FAC, p. 259.

From the widow she learns how it is she, the Queen, who has killed Bardia with her jealous, selfish, demanding love. The widow tells her how he was a weary man who had been worked into an early old age. When Orual retorts that he never looked or spoke like an old man at the palace, the widow explains how "'He was too well-mannered, you know, to nod and yawn in a Queen's house'".[235] The widow goes on to detail how the Queen's love has sucked the life out of her husband,[236] how the husbandless, childless Orual has done all she could, short of an affair, to steal Bardia from his wife and destroy the man himself: "'your queenship drank up his blood year by year and ate out his life'".[237] And so even before Orual sees her self and her 'love' as it really is, Bardia's widow reveals it to her in words: "'Perhaps you who spring from the gods love like the gods. Like the Shadowbrute. They say the loving and the devouring are all one, don't they? [...] You're full fed. Gorged with other men's lives, women's too: Bardia's, mine, the Fox's, your sister's—both your sisters'".[238]

Eventually, Orual comes to agree about the nature of her former loves: 'Did I hate him, then? Indeed, I believe so. A love like that can grow to be nine-tenths hatred and still call itself love'.[239] She begins to smell in her love the stench of hell: 'My love for Bardia (not Bardia himself) had become to me a sickening thing. I had been dragged up and out onto such heights and precipices of truth, that I came into an air where it could not live. It stank; a gnawing greed for one to whom I could give nothing, of whom I craved all'.[240]

Only now, when it is too late, does she begin to really care for Bardia's best good: 'Heaven knows how we had tormented him, Ansit and I. For it needs no Oedipus to guess that, many and many a night, her jealousy of me had welcomed him home, late from the palace, to a bitter hearth'.[241] And only now does Orual submit to the death of her old craving passions and her old, hellish self: 'When the craving went, nearly all that I called myself went with it. It was if my whole soul had been one tooth and now that tooth was drawn. I was a gap. And now I thought I had come to the very bottom and that the gods could tell me no worse'.[242]

---

235 FAC, p. 260.
236 See FAC, pp. 260-261.
237 FAC, p. 264.
238 FAC, pp. 264-265.
239 FAC, p. 266.
240 FAC, p. 267.
241 FAC, p. 267.
242 FAC, p. 267.

The Great Escape

None of this was new to Lewis. Before he wrote of the nature of passions and the need to have them killed, he read of it in MacDonald's books. That which is hideous and false within the ghosts, the Studdocks, and Orual are the same things one finds in Robert Bruce and his wife, Fergus Duff, the Sclaters, Laird Galbraith, Baron Rothie and many other characters of MacDonald's. The good death that Orual, the Studdocks, and some of the ghosts submit to is the same good death that Anodos, Murdock Malison, Lilith and many others submit to in MacDonald's stories. Lilith, before Orual, was a vampiress who attempts to suck the life out of those she 'loves'. Orual's passion, 'for years [...] wrapped round the whole heart', dries up and withers.[243] But only as Anodos's passions died in much the same way, in a story written a hundred years earlier.[244]

Long before Lewis wrote of Orual viewing her own hideousness in a mirror, MacDonald wrote of the same thing in a sermon: 'The one deepest, highest, truest, fittest, most wholesome suffering must be generated in the wicked by a vision, a true sight, more or less adequate, of the hideousness of their lives, of the horror of the wrongs they have done'.[245] Lewis read of this mirror-like hell of truth in many of MacDonald's stories, too, as in the tale 'The Wise Woman' when the self-absorbed Agnes is forced to look upon herself in a great hollow, mirror-like sphere. There is neither door nor window to interrupt the perfect roundness of the sphere, or to interrupt Agnes's meeting and living with the self others have had to live with. As Lewis came to write in *The Problem of Pain*, the soul that forever insists on his own way and passions will get it: 'He has his wish—to live wholly in the self and to make the best of what he finds there. And what he finds there is Hell'.[246] Agnes, in MacDonald's tale, who 'had cared only for Somebody'—that is, herself—is now 'going to have only Somebody'.[247] She walks and walks inside the ball but gets nowhere as the sphere simply rotates with every step she takes.[248] She cries aloud but no one seems to hear or take heed of her. Slow hours drift by as she loses all sense of time.

On the third day, however, she becomes aware of a mysterious companion beside her. Agnes notes how ugly this little girl is, but is glad to have any sort of company. When she reaches her hand out toward the girl, however, she finds that she cannot touch her. Her companion also reaches out with her

243 FAC, p. 267.
244 See PHA, p. 180.
245 US, p. 513 (third quarter of par. 31 in 'Justice', third series).
246 PP, p. 123.
247 CFT, p. 259.
248 Lewis achieves much the same thing in *The Great Divorce* by expanding, instead of limiting, the sense of space. See GD, pp. 10-11.

hand, but in the opposite direction to Agnes. She mimics every movement and word of Agnes because she is Agnes. Agnes is condemned to be with what she has made herself. She flies at the girl for mocking her but finds herself pulling at her own hair and biting into her own arm. After every such attack the other Agnes reappears 'tenfold uglier than before' and Agnes begins to hate her companion 'with her whole heart'.[249]

At this point she realises the truth of her situation: 'it flashed upon her with a sickening disgust that the child was not another, but her Self, her Somebody, and that she was now shut up with her for ever and ever'.[250] When she sees her companion across from her 'staring at her own toes' and smiling with an 'odious, self-satisfied expression', Agnes feels ashamed. She sees the 'heedless, ugly, miserable' little girl patting her own cheeks, stroking her own body, and examining her finger-ends—all the while 'nodding her head with satisfaction', and realises that the 'hateful, ape-like creature' is only 'doing outside of her what she herself had been doing, as long as she could remember, inside of her'.[251]

Something very similar happens to Lilith in one of the darkest chapters MacDonald ever wrote. In 'That Night' Lilith defiantly boasts to Mara of her allegiance to the one principle of hell. She tells Mara that she will not 'turn away from the wicked things' she has been doing: '"I will not [...] I will be myself and not another!"'.[252] When Mara retorts that Lilith is already 'another' and not her '"real self"', Lilith replies that she '"will be what I mean myself now"'.[253] She will not yield after being reminded that she has killed her daughter: '"I have killed thousands. She is my own!"'.[254] She will not yield after being told that her daughter was never hers '"as you are another's"', that is, the One who made her.[255] She will not yield to God, his goodness, or anything that threatens her own control over her self. Simultaneously denying and defying God, Lilith escapes into her own sphere of existential, subjective unreality:

> "So long as I feel myself what it pleases me to think myself, I care not [what her true self is]. I am content to be to myself what I would be. What I choose to seem to myself makes me what I am. My own thought makes me me; my own thought of myself is me [...] No one ever made me. I defy that Power to unmake me from a free woman!"[256]

---

249 CFT, p. 261.
250 CFT, p. 261.
251 CFT, p. 261.
252 LIL, p. 314.
253 LIL, p. 314.
254 LIL, p. 315.
255 LIL, p. 315.
256 LIL, pp. 315-316.

She rejoices in this sort of freedom until she is made to see what she has actually made of herself with it. A white-hot worm-like thing, 'the live heart of essential fire' with 'a soundless presence as of a roaring flame', creeps up and into her bosom, 'piercing through the joints and marrow to the thoughts and intents of the heart'.[257] As Mara tells Vane, the objective ugliness of Lilith's subjective, Prideful self is being revealed to her. Like Orual and Lewis's ghosts, she has been cast, as a last resort, into the torment of her own worst self:

> "She is far away from us, afar in the hell of her self-consciousness. The central fire of the universe is radiating into her the knowledge of good and evil, the knowledge of what she is. She sees at last the good she is not, the evil she is. She knows that she is herself the fire in which she is burning, but she does not know that the Light of Life is the heart of that fire. Her torment is that she is what she is."[258]

Lilith's hell of self-consciousness is a model for that which Orual experiences and a picture of what the two men actually believed must happen to those who refuse to yield their selves up to God and his goodness. Lewis, it is clear, followed MacDonald closely in stressing that this move towards hell involves a shrinking away from objective reality into a subjective, ghostly state of mind. If the passages cited thus far are not enough to prove this, then surely the following passage from *The Great Divorce*, in which MacDonald addresses Lewis, will help: "'A damned soul is nearly nothing: it is shrunk, shut up in itself. Good beats upon the damned incessantly as sound waves beat on the ears of the deaf, but they cannot receive it. Their fists are clenched, their teeth are clenched, their eyes fast shut. First they will not, in the end they cannot, open their hands for gifts, or their mouth for food, or their eyes to see'".[259] These sentences, of course, describe exactly what happens to Lilith towards the end of the story, and could very well be mistaken as a passage *from Lilith*.

Lewis, through MacDonald's character in *The Great Divorce*, notes how such a state of mind begins before death.[260] And he explains the same thing without the mediation of a character in *Mere Christianity*: 'Perhaps my bad temper or my jealousy are gradually getting worse—so gradually that the increase in seventy years will not be very noticeable. But it might be absolute hell in a million years: in fact, if Christianity is true, Hell is the precisely correct technical term for what it would be'.[261] The eternal picture of ourselves, in other words, is beginning to be sketched now. As he wrote in an address entitled 'The Weight of Glory',

257 LIL, pp. 317, 318. MacDonald quotes here from Heb. 4.12. See also Luke 2.29-35, Eph. 6.17.
258 LIL, p. 319. Compare John 1.4 , 8.12. See also P&C, p. 75.
259 GD, p. 104.
260 See GD, p. 55.
261 MC, p, 73.

It is a serious thing to live in a society of possible gods and goddesses, to remember that the dullest and most uninteresting person you can talk to may one day be a creature which, if you saw it now, you would be strongly tempted to worship, or else a horror and a corruption such as you now meet, if at all, only in a nightmare [...] There are no ordinary people. You have never talked to a mere mortal [...] it is immortals whom we joke with, work with, marry, snub, and exploit—immortal horrors or everlasting splendours.[262]

In all of this Lewis is only saying, in a different way, what MacDonald said many times before. As Robert Falconer, in *David Elginbrod*, says of his vision of hell: 'the only devil that can make hell itself a torture [is] the devil of selfishness,—the only one that can *possess* a man and make himself his own living hell'.[263]

There were, of course, differences. But as we have seen, the principal difference between the two writers on hell concerns, paradoxically, their agreement upon the probability of total annihilation of a soul. Lewis didn't think it likely because of the intrinsic difficulty of reducing a soul to utter non-being.[264] The lowest one could ever sink to was a state of '*having been* a human soul'.[265] MacDonald did not believe annihilation was probable for a different reason. He believed a living soul, however low it had sunk in hell, would ultimately yield at the prospect of annihilation. Lilith, it will be remembered, only begins to repent after 'a horrible Nothingness, a Negation positive' enfolds her.[266] Her 'being' recoils from 'Annihilation', 'Death Absolute', and the 'presence of Nothing'.[267] It would have been an interesting question to put to Lewis whether he thought this sort of repentance would have been real: whether this kind of help from God in the form of a taste of annihilation would have been intrinsically possible as well as consistent with a soul's free will choice to yield.

But it will profit us little here to dwell on such differences. Already we have seen how both men understood repentance to be impossible without a man's free will choice, but also believed that God would do all he possibly could to bring a man to this point of choosing, even if it hurts (both the man and God). It will also be noticed that there can be little discernible difference, in the end, between MacDonald's taste of 'Annihilation' and Lewis's 'state of *having been*'. If a being has tasted annihilation, surely he has been very close to '*having been*'. And *vice versa*: if one is in a state of '*having been*', surely she or

262 WG, p. 39.
263 DE, p. 371.
264 See above, p. 173.
265 PP, p. 125.
266 LIL, p. 322.
267 LIL, p. 322.

it knows as much as can be known about 'Death absolute' or 'the presence of Nothing'. The only important difference, as we have noted, involves different notions as to whether such a lowest state could ever be more than simply tasted, whether it could decay into a permanent condition of not being, or having been.

Much more important to note is that both men agreed intensely that it didn't do much good to talk or write of hell as anything other than separation from God and his good reality. As we have seen, their idea of hell is the self moving away from the love and reality of God—'away from the Light and into the Nothing'.[268] As Lewis writes in *Reflections on the Psalms*, it is arguable that 'the moment "Heaven" ceases to mean union with God and "Hell" to mean separation from Him, the belief in either is a mischievous superstition'.[269] This follows the view of his master, who wrote of hell as that 'horror of being without God—that one living death'.[270]

MacDonald writes in a sermon entitled 'The Last Farthing' of his own vision from afar of 'the final prison of all': 'the vast outside' beyond 'the gates of the city of which God is the light'.[271] It is 'absolute loneliness' where 'not a hint, not a shadow of anything outside [one's] consciousness reaches him'.[272] MacDonald envisions a soul so far away from God that 'he is conscious only of that from which he has withdrawn'.[273] It is very similar indeed to Lewis's 'state of *having been*'. Such a soul sinks into the tiny pretend world of his own selfish imagination, at once a 'Poor helpless dumb devil' *and* 'his own glorious lord god'.[274] He is unable to 'rule, direct, or even distinguish' between 'real presences' and the miserable, woeful fancies of his own mind.[275] Withdrawn from the objective reality of God and others, the soul that 'has cared for nothing but himself'[276] finds his own existence a terror: 'Without the correction, the reflection, the support of other presences, being is not only unsafe, it is a horror—for anyone but God, who is his own being'. Such an existence is 'huge, void, formless'.[277]

---

268 SCL, p. 56 (Letter XII).

269 C.S. Lewis, *Reflections on the Psalms* (London: Harper Collins, 1998), p. 35. First published in 1958.

270 US, p. 31 (fourth quarter of par. 24 in 'The Consuming Fire', first series).

271 US, pp. 268-269 (first quarter of par. 27 in 'The Last Farthing', second series).

272 US, p. 269 (second quarter of par. 27 in the same sermon).

273 US, p. 269 (third quarter of par. 27 in the same).

274 US, pp. 269-270 (first quarter of par. 28 in the same).

275 US, p. 270 (fourth quarter of par. 28 in the same). Lewis marks the portion quoted in this sentence, in his copy of the sermon.

276 US, p. 269 (third quarter of par. 27 in the same).

277 US, p. 271 (third and fourth quarters of par. 30 in the same). Lewis marks all of the passage quoted in this sentence.

It is this kind of outer darkness that shows up in *Perelandra*, in the tortured recollection of Weston who has apparently been to such a place, only he confuses it with the inner core of ultimate reality. As the narrator comments, 'what Pantheists falsely hoped of Heaven bad men really received in Hell'.[278] Weston has been to hell and become a jumbled mix of things called the Un-man. He babbles about trying to connect things but not being able to do so in the mad, chaotic nothing that comes after death.[279] He has been to the hell of his own naked consciousness and mistaken it for ultimate reality.

Both MacDonald and Lewis, we have seen, do all they can in their writing to expose this kind of mistake. To their understandings God's love was the ultimate reality. The degree to which one refused to get into this reality, or have it put into them, is the degree to which one was living in hell and its philosophy of 'me' and 'mine'. As Lewis writes in *The Four Loves* of those who would keep a tight grasp on their hearts:

> To love at all is to be vulnerable. Love anything, and your heart will certainly be wrung and possibly broken. If you want to be sure of keeping it intact, you must give your heart to no one, not even to an animal. Wrap it carefully round with hobbies and little luxuries; avoid all entanglements; lock it up safe in the casket or coffin of your selfishness. But in that casket—safe, dark, motionless, airless—it will change. It will not be broken; it will become unbreakable, impenetrable, irredeemable. The alternative to tragedy, or at least to the risk of tragedy, is damnation. The only place outside Heaven where you can be perfectly safe from all the dangers and perturbations of love is Hell.[280]

MacDonald and Lewis, however, believed that the story need not end this way. Both men believed that not one soul need be trapped in such a prison. Even Lewis, who believed in the possibility of final damnation, believed every soul God made has a real chance to yield. 'There is no spirit in prison', as George MacDonald tells Lewis in *The Great Divorce*, 'to whom He did not preach'.[281] It is possible, they both believed, that the door of anyone's hell— 'locked on the *inside*'—may be unlocked.[282]

One of Lewis's best summations of this possible unlocking of the door to hell comes, interestingly, in a book of literary criticism. In the last chapter of one of the last books he published, *An Experiment in Criticism*, he writes of how the substantive good, or Logos, of literature (as opposed to the Poiema, or style) lies in readers wanting 'to see with other eyes, to imagine with other

278 PER, p. 173.
279 See PER, p. 170.
280 4L, p. 121.
281 GD, p. 105. As in the title to his first publication, *Spirits in Bondage*, Lewis alludes here to 1 Peter 3.19 and 4.6.
282 PP, p. 127.

imaginations, to feel with other hearts, as well as with our own'.[283] It is a 'series of windows, even of doors' by which the reader 'gets out' of his mere self and 'gets in' to the imagination, eye, and heart of another.[284] This literary way of reading, he writes, while not essentially 'an affectional or moral or intellectual activity', has something in common with all these things. What all three activities have in common is, by no accident, a good description of what Lewis thought opening the prison door to self would involve:

> In love we escape from our self into one other. In the moral sphere, every act of justice or charity involves putting ourselves in the other person's place and thus transcending our own competitive particularity. In coming to understand anything we are rejecting the facts as they are for us in favour of the facts as they are. [...] Obviously this process can be described either as an enlargement or as a temporary annihilation of the self. But that is an old paradox; 'he that loseth his life shall save it'.[285]

Lewis, as we have seen, learned much about this process of 'transcending our own competitive particularity'[286] in MacDonald's books. Having picked up *Phantastes* as a reader interested only in imaginative escape into fantasy and the Ideal, he was confronted with a similar, but greater escape. Like Anodos, he began to learn the Christian paradox of good death: that one can only get into the Ideal by becoming one's Ideal, or true self—by having one's jealous passions killed and escaping the hell of one's mere subjective self. The spirit truly in bondage, Lewis would come to believe and to illustrate, is that spirit who will not yield and unlock the prison door of self.

The next chapter's concern will be, quite simply, what may be on the other side of the door.

---

283 C.S. Lewis, *An Experiment in Criticism* (Cambridge: Cambridge University Press, 2000), p. 137.
284 EC, p. 138.
285 EC, p. 138. Lewis quotes Christ. See Mat. 10.39.
286 EC, p. 138.

CHAPTER 5

THE CHIVALRY OF GOD

Lyons in the felde and lambes in chambre: egles at assaute
and maydens in halle
–Thomas Usk, *Testament of Love*, 1.5[1]

A poor cow,
An ox and mule stand and behold,
    And wonder
That a stable should enfold
    Him that can thunder.
–Jeremy Taylor, *A Dialogue Between Three
        Shepherds*[2]

Take my yoke upon you, and learn of me, for I am meek
and lowly in heart.
–Matthew 11.29[3]

Hide us from the face of him that sitteth on the throne,
and from the wrath of the Lamb
–Revelation 6.16[4]

There may have been no marriage of heaven and hell in MacDonald's and
Lewis's works, but it does not follow that there are no marriages. A metaphor
that conveys the idea of a kind of marriage will be used in this chapter in an
attempt to sum up what both authors thought and wrote about the goodness
they believed in. Both authors believed this goodness to be that which lies on
the other side of the locked door of mere self.

Beyond Mere Morality

Before we begin using the metaphor, however, it will be needful to observe that
goodness, to these authors, is never simply an abstract ethic, never simply duty
for duty's sake, however much it may sometimes feel like it in emotionally dry
periods. In his sermon 'The Truth', for example, MacDonald speaks of man's
relationship to the truth of goodness as one that grows in stages of increased
intimacy. In the beginning, he writes, men understand the truth of duty more
than they can love the duties themselves, 'with the resulting advantage of
having thereby the opportunity of choosing them purely because they are true'.[5]

1   A description of Love's servants. Quoted in AL, p. 228.
2   Quoted in AQN, p. 312; and EA, p. 219.
3   Quoted in HG, p. 144.
4   Quoted in CHR, p. 154.
5   US, p. 472 (last quarter of par. 12 in 'The Truth', third series).

In this way the man can actually choose to love the good duty for the sake of the truth of the duty, rather than loving it for any gratification he may receive from doing so. Then, as the man does these good duties, he is somehow enabled to love them in another way: 'Then [the duties] cease to show themselves in the form of duties, and appear as they more truly are, absolute truths, essential realities, eternal delights'.[6] A man who goes out of his mere self to the world of moral duty, MacDonald writes, will eventually be able to step out of the world of dry duty, as one who has learned to ride a bike can dispense with the training wheels: 'The man is a true man who chooses duty; he is a perfect man who at length never thinks of duty, who forgets the name of it'.[7]

According to MacDonald, the lowest degree of intimacy with goodness is that of 'the moral philosopher who regards duties only as facts of his system', or of any man who admits them as facts without attempting to do them.[8] A higher level of intimacy is granted to the man who attempts to do his duty and thus makes moral duty a truth of his own existence, rather than simply a fact to be contemplated in the abstract. But higher still, as we have already begun to see, is that man who knows more, even, than the doing of his duty. Even if a man did 'everything required of him' in fulfilling all the duties and 'relations to his fellows', the man, MacDonald says, 'would yet feel, doubtless would feel it the more [that is, feel it the more because he does his duty], that something was lacking to him'.[9] A man of perfect duty, he writes, would still lack the fulfilling of the 'deepest, closest, and strongest' relation possible: that between himself and God, his own maker and eternal Father.[10] 'Sooner or later', writes MacDonald, the 'soul, or heart, or spirit' or 'the man himself' realises 'that he needs some one above him, whom to obey, in whom to rest, from whom to seek deliverance from what in himself is despicable, disappointing, unworthy even of his own interest'.[11] In short, men need to be rightly related to more than simple 'duty'. According to MacDonald, they need to be rightly related to the One who is the root of goodness and the root of their own existence.

Lewis makes the same point in an essay where he writes how '"leading a decent life"' and '"being kind"' isn't 'quite the magnificent and all-important affair' that some might suppose it to be.[12] According to his understanding, a man, even if he could really be '"good"' on his 'own moral efforts', would still not have 'achieved the purpose for which [he was] created':

---

6 US, p. 472 (last quarter of par. 12 in the same sermon).

7 US, p. 472 (last quarter of par. 12 in the same). Lewis marks all of what has so far been quoted from 'The Truth' in his copy of the sermon.

8 US, pp. 472-473 (last quarter of par. 12 in the same).

9 US, pp. 473-474 (first quarter of par. 15 in the same).

10 US, p. 474 (second quarter of par. 15 in the same).

11 US, p. 475 (first and second quarter of par. 17 in the same sermon).

12 GDK, p. 112.

Mere *morality* is not the end of life. You were made for something quite different from that. J.S. Mill and Confucius (Socrates was much nearer the reality) simply didn't know what life is about [...] if they did they would know that 'a decent life' is mere machinery compared with the thing we men are really made for. Morality is indispensable: but the Divine Life, which gives itself to us and which calls us to be gods, intends for us something in which morality will be swallowed up.[13]

According to Lewis, we are to be 're-made' into something that is more than a mere 'rabbit'.[14] Both the 'worried, conscientious, ethical rabbit' and the 'cowardly and sensual rabbit' will be transformed into a creature rightly related to its God: 'a real Man, an ageless god, a son of God, strong, radiant, wise, beautiful, and drenched in joy'.[15]

Lewis expresses this belief in several ways in *The Pilgrim's Regress*. At one point John, the protagonist, tells the anti-romantic Mr. Humanist that one cannot defeat the Nazi-like Savage with mere secular, civil improvement: "'You see that Savage is scalding hot and you are cold. You must get heat to rival his heat. Do you think you can rout a million armed dwarfs by being 'not romantic'?'".[16] At another point Vertue, John's companion in the journey, becomes sick when he begins to doubt the wisdom of having left God out of the question. As he tells John how he almost decided to stay behind with cruel Savage, he reveals his own doubts as to whether his own personal moral improvement is all there is:

"Supposing there is no Landlord, no mountains in the East, no Island in the West, nothing but this country. A few weeks ago I would have said that all those things made no difference. But now—I don't know [...] there is the life I have been leading myself—marching on I don't know where. I can't see that there is any other good in it except the mere fact of imposing my will on my inclinations. And that seems to be good *training*, but training for what?"[17]

Vertue and John go on in the story to discover that there is indeed more than mere training for training's sake, more than a rootless morality. There is Someone to kneel to, to desire and to be filled with: God and the romantic beauty of his holiness. More will be said of this later in this chapter, but it is sufficient here to point out that Lewis followed MacDonald in pointing beyond mere morality. Unlocking the door to the hell of mere self, to them, did not simply mean walking into a dry desert of abstract justice, or personal morality, or secular ethics. To them it meant the first steps toward the unfathomable

13   GDK, p. 112.
14   GDK, p. 112.
15   GDK, p. 112.
16   REG, p. 102.
17   REG, pp. 105-106.

Plentitude they both believed God to be.

Beyond Mere Spirituality

With this observation made, however, it will be necessary to make another one that will lead us to the main business of this chapter and the metaphor that will be used to help accomplish this business. Though both MacDonald and Lewis were romantic, or religious, in believing that reality involved more than mere morality, both men believed it was not enough to simply believe in a God. However much God is more than dry goodness, he is never less than totally good in their view. Both men believed that bowing down before an idea of God that made him less than perfectly good was akin to devil worship.

MacDonald, for example, speaks in a sermon of the greatest heresy being 'that of dividing religion and righteousness'.[18] It is never good, MacDonald thought, to follow a God who is not all good. God may be much more than we understand, but he is never less than our best understandings of what goodness is. To him it is no excuse to argue that God's ways are higher than our ways.[19] As he writes in another sermon, 'I acknowledge no authority calling upon me to believe a thing of God, which I could not be a man and believe right in my fellow-man. I will accept no explanation of any way of God which explanation involves what I should scorn as false and unfair in a man'.[20] God's ways are indeed higher than man's, he believed, but then this always means 'More and higher justice and righteousness' that is 'required of him by himself', and 'greater nobleness, more penetrating sympathy; and *nothing* but what, if an honest man understood it, he would say was right'.[21] And so he urges his readers in another sermon to never go against the light of God-given conscience in believing evil of God, or worshipping a God who is not all good: 'Whatever seems to me darkness, that I will not believe of my God [...] To say that what our deepest conscience calls darkness may be light to God, is blasphemy; to say light in God and light in man are of differing kinds, is to speak against the spirit of light'.[22]

Lewis says much the same in *The Problem of Pain* when he argues that we can mean nothing by calling God good if we say that 'God's moral judgement differs from ours so that our "black" may be His "white"'.[23] If God is wholly different from what our conscience tells us, he argues, our calling him good 'is

---

18   US, p. 300 (third quarter of par. 6 in 'Life', second series).
19   See Isaiah 55.9.
20   US, p. 506 (third quarter of par. 14 in 'Justice', third series).
21   US, p. 507 (third quarter of par. 14 in the same sermon).
22   US, pp. 544-546 (first and second quarters, and then the third quarter, of par. 4 in 'Light', third series).
23   PP, p. 37.

really only to say "God is we know not what"'.[24] Lewis agrees with MacDonald that one has no business following such a God: 'an utterly unknown quality in God cannot give us moral grounds for loving or obeying Him. If He is not (in our sense) "good" we shall obey, if at all, only through fear—and should be equally ready to obey an omnipotent Fiend'.[25]

And so, according to Lewis, moving away from the mere self to 'the spiritual' or 'religion' may possibly make a man very much worse. He highlights this in *Reflections on the Psalms* within the context of a discussion of the many cursings found in the Psalms. He writes how a man who is religious or otherwise dedicated to 'some great Cause' outside himself can be either very much better or very much worse than the '"average sensual man"' dedicated only to his appetites, his safety and his self.[26] It is the man who has given himself to a higher something who can be made into something 'really fiendish': 'It is great men, potential saints, not little men, who become merciless fanatics. Those who are readiest to die for a cause may easily become those who are readiest to kill for it'.[27] As Lewis thinks, devotion to a 'God', simply because it is spiritual, supernatural or 'bigger' than one's self, may simply be a way of moving from the mere sensual or selfish self to the demonic self who adds '"Thus saith the Lord" to the expression of his own emotions or even his own opinions'.[28] As he writes: 'the Supernatural, entering a human soul, opens to it new possibilities of both good and evil. From that point the road branches: one way to sanctity, love, humility, the other to spiritual pride, self-righteousness, persecuting zeal. [...] Of all bad men religious bad men are the worst'.[29]

This belief is clearly manifested in Lewis's space trilogy, where he follows MacDonald in making the worst villains religious. In *That Hideous Strength* Filostrato the scientist and Straik the clergyman are both religious in their own ways. Straik's language is more obviously religious in the usual sense of the word, but it is clear that both men are dedicated to something outside themselves. They are both members of a society (the National Institute of Co-ordinated Experiments) dedicated to the 'conquest of organic life'.[30] Specifically, they are working to give life to a guillotined man's head in an effort to produce a kind of eternal life 'free from nature'.[31] Straik speaks of 'The Head' with eschatological zeal[32] and Filostrato, just as dedicated to the cause,

24 PP, p. 37.
25 PP, p. 37.
26 RPS, p. 24.
27 RPS, p. 24.
28 RPS, p. 26.
29 RPS, p. 27.
30 HS, p. 177.
31 HS, p. 177.
32 See HS, pp. 177-178.

sounds like Nietzsche or Hitler: "'Our Head is the first of the New Men [...] It is the beginning of all power'".[33] The story's action shows that they are both, like Uncle Andrew in *The Magician's Nephew*, willing to ignore conscience for the sake of the Cause. As Straik says earlier in the book:

"The Kingdom is going to arrive: in this world [...] The powers of science are an [...] irresistible instrument in His hand [...] That is what I couldn't get any of the churches to see. They are blinded. Blinded by their filthy rags of humanism, their culture and humanitarianism and liberalism, [...] And that is why I find myself joining with communists and materialists and anyone else who is really ready to expedite the coming. The feeblest of those people here has the tragic sense of life, the ruthlessness, the total commitment, the readiness to sacrifice all merely human values, which I could not find amid all the nauseating cant of the organised religions."[34]

Straik and the other members of N.I.C.E., ignoring that connection between a good God and men called conscience, are dedicated to supernatural power—the 'hideous strength' of the book's title.[35]

In the first book of the trilogy, *Out of the Silent Planet*, Lewis emphasises this greater possibility for wickedness by comparing Devine, a capitalist dedicated to his own greed, to Weston, a scientist religiously and ruthlessly dedicated to the survival and expansion of the human race. In Devine's mind there is little to be found other than "'fear and death and desire'".[36] Weston's will is "'less bent'" than Devine's, he is told, because "'It is not for yourself that you would do all this'".[37] Oyarsa, the ruling angel of the planet Malacandra, tells Weston, however, that he is therefore capable of greater evil:

"a bent *hnau*[38] can do more evil than a broken one. He [that is, the devil, Earth's fallen angel] has only bent you; but this Thin One who sits on the ground [that is, Devine] he has broken, for he has left him nothing but greed. He is now only a talking animal and in my world he could do no more evil than an animal."[39]

---

33   HS, pp. 177-178.
34   HS, p. 79.
35   The title is inspired by a passage from *Ane Dialog betuix Experuence and ane Courteour* (1553), by the Scottish poet Sir David Lyndsay (1490-1555): 'The Shadow of that hyddeous strength / sax myle and more of it is of length'. See HS, p. 3. The passage describes the biblical tower of Babel (Gen. 11.1-9).
36   OSP, p. 134.
37   OSP, p. 137.
38   A phonetical rendering of the Malacandrian word for a talking, rational, and moral being.
39   OSP, p. 139.

It is the devout Weston, of course, who is eventually possessed by a dark power and un-made into the Un-man in the second book of the trilogy.

What Lewis and MacDonald oppose to the 'broken'-ness of mere sensuality and selfishness on the one hand, and the 'bent' spirituality or religious wickedness on the other hand, is the 'sanctity, love, and humility'[40] of God as revealed in Christ. While admitting that a large measure of truth resides in most all religions, both MacDonald and Lewis firmly believed Christ to be a unique and superior revelation of who God is. MacDonald, for example, writes in a sermon how 'Every man who tries to obey the Master is my brother, whether he counts me such or not, and I revere him', but also that he dare not give in to any idea of God that appears to him as untrue or unworthy: 'but dare I give quarter to what I see to be a lie, because my brother believes it? The lie is not of God, whoever may hold it'.[41] Both authors believed Christ to be God's unique revelation of himself to men, though they believed all men were not equally convinced of, or knowingly following, the truth of this revelation. However aware MacDonald and Lewis were of other pictures of God, they wrote over seventy books between them emphasising the Christian picture of God found in Christ. If they have warned their readers away from the hell of self, it is to this idea or reality of God that they urged them to. It will be impossible in this space, of course, to fully describe and explain all that MacDonald and Lewis wrote about this God and his goodness in their seventy or so books. But an effort to suggest and sum up some of the more important and distinctive elements of their depictions of God's character, and its relation to human goodness, will now be made with the help of a metaphor.

A Useful Metaphor

Lewis, in the preface to his anthology of MacDonald's writings, speaks of the 'Divine Sonship' as the 'key-conception which unites all the different elements' of MacDonald's thought.[42] Lewis writes of how he knew of 'hardly any other writer who seems to be closer, or more continually close, to the Spirit of Christ Himself'.[43] The result of this closeness, he writes, produces in MacDonald's writings a 'Christ-like union of tenderness and severity'.[44] 'Nowhere else outside the New Testament have I found terror and comfort so intertwined', he

---

40   RPS, p. 27. See p. 214, above.

41   US, pp. 531-532 (fourth quarter of par. 53 in 'Justice', third series). Lewis marks this and includes it in his anthology (ANTH, reading 210). See also George MacDonald, *The Miracles of Our Lord* (Whitehorn: Johannesen, 1995), p. 282; GDK, p. 102; and MC, pp. 43, 176. *Miracles of Our Lord* first published in 1870.

42   ANTH, p. xxx.

43   ANTH, pp. xxx-xxxi.

44   ANTH, p. xxxi.

writes.[45] It will be the purpose of his chapter to show how Lewis is right about the Divine Sonship uniting MacDonald's writings, and also how it unites all of Lewis's writing on the character of God and his goodness.

Lewis, in his first major work of criticism, *The Allegory of Love*, speaks of the closing scene from Gower's *Confessio Amantis*[46] as 'one of these rare passages in which medieval allegory rises to myth, in which the symbols, though fashioned to represent mere single concepts, take on new life and represent rather the principles—not otherwise accessible—which unite whole classes of concepts'.[47] As the different symbols in Gower's closing passage, according to Lewis, suggest many senses of 'death as new life',[48] so the many senses of the word 'chivalry' will be used here to help throw light on what MacDonald and Lewis thought and wrote of God's character.

From the outset it would seem a fitting symbol to use. Both authors' stories and poems are full of battles, lords, ladies, and distressed damsels in need of heroes on horseback. But it is a very short essay Lewis wrote for *Time and Tide* in 1940 that will help us understand best how the different senses of chivalry help illustrate MacDonald's and Lewis's ideas of God.

In this wartime article Lewis argues for the necessity of chivalry, but first mentions the different senses of the word. It can mean, he writes, either 'heavy cavalry', 'giving a woman a seat in a train', or the distinct medieval concept that married severity and tenderness together in the ideal knight.[49] All of these senses will be used in this chapter, but it is especially important to lay hold of Lewis's understanding of the medieval ideal. The important thing about the ideal, he writes, is the 'double demand it makes on human nature'.[50] As he explains:

> The knight is a man of blood and iron, a man familiar with the sight of smashed faces and the ragged stumps of lopped-off limbs; he is also a demure, almost a maidenlike, guest in hall, a gentle, modest, unobtrusive man. He is not a compromise or happy mean between ferocity and meekness; he is fierce to the *n*th and meek to the *n*th'.[51]

As an example of this paradox Lewis turns to Sir Ector's words to the dead Lancelot, 'the greatest of all the imaginary knights': '"Thou wert the meekest man that ever ate in hall among ladies; and thou wert the sternest knight to

---

45   ANTH, p. xxxi.
46   John Gower (1330-1408) completed *Confessio* in 1390, revising it in 1393.
47   AL, pp. 220-221.
48   AL, p. 221.
49   C.S. Lewis, *Present Concerns* (San Diego: Harcourt Brace & Company, 1986), p.13.
50   PRC, p. 13.
51   PRC, p. 13.

thy mortal foe that ever put spear in the rest"'.[52]

When thinking of this mixture of the hard with the soft, the reader of MacDonald may naturally think of how his God-like characters are very feminine indeed. North Wind of *At the Back of the North Wind* and Queen Irene, the great-great-grandmother of the two Curdie books, immediately spring to mind. William Raeper in his biography has provided an excellent account of the feminine qualities in MacDonald's idea of God without making the mistake of tying MacDonald too closely to any feminist revolt against that great bugbear spoken of in postmodern circles today: patriarchy.[53] MacDonald's depictions of God, as Raeper notes, are all softer, gentler and humbler than the Scotch Calvinist idea of God he was taught as a boy.[54] As Raeper also notes, MacDonald believed that both 'men and women were born out of the heart of God, not *ex nihilo* as traditionally held by the church'.[55] Since women and femininity itself could have no other source but the heart of God, it must follow that God himself is not simply a himself as some understand the term. He is the heart of all womanly tenderness and therefore infinitely more tender than any woman whom he creates with a capacity for tenderness.

But MacDonald, a father and grandfather who sported one of the most patriarchal of beards, never forgot about God as Father. He never believed God was less fatherly simply because he was also the source of all good

---

52 PRC, p. 13. Sir Thomas Malory, *Le Morte Darthur* (1485), XXI, xii [from W. Hooper's note in PRC, p. 13]. Lewis, of course, was a professional literary critic who was very familiar with the medieval ideal of chivalry and manifestations of it in medieval and renaissance literature [See AL, especially chp. 1, 'Courtly Love']. As one of the most influential medievalists of his day, he would have been familiar with chivalry, and images of chivalry, had he never read any of MacDonald's stories. The argument in this chapter, it is important to note, is not that MacDonald was the sole influence upon Lewis in this regard, but that he was one important influence on his fiction, and that the metaphor of chivalry is useful in helping to explain how both authors depict God's character. Where there is a high probability of direct influence, it is duly noted in this chapter. But every instance of likeness should not be taken to indicate direct influence of MacDonald upon Lewis, though the likeness may still be worth mentioning. And it would be an error to suppose that Lewis's critical understanding of chivalry was influenced significantly by MacDonald. Both were familiar with medieval and renaissance literature, it is clear, but it is also clear that Lewis, not MacDonald, was the professional expert on the subject of chivalry. This critical expertise does not mean that Lewis was any better at depicting chivalrous things in his fiction, of course, but it is important to distinguish here between literary depictions and critical expertise.

53 See chp. 24, 'God our Father and Mother—MacDonald's Theology' (RAEP, pp. 237-263).

54 See RAEP, pp. 242-243.

55 RAEP, p. 243.

motherhood. As Raeper observes, MacDonald most often presents God as a grandmother, 'that is, Grand Mother' and not simply as a woman.[56] The age and frequent severity of both North Wind and Great-Great-Grandmother in the Curdie books, for example, reminds us that these characters are not simply femininity writ large. North Wind can appear as the most lovely and feminine of mothers, but she can also appear as a stern giant or frightful wolf. Curdie, when he looks upon his Great Grandmother, sees a 'tall, strong woman— plainly very old, but as grand as she was old, and only *rather* severe-looking', a character with motherly tenderness *and* patriarchal grandeur.[57] As Raeper has quoted from *Adela Cathcart*, MacDonald has called God 'Him who is Father and Mother both in one'.[58]

False Gods

We will return later to consider ways in which MacDonald and Lewis combine tenderness and severity together in their books, but we move now to focus on the distinctive tenderness, or softness, of MacDonald's conception of God and how Lewis was influenced by it.

This brings us again to the symbol of chivalry. Not only does it suggest the marriage of severity and tenderness, but also one specific example of the tenderness: the knight kneeling in humble submission before his lord or lady. This kneeling, in turn, suggests something of the eternal Sonship and Fatherhood which both authors believed to be the root of all tender love. All that can be called feminine, humble or child-like, they believed, exists only because there is a gentleness and humility in what the Father and Son have been from all eternity.

Jesus Christ, the eternal Son come into time and space on Earth, MacDonald explains in a sermon, is the 'express image of the Father' by which humans—'his imperfect images'—'read and understand' who God is.[59] As he writes in another sermon, one 'whose heart can perceive the essential in Christ' has 'the essence of the Father' because 'the Son is as the Father'.[60] Regarding Christ's miracles MacDonald writes how Christ 'came to reveal his Father in miniature', to 'do briefly and sharply' before men's eyes what the Father 'does so widely, so grandly that they transcend the vision of men'.[61] Christ's changing water to wine and producing bread and fish for the multitudes, for

---

56   RAEP, p. 261.
57   P&C, p. 30.
58   RAEP, p. 262.
59   US, p. 294 (last quarter of penultimate paragraph of 'Abba, Father!', second series).
60   US, p. 9 (third quarter of par. 13 in 'The Child in the Midst', first series).
61   MOL, p. 234.

example, are only sped-up and miniature versions, with human hands, of what God the Father does 'in making the corn to grow in the valleys, and the grapes to drink the sunlight on the hill-sides of the world, with all their infinitudes of tender gradation and delicate mystery of birth'.[62]

It is clear that Lewis thought similarly when we read a passage in *Miracles* that seems to imitate and elaborate on this thought of MacDonald's on Christ's miracles. Regarding the conversion of water into wine, Lewis writes how it 'proclaims that the God of all wine is present':

> Every year, as part of the Natural order, God makes wine. He does so by creating a vegetable organism that can turn water, soil, and sunlight into a juice which will, under proper conditions, become wine [...] Once, and in one year only, God, now incarnate [in Christ] short circuits the process: makes wine in a moment: uses earthenware jars instead of vegetable fibres to hold the water. But uses them to do what He is always doing.[63]

And with the multiplication of fish to feed the five thousand, Christ 'does close and small, under His human hands, a workman's hands, what He has always been doing in the seas, the lakes and the little brooks'.[64]

MacDonald and Lewis believed, therefore, that Christ the Son was no innovator in anything he was or did. He always showed men what God in eternity always is. As MacDonald wrote in a sermon, 'Our Lord never thought of being original'[65]; and as Lewis wrote about Christ in *Reflections on the Psalms*: 'The Light which has lightened every man from the beginning may shine more clearly but cannot change. The Origin cannot suddenly start being, in the popular sense of the word, "original"'.[66]

But what Christ may have revealed of God can certainly be seen as original in another sense: in relation to other, less clear ideas of who God is. Though MacDonald and Lewis wrote many words on how Christ's moral teachings square with other moral teachings, especially 'morality between man and man',[67] they are both quite clear in their belief that Christ's revelation of the character of God in himself is an advance over all other ideas. If Christ is the eternal and perfect Son of God, there can of course be no advance from his eternally perfect perspective—only a progressive working out or unrolling in time of that perfect character's timeless purposes. But in contrast with other ideas of God that do not come directly from the incarnate Origin himself,

---

62 MOL, p. 235.

63 MIR, p. 136.

64 MIR, p. 137.

65 US, p. 128 (first paragraph of 'Love Thy Neighbour', first series). Lewis marks and underlines in his copy.

66 RPS, p. 23.

67 MC, p. 78.

God's direct revelation of himself can certainly be seen as an advance, or 'original'.

In this context we can return to Lewis's essay on chivalry in which he speaks of the 'novelty and originality of the medieval demand upon human nature'.[68] Homer's Achilles, he writes, 'knows nothing of the demand that the brave should also be the modest and the merciful', killing men as they 'cry for quarter' and taking prisoners to kill at his leisure. Neither do the heroes of the Icelandic Sagas, Atilla, or even the Romans, who led their gallant prisoners of war 'through the streets for a show, and cut their throats in cellars when the show was over'.[69]

Just as Lewis describes the medieval ideal of chivalry as introducing courtesy to the cruel warrior, so do MacDonald's and Lewis's understandings and depictions of a humble and tender God—a child-like and even maiden-like God—contrast sharply with other views of God they had known of.

MacDonald, unsurprisingly, contrasts the humble and tender God he believed in with the old Scotch Calvinist idea of God that he grew up with. In one sermon he writes how one of his earliest memories is of 'beginning to be at strife with' such a 'false system'.[70] As an adult he continued to scorn it, if not its believers, 'as heartily in the name of Christ, as I scorn it in the name of righteousness'.[71]

One reason he scorns it so is its doctrine of predestination which teaches that God is only Father to some and not to others and therefore loves only a chosen few.[72] Another reason he gives is its saying that God punishes for the sake of punishment and that he takes pleasure in seeing the wicked suffer.[73] But all of MacDonald's objections can be summed up by observing that he thought the Scotch Calvinist God much too proud a being to be the humble God he believed in. The reason he loathed this picture of God so much is because it ascribes to God himself what MacDonald believed to be the one principle of hell: Pride. Both the intensity of MacDonald's abhorrence, and the reasons for it, can be clearly seen in these words near the end of a sermon entitled 'Justice': 'They yield the idea of the Ancient of Days, "the glad creator", and put in its stead a miserable, puritanical martinet of a God, caring not for righteousness, but for his rights; not for the eternal purities but the goody proprieties. The prophets of such a God take all the glow, all the hope, all the

---

68   PRC, p. 14.
69   PRC, p. 14.
70   US, pp. 385-386 (par. 4 in 'The Truth', second series).
71   US, p. 386 (same paragraph in the same sermon).
72   See US, pp. 127 (par. 9 in 'The Hands of the Father', first series), 131 (par. 7 in 'Love Thy Neighbour', first series).
73   See US, pp. 509-510, 514, 517 (paragraphs 27-28, the third and fourth quarters of par. 31, and the second through fourth quarters of par. 38 in 'Justice', third series).

colour, all the worth, out of life on earth, and offer you instead what they call eternal bliss—a pale, tearless hell'.[74]

The Calvinistic idea of God, MacDonald believed, was very much off the mark because it presented God as being obsessed with his own sovereignty, power and dignity. As he writes in another sermon, Calvinistic theologians have 'misrepresented' God as 'a great King on a grand throne, thinking how grand he is, and making it the business of his being and the end of his universe to keep up his glory, wielding the bolts of Jupiter against them that take his name in vain'.[75] The 'simplest peasant who loves his children and his sheep', MacDonald writes, could be said to be a truer type of God in comparison, if it were not for the fact that this 'monstrosity of a monarch' is an altogether 'false' picture.[76]

Unfavourable portrayals of this 'Scotch God, whose nature was summed up in a series of words beginning with *omni*',[77] spring up on all sides in MacDonald's stories, but especially so in his Scottish novels. A belief in such a God is what plagues Murdoch Malison in *Alec Forbes*, for example. It is the driving force behind his tyrannical rule of his classroom. As he believes God to be, so he rules his students: with a cold heart and a sovereign tawse. 'Murder Malison', as his students call him,[78] pleasures in the law 'irrespective of right and wrong', glories in punishment for his own dignity's sake, and chooses his favourites according to the 'inexplicable' workings of his will.[79] It is only after he cripples a weak orphan that he realises how ungodly his shadowy character really is.

But it is another of his Scottish novels, *Robert Falconer*, in which MacDonald expresses his hatred for this old Scotch idea of God most thoroughly. It is stern Mrs. Falconer's belief in such a God that afflicts both her and her grandson Robert. Early in the story, for example, Robert by accident overhears a prayer of his grandmother's to this kind of God. He listens in terror to her agonising prayer for her son Andrew, Robert's long-lost father. It is clear that her tender, motherly love for her son is struggling against, while also trying to pray to, a God who has predestined that some should never taste his mercy and forgiveness. MacDonald highlights this tension with the contrast between the woman's homely Scottish vernacular and her belief in the proud, haughty Scotch God:

74　US, p. 540 (last quarter of the penultimate paragraph in the same sermon). Lewis marks.
75　US, p. 15 (par. 30 in 'The Child in the Midst', first series).
76　US, p. 15 (first two quarters of par. 30 in the same sermon).
77　GIB, p. 195.
78　AFH, p. 48.
79　AFH, p. 117.

"To think o' my bairnie that I cairriet i' my ain body, that sookit my briests, and lech i' my face—to think o' 'im bein' a reprobate! O Lord! Cudna he be eleckit yet? Is there *nae* turnin' o' thy decrees? [...] the torments o' that place! And the reik that gangs up for ever an' ever, smorin' (*smothering*) the stars! And my Andrew doon i' the hert o' 't cryin'! And me no able to win till[80] him! O Lord! I *canna* say thy will be done [...] I beg yer pardon. I'm near oot o' my min'."[81]

Devotion to this kind of God makes the atmosphere of his grandmother's house austere and always 'douce', that is, sedate, sober and respectable. There are fits of tenderness that break out from her heart of love, but her theology represses it and even threatens to 'harden her heart' toward her lost son Andrew.[82] Her 'rebellious mother heart', the narrator tells us, is constantly being pulled down from its 'own large light' by the 'glimmer from the phosphorescent brains of theologians' that threaten to obscure the words and truth of Christ.[83]

We are also told how a belief in this sort of God affects Robert's behaviour. He strictly keeps the Sabbath by going to church no less than three times on Sunday and 'never walking a step save to or from church'; never saying a word 'upon any subject unconnected with religion', especially 'theoretical' religion; never reading 'any but religious books'; never whistling; never thinking of his lost fiddle.[84] All of these 'vain endeavours', the narrator tells us explicitly, deny God 'altogether as the maker of the world' and as the creator of Robert's own 'soul and heart and brain', and are an attempt to worship him 'as a capricious demon'.[85] This idea of God also suppresses poetry, dancing, play acting, all music but 'the most unmusical of psalm-singing', and many more '"wardly vainities an' abominations"'.[86] Mrs. Falconer, for example, burns Robert's 'bonny leddy' of a violin.[87] When Robert discovers this, she is sitting beside the burning mass of shriveled strings and wood, 'stern as a Druidess' and 'feeding her eyes with grim satisfaction on the detestable sacrifice'.[88] As Robert flees from this scene in agony and horror, he imagines his grandmother as a haunting symbol of the horrible Scotch God: 'There was no escaping her. She was the all-seeing eye personified—the eye of the God of the theologians of his country, always

---

80   That is, allowed to go to.
81   RF, p. 44.
82   RF, p. 91.
83   RF, p. 92.
84   RF, p. 78.
85   RF, p. 78.
86   RF, p. 95.
87   See RAEP, p. 19, on how Mrs. Falconer is inspired by MacDonald's own grandmother, who actually did burn one of her son's violins.
88   RF, 151.

searching out the evil, and refusing to acknowledge the good'.[89] Though he knows his granny's heart isn't cruel, he flees from the woman whose cruel theology has burnt his 'bonny leddy', and seeks out Mary St. John, the novel's chief human manifestation of feminine beauty and tenderness.

Mrs. Falconer's 'crabbed religion' sends young Robert into frequent bouts of gloom and threatens to crush all of his child-like wonder and joy.[90] He dreams of a life at sea,[91] or anything that will help him escape life under the shadow of such a God, but this proud God does not cooperate:

> God did not heed. He leaned over the world, a dark care, an immovable fate, bearing down with the weight of his presence all aspiration, all budding delights of children and young persons: all must crouch before him, and uphold his glory with the sacrificial death of every impulse, every admiration, every lightness of heart, every bubble of laughter.[92]

Even worse for Robert is the probability that this God will not punish for these things because 'they came not within the sphere of his condescension, were not worth his notice'.[93] Later, Robert forbears knocking on Mary St. John's door partly because he suspects that 'violins, pianos, moonlight, and lovely women were distasteful to the over-ruling Fate, and obnoxious to the vengeance stored in the grey cloud of his providence'.[94]

Robert eventually abandons his grandmother's God, though not his grandmother. He turns his back on this aloof, proud and vengeful 'monstrosity of a monarch'[95] and leaves town, searching for his father Andrew and, as it turns out, his real heavenly Father. Like MacDonald himself he turns away from any Great Almighty who is not also all loving: 'I love the one God seen in the face of Jesus Christ. From all copies of Jonathan Edwards's[96] portrait

---

89 RF, p. 152.

90 RF, p. 152.

91 As MacDonald himself did as a boy. See RAEP, pp. 38-39.

92 RF, p. 156.

93 RF, p. 156.

94 RF, p. 164.

95 US, p. 15 (last quarter of par. 30 in 'The Child in the Midst', first series).

96 Jonathan Edwards (1703-1758), American Puritan minister and religious philosopher who contributed to the 'Great Awakening' revival in 1740 and who fused an 'orthodox Calvinism with Lockean psychology and Newtonian physics' [Ian Ousby, (ed.), *Wordsworth Companion to Literature in English* (Cambridge: Wordsworth, 1992), p. 288]. His being a staunch Calvinist and something of a Lockean/Newtonian rationalist makes him two things that MacDonald reacted strongly against and helps one understand why his portrait of God is so loathed by MacDonald. See Edwards's sermon 'Sinners in the Hands of an Angry God' (1741): 'And though he will know that you cannot bear the weight of omnipotence treading upon you, yet he will not regard that, but he will crush you under his feet without mercy; he will crush out

of God, however faded by time, however softened by the use of less glaring pigments, I turn with loathing'.[97]

We see in other writings of MacDonald's how following an aloof, untender and proud God can actually transform the 'me' and 'mine' of individual hell into the 'us' and 'ours' of a hellish community. Devoted members of such a community may have been taken out of themselves, but it does not follow, he thought, that they have moved much closer to Love Himself.

MacDonald is very clear about this throughout his last collection of published sermons. In one of these he refers to Christ's reading of a portion of Old Testament Scripture to the congregation of the synagogue in his home town of Nazereth, and its result: the wrathful rejection of Jesus by his fellow townsmen.[98] MacDonald suggests that these religious folk of Nazareth were stirred to wrath, in part, by where in Isaiah Jesus stopped reading. He closed the book, or scroll, before reading the portion of Isaiah that portrays the coming redeemer as proclaiming 'the day of vengeance of our God'.[99] MacDonald writes that Jesus's listeners were not interested in a Messiah who was not interested in vengeance, especially vengeance against their unholy oppressors on Earth. Preaching to the poor, healing the broken hearted, preaching deliverance and declaring the acceptable year of the Lord[100] were all well and good, but these Nazarenes, writes MacDonald, wanted a Messiah on their own terms: one who would throw off the yoke of their political oppressors and return the Israelites to the dignity they deserved as God's chosen. At one point he paraphrases what he imagines to be the thoughts of the congregation. It will be noticed how similar this paraphrase is to the creed of hell in his sermon 'Kingship'.[101] The pronouns 'us' and 'our' appear here as frequently as the 'me' and 'mine' of that declaration. I italicize the pronouns here, as MacDonald often italicised the pronouns in 'Kingship', to highlight this similarity:

> "These things [that is, Jesus's idea of what kind of Messiah he would be] are good, it is true, but they must come after *our* way. *We* must have the promise to *our* fathers fulfilled—that *we* shall rule the world, the chosen of God, the children of Abraham and Israel. *We* want to be a free people, manage *our* own affairs, live in plenty, and do as *we* please.

your blood, and make it fly, and it shall be sprinkled on his garments, so as to stain all his rainment [...] when the great angry God hath risen up and executed his awful vengeance on the poor sinner [...] then will God call upon the whole universe to behold that awful majesty and mighty power that is to be seen in it'. Compare to Isaiah 63. 1-6.

97 US, p. 540 (last paragraph of 'Justice', third series).
98 See Luke 4.16-30. MacDonald quotes verses 14-21 to begin his sermon.
99 See Isaiah 61.2b.
100 See Isaiah 61.1-2.
101 See pp. 164-165, above.

Liberty alone can ever cure the woes of which you speak. *We* do not need to be better; *we* are well enough. Give *us* riches and honour, and keep *us* content with *ourselves*, that *we* may be satisfied with *our* own likeness, and thou shalt be the Messiah."[102]

The one principle of hell—'I am my own'—has simply been changed to 'we are our own'. Thinking of themselves as God's chosen, they have added 'Thus saith the Lord' onto the philosophy of hell.[103] As MacDonald writes in the same sermon, 'Their Messiah would make of their nation the redeemed of the Lord, themselves the favourites of his court, and the tyrants of the world!'.[104] Like the predestinarian Scotch Omni-God described in his novels, the Nazarenes' idea of God stands in stark contrast to the God that MacDonald sees revealed in Christ:

> The very beams of their ugly religion were party-spirit, exclusiveness, and pride in the fancied favour of God for them only of all nations: to hint at the possibility of a revelation of the glory of God to a stranger[105]; for more, to hint that a stranger might be fitter to receive such a revelation than a Jew, was an offense reaching to the worst insult; and it was cast in their teeth by a common man of their own city![106]

Jesus's mission of humility, servanthood, and forgiveness of sins may have been God's mission, but this tenderness of God was not going to be *their* mission, as MacDonald writes to close the sermon:

> The men of Nazareth could have believed in Jesus as their saviour from the Romans; as their saviour from their sins they could not believe in him, for they loved their sins. The king of heaven came to offer them a share in his kingdom; but they were not poor in spirit, and the kingdom of heaven was not for them. Gladly would they have inherited the earth; but they were not meek, and the earth was for the lowly children of the perfect Father[107]

It can be proven in many ways how Lewis followed MacDonald in this in both his fiction and non-fiction. We have already seen in *Reflections on the Psalms* where he mentions the danger of spiritual or religious pride in his discussion of the cursings in the Psalms.[108] He mentions something

---

102 HG, pp. 69-70. Compare US, p. 495 (first half of par. 3 in 'Kingship', third series).
103 See RPS, p. 26; p. 214, above.
104 HG, p. 73.
105 As Christ goes on to do in Luke 4.23-27. See MacDonald's exposition of this, HG, pp. 74-75.
106 HG, p. 76.
107 HG, p. 78. See Mat. 5.3, 5.5, 11.29 for the meekness of Christ and his kingdom. See also Mat. 21.5, Zech. 9.9, Phil. 2.5-8.
108 See RPS, pp. 17-28; p. 214, above.

very similar in his discussion of friendship in *The Four Loves*. Friendship, the most spiritual of loves, he writes,[109] can go wrong—like religious or spiritual devotions—if it forgets to humble itself before God's unconditional love. Just because friendship is 'spiritual and therefore faces a subtler enemy', Lewis writes, it needs, more so than other loves, the help of Love Divine if it is to 'remain sweet'.[110] Because friends choose each other on grounds other than natural necessity, the temptation, according to Lewis, is to think that their group, by their 'native powers', have 'ascended above the rest of mankind'.[111] They may indeed have been given qualities or insights that other groups lack, but the danger is, especially in 'an explicitly religious friendship', that the group forgets that the distinct beauties they discover in one another are no greater than the distinct, God-given beauties 'of a thousand other men'.[112]

Friendships must of necessity exclude, Lewis writes: 'People who bore one another should meet seldom; people who interest one another, often'.[113] The danger is when the 'easy step' is taken from the 'innocent and necessary act of excluding' to the '"spirit"' and 'degrading pleasure' of Pridefull exclusivity: 'We shall be a *coterie* that exists for the sake of being a *coterie*; a little self-elected (and therefore absurd) aristocracy, basking in the moonshine of our collective self-approval'.[114]

Lewis's fiction, like MacDonald's, portrays the hideousness of spiritual devotions that have little of God's humble love in them. We've already shown this with examples from his space trilogy,[115] but the instance which best reveals his affinity to MacDonald is his portrayal of the Calormenes and their devotion to the god Tash in two of his Narnia books. As MacDonald contrasts the lack of humility and tender love in the Calvinist God with something better in his Scottish novels, so in *The Horse and His Boy* and *The Last Battle* does Lewis contrast devotion to Tash with all true devotion to Aslan.

Many readers will be excused for thinking Lewis to be anti-Arab in his portrayal of the Calormenes. All readers will notice that the Calormenes are in fact very Arab-like. They inhabit a sun-baked land south of Narnia. They use crescents for money and swing scimitars in battle. Their cities bear names like Azim Balda, Tehishbaan, and Tashbaan. They themselves are called by names like Arsheesh, Emeth, Alimash and Rabadash. They go by titles such as Tarkaan, Tarkeena and Grand Vizier. Like the Turks, they have famous

---

109   As Lewis puts it, 'the least natural of loves; the least instinctive, organic, biological, gregarious and necessary' [4L, p. 58].
110   4L, p. 88.
111   4L, p. 89.
112   4L, p. 89.
113   4L, p. 81.
114   4L, p. 86.
115   See above, pp. 214-216.

baths.[116] They have a very formal, dignified way of speaking, especially when telling stories.[117]

But the accusation that Lewis was anti-Arab is as incredible as would be the claim that MacDonald was anti-Scot. Lewis's Emeth, a Calormene in *The Last Battle*, like MacDonald's Mrs. Falconer, is portrayed as honourable, virtuous, and an honest seeker after God and his ways. He is a courageous warrior who looks forward to battle with the Narnians until he becomes disillusioned with the dishonourable methods and trickery his commander has resorted to.[118] Even proud Aravis in *The Horse and His Boy* is not without her good qualities. She is courageous in the midst of those who seek only ease.[119] And there are many wicked Narnians, Archenlanders and Earthlings in the Narnia tales to go along with any Calormene villainy. Any anti-Arab charge is simply unsupportable.

An entirely credible charge, however, is that Lewis is against the Islamic conception, or at least some elements inherent in middle-eastern or eastern conceptions, of God. That is, to the degree that Islam or other devotions present an aloof, proud and merely majestic God, Lewis is against it. It is a charge that he is as guilty of as MacDonald is guilty of loathing Calvinism's 'miserable, puritanical martinet of a God'.[120] Again, one must be careful to distinguish between what these writers believed to be pernicious doctrine and its effects, and those devoted to such doctrines. Both MacDonald and Lewis thought it was entirely possible, even if more difficult, for believers of such doctrines to truly serve God. As MacDonald writes in a sermon:

> I would rather have a man holding, as numbers of you do, what seem to me the most obnoxious untruths, opinions the most irreverent and gross, if at the same time he *lived* in the faith of the Son of God, that is, trusted in God as the Son of God trusted in him, than I would have a man with every one of whose formulas of belief I utterly coincided, but who knew nothing of a daily life and walk with God.[121]

---

116 See HB, p. 106. A 'Turk' is not synonymous with an 'Arab', of course. Anti-Arab is perhaps the best term available here to describe the charge. It is not perfect, for Lewis's depiction of the Calormenes cannot be said to be exclusively Arab-like. They are a fictional people who share characteristics with many mid-eastern and eastern peoples, past and present.

117 Calormenes, for example, invariably say 'the sun appeared dark in my eyes' instead of 'I despaired'. Prince Rabadash addresses his father, the Tisroc, as 'Oh-my-father-and-oh-the-delight-of-my-eyes' (HB, p. 117).

118 See LB, pp. 200-202.

119 See HB, pp. 107-108.

120 US, p. 540 (penultimate paragraph of 'Justice', third series).

121 US, pp. 389-390 (last half of par. 9 in 'The Truth in Jesus', second series).

One may 'hold doctrines of devils' and yet still be 'a child of God', just as one can hold 'the doctrines of Christ and his Apostles' and still be a child of 'the world' or even 'the devil'.[122]

Lewis echoes this thinking in *Mere Christianity*,[123] and we have seen how his sympathetic portrayal of Emeth echoes MacDonald's portrayal of Mrs. Falconer. He makes the point explicit, however, in the penultimate chapter of *The Last Battle* when Emeth finds that Tash and Aslan are not the same at all. Tash, the god Emeth has sought to serve since boyhood, is revealed to be a monstrous devil, and he discovers that Aslan, the Golden Lion he had grown up hating, is actually the real 'Glorious One'.[124] He fears for his life when he meets Aslan, having served the wrong god for so long, until Aslan comforts him with words like these:

> "Child, all the service thou hast done to Tash, I account as service done to me [...] if any man swear by Tash and keep his oath for the oath's sake, it is by me that he has truly sworn, though he knew it not, and it is I who reward him. And if any man do a cruelty in my name, then, though he says the name Aslan, it is Tash whom he serves and by Tash his deed is accepted [...] Beloved [...] unless thy desire had been for me thou wouldest not have sought so long and so truly."[125]

But still, we have learned that both authors believed it is important what kind of a God one believed in and followed, and that they did not think all ideas of God equally worthy. They both believed that some doctrines of God, or portions of doctrines, were loathsome and potentially poisonous. They both spilled considerable amounts of ink in their fiction and non-fiction attacking any idea of God that viewed him as proud, untender and unloving. It is no mistake that MacDonald wrote so much against Calvinistic ideas of God, and it is perhaps no mistake that Lewis's Arab-like Calormenes are portrayed as worshipping a devil. Tash is clearly a fiend, even if all Calormene devotion to him is not fiendish.[126]

---

122 US, p. 390 (last quarter of par. 9 in the same sermon).
123 See MC, pp. 176-177.
124 LB, p. 205.
125 LB, pp. 205-206.
126 It is only speculation, but there may be clues to show that Lewis's target was not simply the Islamic conception of God, but all conceptions of God that he saw as proud and cruel misrepresentations. The Calormenes do resemble many Muslim peoples, but then the first three letters of their name, 'Cal', are the same three letters of the word 'Calvin', or 'Calvinism'. The province of Calormen that Aravis runs away from, 'Calavar' (HB, p. 37), shares an additional 'v'. Similarities of emphasis (e.g., God's omnipotence, majesty and predestination) in Calvinist and Muslim teaching, and Lewis's acknowledged opposition to such emphasis [See, for example, one of his letters in C.S. Lewis (W.H. Lewis and W. Hooper, eds.), *Letters of C.S. Lewis* (San

The distinction between Tash and the Christ-like Aslan is clearly emphasised by Aslan himself during Emeth's encounter with the Lion. Although he counts Emeth's honest devotion to Tash as true service to him, he does not react kindly when Emeth mentions the Ape's preaching that he and Tash are one. As Emeth's account tells us,

> "The Lion growled so that the earth shook (but his wrath was not against me) and said, It is false. Not because he and I are one, but because we are opposites, I take to me the services which thou hast done to him. For I and he are of such different kinds that no service which is vile can be done to me, and none which is not vile can be done to him."[127]

It is significant, and fits well with our symbol of chivalry, that a lamb as well as a lion expresses Lewis's reaction to the kind of God that Tash is. Earlier in *The Last Battle*, when the Ape is attempting to convince the Narnians that Tash and Aslan are one, a gentle lamb speaks up for Aslan, and against Tash: "'They have a god called Tash. They say he has four arms and the head of a vulture. They kill Men on his altar. I don't believe there's any such person as Tash. But if there was, how could Aslan be friends with him?'".[128] And so we see Lewis expressing, through the words of a great Lion *and* a meek lamb, his idea of a 'chivalrous' God who is both strong and tender, but never simply strong, and not at all proud or cruel. The Ape jumps up and spits at the lamb, calling it a "'Baby!'" and "'Silly little bleater!'" and telling it to "'Go home to your mother and drink milk'".[129] But not everyone reacts to the lamb's reasoning in such a way. Tirian, king of the Narnians, speaks up and tells Shift that he lies "'damnably'", and means to go on and ask 'how the terrible god Tash who fed on the blood of his people could possibly be the same as the good Lion by whose blood all Narnia was saved'—until he is struck down by a few Calormenes.[130] The whole point of Lewis's depiction of Tash and devotion to Tash seems to be uttered by Jewel the unicorn, who whispers into the king's ear these words about Emeth: "'By the Lion's Mane, I almost love this young warrior, Calormene though he be. He is worthy of a better god than Tash'".[131] What Jewel says here of Emeth is essentially the same thing that MacDonald expresses throughout *Robert Falconer* concerning Mrs. Falconer. Both of these characters, according to both authors, are worthy of a better God.

Diego: Harcourt Brace and Company), pp. 339-340 (18 Feb. 1940)] do not make this possibility any less probable.
127 LB, p. 205.
128 LB, p. 40.
129 LB, p. 40.
130 LB, p. 42.
131 LB, pp. 140-141.

Lewis also followed MacDonald in depicting the ill effects of following such proud gods. Tash, "'the inexorable, the irresistible'", like the inexorable and irresistible Scotch God of MacDonald's novels, encourages neither humility nor true love amongst his followers. They invariably display the courage and severity of a proud warrior, but in general very little of the meekness and mercy of the ideal knight.

The capital of Calormen, Tashbaan, for example, is imposing and proud. There is little meekness to its beauty. Strong, solemn and frightening horns that seem to sway the earth with their throbbing blasts signal the opening of the city gates.[132] The finer streets of the city contain great statues of Calormene gods and heroes who are 'mostly impressive rather than agreeable to look at'.[133] The one traffic regulation is that everyone less important has to make way for everyone more important 'unless you want a cut from a whip or punch from the butt end of a spear'.[134] The manner of some visiting Narnians—their walking with a swing, letting arms and shoulders go free, chatting, laughing, whistling, and readiness 'to be friends with anyone who was friendly'—is contrasted with the 'grave and serious' manner of the city's inhabitants.[135] After leaving Tashbaan Shasta looks back at all of its 'splendour and strength and glory', but these things also make him remember its 'dangers'.[136]

And we have already alluded to the dangers of Aravis's cruelty and arrogance in *The Horse and His Boy*.[137] She has enough courage to escape and flee from a fate dreadful to her self, but she drugs a maid of hers in order to do it, knowing all along that the maid will probably be beaten for it.[138] Aravis's friend Lasaraleen shares this propensity to cruelty. To keep Aravis's presence in Tashbaan a secret, she threatens her slaves: "'anyone I catch talking about this young lady will be first beaten to death and then burned alive and after that be kept on bread and water for six weeks. There.'"[139]

These impossible threats of Lasaraleen's show another way Lewis treats

---

132 See HB, pp. 54-55.
133 HB, p. 58. This passage proves that Lewis's portrayal of Calormene devotion is not wholly congruent with Islamic devotion, given Islam's emphasis on the one-ness and transcendence of Allah and hence its strict iconoclasm. There are daemons, or jinn, but no Muslim is permitted to make a statue of these spirits. But the proud, imposing nature of the statues, the city, and the Calormenes themselves is surely patterned after many tendencies common to Islamic culture as Lewis understood it.
134 HB, p. 59.
135 HB, pp. 60-61.
136 HB, p. 97.
137 See above, p. 139.
138 See HB, p. 44.
139 HB, p. 106.

the Calormene temperament: with humour. As he lampooned the pride of devils in *Screwtape*, so he makes fun of Calormene pride in this story. The story culminates, in fact, with the comic humiliation of the proud, corrupt and cruel Prince Rabadash. When Rabadash meets Aslan in the book's final chapter, Aslan gives him another chance to repent and humble himself. But instead of humbling himself, as Aravis has learned to do, he continues to make an ass of himself before the great Lion.[140] He attempts to frighten Aslan by contorting his face into an absurd shark-like grin and wagging his ears up and down. When Rabadash realises his efforts have achieved less than he hoped for, he lets loose with a number of idiomatic insults and curses. Even in the midst of this fulmination, Aslan gives Rabadash another chance. But when he continues, Aslan unleashes his punishment: Rabadash is turned into a real ass. The prince who loved to intimidate is now simply laughed at.[141] Even then Aslan's tender mercy is not exhausted. He sends Rabadash the donkey on a mission of humility to the temple of Tash where he will be healed.[142] We are told that this happens, but none of his subjects ever forget that he had been a donkey. The proud prince has been humbled in the sight of his people.

The humility and tenderness of Aslan, and other characters,[143] stand in sharp relief against the pride and mere severity of Tash and many of the Calormenes. One example is the enduring mercy of Aslan next to the tirade of insults and cursings of Rabadash. Another example, in *The Last Battle*, is Emeth's expectation of utter destruction from the Great Lion followed by what the Great Lion actually does. As Emeth recounts, "'But the Glorious One bent down his golden head and touched my forehead with his tongue and said, Son, thou art welcome'".[144]

The Divine Sonship

This example of Aslan calling Emeth his 'Son' gives us the perfect opportunity to examine more closely the Divine Sonship, the distinct concept that lies at the heart of all that Lewis and MacDonald wrote about God's tender and humble love. Both authors believed God was personal. To their minds he was certainly more than personal, but not less. He *is* the great Unfathomable and Transcendent Other that humans will never fully comprehend, but he is also *more* than an incomprehensible, impersonal, almighty being. He is also the one

---

140 See HB, p. 233.

141 Calling someone a donkey is an Arabic insult, and it seems likely that Lewis knew this, considering Rabadash's last words before losing his powers of speech: "'Oh, not a Donkey! Mercy! If it were even a horse—e'en—a—hor—eeh—auh, eeh-auh'" (HB, p. 235).

142 Compare Christ's healing of the ten lepers: Luke 17.12-14, Mat. 8.2-5.

143 See especially Hwin the horse in HB and Puzzle the donkey in LB.

144 LB, pp. 204-205.

who reveals much of himself to us: his goodness as well as his majesty, the Love that he is as well as the great Other that we are not. It was this kind of God that MacDonald and Lewis believed in bowing down to, as sons who can understand something of their Father and be like him in love and goodness.

It is important at this point to note how Lewis believed that God was not simply a Person, but three Persons: the Father, the Son, and the eternal Spirit of that eternal relationship. This doctrine of the Trinity, he admits, does not please his imagination as much as either the 'monolithic grandeur of strictly Unitarian conceptions' or 'the richness of Polytheism', but he believed it to be true.[145] He also believed that this kind of God is the only one, or three, who could have been Love from all eternity. As Lewis explains in *Mere Christianity*, 'Love is something that one person has for another person. If God was a single person, then before the world was made, He was not love'.[146] The three-person God, he writes, 'is perhaps the most important difference between Christianity and all other religions: that in Christianity God is not a static thing—not even a person—but a dynamic, pulsating activity, a life, almost a kind of drama. Almost, if you will not think me irreverent, a kind of dance'.[147]

Lewis believed that a strictly one-person God, or non-personal God, could not have been love from before all time because love, like dances (as opposed to solo jigs), requires at least two. No matter how inexorable and irresistible in his unity and power, God could not have been love from all eternity unless he were not also more than one from all eternity. If he were only One, he would have had to learn love right along with his creatures, Lewis reasons. He, like his creatures, would not have known what he was doing, and love could not have been at the heart of reality. But in the doctrine of the Blessed Trinity, as he writes in *The Problem of Pain*, one learns that 'something analogous to "society" exists within the Divine Being from all eternity—that God is Love, not merely in the sense of being the Platonic form of love,[148] but because, within Him, the concrete reciprocities of love exist before all worlds and are thence derived to the creatures'.[149]

But none of this from Lewis is new. One need only go back sixty or so years to find very similar words from MacDonald. In one sermon MacDonald writes of how love is deepest in God, deeper than either his power or even his 'righteousness'.[150] In a passage of this sermon that Lewis marked in his own copy and included in his anthology,[151] MacDonald writes:

145 WG, p. 91. From the address 'Is Theology Poetry?'.
146 MC, p. 151.
147 MC, p. 152.
148 See, for example, Diotima's speech about Love, in *Symposium*, 202B-211C.
149 PP, p. 29.
150 US, p. 421 (last half of par. 13 in 'The Creation in Christ', third series).
151 ANTH, reading 172.

let us understand very plainly, that a being whose essence was only power would be such a negation of the divine that no righteous worship could be offered him: his service must be fear, and fear only. Such a being, even were he righteous in judgement, yet could not be God. The God himself whom we love could not be righteous were he not something deeper and better still than we generally mean by the word.[152]

What God is, 'in one word', MacDonald writes, is 'Love'.[153] Love is God's 'deepest depth, the essence of his nature, at the root of all his being'.[154] And this Love that God is, what Lewis would later refer to as an eternal dance, is according to MacDonald the relation, or interaction between, the eternal Father and eternal Son:

> Jesus has God to love; the love of the Son is responsive to the love of the Father. The response to self-existent love is self-abnegating love. The refusal of himself is that in Jesus which corresponds to the creation of God. His love takes action, creates, in self-abjuration, in the death of self as motive; in the drowning of self in the life of God, where it lives only as love.[155]

It is this eternal kneeling of the Son before his Father, MacDonald and Lewis believed, that was the root of all humble love which, unlike the competitive spirit of hell, looks to and defers to another. As a knight bows before his lord or lady in humble and obedient service, so too has the Son ever bowed in service and loving submission before his Father who loves him, not before a mere tyrant who only rules him. This eternal 'chivalry' within the godhead is the reason that Christ, the Son on Earth, bowed to his Father's will in submitting to human death. As MacDonald writes later in the sermon, 'When [Jesus] died on the cross, he did that, in the wild weather of his outlying provinces in the torture of the body of his revelation, which he had done at home in glory and gladness [...] he completed and held fast the eternal circle of his existence in saying, "Thy will, not mine, be done!"'.[156] Such love, humility and self-abnegation would have never appeared in the universe, MacDonald

---

152 US, pp. 420-421 (first half of par. 13 in the same sermon). Lewis marks from 'let us' to 'be offered him'.

153 US, p. 421 (second and third quarters of par. 13 in the same). Compare 1 John 4.8.

154 US, p. 421 (third quarter of par. 13 in the same sermon).

155 US, pp. 421-422 (second quarter of par. 14 in the same). Lewis marks all of this in his copy and includes the second and third sentence in his anthology (ANTH, reading 173).

156 US, p. 423 (second and third quarters of par. 16 in the same). Lewis marks and underlines from 'when he died' to 'glory and gladness' and includes it in his anthology (ANTH, reading 173). For 'Thy will, not mine, be done', see Mat. 26.39, Mark 14.36; Luke 22.42.

writes, had it not been eternally occurring in the Divine Relation between the Father and Son. As Lewis would write decades later, MacDonald writes in this sermon that the central fact of the universe is the Love between the Son and His Father:

> It is not the fact that God created all things, that makes the universe a whole; but that he through whom he created them[157] loves him perfectly, is eternally content in his father, is satisfied to be because his father is with him. It is not that God is all in all, that unites the universe; it is the love of the Son to the Father. For of no onehood comes unity; there can be no oneness where there is only one. For the very beginnings of unity there must be two. Without Christ, therefore, there could be no universe.[158]

From this central fact of reality, he writes, springs all the hope that humanity can have of loving humbly:

> But for the Father and the Son, no two would care a jot the one for the other [...] Even had I come into being as now with an inclination to love, selfishness would soon have overborne it. But if the Father loves the Son, if the very music that makes the harmony of life lies, not in the theory of love in the heart of the Father, but in the fact of it, in the burning love in the hearts of Father and Son, then glory be to the Father and to the Son, and to the spirit of both, the fatherhood of the Father meeting and blending with the sonhood of the Son, and drawing us up into the glory of their joy, to share in the thoughts of love that pass between them, in their thoughts of delight and rest in each other, in their thoughts of joy in all the little ones.[159]

A Lamb to the Rescue

And so while MacDonald and Lewis believed God to be transcendent and unfathomable, they believed him to have revealed his loving essence in the person of Christ the Son, and in other ways. 'Self-existence and creation' for example, 'no man will ever understand', MacDonald writes.[160] But 'nevertheless, if I be a child of God, I must be *like* him'.[161] That is, any love between a human father and son, or any love that one has for another, is something like the eternal Love of the Father and Son. To the degree that we know and do this love is the degree to which we know, and are united with, the Love at the heart

---

157 That is, Christ. See John 1.3.
158 US, p. 428 (second quarter of par. 23 in 'The Creation in Christ', third series). Lewis marks all this and includes in anthology (ANTH, reading 176).
159 US, p. 429 (last half of par. 23 in the same sermon). Lewis marks from 'I cannot for a moment' to 'overborne it' and underlines 'selfishness would have overborne it'.
160 US, p. 420 (second quarter of par. 12 in the same).
161 US, p. 420 (last quarter of par. 12 in the same).

of reality. The degree to which we become courteous in supernatural love, rather than hateful or competitive, is the degree to which we are sons of God as Christ is the Son of God.[162]

As Lewis writes in *Miracles*, 'Divine Sonship is, so to speak, the solid of which biological sonship is merely a diagrammatic representation on the flat'.[163] And as he explains in *Mere Christianity*, Christ came to make humans more than mere biological representations of the Sonship. He came to take humans, if they will let him, beyond mere natural competitiveness and diagrammatic representations of love, to the supernatural life and love that he has always been:

> The Spiritual life which is in God from all eternity, and which made the whole natural universe, is *Zoe*. *Bios* has, to be sure, a certain shadowy or symbolic resemblance to *Zoe*: but only the sort of resemblance there is between a photo and a place, or a statue and a real man. A man who changed from having *Bios* to having *Zoe* would have gone through as big a change as a statue which changed from being a carved stone to being a real man. [...] And that is precisely what Christianity is about. This world is a great sculptor's shop. We are the statues and there is a rumour going round the shop that some of us are some day going to come to life.[164]

A few years after these words were written, Lewis wrote of such a thing happening in his most famous book, *The Lion, the Witch, and the Wardrobe*. In a chapter entitled 'What Happened about the Statues', he writes of Aslan, son of the Emperor-Beyond-the-Sea, breathing upon statues to quicken them into new life and release them from the curse of the White Witch who has cast all of Narnia into perpetual winter.[165]

This new life comes after Aslan's supreme act of humility and good death: allowing himself to be killed upon the Stone Table by the Witch. Like Christ at his crucifixion, he makes no 'resistance at all' in allowing his great paws to be bound, his great mane to be shaven off.[166] This humble sacrifice of Aslan's, and the very fact of Aslan's presence in Narnia, gives us the opportunity, again, to put things into context with another sense of chivalry. We have just seen how the love of the eternal Father and Son is like a knight kneeling before and obeying his lord or lady; or, if the Father and Son be true, how a knight kneeling and obeying is like that which goes on between the Father and Son.

---

162 See also John 1.12; Rom. 8.14, 19; Phil. 2.15; 1 John 3.1, 2.
163 MIR, p. 91.
164 MC, p. 140.
165 In John 20.21, Christ breathes on his disciples in imparting to them the Holy Spirit. This is also how Lewis describes the process of 'good infection' in *Mere Christianity* (See MC, p. 153).
166 LWW, p. 166.

Now, in Aslan and his sacrifice, we can see how the goodness and love of God, as Lewis portrayed it, is at once like a knight kneeling *and* a knight coming to the aid of, and perhaps sacrificing himself for, someone weaker. The images that come to mind are of a man 'giving a woman a seat in a train',[167] of Raleigh throwing his cape in the mud for a lady to walk upon, or of any knight coming to the aid of any distressed damsel.

Such images abound in Lewis's writing. There is Aslan, of course, but there is also Ransom coming to the aid of the Lady of Perelandra. There is even Reason, depicted in *The Pilgrim's Regress* as an armed woman on horseback, coming to save John from the giant Spirit of the Age.[168]

And before these were countless images of the same kind in MacDonald's books: the rusty knight coming to Anodos's aid in *Phantastes*, Dr. Anderson and others coming to help Adela Cathcart; Gibbie saving Ginevra Galbraith from flood waters and Alec Forbes doing the same for Annie Anderson; Robert Falconer and Mary St. John coming to the aid of the poor in London; Diamond helping little Nanny; North Wind helping little Diamond; Queen Irene taking little Irene, all dirty and wet with tears, to her bosom; Curdie and Princess Irene helping each other at different points; Hugh Sutherland saving Margaret Elginbrod from snow drifts; Gibbie as a man coming to the aid of Mistress Croale and other poor, drunk folk in the town; Shargar waylaying a man who insults his mother, a poor gypsy woman. The examples are too numerous to list here, but the one example which may help sum them all up, and show how they are similar to Lewis's images, is the prince saving the princess in his fairy tale 'The Light Princess'.

In one sense the tale resembles Beauty and the Beast, except it is the light princess, born relatively immune to the effects of gravity, who is the beastly one. As she is physically unable to fall, so is her character, like Agnes in 'The Wise Woman',[169] devoid of any humility or real love for others. She has as little humility and love as she has weight until the prince comes along. His heroic deed is to save the kingdom from ruin at the hands of an evil witch who is draining all the water and life from the land, but the way in which he does it helps the princess to fall in more than one way.

This fall into humility that the prince leads her to is partially accomplished, or symbolised, by his falling with her into a lake earlier in the story. She physically falls for the first time when he takes her in his arms, therefore

---

167　PRC, p. 13.

168　'Then the rider threw back the cloak and a flash of steel smote light into John's eyes and on the giant's face. John saw that it was a woman in the flower of her age: she was so tall that she seemed to him a Titaness, a sun-bright virgin clad in complete steel, with a sword naked in her hand' (REG, p. 52). Compare to Spenser's Britomart.

169　See above, pp. 203-204.

lending her some of his gravity, and leaps off of a high rock into a lake, to the princess's great delight. This baptism does wonders while she's in the water: she is not so 'forward' or 'pert' as she is on land, and she laughs more gently.[170] 'She seemed altogether more modest and maidenly in the water than out of it', MacDonald writes.[171] But when he talks to her of love while in the lake, the princess just laughs her old laugh and looks puzzled. She has not learned enough.

And so the prince comes to save her, and the kingdom, from ruin. The ways in which he, like Aslan, resembles Christ in his mission are fairly obvious. He comes disguised as a common servant: a shoe-black.[172] A plate of gold found at the bottom of the sinking lake is inscribed with these words which tell of the sacrificial act required to save the lake and the kingdom: *"The body of a living man could alone staunch the flow. The man must give himself of his own will; and the lake must take his life as it filled"*.[173] This is very much like the 'deeper magic from before the dawn of time' that Aslan accomplished: *"that when a willing victim who had committed no treachery was killed in the traitor's stead, the Table would crack and Death itself would start working backward"*.[174] It seems likely that Lewis had the inscription on the gold plate and the situation of 'The Light Princess' in his head when conceiving this. Both situations, after all, involve the son of a king or emperor sacrificing himself to save both an individual (the light princess, and Edmund) and a country (the princess's kingdom which is being drained of life, and Narnia which is oppressed by perpetual winter). And the hole on the bottom of the lake which the prince must plug with his body is in the middle of a stone. Aslan's body dies upon a table of stone.

What is certain, though, is that both writers had Christ's sacrifice in mind when they wrote. The humility of MacDonald's prince, for example, stands out distinctly amidst those who are proud, as Christ in the New Testament stands out distinctly in comparison to chief priests, doctors of law, and other men of power. The princess's father, the king, when he opens his door and sees only the shoe-black, draws his sword: his 'usual mode of asserting his regality when he thought his dignity was in danger'.[175] But the prince, like Christ, does not assert his own regality[176] and is not careful for his dignity. He comes as a shoe-black. His willing surrender to death finally opens up the princess's eyes to the

---

170 AC, p. 87.
171 AC, p. 87.
172 Compare John 13.4-17.
173 AC, p. 93.
174 LWW, p. 179.
175 AC, p. 94.
176 Compare Phil. 2.6-8.

reality of humility and sacrificial love, and enables her to find her own gravity: to fall down from her self-regard and begin caring for others as he does.

The princess's salvation and learning to walk is a picture of how MacDonald believed people are saved into humility and love. In the tale the princess learns to walk from the prince, one who is used to gravity.[177] She, the weaker, gains strength from the strong who has sacrificed himself. It is very much like the salvation he speaks of in one of his sermons when he refers to Christ in his eucharistic function: 'Their souls must live on his soul',[178] and God in Christ 'bestows his very being for the daily food of his creatures'.[179] The natural or hellish order of things, in which the stronger eats the weaker, is turned upside down by the Strongest sacrificing himself to feed the weak with what he is. The weak eat the strong by his consent, and the weak become strong in love and humility, offering themselves in love to others as he has done.[180] Another way he speaks of it is by referring to Christ's invitation to those who would follow him to 'take my yoke upon you, and learn of me; for I am meek and lowly in heart'.[181] As MacDonald writes, 'When he says, "Take my yoke upon you," he does not mean a yoke which he would lay upon our shoulders; it is his own yoke he tells us to take, and to learn of him—it is the yoke he is himself carrying, the yoke his perfect Father had given him to carry'.[182] In other words, God does not invite humans to do something that he himself is not used to doing. Dying to self and living in strong love is something the Son has been forever doing with his Father, and he as Christ has done it as a human to enable humans to grow strong in love as he is.

Lewis, in a chapter of *Mere Christianity* entitled 'The Perfect Penitent', expresses something similar while attempting to illustrate what the Son, by living and dying as a human, can do for all other men who live and die. What he can do, Lewis writes, is lift men out of the '"hole"' they've fallen into by behaving as if they belonged to themselves.[183] What men have to do is to surrender and repent, or as MacDonald might have put it, turn away from the one principle of hell: '"I am my own"'.[184] As Lewis writes, it means 'unlearning all the self-conceit and self-will that we have been training ourselves into for

---

177 The fact that she has to learn to walk before she can be married 'with any propriety' to the prince follows New Testament imagery of the bride, Christ's church, learning love from the bridegroom, Christ, before the consummation in paradise. See Mat. chp. 25; Rev. 21.2, 9. See also Isaiah 61.10.
178 MOL, pp. 408-409.
179 MOL, p. 409.
180 See the same idea in Lewis's *The Four Loves*, p. 127.
181 Mat. 11.29.
182 US, pp. 371-372 (last half of par. 8 in 'Self-Denial', second series).
183 MC, p. 59.
184 US, p. 495 (first quarter of par. 3 in 'Kingship', third series).

thousands of years'.[185] It is the essence of the spiritually good death that we read so much about in both authors' books: 'It means killing part of yourself, undergoing a kind of death'.[186]

The paradoxical difficulty of achieving this sort of good death, according to Lewis, is that while only bad, prideful people need to repent, only a wholly good person 'can repent perfectly'.[187] As he writes, 'The worse you are the more you need it and the less you can do it. The only person who could do it perfectly would be a perfect person—and he would not need it'.[188] The only solution to such a problem, Lewis writes, would be for perfect God, who in his perfect existence never needs to repent, to become a man. A person 'in whom our human nature was amalgamated with God's nature could help', he explains: 'He could surrender His will, and suffer and die, because He was a man; and He could do it perfectly because He was God. You and I can go through this process only if God does it in us; but God can do it only if He becomes a man'.[189] As MacDonald symbolised such a process in the light princess learning to walk from the loving prince who knew how, so does Lewis use a similar analogy here to describe the process by which proud creatures are made into sons and daughters of an eternally meek and loving God: 'When you teach a child writing, you hold its hand while it forms the letters: that is, it forms the letters because you are forming them [...] The teacher is able to form the letters for the child because the teacher is grown-up and knows how to write'.[190]

We begin to see here where Lewis and MacDonald believed the incarnation and death of Christ to be *the* great act that is imitated by all other 'knights' who leave 'castles' in order to save 'damsels'. They believed that God came down from his transcendent Paradise into the shadowy realm of suffering, temptation and death to save men and women from their own proud selves, and eventually all else that ails them. He gets his hands (or his cloak) dirty, so to speak, in order to lift men, women and all of nature out of the muck. To Lewis and MacDonald he is no mere Transcendence, Numen, Omnipotence or Aloofness content to remain in a distant heaven.[191]

As we've mentioned above, it is the very fact of Aslan's presence in Narnia, not just what he does, that helps distinguish Lewis's depiction of God from other depictions. He is the Son of the Emperor-Beyond-the-Sea

---

185 MC, p. 59.
186 MC, p. 59.
187 MC, p. 59.
188 MC, p. 59.
189 MC, p. 60.
190 MC, pp. 60-61.
191 Contrast to Lewis's 'Satan Speaks' (XIII) in SIB. See p. 26, above.

who did not stay beyond the sea. The Emperor demonstrates his essential love by going out across the sea to reveal himself and his saving love in his son Aslan. Aslan's death and humiliation on the Stone Table is a working out of this love. Aslan is simply Lewis's greatest literary illustration of the kind of goodness that he and MacDonald thought God to be. Lewis speaks of this in *Miracles* as 'the great' entering 'the little' and its power to so descend being 'almost the test of its greatness'.[192] This same passage, in a chapter entitled 'The Grand Miracle', also contains perhaps the best non-fiction description of the Incarnation, Death and Resurrection that Lewis ever wrote: '[God] comes down; down from the heights of absolute being into time and space, down into humanity; down further still, if embryologists are right, to recapitulate in the womb ancient and pre-human phases of life; down to the very roots and sea-bed of the Nature He has created. But he goes down to come up again and bring the whole ruined world up with Him'.[193] He compares this rescue at one point to a diver stripping down and plunging to unfathomably dark depths to recover a precious object,[194] and at another point to a strong man stooping lower and lower to get himself underneath a 'great complicated burden': 'He must stoop in order to lift, he must almost disappear under the load before he incredibly straightens his back and marches off with the whole mass swaying on his shoulders'.[195]

God's goodness, then, according to Lewis and MacDonald, is not stand-offish. It is not the sort of goodness that is content to demand that humans be 'good'; it is Love that reaches out and down to save, heal and enliven those who would be sons and daughters of Love. As MacDonald wrote before Lewis was born, God is not simply a monarch who issues decrees from afar, who sits back on his throne watching his creatures sin, suffer and die by themselves. He is accessible.[196] He is infinitely closer in his relation to us than a human father, though we feel it not.[197] He is necessarily bound to us of his own free will because he is Love.[198] His forgiveness and love are given according to need, not merit.[199] He is the source of all our true humanity.[200] He is the well-spring for all womanly love[201] and more like a mother than any mother.[202] He

---

192 MIR, p. 111.
193 MIR, p. 111.
194 MIR, pp. 111-112.
195 MIR, p. 111.
196 See US, pp. 335-336 (par. 8-9 in 'The Voice of Job', second series).
197 See US, p. 338 (par. 12 in the same sermon).
198 See US, p. 343 (first quarter of par. 17 in the same).
199 See US, pp. 52-53 (last half of par. 20 in 'It Shall Not Be Forgiven', first series).
200 See US, p. 13 (first half of par. 24 in 'The Child in the Midst', first series).
201 See US, p. 16 (last quarter of par. 31 in the same sermon).
202 See US, p. 547 (third quarter of par. 6 in 'Light', third series).

gives refuge to the oppressed and a hearing to women.[203] He is motivated by love, not fame.[204] He smiles,[205] gives himself for his children,[206] is quiet and tender.[207] He rejects visions of grandeur,[208] and his miracles are examples of love, not showy displays of power.[209] The 'sweet colour of the divine light in courtesy' is his.[210] He is the inventor of laughter[211] and transmitter of 'that divine disease' called '*humility*'.[212]

With belief in this kind of God, it is no surprise that MacDonald came to write against the Calvinist Omni-god, or that he consistently portrayed pride and snobbery, religious or otherwise, in a bad light. Or that he always portrayed womanhood and child-likeness in a good light. In *Lilith*, the Little Ones, or Lovers, are good because they are humble and know that they are children. The giants in the story turn bad because they become proud and forget that they are children.[213] David Elginbrod prays for God to 'Be thou by us, even as a mother sits by the bedside o' her ailin' wean a' the lang nicht; only be thou nearer to us'.[214]

And *Robert Falconer*, just as it expresses much of what MacDonald thought God is not, thoroughly expresses, perhaps more than any other novel of his, who he thought God is and what his goodness is like. Soon after Robert abandons his grandmother's conception of God, he leaves home on an adventure to Aberdeen and beyond, much as MacDonald himself did. Through his adventures, much like Julian in *Within and Without* and Anodos in *Phantastes*, he comes to a greater understanding of who God is and who he, Robert, can be. After spending six weeks in a quiet place in the Alps, reading the New Testament every day by a stream, he comes to the conclusion that God's will was 'to be found and done in the world', as Christ had done his Father's will in the world.[215] And so from this retreat in the Alps to the streets of London he descends to live the kind of chivalrous love that he reads about in the New Testament. His resolution to do so is revealed in a conversation he has with his grandmother during a brief visit back home. Here, in Scots, we

---

203 See HG, pp. 65-66.
204 See HG, p. 176.
205 See MOL, p. 238.
206 See MOL, p. 246.
207 See MOL, p. 248.
208 See MOL, p. 242.
209 See MOL, pp. 248, 260.
210 HG, p. 167.
211 See MOL, p. 249.
212 MOL, p. 336.
213 See LIL, pp. 99-100, 102-105, 262.
214 DE, p. 20.
215 RF, p. 304.

get a good summary of what we have been describing as the chivalry of God, and how it contrasts with other, proud ideas of God and his glory:

> "ye speyk aboot him as gin he was a puir prood bailey-like body,[216] fu' o' his ain importance, an' ready to be doon upo' onybody 'at didna ca' him by the name o' 's office—ay think-thinkin' aboot 's ain glory; in place o' the quaiet, michty, gran', self-forgettin', a'-creatin', a'-uphaudin', eternal bein', wha took the form o' man in Christ Jesus, jist that he micht hae't in 's pooer[217] to beir[218] and be humblet for oor sakes. Eh, grannie! think o' the face o' that man o' sorrows, that never said a hard word till a sinfu' wuman, or a despised publican[219]: was he thinkin' aboot's ain glory, think ye? An we have no richt to say we ken God save in the face o' Christ Jesus. What ever's no like Christ is no like God."[220]

And so Falconer goes down into London acting like a little Christ himself. He learns law and medicine so that he can defend and heal the poor people he knows. He visits people in rat-infested flats where children sleep upon the floors. In Bethnal Green he goes from 'house to house till it grew very late', and everyone in every house knows him.[221] His old ideal of feminine beauty, Mary St. John, he finds in London too, caring for the motherless.[222] He shows tenderness to a girl contemplating suicide and gives her reasons not to go through with it.[223] A young child in one section of town, where all the children know him, thinks he actually is Jesus Christ.[224] To sum up, Falconer becomes his ideal, as Anodos is urged to do in *Phantastes* and as the youth in Melchah's dream struggled to do in *Within and Without*.[225] The faith he came to in the Alps—in a tender-hearted God who descends to love—has worked itself out in his person. He is becoming the song he would sing[226] in the world of men. Believing and trusting in God's chivalry, he has become chivalrous himself.

A Lion to the Rescue

It also needs to be noted here, though, how MacDonald's and Lewis's idea of

216 That is, like a town magistrate next in line to a provost.
217 Power
218 Bear, as in bearing burdens
219 Generally despised Jewish tax collectors employed by the occupying Romans in Christ's day.
220 RF, p. 328.
221 RF, p. 358.
222 See RF, p. 360.
223 See RF, pp. 379-381.
224 See RF, p. 384.
225 See p. 41, above.
226 See pp. 41, 98, 109-112, 147-148, above.

God was not tender *only*. The 'chivalry' that they believed God to be may have stood out distinct from other, merely severe ideas of God, but it does not follow that they believed God and the Love that he is to be simply 'soft'. The Christian idea of God they espoused, when compared to a 'monstrosity of a monarch',[227] may indeed be much more 'feminine' and child-like. But a God who is not aloof or proud does not denote a God who is a milksop, they believed.[228] That he is the root of all femininity does not make him effeminate; that he is eternally child-like does not make him the least bit childish. They both believed, we shall find, that the tenderness and humility of God's love does not cancel out his transcendence, majesty or severity.

We will begin to see the foundation for this belief if we look more closely at the last sense of chivalry that we have just used: that of a knight, or any other strong person, sacrificing himself to save someone weaker. The Great Example of this in MacDonald's and Lewis's eyes is of course the incarnate Christ on the cross. In one sense this can be seen as passive. Christ submits to the will of his Father and allows himself to be ridiculed, beaten and killed without the least resistance. Now however passive this may be, it certainly proves, if Christ is God, that God is humble and not proud. Almighty God hanging naked and bloody on a cross in front of an audience surely proves this. His washing of human feet,[229] and the very fact that the Transcendence has had human feet, does the same thing. But do these things also prove that he is 'soft' only? Or passive at his deepest core? MacDonald and Lewis thought not.

Such can be seen at a glance in Lewis's poem 'Love's as Warm as Tears'. The poem's title may seem to introduce an ode to simple softness, but the poem's content proves otherwise. Love *is* as warm as tears, but the poet reminds us of what often comes with the tenderness of tears: 'Pressure within the brain, \ Tension at the throat'.[230] Human tears, he notes, are like nature's: 'weeks of rain' that send 'Haystacks afloat' and make 'Featureless seas between \ Hedges' where all was once green.[231] Both kinds of tears involve the active disruption of what was passively calm. Love is also as 'fierce as fire'.[232] All our loves, however impure we make them, originally spring from an 'empyreal flame'.[233] Love also is 'as fresh as spring', a spring that is feminine in its lovely sounds and 'cool smells', but which whispers to 'sap' and 'blood' the exhortation to '"Dare!

---

227 US, p. 15 (last quarter of par. 30 in 'The Child in the Midst', first series).
228 See Lewis's 'Necessity of Chivalry' (PRC, p. 14).
229 See John 13.4-17.
230 C.S. Lewis, *Poems* (San Diego: Harcourt Brace & Company, 1992), p. 123. First published, posthumously, in 1964.
231 POE, p. 123.
232 POE, p. 123.
233 POE, p. 123.

Dare!'".[234] Ease and safety and rest, it whispers, are good but 'not best'.[235] And finally, we are bluntly told, love is 'as hard as nails':

Love is nails:
Blunt, thick, hammered through
The medial nerves of One
Who, having made us, knew
The thing He had done,
Seeing (with all that is)
Our cross, and His.[236]

God's supreme act of sacrificial love, according to the poem, is not simply soft. The great Act of which the ideal of chivalry is an imitation is at once tender *and* severe. Christ in Gethsemane and on the cross is at once God in meekness and God at battle: meek submission but also fierce gallantry in a man who is also God.[237]

Lewis also stresses this hardness in his mentioning Christ's fulfillment as the conquering Messiah of the Old Testament. The modern sentiment that emphasises Christ as a baby in a manger, while 'excellent in itself', does less than justice if it stops at the nativity: 'For those who first read these Psalms as poems about the birth of Christ, that birth primarily meant something very militant; the hero, the 'judge'[238] or champion or giant-killer, who was to fight and beat death, hell and the devils, had at last arrived, and the evidence suggests that Our Lord also thought of Himself in these terms'.[239]

Christ, to Lewis's understanding, does not cease to be a lion because he is also a lamb. As he writes in *The Problem of Pain* concerning Paradise, the lion lying down with the lamb will not mean that the lion ceases to exist. It may no longer 'live by the destruction of the lamb', but it will keep all of the 'energy' and 'exulting power' that makes it a lion to begin with: 'I think the lion, when he has ceased to be dangerous, will still be awful: indeed, that we shall then first see that of which the present fangs and claws are a clumsy, and satanically perverted, imitation. There will still be something like the shaking of a golden mane: and often the good Duke will say, "Let him roar again."'.[240]

---

234 POE, p. 123.
235 POE, p, 123.
236 POE, p. 124.
237 See also Lewis's comments on the hard 'comfort' Christ received from the angel in Gethsemane (LM, p. 42; Letter VIII) and MacDonald's idea that Jesus being God made suffering more difficult, not easier, for him to bear (US, pp. 111-112 [second paragraph of 'The Eloi', first series]).
238 Not a judge in the modern juridical sense, but in the old Hebrew sense of one who defends and rescues the poor. See RPS, p. 10.
239 RPS, p. 108.
240 PP, p. 143.

This, of course, is how Lewis drew Aslan in the Narnia books. At the very end of *Dawn Treader*, for example, Edmund, Lucy and Eustace meet Aslan in the form of a lamb who invites them in a sweet milky voice to come and have breakfast.[241] But eventually, as the Lamb speaks to the children, 'his snowy white flushed into tawny gold and his size changed and he was Aslan himself,[242] towering above them and scattering light from his mane'.[243] Aslan is a Lion as well as a Lamb, and he is never a 'tame lion'.[244] He is all good and more gentle than a mother, but he is not to be trifled with. As Mrs. Beaver tells Susan in the first Narnia book that Lewis wrote: '"if there's anyone who can appear before Aslan without their knees knocking, they're either braver than most or else just silly"'.[245] In this same book Aslan humbles himself to an undignified death on the Stone Table, but he also, after coming back to life and cracking the Table, leads the Narnians in furious battle against the White Witch.[246]

But Aslan's magnificence and severity is only the most obvious example. This 'hard' side of chivalry springs up everywhere in Lewis's writing. One will remember, for example, the severity with which the Bright Ones in *The Great Divorce* deal with those things which dominate the ghosts. In *Reflections on the Psalms*, we can see the foundation for this kind of hostility when Lewis writes that he can even take the cursings in the Psalms as a word from God if it is applied to wickedness, 'especially our own'.[247] Even the ninth verse of Psalm 137, in which the psalmist speaks of dashing Babylonian babies against stones, can be used thus if it is applied to one's own evil: 'I know things in the inner world which are like babies; the infantile beginnings of small indulgences, small resentments, which may one day become dipsomania or settled hatred, but which woo us and wheedle us with special pleadings and seem so tiny, so helpless that in resisting them we feel we are being cruel to animals'.[248] Like the lizard that whispers into the ghost's ear in *Divorce*:[249] 'They begin whimpering to us, "I don't ask much, but", or "I had at least hoped", or "you owe yourself *some* consideration"'.[250] 'Against all such pretty infants', Lewis writes, 'the advice of the Psalm is the best. Knock the little bastards' brains

---

241 See VDT, pp. 267-268. Compare Rev. 7.17.
242 The children have hitherto known him only as a Lion.
243 VDT, p. 269.
244 As we are told in several Narnia books.
245 LWW, p. 86.
246 See, for example, LWW, p. 194.
247 RPS, p. 117.
248 RPS, p. 118.
249 See GD, pp. 84-85.
250 RPS, p. 118.

out'.[251]

Similarly, in *The Problem of Pain* Lewis writes of how God's love for men motivates more than his tenderness, or how 'disinterested' love, when describing God's love, does not mean 'indifferent':

> You asked for a loving God: you have one. The great spirit you so lightly invoked, the "lord of terrible aspect,"[252] is present: not a senile benevolence that drowsily wishes you to be happy in your own way, not the cold philanthropy of a conscientious magistrate, nor the care of a host who feels responsible for the comfort of his guests, but the consuming fire Himself, the Love that made the worlds, persistent as the artist's love for his work and despotic as a man's love for a dog, provident and venerable as a father's love for a child, jealous, inexorable, exacting as love between the sexes.[253]

This talk of inexorable love and God as a consuming fire reminds us of similar talk from MacDonald. In a sermon entitled 'The Consuming Fire', MacDonald writes of fear being nobler than sensuality,[254] how love does not exclude all fear,[255] how the Love that God is must purify.[256] In another sermon, in a sentence that Lewis marks and underlines in his copy, MacDonald—who unfailingly speaks of Christ's tenderness and humility—speaks against too-delicate pictures of Christ. If Jesus were to come to England today, MacDonald writes, 'he would not come in the halo of the painters, or with that wintry shine of effeminate beauty, of sweet weakness, in which it is their helpless custom to represent him'.[257]

As Lewis did after him, he writes of a man making war with God against his own shadowy self: 'The man himself must turn against himself, and so be for himself'.[258] A man is to resist 'unto blood' with his Lord against his own sin.[259] There is no self-denial for denial's sake, but there is surely self-denial for God's and others' sake. One must stand ready to receive the 'blows of his mallet' as a statue stands before the chisel of a sculptor until he has made us

---

251 RPS, p. 118.
252 From Dante's *La Vita Nuova*, chp. 2.
253 PP, pp. 46-47. For more on this aspect of divine love, see PP, p. 39-41.
254 See US, p. 24 (second quarter of par. 15 in 'The Consuming Fire', first series).
255 See US, p. 29 (par 20 of the same sermon).
256 See US, p. 30 (par. 22 of the same).
257 US, p. 444 (par. 22 in 'The Knowing of the Son', third series).
258 US, p. 257 (last quarter of par. 26 in 'Man's Difficulty Concerning Prayer', second series).
259 US, p. 264 (last quarter of par. 6 in 'The Last Farthing', second series). See also Lewis's discussion of the *bellum intestinum* in reference to the development of allegory in AL, chp. 2, especially 2.3.

into our true selves.[260] A man's anger against his false self must be like the 'divinely beautiful' anger of God: 'helpful, healing, restoring', but 'verily and truly what we call anger'.[261] A man is to cooperate with this loving anger in order to 'beat down your sin, and trample it to death'.[262] He writes about how we have a right 'to be hedged in on every side; to have one after another of the strong, sharp-toothed sheep-dogs of the great shepherd sent after' us, to 'thwart' and 'frustrate' us until we are brought into harmony with his love and goodness.[263]

This last example of sharp-toothed sheep-dogs will help us to see how MacDonald transposed such an image, and such 'hard' chivalry, into his fiction.[264] MacDonald never wrote about a great and good Lion who was also fierce, as Lewis did with Aslan,[265] but he did write about a strong, sharp-toothed sheep-dog named Prince who acts similarly. It is he who in the 'Wise Woman' thwarts and frustrates proud little Princess Agnes until she grows into something stronger and humbler, much as Aslan does with the proud and haughty Aravis in *The Horse and His Boy*. The parallels are surely not a coincidence. Both girls are princesses. Their names sound alike. The dog is named Prince, and the Lion is the Son of an Emperor. At one point the dog flies at the princess, knocks her down, and commences to shake her 'so violently as to tear her miserable clothes to pieces'.[266] He takes care not to hurt her, though, only giving her, 'for her good', 'a blue nip or two by way of letting her imagine what biting might be'.[267] This scene is very close indeed to when Aslan gives Aravis ten scratches—'sore, but not deep or dangerous'—across her back to let her know what her stepmother's slave received because of the drugged sleep Aravis cast on her.[268]

The manifestations of this kind of severity in their fiction are legion. Nearly all of their stories include some sort of good violence, just as there is much good death in them. No tale of Narnia, for instance, is complete without a battle. A look at some of the chapter titles is enough to suggest the quantity: 'The Fight at the Lamp-post', 'Sorcery and Sudden Vengeance', 'The Fight

---

260 US, p. 591 (last quarter of par. 16 in 'Righteousness', third series). Lewis marks in his copy.

261 US, p. 561 (second and third quarters of par. 11 in 'The Displeasure of Jesus', third volume).

262 US, 591 (last quarter of par. 16 in 'Righteousness', third series).

263 US, p. 348 (last half of par. 19 in 'The Voice of Job', second series).

264 Or vice versa, perhaps, given that his story containing the image was first published eleven years before the sermon was (1874, 1885).

265 Though he did write of such a leopardess (Lona) in *Lilith*.

266 CFT, p. 268.

267 CFT, p. 268.

268 HB, pp. 158, 216. See pp. 139, 231, above.

at Anvard', 'Peter's First Battle', for instance. And of course the last book of the series is entitled *The Last Battle*.[269] There are decapitations[270] and piercings of warriors with the horn of a unicorn.[271] Jill Pole shoots an evil bull in the eye with one of her arrows.[272] Prince Rilian, Eustace and Puddleglum with repeated blows hack off the head of a giant green serpent (formerly the Queen of Underland) that threatens to squeeze the prince to death.[273] Everything is 'blood and heat and hair' as Peter struggles to kill an evil wolf.[274] And there is of course Aslan's own violent death on the Stone Table which he permits, and the death of the Witch which he brings about in *The Lion, the Witch, and the Wardrobe*.

It is not surprising to see Lewis continuing this pattern in his books written specifically for adults. Angels kill evil lizards in *The Great Divorce*, John and Reason kill giants and dragons in *The Pilgrim's Regress*, and Orual and Psyche take the long, hard route in killing Orual's false self in *Till We Have Faces*. Ransom kills the Un-man who threatens the Lady of Perelandra and Perelandra itself. In *That Hideous Strength*, a zoo of animals is unleashed to help thwart a banquet meeting of N.I.C.E., and to trample to death their plans to trample upon nature. Our list could go on, but the point is clear. Lewis obviously believed that some things were worth saving and that, therefore, some things were worth struggling against to the death. He also believed that this struggle and death were patterned after the assertive love of a God of splendour who is strong even when he humbly suffers and serves. As Oyarsa sums it up to Ransom in the first book of the space trilogy, God will not give up Earth '"utterly to the Bent One"'.[275] There are stories going about, he says, that '"He has taken strange counsel and dared terrible things, wrestling with the Bent One in Thulcandra[276]"'.[277]

We have already begun to note similar strife in MacDonald's stories. The love of God must strive against that which is proud and unloving, he thought. It will not be forgotten that the Little Ones in *Lilith*, the child-like ones who are also called 'the Lovers', carry out an assault on Bulika, the proud capital city of the cruel Princess Lilith. These Little Ones are child-like in their wonder, joy and humble love, but they are never simply childish. They

269 Which does, however, strongly suggest that there will come a day when no more battles will be fought, evil having finally been exterminated from reality.
270 See PC, p. 182; HB, p. 204.
271 See LB, p. 150.
272 See LB, p. 151. This is of course a joke: she hits a 'bull's eye'.
273 See SC, pp. 192-193.
274 LWW, p. 144.
275 OSP, p. 121.
276 That is, Earth, the Silent Planet.
277 OSP, p. 121.

are innocents who are also wise in their battles against the giants of Bulika.[278] They come to rescue proud Vane who thought he could rescue them.[279] They stab giants with their spears,[280] and in a scene that Lewis would echo in *That Hideous Strength*, they lead an army of animals to take the city and capture Lilith. As Lewis would come to write of an elephant trampling upon folk at the interrupted N.I.C.E. banquet,[281] so in *Lilith* does an elephant trample upon a 'brute' of a giant who had just waylaid a horse with his hammer.[282] It is upon these elephants that the proud vampiress Lilith is ridden out of her city, bound hand and foot.[283]

And we have already seen in a tale for children, 'The Giant's Heart',[284] where little Buffy-Bob is not as harmless as his name might imply. He ends the story by burying his knife in a rapidly expanding giant's heart.[285] There is pity, in Tricksey-Wee's being sorry for the slain giant, but the slaying had to be done. The giant was lying when he promised not to keep eating children and proved it by trying to eat these two. MacDonald's meaning, or moral, is not difficult to guess. The wicked giant ate children; that is, he destroyed child-likeness. His heart swells to the 'size of a bullock'.[286] He is proud and pride must be killed, however sorry one may be for those who are proud. The child-likeness of Buffy-Bob and Tricksey-Wee may be humble, but it is strong and has the capacity to kill.

This point is driven home by MacDonald in *Adela Cathcart*, the original context of 'The Giant's Heart'. It is a tale told within a story, and one can tell clearly from the dialogue and narrative that follows the tale that MacDonald anticipated that some readers might not like the tale or its ending. One of the listeners replies, "'What a horrible story!'", and another, "'I don't think it at all a nice story for supper, with those horrid spiders, too'".[287] But one little girl comes up to Mr. Smith, the teller of the tale, and whispers very gently into his ears her gratitude for such a "'nice story'".[288] From this 'darling little blue-eyed girl', who hugs and kisses and whispers gently to Mr. Smith, we hear these

---

278 LIL, p. 283. See also LIL, pp. 224, 267.
279 See LIL, p. 255.
280 See LIL, p. 283.
281 See HS, p. 349.
282 LIL, p. 284.
283 See LIL, p. 292. A similar scene, of a troupe of animals laying waste to evil, occurs in *The Princess and Curdie*, published thirteen years earlier than *Lilith*. See chapters entitled 'The Avengers' and 'The Vengeance'.
284 See p. 130-131, above.
285 See AC, p. 337.
286 AC, p. 337.
287 AC, p. 337.
288 AC, p. 338.

words: "'Thank you, dear Mr. Smith [...] If I was a man, I would kill all the wicked people in the world. But I am only a little girl, you know; so I can only be good'".[289]

In his comment on the little girl's words, Smith the narrator reveals to us much of how MacDonald viewed God's goodness: 'The darling did not know how much more one good woman can do to kill evil than all the swords of the world in the hands of righteous heroes'.[290] In other words, to return to our metaphor, MacDonald's idea of God's goodness is that it is chivalrous. It is not evil people who must necessarily be killed; it is the 'evil' of the people, as Smith's reply reveals. And many swords 'in the hands of righteous heroes' are nothing in comparison to the actions of a single 'good woman' in accomplishing this. This is MacDonald showing where the letter of the little girl's response was inaccurate and thereby explicitly drawing attention to the allegorical meaning of his tale. But it is also MacDonald declaring that the spirit of the little blue-eyed darling is very accurate indeed in relation to what God's goodness is. In this gentle little Joan of Arc we get an excellent example of how MacDonald, before Lewis, portrays God's good love time after time. It is tender: child-like, gentle, courteous and maidenly. But it is no less fierce against that which is proud and unloving.

As in Lewis's poem, love is both 'warm as tears' and 'hard as nails'.[291] It voluntarily kneels before that which is good but has the mettle to struggle against that which is not. As MacDonald wrote, '[God] is love when he gives, and love when he withholds; love when he heals, and love when he slays'.[292] Power and strength may not be deepest in Love, but Love is powerful and strong, they believed. Even self-surrender, like that of the eternal Son to the Father, has always been strong. It is not proud or showy, but it is grand and strong in a deeper sense. Heaven's harmony may harbour no strife, but in strife on Earth Love has revealed its inherent strength, they believed. Love is not essentially competitive, but it has the wherewithal within its own essence to 'compete' against competition. Its meekness will kill pride and inherit the earth.[293] It stoops to conquer, but still it conquers.

Both authors believed all these things about the good and holy love of God: that he and those who follow him, in their own capacities, were all these things at once, or striving to become so. It is appropriate, then, to end our relatively isolated overviews of either tenderness or severity in their works, and begin to conclude the chapter with a review of how they depicted both things together.

---

289 AC, p. 338.
290 AC, p. 338.
291 POE, pp. 123-124.
292 US, p. 564 (last quarter of par. 14 in 'The Displeasure of Jesus', third series).
293 See Mat. 5.5.

Pictures of God

In *Phantastes*, the first book of MacDonald's that Lewis read, Anodos resolves to become squire to a rusty knight. The armoured, singing warrior, who drags a slain dragon behind his steed, accepts Anodos's request, significantly offering his gauntleted hand and saying, "'Squire and knight should be friends'".[294] The knight wishes to be lord *and* friend to Anodos, just as MacDonald stressed that God wanted 'sons' and 'daughters' to share in the 'divine nature', not simply slaves who crouch before him in fear.[295] Anodos soon discovers more thoroughly how his fealty has not been pledged in vain. He knows by watching the knight's familiar conversation with a simple peasant in a cottage that the white lady has made no mistake in preferring the knight to himself: 'A nobler countenance I never saw. Loving-kindness beamed from every line of his face. It seemed as if he would repay himself for the late arduous combat, by indulging in all the gentleness of a womanly heart'.[296]

But then the knight's gentle countenance grows strong and determined when he learns from his host that there is a severely injured child under the same roof. After falling into a moment of reverie,

> the exquisite curves of the upper lip vanished. The lip was lengthened and compressed at the same moment. You could have told that, within the lips, the teeth were firmly closed. The whole face grew stern and determined, all but fierce; only the eyes burned on like a holy sacrifice, uplift on a granite rock.[297]

The knight's chivalrous combination of strength and tenderness, and readiness to serve and save the weak, is made manifest in his actions toward the girl and her family, as Anodos recounts:

> The knight rose. The light that had been confined to his eyes, now shone from his whole countenance. He took the little thing in his arms, and, with the mother's help, undressed her, and looked to her wounds. The tears flowed down his face as he did so. With tender hands he bound them up, kissed the pale cheek, and gave her back to her mother. When he went home, all his tale would be of the grief and joy of the parents; while to me, who looked on, the gracious countenance of the armed man, beaming from the panoply of steel, over the seemingly dead child, while the powerful hands turned it and shifted it, and bound it, if possible even more gently than the mother's, formed the centre of the story.[298]

---

294 PHA, p. 169.
295 US, p. 299 (first quarter of par. 6 in 'Life', second series). See also US, p. 482 (first quarter of par. 3 in 'Freedom', third series).
296 PHA, p. 169.
297 PHA, p. 170.
298 PHA, p. 170.

Anodos, who in the beginning of the book is only concerned with possessing and imagining his Ideal—the white lady—is content to follow the lady's husband, this ideal knight who has become the song he sings[299]: "'This [...] is a true man. I will serve him, and give him all worship, seeing in him the imbodiment of what I would fain become. If I cannot be noble myself, I will yet be servant to his nobleness'".[300] Anodos is now pleased to follow this rusty knight in humility, in the same rainy, strife-filled world in which the knight gained his rustiness.

It is no surprise that one who was so taken with this book should create a golden Lion to match MacDonald's rusty knight. Aslan is the great king who brings the world of Narnia into being;[301] he is also the one whose eyes, when Digory looks up beyond his great paws and huge claws, are seen to contain 'great shining tears' due to his love for Digory and his suffering mother.[302] His roar is mighty enough to end all time,[303] as the rusty knight was mighty in slaying the dragon. But like the rusty knight with the family in the cottage, Aslan can be tenderly intimate with his sons and daughters: 'The great beast rolled over on his side so that Lucy fell, half sitting and half lying between his front paws. He bent forward and just touched her nose with his tongue. His warm breath came all round her'.[304]

Similar chivalry, as mentioned at the beginning of this chapter,[305] can be found in two of MacDonald's most famous characters: North Wind of *At the Back of the North Wind* and Queen Irene of the Curdie books. Both are represented as women, but they are mythical characters that represent more. Queen Irene, young Irene's great-great grandmother, is very tender when attending to Irene's hurt finger, and letting her head rest on her bosom as the two sleep together in the Queen's bedroom. But she is also severe, ordering Curdie at one point to thrust his hands into a mystical fire of burning roses.[306] She lifts a stone twenty men could not lift, but with fingers that are 'white and smooth as any lady's in the land'.[307] And in her penultimate appearance in the books, Curdie gets a glimpse of the lady in all her glory. It is a 'glorious terrible sight!' of her purifying and reviving the old befeebled king of Gwyntystorm.[308] At first sight it is too bright for him to see who is dropping the burning

---

299 Hence his singing after having slain the dragon. See WW, pp. 73-75 (III.i).
300 PHA, p. 174.
301 See *The Magician's Nephew*, chp. 9, for his creation of Narnia.
302 MN, p. 168.
303 See LB, pp. 186-188.
304 PC, p. 148.
305 See pp. 218-219, above.
306 See P&C, chp. 8.
307 P&C, p. 55.
308 P&C, p. 235.

roses upon the king's face and showering tears from her hair down upon the flames.[309] When the fire dies down Curdie can see that it is the old Queen, the Mistress of the Silver Moon, only now she shines golden, much like Lewis's Aslan would come to do: 'The room was lighted with the splendour of her face, of her blue eyes, of her sapphire crown. Her golden hair went streaming out from her through the air till it went off in mist and light. She was large and strong as a Titaness'.[310]

But the great mythical kings, queens and knights of these authors' books are not the only ones who unite both glory and grace in their characters. There are a number of examples in the two Curdie books themselves. In the second book MacDonald indicates the chivalry of Curdie's mother in one of the same ways he shows the chivalry of Queen Irene: by contrasting the inside with the outside. Her hands are hard and worn with work on the outside, but Curdie, by a magical gift he has just acquired, discovers that he is holding the hands of a beautiful princess. His mother jokes about her hard and horny hands being like those of a princess, but her husband Peter, Curdie's father, confirms the fact with his own knowledge: "'Curdie, your mother's foot is as pretty a foot as any lady's in the land, and where her hand is not so pretty it comes of killing its beauty for you and me, my boy'".[311] The miner knows his wife to be a "'true lady'".[312]

In another instance MacDonald creates a picture of chivalry with two characters. In the first book, Princess Irene runs to meet her papa the king after he's just ridden up on a white horse along with a troupe of his men. To the sound of bugle blasts her papa rides up the hill amidst a galloping vision of shining armour, gleaming spears and helmets, with banners flying and horses prancing. The king is delighted to see his little girl and stoops down from his mount to lift her up into the saddle with him. The two of them together are an image of chivalry, a mingling of seeming opposites on horseback:

> [the king] had gentle, blue eyes, but a nose that made him look like an eagle. A long dark beard, streaked with silvery lines, flowed from his mouth almost to his waist, and as Irene sat on the saddle and hid her glad face upon his bosom it mingled with the golden hair which her mother had given her, and the two together were like a cloud with streaks of the sun woven through it.[313]

---

309 Tears and flames, so closely intermingled in this scene, are also intermingled in Lewis's poem 'Love is as Warm as Tears'. See POE, p. 123.
310 P&C, p. 235.
311 P&C, p. 82.
312 P&C, pp. 82-83.
313 P&G, pp. 76-77.

And sometimes MacDonald doesn't even need people to paint such a picture. There is such a thing as the chivalry of a mountain, if the opening words of *The Princess and Curdie* can be believed. After telling the reader in the first paragraph of the book that Curdie's family lives in a cottage on a mountainside, and that Curdie and his father work as miners inside the mountain, MacDonald uses the same inside-out contrast as he does with Queen Irene and Curdie's mother to describe what a curious combination of awful severity and tender beauty a mountain really is.

People of old, we are told, were more sensitive to the awfulness of a mountain. They were afraid of mountains and unable to see how 'beautiful they are as well as awful'.[314] Likewise, the narrator tells how people in his day, now that they have learned to admire a mountain's beauty, may perhaps 'not feel quite awe enough of them'.[315] MacDonald, in the paragraphs that follow, makes sure that neither part is neglected, just as his representations of God and his goodness are both grand and tender. To him mountains are 'beautiful terrors'.[316]

Mountains are portions of the earth that originate deep down in the earth: a 'great wallowing mass' of 'glowing hot, melted metals and stones'.[317] From this great dark 'cauldron', where bubbles would be as big as the Alps if they had room to boil, from this heat of 'endless tumult' and 'boiling unrest' the portions of earth shoot up heavenward to cool in the cold 'everlasting stillness' of the starlit open air.[318] The masses of earth that were once 'molten and soft, heaving and glowing', become hard, shining and cold.[319] It becomes the home of creatures that scamper over and burrow in it, birds that build their nests upon it, and trees that grow out of its sides. These trees are like 'hair to clothe it', just as 'the lovely grass' in the valleys and 'gracious flowers' act as the 'rich embroidery' of its garment.[320] We see here, then, both the awful, fiery beginnings of a mountain and the delicate loveliness that it becomes. The finished product, too, maintains a paradoxical mingling of elements. The mountain on the outside is full of the loveliness of trees, grass, flowers and 'rivers galloping down the valleys in a tumult of white and green'.[321] The inside, though, retains the mountain's awful mysteries. There are 'caverns of awfullest

---

314 P&C, p. 1. See also the second essay on Dante in Ruskin's *Modern Painters, III* (1856).
315 P&C, p. 1.
316 P&C, p. 1.
317 P&C, p. 1.
318 P&C, p. 2.
319 P&C, p. 2.
320 P&C, pp. 2, 3.
321 P&C, p. 3.

solitude' with walls 'miles thick'.[322] There are underground brooks with 'eyeless fish' and masses of rock sparkling with precious metals and stones.[323] There are caverns full of both 'numbingly cold' and 'fiercely hot' water.[324]

Even if one limits mountains to their outsides, there remain chivalrous contrasts. The maidenly and welcoming loveliness of trees, grass, flowers and streams sits alongside 'terrible precipices' and 'dark profound lakes'.[325] 'Gracious' flowers lie on the very edge of the mountain's 'armour of ice',[326] much as the rusty knight's 'gracious countenance' beamed from beneath a 'panoply of steel'.[327]

What MacDonald sees in and on the mountain is often seen in and on the characters in his more realistic novels. Having written many novels with realistic settings, he of course had more opportunities than Lewis to express such chivalry in 'realistic' terms. We have already seen in several characters, especially in Robert Falconer, the heroic or rescuing sense of chivalry that does not hesitate to stoop or 'get its hands dirty' in serving others. But there are just as many examples of the sense that denotes the mingling of seeming opposites.

A good example of this is Peter Whalp, the blacksmith in *Alec Forbes* who stands as if he were the 'gnome-king of molten iron' before his fiery furnace.[328] Alec takes Annie Anderson to him so the cold child can warm herself near the 'murky' smith's fire.[329] She is at first afraid, shrinking to draw nigh to this burly man with his 'brawny arms that twisted and tortured iron bars all day long'.[330] Like the heart of the earth that produced the mountain upon which Curdie lives, there is 'a certain fierceness about the whole affair' with this 'giant smith' and his dragon of a furnace.[331] One look at the man's 'black-looking face' seems enough to have put the forge-fire 'out of countenance', but Alec leads Annie right up to the man who makes the fire hiss and sputter into a 'perfect insanity of fury'.[332]

Annie remains afraid until she hears the great Vulcan reply to Alec in kindly Scots. He wipes his hands on his apron, and lifts her up on it 'as tenderly as if she had been a baby'.[333] In between blowing the fire with the bellows

---

322 P&C, p. 3.
323 P&C, p. 3.
324 P&C, p. 3.
325 P&C, p. 3.
326 P&C, p. 3.
327 PHA, p. 170.
328 AFH, p. 88.
329 AFH, p. 88.
330 AFH, p. 88.
331 AFH, p. 88.
332 AFH, pp. 88-89.
333 AFH, p. 89.

and beating away at the red-hot sparking iron on his anvil, he carries on a conversation with Annie. Each succeeding question he asks her about herself is put 'in a yet kindlier voice' and he gives careful attention to look into her face with eyes that shine as if they might cry, in between bouts of work with fire and iron.[334] This 'terrible smith's heart' is 'just like his fire'; to Annie 'his ways were as soft and tender as a woman's'.[335] He is a man who can 'burn or warm'.[336]

This smith shows us something of one of MacDonald's favourite methods of depicting chivalry: by describing a particular human face, voice, form or manner. There is also the six-foot, square-shouldered, long-armed Robert Falconer with uncommonly large and powerful hands. His broad forehead projects over 'deep-sunk eyes' that shine 'like black fire'.[337] All of his features are large, especially his 'Roman nose', and finely 'though not delicately' modeled.[338] His nostrils, when he is excited, expand in a 'wild equine manner'.[339] His mouth expresses 'tender power, crossed with humour'.[340] He is a man of obvious gravity but is not merely grave: 'He kept his lips a little compressed, which gave a certain sternness to his countenance: but when his sternness dissolved into a smile, it was something enchanting'.[341]

In the same book Falconer's old friend, Dr. Anderson, has a face that expresses something similar in a distinctively Scottish way. As the narrator makes clear, Anderson's face is essentially the face of Scotland, or rather, the best elements of the Scottish character combined. This 'face of his ancestors', described just before his death, is tender and lofty: 'noble, sensitive, heart-full'.[342] But also hard and earthy: 'rugged, bucolic, and weather-beaten through centuries of windy ploughing, hail-stormed sheep-keeping, long-paced seed-sowing, and multi-form labour'.[343]

All of this, in one sense, goes back to MacDonald's own father, George Sr., the model for the title character of his first realistic novel.[344] As the younger MacDonald described David Elginbrod:

> His carriage was full of dignity, and a certain rustic refinement; his voice was wonderfully gentle, but deep; and slowest when most impassioned. He seemed to have come of some gigantic antediluvian breed: there

334 AFH, p. 89.
335 AFH, p. 89.
336 AFH, p. 89.
337 RF, p. 348.
338 RF, p. 348.
339 RF, p. 348.
340 RF, p. 348.
341 RF, p. 348.
342 RF, p. 320.
343 RF, pp. 320-321.
344 See RAEP, p. 22.

was something of the Titan slumbering about him. He would have been a stern man, but for an unusual amount of reverence that seemed to overflow the sternness, and change it into strong love.[345]

But in another sense that does not exclude what MacDonald learned from his father, all of this tenderness and severity goes back to Christ, the perfect living picture of who the Father is. We can see this in the face of Someone a young boy encounters in a dream in 'A Child's Holiday', one of MacDonald's realistically-set short stories. Herbert, in his dream, is being carried over the tumultuous storms and waves of a sea, much like Diamond is often carried in *North Wind*. When the boy looks up from the tumult, he sees the face of one whom we see again and again, in different forms, throughout MacDonald's works:

> And lo! a shadowy face bent over him, whence love unutterable was falling in floods, from eyes deep, and dark, and still, as the heavens that are above the clouds. Great waves of hair streamed back from a noble head, and floated on the tides of the tempest. The face was like his mother's and like his father's, and like a face that he had seen somewhere in a picture, but far more beautiful and strong and loving than all.[346]

Suddenly Herbert realises that the face he has been looking into is the face of his 'Lord' and 'Master',[347] the face which MacDonald and Lewis attempt to depict in one way or another in all their books. All of their representations of God and his goodness, from the rusty knight to Aslan, strive to show something of the eternal union of severe and tender love revealed in the face of Jesus Christ.

Lewis's stories, as mentioned, are less frequently set in very realistic places, and so there are not that many realistic parallels to what MacDonald has written in his novels. But it is clear in perhaps his most realistically set book, *That Hideous Strength*, that Lewis took note of all of MacDonald's methods of expressing the chivalrous love we have been speaking of. In this book the appearance and manner of Ransom[348] helps Jane Studdock see the sort of splendour and tenderness that shows up in so many ways in MacDonald's books.

It might have been difficult to determine which situation of which book of MacDonald's Jane Studdock's encounter with Ransom most closely resembles, since all such situations in MacDonald's books, as we have seen, resemble each other. It might have been difficult, that is, if Lewis hadn't included clear hints

345 DE, p. 70.
346 AC, pp. 363-364.
347 AC, p. 364.
348 Excepting Aslan, Lewis's most obviously Christ-like character.

himself, as if he were paying homage to a particular book of MacDonald's. The most obvious clue is when Ransom, called mostly 'The Director' in *Hideous Strength*, specifically mentions *The Princess and Curdie* to Jane in conversation.[349] But there are other hints that are also similarities. What Jane's encounter with the Director resembles most are Princess Irene's and Curdie's encounters with their great-great grandmother in both the Curdie books.

Jane's encounter, for example, requires her to ascend several flights of stairs to reach the 'upper floors' of a large house, just as Irene and Curdie must wind their way up staircases in the castle to reach Queen Irene.[350] The predominating colour of Ransom's room, like Queen Irene's, is blue.[351] To Jane it seems as if she and the Director are 'perched in a blue tower overlooking the world', as in fact Queen Irene's room is a blue tower overlooking the world.[352] In place of the usual silvery moonlight that brightens Queen Irene's tower, golden light, like that of the glorified Queen Irene in the second Curdie book,[353] brightens the Director's room and the path to it.[354] As with MacDonald's Mistress of the Silver Moon, the light in Ransom's room seems difficult to separate from Ransom himself: 'all the light in the room seemed to run towards the gold hair and the gold beard of the wounded man'.[355] And like Queen Irene, the Director seems both old and young at once. At first glance he looks to be a boy of twenty years with fresh skin on his forehead, cheeks and hands. But Jane finds that he, like the smithy Annie encounters in *Alec Forbes*, is no mere boy: 'no boy could have so full a beard. And no boy could be so strong. She had expected to see an invalid [...] imagination suggested that those arms and shoulders could support the whole house'.[356]

It eventually dawns on Jane with 'quick fear' that the Director's face has no age whatsoever.[357] His golden beard brings back to her the forgotten images of her childhood of bearded kings, especially Solomon, the 'bright solar blend of king and lover and magician'.[358] From the Director Jane receives her first real taste of 'the word king itself', and this taste is like that which the princess and Curdie encounter in their great-grandmother.[359] In the Director there is both

---

349 See HS, p. 149.
350 HS, p. 141.
351 See HS, p. 141; P&G, p. 89.
352 HS, p. 142.
353 See P&C, chp. 31, 'The Sacrifice'; p. 253-254, above.
354 See HS, pp. 141-142.
355 HS, p. 142. Compare P&G, p. 86.
356 HS, p. 142.
357 HS, p. 143.
358 HS, p. 143.
359 HS, p. 143.

'mercy' and 'power'.[360] His voice reveals him to be much like the smithy of *Alec Forbes* who could burn or warm: 'the voice also seemed to be like sunlight and gold. Like gold not only as gold is beautiful but as it is heavy: like sunlight not only as it falls gently on English walls in autumn but as it beats down on the jungle or the desert to engender life or destroy it'.[361] And so Jane alternatively thinks throughout her encounter how it is impossible to regard him as either young—as when she sees his beard and the strength in his countenance, or old—as when she sees the 'laughter in his eyes' after he's fed crumbs to a group of mice.[362]

Jane finds in the Director the same distinctive combination of severity and tenderness that readers encounter in all of MacDonald's books: that mingled beauty of holy love which we have been calling chivalry. As Ransom in *Hideous Strength* resembles so many of MacDonald's characters in this, so would Aslan and many characters of the Narnia books[363] come to resemble Ransom, the rusty knight of *Phantastes,* and Queen Irene. And Lewis, of course, depicts a glorified George MacDonald this way in *The Great Divorce.* He is 'an enthroned and shining god, whose ageless spirit weighed upon mine like a burden of solid gold', but at the same time 'an old weather-beaten man, one who might have been a shepherd'. All of these characters are different, but all of them have the capacity for gravity *and* gladness. They are all in their various ways both fierce and meek 'to the *n*th'.[364] And they are all ready to save, and ready to stoop and suffer in order to do it.

The Art of Love

There are two last observations that need to be made, however, before this study of their ideas and depictions of God's goodness can be complete. The first is that neither MacDonald nor Lewis thought it was easy or natural. Becoming a son of God like the Son of God, with all of the humility and strength that this demands, is very difficult indeed. Lewis makes specific reference to this in his essay on chivalry. The 'medieval ideal', he writes, 'brought together two things which have no natural tendency to gravitate towards one another'.[365] The great warrior needed to be taught humility 'because everyone knew by experience how much he usually needed that lesson', and the 'urbane and modest' man needed to be urged to valour since 'everyone knew that he was as likely as not to be a milksop'.[366]

---

360 HS, p. 143.
361 HS, p. 143.
362 HS, p. 149.
363 The first was published four years later than *Hideous Strength*.
364 See PRC, p. 13; pp. 217, above.
365 PRC, p. 14.
366 PRC, p. 14.

In relation to 'any lasting happiness or dignity' in human society, Lewis writes how the Middle Ages 'fixed on the one hope of the world' in the ideal of chivalry.[367] It may not be possible, he says, to produce very many Lancelots, but if society doesn't, then history is doomed to never-ending cycles of barbarism: 'Hardy barbarians swarm down from their highlands and obliterate a civilisation. Then they become civilised themselves and go soft. Then a new wave of barbarians comes down and obliterates *them*. Then the cycle begins over again'.[368] The only escape from 'a world divided between wolves who do not understand, and sheep who cannot defend, the things which make life desirable', he writes, is the art of chivalry.[369]

This study, of course, is neither historical nor sociological, but this point of Lewis's about chivalry being civilization's only hope helps isolate an important aspect of the human share in the Divine Character. The art of becoming more loving, or more like what Love himself is, is very well symbolised by the art of chivalry. As we have already learned in this and previous chapters, both authors believed that one must be ruthless with God against one's own wickedness and pride while at the same time humble in obedience to the good will of God. As Lewis writes of the paradoxical ideal of chivalry, it is something that we are not naturally inclined to do: 'The man who combines both characters—the knight—is a work not of nature but of art; of that art which has human beings, instead of canvas or marble, for its medium'.[370]

But then the hardness or difficulty in an art, it must also be remembered, is not all there is to art. There is the raw material without which no art is possible. Sculpting is not simply a matter of crushing stone, as the art of singing is not simply a matter of removing and disposing of one's vocal chords. Stone must be ruled and shaped by someone who is more than mere stone, and vocal chords cannot teach themselves to sing. But still there is stone to form and throats to discipline. Art is not accomplished with a simple despising of the medium. And in this sense, the combined hardness and softness of the knight is again helpful in symbolising how the art of love, to MacDonald's and Lewis's understandings, relates to the medium: that is, man's natural self. As we have already mentioned, neither author believed in self-denial for the sake of denial.[371] With these two there is no question of simply despising nature and attempting to escape to the purely spiritual.

The most frequent way Lewis describes this art being accomplished is by prioritising God's will, or God's love. All other things, he is always

---

367 PRC, pp. 14-15.
368 PRC, p. 15.
369 PRC, p. 16.
370 PRC, p. 15.
371 See pp. 210-213, above.

writing, must die or abdicate in submitting to the rule of God and his love. As MacDonald the character tells Lewis in *The Great Divorce*, explaining both the title and the point of the book: "'Nothing, not even the best and noblest, can go on as it now is. Nothing, not even what is lowest and bestial, will not be raised again if it submits to death [...] Flesh and blood cannot come to the Mountains. Not because they are too rank, but because they are too weak'".[372] All things, including all natural things, will be made pure and strong, but they must first submit to God's art.

In *The Four Loves*, for instance, Lewis notes how romantic love, the most 'god-like' and boasting natural love,[373] cannot be all it promises without submitting to God's love. Eros is right in a sense to make so many promises: 'The event of falling in love is of such a nature that we are right to reject as intolerable the idea that it should be transitory. In one high bound it has overleaped the massive wall of our selfhood; it has made appetite itself altruistic, tossed personal happiness aside as a triviality and planted the interests of another in the centre of our being'.[374] But this escape from hell's philosophy may be short-lived, he writes, if something stronger than Eros isn't allowed to help her keep her many promises:

> Can we be in this selfless liberation for a lifetime? Hardly for a week. Between the best possible lovers this high condition is intermittent. The old self soon turns out to be not so dead as he pretended [...] In either he may be momentarily knocked flat; he will soon be up again; if not on his feet, at least on his elbow, if not roaring, at least back to his surly grumbling or his mendicant whine.[375]

Those couples most likely to fall prey to this revived hellish self, he writes, are those who have idolised the state of 'Being in Love': 'They thought [Eros] had the power and truthfulness of a god. They expected that mere feeling would do for them, and permanently, all that was necessary'.[376] Instead, Lewis writes, they find that Eros, 'having made his gigantic promise and shown you in glimpses what its performance would be like', has quit the field: 'He, like a godparent, makes the vows; it is we who must keep them. It is we who must labour to bring our daily life into even closer accordance with what the glimpses have revealed. We must do the works of Eros when Eros is not present'.[377]

At one point Lewis uses the analogy of a garden to suggest this art of love: 'It is no disparagement to a garden to say that it will not fence and weed

---

372 GD, p. 87.
373 4L, p. 110.
374 4L, p. 114.
375 4L, p. 114.
376 4L, p. 114.
377 4L, p. 115.

itself, nor prune its own fruit trees, nor roll and cut its own lawns. A garden is a good thing but that is not the sort of goodness it has. It will remain a garden, as distinct from a wilderness, only if someone does all these things to it'.[378] Just as the great warrior needs to learn courtesy, so does the wilderness of our natural loves, as vigorous and brave as they may be, need something more. Gardens need both the vigour of nature and the nurturing discipline of our gardening. As Lewis writes of these necessary elements, there is the 'beauty, energy and fecundity' of even the 'commonest weed' of nature in contrast to the dead and sterile tools of a gardener: 'hoes, rakes, shears, and packet of weed killer'.[379] But both are necessary, just as both natural and divine elements are necessary in the art of loving: 'When [God] planted the garden of our nature and caused the flowering, fruiting loves to grow there, He set our will to "dress" them'.[380] Compared with the natural beauties of our loves, our 'dressing' them, he writes, is 'dry', 'cold', 'laborious', and 'largely negative', but it is nonetheless 'indispensable' to the perfecting and strengthening of our loves.[381]

What all this gardening means in non-figurative terms, Lewis writes, is loving God more than anything else, or putting his love first. This prioritisation, however, means neither loving others *less*, nor always *feeling* towards God what one does for others. If our natural loves become inordinate, he writes, it will only be so relative to how much we love God: 'It is probably impossible to love any human being simply "too much". We may love him too much *in proportion* to our love for God; but it is the smallness of our love for God, not the greatness of our love for the man, that constitutes the inordinacy'.[382] Or as Lewis once wrote in a letter, this first allegiance to God's love, though it requires all other loves to bow, actually makes them stronger:

> When I have learnt to love God better than my earthly dearest, I shall love my earthly dearest better than I do now. In so far as I learn to love my earthly dearest at the expense of God and *instead* of God, I shall be moving towards the state in which I shall not love my earthly dearest at all. When first things are put first, second things are not suppressed but increased.[383]

But as mentioned, this loving God more than one's earthly dearest, Lewis believed, is not about 'the comparative intensity of two feelings'.[384] 'Otherwise', Lewis writes in *Four Loves*, 'we shall trouble some who are very

---

378 4L, p. 116.
379 4L, p. 117.
380 4L, p. 117.
381 4L, pp. 117-118.
382 4L, p. 122.
383 LLET, p. 429 (8 Nov. 1952).
384 4L, p. 122.

much on the right road but alarmed because they cannot feel towards God so warm a sensible emotion as they feel for the earthly Beloved'.[385]

What the subordination, or good death, of our natural loves to God and his love boils down to, he writes, is the question of 'which (when the alternative comes) do you serve, or choose, or put first? To which claim does your will, in the last resort, yield?'.[386] It is to be hoped, he writes, that all one's loves can be ordered so as to avoid any conflict, ordered so that all natural loves are lived in the light of God's unconditional Gift-love,[387] but that if the conflict in the end does come, 'we must turn down or disqualify our nearest and dearest when they come between us and our obedience to God'.[388]

We have already made reference in this study to Lewis's fictional expression of what may result if God and his love is not put first: the weak or oppressive loves of Mark and Jane Studdock, Orual, and the ghosts of *The Great Divorce*. One could say that these loves, as Lewis portrayed them, forgot their Lord, or refused to acknowledge or obey anything above themselves. Like a wilderness that refuses the shears and weed killer of the gardener, they remain wild and weak, much as the great warrior whose passions rule him will never become a knight.

It may be argued that MacDonald does not stress this sort of prioritisation as much as Lewis, and one can certainly see why it may go unnoticed. His Wordsworthian love and appreciation for nature and his Burns-like emphasis on homely, often vernacular, authenticity does not immediately bring to mind the shears or weed killer of a gardener. But we have already learned enough here to see that MacDonald is not simply a Romantic who worships nature or feeling. Nature, to him, is inadequate, and authenticity does not come simply by following one's moods.[389] As he illustrates in his last adult fantasy, *Lilith*, 'child-like' is not synonymous with 'childish',[390] and Lilith is more than what she *feels* herself to be.[391] MacDonald, though he is very much like Wordsworth, Burns, Coleridge and Novalis, is by no means a Rousseau. Society and civilisation may oppress the child-like in his books, but his child-like characters are not noble because they are simpletons or savages. They are giant killers who, unlike the giants, know how to look up, and how to bow down to something other than natural feeling, appetite or pride.[392] They learn

---

385 4L, p. 122.
386 4L, pp. 122-123.
387 For Gift-love, see 4L, pp. 1-9, 128-129; p. 188-189, above.
388 4L, p. 124.
389 See above, pp. 111-112.
390 See the Little Ones in *Lilith*: pp. 249-250, above.
391 See LIL, chp. 39; pp. 204-205, above.
392 See Little Ones and giants in *Lilith*: LIL, p. 262.

to kill their self-serving passions.[393] They lose their childish weightlessness and learn to walk in the gravity of self-sacrificial love.[394]

If we look closely enough, we can find MacDonald writing very similar things indeed to the kind of prioritisation that Lewis would come to write of. As Lewis would write in *The Four Loves* of the most 'god-like' loves being potentially the most demon-like,[395] so does MacDonald write in a sermon that it is not the 'fetters that gall', but the 'fetters that soothe' or those 'of gold' that threaten to 'eat into the soul'.[396] As Lewis would come to write of all things and all loves being increased in the light of God and his love, so MacDonald writes of no thing or no love reaching its potential without our giving pre-eminence to God:

> no man who has not the Father so as to be eternally content in him alone, can possess a sunset or a field of grass or a mine of gold or the love of a fellow-creature according to its nature—as God would have him possess it—in the eternal way of inheriting, having, and holding. He who has God, has all things, after the fashion in which he who made them has them.[397]

In another sermon we see how MacDonald, before Lewis, indicates that this first allegiance to God is something other than a greater intensity of feeling. In another passage that Lewis marks and underlines in his own copy, MacDonald writes: 'The true man trusts in a strength which is not his, and which he does not feel, does not even always desire'.[398] MacDonald's direct influence here is unmistakable. What we find in Lewis we find first in MacDonald.

The good death, or submission, of all things and loves to God, is most clearly seen in MacDonald's sermon 'Self-denial'. What is also clear is how he, before Lewis, understood God's goodness and our following him in it. Towards nature, our natural selves and natural loves, Christian self-denial is both softer and harder than the old Manicheans and others who have viewed nature as something to be escaped or denied as an evil itself. As MacDonald writes, 'Neither nature, art, science, nor fit society, is of those things a man will lose in forsaking himself: they are God's, and have no part in the world

---

393 See Anodos in *Phantastes*.
394 See 'The Light Princess'.
395 4L, p. 110.
396 US, p. 202 (first quarter of par. 25 in 'The Hardness of the Way', second series).
397 US, p. 201 (second and third quarters of par. 21 in the same sermon). Lewis underlines the last sentence in his copy.
398 US, p. 305 (third quarter of par. 11 in 'Life', second series). Lewis marks all, and underlines 'does not even always desire'.

of evil'.[399] Some of these things may have to be denied at times in order to kill the evil, inaccurate tendency that calls all things 'my own', but the things denied are not evil in themselves, no more than a plant that has to be pruned is evil in itself. As MacDonald writes, one 'may have to deny himself in leaving them—not as bad things, but as things for which there is not room until those of paramount claim have been so heeded, that these [the things denied] will no longer impede but further them'.[400]

In other words the Christian 'gardener', like the Christian knight, is distinct in that he strives to rule his nature and perfect it, not simply destroy it. Denial of things natural in this Christian sense is a chivalrous strife. The total war is against the philosophy of hell, not nature herself or our natural loves. As Lewis writes in *The Problem of Pain* concerning denial, 'where other systems expose our total nature to death (as in Buddhist renunciation) Christianity demands only that we set right a *misdirection* of our nature'.[401] In a sermon later published as an article, he characterises the Christian attitude toward nature as at once more severe than nature religions, which 'simply affirm my natural desires', and more tender than 'anti-natural' religions 'that simply contradict them'.[402]

This attitude is clearly evident in MacDonald's sermon on self-denial, where he writes how learning to forsake things 'where the Master says one thing and they another', is to learn to love the things or people denied 'in a far higher, deeper, tenderer, truer way than before'.[403] As Lewis would write of one's earthly dearest being loved more when one puts God first, so MacDonald writes here. And so we see where Lewis followed MacDonald in seeing good death as an art, an art that actually leads to 'more life'.[404]

It must also be mentioned, though, that both writers believed that this art of becoming more loving was too hard for humans to accomplish on their own. They both believed it to be impossible, in fact, without divine intervention. As Lewis writes in an essay, personal morality 'is a mountain which we cannot climb by our own efforts'.[405] And even if one could reach the summit of moral perfection, he would not have become all that Divine Love requires: 'we should only perish in the ice and unbreathable air of the summit, lacking those wings with which the rest of the journey has to be accomplished'.[406]

---

399 US, pp. 380-381 (first quarter of par. 15 in 'Self-Denial', second series).
400 US, p. 381 (second quarter of par. 15 in the same sermon).
401 PP, p. 104.
402 GDK, p. 86.
403 US, pp. 381-382 (last quarter of par. 15 in 'Self-Denial', second series).
404 CFT, p. 143. Mossy learns how tasting of death in a magic bath is actually more life.
405 GDK, p. 113.
406 GDK, p. 113.

We can see this in his fiction when a space-travelling monk in one of his short stories asks forgiveness from God for his isolated pursuit of piety: "'I had been supposing you sent me on a voyage of forty million miles merely for my own spiritual convenience'".[407] The monk's concern for God and his own personal holiness, he learns, is only the very beginning of following God in love. In a real sense it is even opposed to following the Love that God is and may very well add to his pride and self-centredness. As Lewis writes in *Mere Christianity*: 'The devil laughs. He is perfectly content to see you becoming chaste and brave and self-controlled provided, all the time, he is setting up in you the Dictatorship of Pride—just as he would be quite content to see your chilblains cured if he was allowed, in return, to give you cancer'.[408] This can also be seen in *Pilgrim's Regress* when Vertue must lose his dignity, be cured of 'playing the Stoic' and descend to humble faith.[409] But even a descent into humility is a treacherously difficult path to keep, as Lewis writes in an essay: 'A man is never so proud as when striking an attitude of humility'.[410] Or as he puts it in *Mere Christianity*, the 'relief' and 'comfort' of taking the 'fancy-dress' of Pride off is impossibly difficult to come by for creatures who are by nature used to thinking of themselves.[411] 'Thinking about humility', he writes, may simply be another way of a man 'thinking about himself'.[412]

The impossible task of killing one's Pride by one's self is symbolised most strikingly by Lewis in *The Voyage of the Dawn Treader* when Eustace, a selfish bully, is changed into a dragon. This change, like Agnes's experience in MacDonald's 'The Wise Woman',[413] opens his eyes to the monstrosity his Pride has made him into: 'He wanted to get back among humans and talk and laugh and share things. He realized that he was a monster cut off from the whole human race. An appalling loneliness came over him'.[414]

Eustace is eventually changed back into a boy again, but not without excruciating difficulty. He is awakened by Aslan one night and follows him to a garden far away on the top of a mountain. In the middle of this garden lies a large well which resembles a bath. Eustace the dragon wants to bathe in it, but Aslan tells him he must first undress. After Eustace guesses what this might mean for a dragon, he begins scratching and peeling away layer after

---

407 C.S. Lewis, 'Ministering Angels', in *The Dark Tower and Other Stories* (London: Harper Collins, 1998), p. 117.
408 MC, p. 112.
409 REG, pp. 196-198.
410 CHR, p. 29.
411 MC, p. 114.
412 MC, p. 114. Compare PHA, p. 166: 'Self will come to life even in the slaying of self'.
413 See above, pp. 203-204.
414 VDT, p. 98.

layer of snaky, scaly skin from himself, as one peels the skin off a banana. He finds, however, that the layers of dragon skin seem to go on forever and that there is no getting down to his true self. But then Aslan tells the dragon that he will have to let him, the Lion, undress him, much as the ghosts in *Divorce* cannot cease to be ghosts without allowing one of the Shining Ones to kill their ghostliness. Even though Eustace is afraid of the Lion's claws, and even though it does hurt dreadfully, he submits to the undressing and emerges 'un-dragoned' after Aslan completes the peeling and throws him into the pool for a bath.[415]

This baptismal scene resembles many scenes in MacDonald's stories, as in 'The Golden Key' where both Mossy and Tangle submit to a magic bath which is both a 'taste of death' and 'more life'.[416] Before Eustace submitted to Aslan's undressing, there is Mossy who allows the Old Man of the Sea to help undress him and lay him a bath.[417] There is also the light princess who allows herself to be embraced by the prince who then falls with her down into a lake. And there is of course *Phantastes*, where Lewis first read of such bathings. Anodos at one point undresses to bathe in a fairy bath in a fairy castle, where the waters 'enter and revive' his heart.[418] At another point he descends, as the light princess does, down and down until he is able to plunge deep into a sea which 'bathed my spirit'.[419] In all of these instances, the bathers, like Eustace, descend into humble child-likeness to allow something or someone to do what he or she cannot do for themselves, as when Lilith allows Adam to cut away the possessive hand that she herself cannot open, try though she may.[420]

This neediness and humble willingness to accept help from above is evident and explicit in MacDonald's more realistic novels. It is most thoroughly expressed in *Robert Falconer* when Falconer attempts to convince a poor London silk weaver named De Fleuri to swallow his pride and stop refusing help for his sick daughter. De Fleuri does not believe in God, will not descend to 'ask a favour' even to help his family, and is 'fond of being hungry' so long as he doesn't have to ask for help.[421] He is 'proud as Lucifer' and provides inspiration for Lewis's dwarves in how he doesn't 'choose to be taken in',[422] not even for a cup of tea under Falconer's roof.[423] But Falconer is persistent and De Fleuri, after having heard Falconer's own story over a

---

415 See VDT, pp. 113-117.
416 CFT, p. 142.
417 See CFT, p. 141.
418 PHA, p. 75.
419 PHA, pp. 120, 124-126.
420 See LIL, pp. 323-324, 345-345; p. 175, above.
421 RF, p. 343.
422 See above, pp. 69-70.
423 RF, p. 344.

cup of tea, acknowledges his need and gives in. He accepts Falconer's help for his daughter and eventually becomes Falconer's assistant in helping other needy folk in the area.[424] It is even stressed how Falconer himself submits to accepting help: 'in all that region of London it became known that the man who loved the poor was himself needy, and looked to the poor for their help'.[425]

When Falconer finally does find his lost father, he meets even stronger resistance than in De Fleuri. Andrew Falconer is absolutely dominated by his addiction to opium and other drugs, but when he is nursed back by his son into a healthy enough state to speak, he utters, like De Fleuri and Lilith, his proud defiance and unwillingness to accept help. His son is a doctor, but this does not keep him from insisting that he is well enough to leave and be on his own again: "'I am quite well enough to go, and have a right to judge for myself [...] I tell you I will not be treated like a child'".[426] Instead of becoming as a little child,[427] like Anodos, Mossy, Tangle and Eustace, who all submit to a humble undressing and bath, the elder Falconer demands "'my clothes'" and "'my liberty'", even if they are the clothes and liberty of a decaying drug addict.[428] Even when he is told that he has been saved from probable death, he will not yield his pride: "'I tell you I *will* go. I do not choose to live on charity. I will *not*. I demand my clothes'".[429]

Andrew does eventually begin to yield to his son's and God's love, and in the last chapter of the book the narrator makes it explicit that although God has given a 'making share'[430] to men in their redemption, no redemption is possible without God. He compares the difficulty of a man redeeming himself to the difficulty of a hyena having the wherewithal to declare that he will become a man and being able to accomplish it.[431] The human need to give into God's help, or to allow one's self to be 'taken in' to him, is to MacDonald's mind *the* fact of human existence, as these words near the end of the story make clear beyond all doubt:

> I heartily believe, though I cannot understand the boundaries of will and inspiration, that what God will do for us at last is infinitely beyond any greatness we could gain, even if we could will ourselves from the lowest we could be, into the highest we can imagine [...] One thing is sure: we are his, and he will do his part, which is no part but the all in all. If man could do what in his wildest self-worship he can imagine,

---

424 See RF, pp. 344-345, 373-374.
425 RF, p. 374.
426 RF, p. 395.
427 See Mark 10.15; Luke 18.17.
428 RF, p. 395.
429 RF, p. 395.
430 DOS, p. 117 (17 Dec.).
431 RF, p. 415.

the grand result would be that he would be his own God, which is the Hell of Hells.[432]

Good Hierarchy

This point regarding the need to be rescued from above leads directly to the last observation this chapter will make: that both MacDonald and Lewis believed that God's goodness was hierarchical. As the Son has eternally subordinated himself to the Father, and delighted in it, so will God preserve the distinctions that make all other such yieldings possible, they believed. That we shall be more like the Goodness he is will neither muddy the distinction between himself and us nor the distinctions between his various creatures. To both writers the advent of universal love will not mean the realisation of absolute equality. God will love all, and all will love each other, but the war God wages to bring this heaven into being is a war against evil, they believed, not a war against variety. Men may have used distinctions in evil ways, but God will no more wage total war on distinctions themselves than he wages total war on nature itself.

Such can be seen, for example, in the passages referred to above in which De Fleuri resists Falconer's help. De Fleuri rejects his help because it is "'charity'", or help from above, not help between "'equals'".[433] Even though Falconer responds by noting that he treats De Fleuri "'as an equal'", the silk weaver remains obstinate: "'But you know that don't make us equals'".[434] To which Falconer responds, "'But isn't there something better than being equals? [...] Do you think now, Mr. De Fleuri, if you weren't something more to me than a mere equal, I would go telling you my own history? [...] Come, don't be a fool. I want you'".[435]

What MacDonald believed to be better than mere equality is the maze of intermingling but distinct beings, and kinds of beings, that he believed God created. As much as MacDonald writes against the abuses and snobbery of class pride, he never advocates the reduction of reality into a morass of sameness. In one sermon, for example, he speaks of the dangers of a superior inflicting torture upon an inferior, but then affirms the 'divine idea of a superior' who 'protects, helps, and delivers'.[436] The right relation of men to animals, for example, is 'that of their superiors in the family' of God's creation who are 'just, helpful', and 'protective' to them as God is to humans and all creation.[437]

---

432 RF, p. 415.
433 RF, p. 334.
434 RF, p. 344.
435 RF, p. 344.
436 HG, p. 219.
437 HG, pp. 219-220.

It is not the superiority or the just rule of superiors he argues against, but the use some have made of inferiors.[438]

All of this, again, goes back to his understanding of the Divine Fatherhood and Sonship that has always been united and always distinct. As he writes in another sermon, the Son's greatness consists in 'his Father being greater than he'.[439] 'The Father was always the Father, the Son always the Son', he writes, and the Son is ever devoted to the Father above him.[440] He does not think of his own goodness, but 'for his Father's goodness, he would spend life, suffering, labour, death, to make that known!'.[441] And the Father has always 'given to the Son' without the distinction between Father and Son ever being lost.[442]

As he believed of the Divine Relation, so MacDonald believed of the relation of children to parents, and even wives to husbands. A parent's relation to his child may be very different from a husband's relation to his wife, but MacDonald thought they both were relations between people who were not equal in all respects. We have already shown where his conception of God and his goodness dictated that all men ought to have some tenderness to them, like the rusty knight, and that all women ought to have some severity to them. As God himself is both severe and tender in love, so should both his sons and daughters be. But this art of chivalry in the man or the woman never means a man is made other than a man, or a woman other than a woman. As he writes of the good transformation of the inhabitants of a castle, who've come under the influence of their Christ-like elder brother, in a parable entitled 'The Castle', 'The voices of the men were deeper, and yet it seemed by their very depth more feminine than before; while the voices of the women were softer and sweeter, and at the same time more full and decided'.[443] The men acquire the tenderness of a woman, but their voices never cease to be the voices of men: they grow even deeper. And the women's softness and sweetness is not decreased by the fact that they become more full and decided. The preponderancies that made them either women or men are maintained. The increase in chivalry is not matched by a decrease in their original identity. Things have been transformed for the better, as a gardener transforms a wilderness, but no good distinction has been marred.[444]

438 Passages of this sermon, 'The Hope of the Universe', are echoed in an essay by Lewis on vivisection, originally published as an anti-vivisection pamphlet. See HG, pp. 190-224; GDK, pp. 224-228.
439 US, p. 172 (first quarter of par. 17 in 'The Way', second series).
440 US, p. 172 (first quarter of par. 17 in the same sermon).
441 US, p. 173 (third quarter of par. 17 in the same).
442 US, p. 172 (first quarter of par. 17 in the same).
443 AC, p. 436.
444 See RAEP, p. 261, for how MacDonald's women characters do not assert their

Lewis is just as clear on this, and more frequent in mentioning it. Along with MacDonald he thought that 'there ought spiritually to be a man in every woman and a woman in every man', as he once wrote to a Sister Penelope, one of his most frequent correspondents. 'And how horrid the ones who haven't got it are: I can't bear a "man's man" or a "woman's woman"'.[445] In *Screwtape* he expresses this by recording the demon's revulsion towards a girl who has acquired the chivalrous combination of sweetness and strength that we've been speaking of:

> I have looked up this girl's dossier and am horrified at what I find. Not only a Christian but such a Christian—a vile, sneaking, simpering, demure, monosyllabic, mouselike, watery, insignificant, virginal, bread-and-butter miss! The little brute! She makes me vomit. She stinks and scalds through the very pages of the dossier [...] We'd have had her to the arena in the old days. That's what her sort is made for. Not that she'd do much good there, either. A two-faced little cheat (I know the sort) who looks as if she'd faint at the sight of blood, and then dies with a smile. A cheat every way. Looks as if butter wouldn't melt in her mouth, and yet has a satirical wit. The sort of creature who'd find *ME* funny! Filthy, insipid little prude—and yet ready to fall into this booby's arms like any other breeding animal.[446]

The demon's uncomplimentary reference to the woman's virginity near the end of the quote allows us a glimpse of the art of human chivalry in microcosm. The girl in her virginity is like the girl as a whole: both severe and tender. She is severe towards whatever sexual desire she may have, unwilling to let it rule her. She denies it. But not for the sake of denial. Her hard denial of her natural sexual desire, as something that would rule her, is motivated not by a hatred of sex, but by a love for something greater that includes and transforms sex. As Screwtape puts it, she is 'ready to fall into this booby's arms'. In this way she is tender towards natural sexuality because she is tender in love towards her beloved.

The willingness of this woman to fall into her man's arms is also a picture of how Lewis believed the individual art of chivalry—that is, acquiring both 'feminine' sweetness and 'masculine' strength in one's self—does not impede the art of chivalry *between* individuals. That a woman should in some senses be 'manly' does not mean she should be unwilling to fall into her man's arms as the woman she is. A woman who was unwilling to do so would not be strong in Lewis's eyes: only weak in her inability to open the closed hand of her arrogance, pride, and competitive spirit. This understanding can be seen in everything from his explanations as to why Christian marriage is not about

equality or superiority.
445 LLET, p. 417 (10 Jan. 1952).
446 SCL, p. 101 (Letter XXII).

utter equality,[447] to what sense husbands should (and should not) be considered the head of their wives,[448] to how Aristotle, Spenser, Shakespeare, Milton and others understood hierarchy.[449] Or as to why Christian marriages and the Christian church (regarding women priests) ought to resist the secular move towards complete equality:

> The innovators are really implying that sex is something superficial, irrelevant to the spiritual life [...] As the State grows like a hive or an ant-hill it needs an increasing number of workers who can be treated as neuters. This may be inevitable for our secular life. But in our Christian life we must return to reality. There we are not homogenous units, but different and complementary organs of a mystical body [...] We have no authority to take the living and semitive figures which God has painted on the canvas of our nature and shift them about as if they were mere geometrical figures.[450]

As MacDonald distinguished between hierarchy and the abuses of hierarchy, so Lewis does here: 'We men may often make very bad priests. That is because we are insufficiently masculine [...] A given man may make a very bad husband; you cannot mend matters by trying to reverse the roles'.[451] And so he believed of all good distinctions that come in contact with the Goodness that God is.[452]

We can see in one of MacDonald's sermons that he thought the same. And we may even discover an inspiration for Lewis's gardening analogy in *The Four Loves*,[453] for MacDonald writes in 'The New Name' of each person as a 'distinct flower or tree in the spiritual garden of God'.[454] Each of these flowers or trees is 'precious, each for his own sake' to the Gardener who waters it and shines upon it and fills it with life.[455] His filling them with his life, far from destroying distinctions and variety, helps each to grow and blossom into its unique 'secret

---

447 See MC, pp. 102-103.

448 See 4L, pp. 102-103, 105-106.

449 See PPL, pp. 72-80. See also ELSC, pp. 12-14, for his discussion of the renaissance neo-Platonists' move away from a hierarchical understanding of man's place in the universe.

450 GDK, pp. 237-238. See also C.S. Lewis, 'Membership', in WG, pp. 122-126.

451 GDK, p. 239.

452 See MC, pp. 188-189, where he uses analogies involving the influence of light and salt to illustrate how Christ's influence means becoming more individual and distinct, not less. Compare this analogy to the effect of God's light on various creatures in Dante's *Paradiso*, Canto 29.136-145. See also, in the preface to GD: 'Good, as it ripens, becomes continually more different not only from evil but from other good' (GD, p. viii).

453 See above, p. 262-263.

454 US, p. 75 (first quarter of par. 17 in 'The New Name', first series). See Dante's *Paradiso*, Canto 30, where souls in the Empyrean first appear as flowers.

455 US, p. 75 (first quarter if par. 17 in the same sermon).

of the Divinity'.[456] And without the pride that breeds competition, these God-given distinctions, far from separating God's creatures, will help bring them together: 'Each will feel', he writes, 'the sacredness and awe of his neighbour's dark and silent speech with his God', without jealously complaining that he or she has not been given the same, or equal, gifts: 'Each will behold in the other a marvel of revelation, a present son or daughter of the Most High, come forth from him to reveal him afresh. In God each will draw nigh to each'.[457]

As with Lewis, so with his 'master'. The influence of God's love, they both believed, refines and unites a vast diversity of unique individuals and kinds of individuals; it does not simply level and unite all reality into a single mass of equal and interchangeable units. As MacDonald writes, 'There is no *massing* of men with God. When he speaks of gathered men, it is a spiritual *body*, not a *mass*. For in a body every smallest portion is individual, and therefore capable of forming a part of the body'.[458]

MacDonald's description of men becoming parts of a spiritual body is a reference to the metaphor used repeatedly by Paul in his New Testament epistles to describe the Church, or those who accept Christ's redemption. Paul speaks of Christ as the head of this body: its founder and that by which it is sustained and preserved.[459] It is to the Head that the body looks for salvation and hope of transformed, eternal life. It is this teaching about God's relation to his creatures, or Christ the Son's relation to sons and daughters of God, that MacDonald and Lewis adhere to in their books. However much humans may become like God in love and goodness, it is still he who is the head. It is still he who saves and we who need saving. He descends in Christ to save humans as a human, but the fact that he descends proves that he is more than human.

As Lewis writes, he is the eternal 'Gift-love' to our creaturely 'Need-love'.[460] He may want to enliven us with his kind of Gift-love, but no creature, even sons and daughters of God, will ever be above him, or will ever cease to need him like the air they breathed on earth. There may be 'no stand-off-ishness' to God, as Lewis wrote of Aslan,[461] but it is still he who is God, not we. We have already seen where MacDonald wrote, concerning the 'one principle of hell', that all evil springs from the proud attempt to think and live as if one's own self were God.[462] Lewis draws attention to this belief

---

456 US, p. 75 (second quarter of par. 7 in the same).

457 US, pp. 77-78 (par. 20 in the same).

458 US, p. 75 (par. 16 in the same). Compare the diversity and unity in Paul's description of Christ's church in 1 Corinthians chp. 12. Lewis refers to 1 Cor. 12.12-30 in PP, p. 150.

459 See Eph. 2.22, 4.15; Col. 1.18, 2.19.

460 See 4L, pp. 1-9.

461 LWW, p. 191.

462 See pp. 164-169, above. See also US, p. 495 (first half of par. 3 in 'Kingship',

in a critical work by noting the 'heresy' which 'lies at the root' of the first sin: Satan's rebellion. He points to Book V of *Paradise Lost*[463] where Satan nonsensically attempts to convince Abdiel that he, Satan, 'is a self-existent being, not a derived being, a creature'.[464] Satan's 'monomaniac concern with himself' leads to the non-sensical doctrine that he, not God, is God.[465] And so he rebels against heaven's hierarchy, resisting the idea that anyone should be above him whom he needs to obey, that he should need to bow to any reality outside his own self-consciousness.

However much Satan ignored this hierarchy, it is clear that Lewis in his own books did not. Aslan gives himself to rescue Edmund; it is not Edmund who saves Aslan or Aslan who needs Edmund. And it is Jane Studdock in *That Hideous Strength* who realises after great difficulty that she is feminine in more than a biological sense, as all creatures are a feminine weakness in need of Him. Throughout the story it is made clear that Jane has tried to 'keep up my own life'[466] in relation to her husband Mark and all else that she feels will 'invade' and 'entangle' the self she calls her own.[467] Ransom puts it to her this way: "'your trouble has been what old poets called *Daungier*.[468] We call it Pride. You are offended by the masculine itself: the loud, irruptive, possessive thing—the gold lion, the bearded bull—which breaks through hedges and scatters the little kingdom of your primness as the dwarfs scattered the carefully made bed'".[469]

At this point he makes it clear to Jane that it is not just Mark, or married life with children, that she fears; and not just she, or women in general, who need to yield: "'The male you could have escaped, for it exists only on the biological level. But the masculine none of us can escape. What is above and beyond all things is so masculine that we are all feminine in relation to it'".[470]

The narrator's record of Jane's thoughts shows that her ideas about 'Religion', after her encounters with Ransom and others, are beginning to change. Before, she had thought it was an upward movement by 'specially gifted souls', like a 'cloud of incense' steaming up to 'a receptive Heaven' where

---

third series); RF, p. 415.

463 *Paradise Lost*, 5.853-871.

464 PPL, p. 95.

465 PPL, p. 100. See also MacDonald's *Lilith* (pp. 204-205, above).

466 HS, p. 72.

467 HS, p. 73.

468 See Lewis's mention of this as an element in medieval allegory: AL, pp. 123-124; 130, 132, 134, 138, 139, 181-182, 253, 268, 343.

469 HS, pp. 315-316. Dwarves scatter a carefully made bed in Snow White.

470 HS, p. 316. For the transcendence of masculinity and femininity beyond the biological, see also PER, p. 200.

she would be free from all entanglements.[471] Now she thinks of how Ransom and his followers never talk about 'Religion', and how many things may be different from what she once thought:

> They talked about God. They had no picture in their minds of some mist steaming upward: rather of strong, skilful hands thrust down to make, and mend, perhaps even to destroy. Supposing one were a *thing* after all—a thing designed and invented by Someone Else and valued for qualities quite different from what one had decided to regard as one's true self?[472]

Lewis's story ends with Jane giving into God, and Jane and Mark 'descending the ladder of humility' and giving into each other.[473] And Lewis's point is clear: God's reality is a loving dance among unequals, and that even the best created dancer must follow His lead, as the uncreated Son has always bowed to his Father.

Human femininity in relation to the masculinity of God may at first glance be more difficult to spot in MacDonald's fiction, due to his woman-like representations of God. But it is certainly there. We have already seen how Queen Irene, North Wind and others are not feminine only, how MacDonald obviously believed it was we who need God, not *vice versa*. It is Anodos who needs to follow the rusty knight and submit to good death. He and other characters grow stronger in chivalrous love, but it is ultimately they who need something other than their own ways. It is Vane, who vainly thinks he can rescue, who needs to be rescued.[474]

But if these and previous examples are not enough, MacDonald is very explicit about it in his sermons. In one he speaks of how a soul, in regard to 'righteousness', 'cannot set itself right', and that it needs that 'which the soul can generate no supply'.[475] He speaks also of a need not having specifically to do with righteousness: the need of *existence not self-existent* for the consciousness of the presence of the causing self-existent', or more succinctly, 'the man's need of God'.[476] In another sermon he asks, 'how shall any man imagine he is complete in himself, and can do without a father in heaven [...]?'.[477] In another he identifies the 'one central wrong in the whole human affair' and the 'one central misery' as 'the refusal to look up to God as our Father'.[478] The only place

---

471 HS, p. 318.
472 HS, p. 318.
473 HS, p. 382.
474 See LIL, p. 255.
475 HG, p. 120.
476 HG, p. 121.
477 MOL, p. 391.
478 US. p. 276 (fourth paragraph of 'Abba, Father!', second series).

where everything is equal, he writes in another sermon, is monolithic hell: 'a vast inane, yet filled full of one inhabitant, that devouring monster, your own false self'.[479] In contrast to this stands the diverse labyrinth of heaven's love. As he asks in another sermon, 'is not knowledge of difference essential to the deepest love?' and 'can there be oneness without difference? harmony without distinction?'.[480] God's ultimate reality, he believed, will not be the equality of 'multitudinous heads with one face' or 'perfect spheres of featureless ivory'.[481] He writes of God's '*logos*' interpenetrating the 'soul' of our '*cosmos*' to make us more of what we are and give us that which we are not but which we need.[482] Before Lewis wrote of the 'gold lion' and 'bearded bull' and 'strong, skillful hands thrust down',[483] MacDonald wrote of how 'his magnificence' must flow down 'into the channels of the indigence he has created'.[484]

And so we see how Lewis must have learned much of what he came to believe of God's love and the human share in it. We are to become chivalrous ourselves, more like the good and holy Love that He is, they believed. As MacDonald writes, we are not simply 'the instrument upon which his power plays a soulless tune'.[485] Our part in His reality is necessarily an intimate and artful mingling of our action and His. We 'must walk',[486] but we must also be carried, they believed: strong to the death in battle against Pride, but also a tender willingness to fall into His arms and yield to the rescue.

---

479 HG, p. 118.
480 HG, p. 103.
481 HG, p. 103.
482 US, p. 227 (second and third quarters of par. 8 in 'The Word of Jesus on Prayer', second series).
483 HS, pp. 316, 318.
484 MOL, p. 296.
485 MOL, p. 267.
486 MOL, p. 275.

CHAPTER 6

INNESS

And on the ground, which is my modres gate,
I knocke with my staf, erlich and late,
And say to hire, Leve mother, let me in.
–Chaucer, 'The Pardoner's Tale'[1]

all things bound in a single book by love
of which creation is the scattered leaves: [...]
I know I saw the universal form,
the fusion of all things[2]
–Dante, *Paradiso*, Canto 33. 85-87, 91-92[3]

He, They, One. All; within, without.
–Tennyson, *In Memoriam A.H.H.*, CXXIII

And having made peace through the blood of his cross,
by him to reconcile all things unto himself [...] whether
they be things in earth or things in heaven.
–Colossians 1.20

His Lord said unto him, Well done, thou good and
faithful servant: thou hast been faithful over a few things,
I will make thee ruler over many things: enter into the joy
of thy Lord.
–Matthew 25.21[4]

There is at least one more marriage we must note before concluding this study. It is the marriage that Lewis yearned for but never achieved in *Spirits in Bondage*, and a marriage that will help us sum up their depictions of heaven and MacDonald's overall influence on Lewis.

Most readers of MacDonald and Lewis will notice the prevalence of magical doors or thresholds in their stories. The most famous of these, without doubt, is the door of a seemingly common-place wardrobe which actually leads to another world in *The Lion, the Witch, and the Wardrobe*. There are many such doors in all of the Narnia books, and all of these resemble similar doorways in MacDonald's stories. In *Lilith*, Vane enters a strange world through a seemingly common-place wooden door to a small chamber in an old garret.[5]

---

1   Quoted in PHA, chp. 25.
2   Mark Musa (tr.), Dante's *Paradiso* (London: Penguin, 1986).
3   Canto 33.91 quoted in C.S. Lewis, *Studies in Medieval and Renaissance Literature* (Cambridge: Cambridge University Press, 1998), p. 86.
4   Quoted in WG, p. 33.
5   See LIL, p. 16.

And in many other of his stories there are strange and beautiful wonders on the other side of a common-place door. Irene finds her great-grandmother in a similar fashion to how Vane entered another world: up a flight of stairs, in what first seems like just an old garret, on the other side of a door.

It will be remembered, of course, how young Lewis, the imaginative atheist, ended *Spirits in Bondage* with a poem in which the speaker is not able to get through to the other side of a doorway. The marriage he pines for is the union of himself with his ideal heaven. He longs for paradise and cries at its gates to be let in:

> Open the gates for me,
> Open the gates of the peaceful castle, rosy in the West,
> In the sweet dim Isle of Apples over the wide sea's breast,
> Open the gates for me![6]

But the speaker cannot get in. The cycle of forty poems ends showing the reader that the spirit of the work remains confined. It hopes and dreams and cries to be let in, but the work ends outside the gates of the longed-for 'Country of Dreams'.[7]

In this context the story of MacDonald's influence upon Lewis might be quickly summarised by pointing out that MacDonald helped Lewis realise that he was looking in the wrong direction. In *Alec Forbes*, for example, we are told by the narrator how 'the door into life generally opens behind us, and a hand is put forth which draws us in backwards'.[8] Alec Forbes, like many of MacDonald's characters, is very much like the young, romantic Lewis who yearned to get into his Ideal but was frustrated. Upon moving away from home and embarking upon his education, Alec feels that he's got to 'the borders of fairy-land'.[9] 'A door would open and admit him into the secret of the world', he thinks.[10] But the narrator tells us how Alec is not so close as he thinks. He must take the long road to heaven: 'The sole wisdom for a man or boy who is haunted with the hovering of *unseen wings*, with the scent of *unseen roses*, and the subtle enticements of *"melodies unheard"* is *work*'.[11] If one follows after only his dreaming, the paradise he dreams of 'will vanish', we are told.[12] Those who simply beat upon the gates of heaven with their imaginations, like young Lewis in *Spirits in Bondage*, will never get in: 'The idle beat their heads

---

6   SIB, p. 74 (XL).
7   SIB, p. 75.
8   AFH, p. 148. Lewis quotes this same passage in PP, p. 148, and in ANTH, reading 261.
9   AFH, p. 147.
10   AFH, p. 147. See note 280 on p. 112, above.
11   AFH, p. 148.
12   AFH, p. 148.

against its walls, or mistake the entrance, and go down into the dark places of the earth [...] For to no onlooker will life any more than Fairy-Land open its secret. A man must become an actor before he can be a true spectator'.[13]

This study has shown how MacDonald helped lead Lewis away from simple imaginative romanticism. He did not lead Lewis away from all romance; if the two authors are to be believed, he led him to a deeper kind of romance. As a romantic atheist, Lewis yearned for what he did not believe in. In becoming a Christian, Lewis came to share with MacDonald a belief in what he had yearned for, as well as a belief that the marriage to heaven began now: an unconsummated marriage, or kind of courtship, in a world of suffering, pride and infant loves that struggle to walk.

A similar development is depicted in *Robert Falconer*, in Falconer's journey to the Ideal. In the early part of the novel Robert, as a boy, is acquainted with many hints of heavenly beauty. There is the lovely music of his fiddle, his 'bonny leddy', and the even greater beauty of Mary St. John, a woman whose room he has access to by an old doorway that joins the Falconer residence to hers. Young Falconer, upon first seeing her, mistakes her for an angel. The door that separates him from the wonders of Miss St. John is to him a magical door, and her room is for him a haven, or heaven, of tender feminine beauty that stands in sharp contrast to the merely 'douce' atmosphere of his usual surroundings. But it is not long before this door is boarded up. Mrs. Falconer burns his 'bonny leddy' and closes up the passageway between the two houses so that Robert, like the speaker in the last poem of *Spirits in Bondage*, is left standing outside the gates of paradise.[14] Even a kite of his resembling a flying dragon, that he flew from inside the house, is cut down. And so the 'string of the sky-soaring kite of his imagination' is cut by the 'shears of Fate'.[15] Every remembrance of these lovely things, since he can no longer get into them, is a pain to Robert's mind, just as beauties are a pain to the imaginative Lewis in *Spirits*.

But MacDonald's stories, as we have learned, did not stop at these points. Young Robert enters a dreary, wintry period of his life afterwards. The 'glow' is 'out of his heart' and 'out of the world' for him.[16] But not all doors are barred. We are told how Robert is driven 'into his garret, into his soul', and how 'a door, out or in, he must find, or perish'.[17] The rest of the action of the novel, as we have already noted,[18] is how Falconer finds and enters in through this door:

---

13   AFH, p. 148.
14   See RF, pp. 162-164.
15   RF, p. 165.
16   RF, p. 165.
17   RF, p. 165.
18   See pp 243, above.

how he works into himself the lovely Beauty that he had once only gazed upon or heard. He himself becomes a loving instrument of beauty by descending into a world of troubles and loving those around him. He has gotten further into heaven by getting heaven's love further into himself, and this has been accomplished, paradoxically, by going out of himself in love. The door back into heaven, or into a deeper heaven, is also the door out. It is the same with Vane in *Lilith*, who is told after entering another world, "'All the doors you had yet seen—and you haven't seen many—were doors in; here you came upon a door out! The strange thing to you [...] will be, that the more doors you go out of, the farther you get in!'".[19]

This study has shown how MacDonald's literature helped Lewis to make a similar escape. By entering into the door of MacDonald's fiction, Lewis began to escape mere escapism. A literary study, of course, is no place to judge how deeply heaven's good love got into Lewis himself, but this study has shown that it deeply entrenched itself in his writing. The literary incarnation of humble goodness that he found in MacDonald's books would come to inspire all the books he would come to be known for. The goodness that characterises MacDonald's books—a strong and sweet love that crushes pride to redeem men and nature—comes to characterise Lewis's.

This influence began straight away with Lewis's first reading of MacDonald. In *Phantastes*, Cosmo, who views his ideal beauty through a magical mirror, is invited by the beautiful woman he views to break the mirror and set her free if he really loves her. 'I am but a slave, while that mirror exists', she tells him.[20] Anodos, too, must stop merely viewing, or imagining, his ideal. The main story of *Phantastes* is how he learns to become his ideal rather than simply chasing it in the white lady. The white lady is married to one better than he: the rusty knight who has worked and striven and slain a dragon. Anodos must follow him in this if he ever hopes to become truly married to his ideal. This is evident at one point after he has stripped off his armour[21] and begun a journey of humility to a deeper romance than his imagination or pride could ever arrive at: 'In nothing was my ideal lowered, or dimmed, or grown less precious; I only saw it too plainly, to set myself for a moment beside it. Indeed, my ideal soon became my life; whereas formerly, my life had consisted in a vain attempt to behold, if not my ideal in myself, at least myself in my ideal'.[22] Anodos begins to lose his shadow by going out of himself and mere imagination to humble love and obedience. His path, we are told, lies 'eastward through the woods'[23] where he meets the Christ-like rusty knight

19 LIL, p. 20. Compare US, p. 363: 'Christ is the way out, and the way in'.
20 PHA, p. 99.
21 See PHA, p. 166.
22 PHA, p. 166.
23 PHA, p. 166.

whom he learns from and follows. It is the opposite direction to which the speaker in *Spirits*'s last poem looked for his 'peaceful castle, rosy in the West'.[24] A peaceful castle for Anodos there may be, but the way to it is anything but peaceful in the strife he must go through. There is arduous combat and more than one kind of death.

The same path, this study has shown, awaits Lewis's characters, from his first to his last. John, the protagonist of the first book he published as a Christian, only reaches his destination by combat and humility. It is a *Pilgrim's Regress*,[25] and the regress is difficult. The same is true for Orual in Lewis's last story. In the end she learns that Psyche—a character very much like the ideal white lady of *Phantastes*—has traveled "'a long journey to fetch the beauty that will make Ungit beautiful'".[26] Orual, it will be remembered, learns that it is she with her hateful passions and so-called loves who is Ungit.[27] Psyche her sister has acted chivalrously on her behalf, "'bringing the casket of beauty from the Queen of Shadows'".[28] But in the very end Orual discovers that Psyche's long, hard journey to peace and wholeness has also been hers, as it had to be. In the end she sees 'two Psyches', both beautiful 'beyond all imagining, yet not exactly the same'.[29] "'You also are Psyche'", a great voice tells her.[30] Like her sister, and like Anodos, she has become her beautiful ideal. Lewis here combines the central meaning of *Phantastes* with the Cupid-Psyche myth to illustrate what the path to heavenly peace and wholeness is like. Orual, like Anodos, moves from wanting to possess her ideal, Psyche, on her own terms, to becoming her beautiful ideal in a world of strife and death. The door to heaven opened behind her and led away from what she once imagined as her true self.

And so many of the magical doors in these authors' stories seem to lead to nowhere, as good death seems to lead to nowhere. Wardrobes usually lead to a cramped, dark space, but the humble, common-looking wardrobe in Lewis's tale leads to Narnia. A stable door, likewise, in his last Narnia book, leads to something greater than either a stable or Narnia. Lucy's words show explicitly that the stable door is patterned on the humility of God's incarnation in Christ: "'In our world too, a stable once had something inside it that was bigger than our whole world'".[31] Scenes like this, walking through a humble door to something unimaginably wonderful, Lewis learned in many of MacDonald's stories. In

24   SIB, p. 74.
25   Italics mine.
26   FAC, p. 306.
27   See p. 201, above.
28   FAC, p. 305.
29   FAC, pp. 307-308.
30   FAC, p. 308.
31   LB, p. 177.

Phantastes, for example, the indoor bath that Anodos swims in is no ordinary bath. When he descends beneath the surface of its waters, he discovers that the basin extends 'on all sides like a sea' to reveal a vast underwater world of caves, pinnacles and sea people.[32] Later, Anodos succeeds in singing his white lady into view as a statue upon a pedestal. But when he attempts to embrace the statue, the lady tells him he shouldn't have touched her and darts away, closing a door behind her. This closed door that Anodos must open to continue his journey is much different from all the other doors of the fairy palace. It has not the ebony, ivory, and silver plating, or ornate, odorous wood that the others do. It is a rough old door of oak with heavy nails and iron studs, and it leads to a hole in the ground. In the hole are descending stairs down which Anodos must walk.[33] And the way to ultimate joy, we are told in the last chapter, is through the most humble door of all: Anodos's own tomb.[34]

The influence here upon Lewis is unmistakable. The kinds of doors he puts in his books are too similar and too many to be a coincidence. But it is to what lies on the other side of the door that we will refer in proving this kind of influence beyond doubt. Both MacDonald and Lewis believed that the resurrection of redeemed men and redeemed nature lies on the other side of death. They are both clear in saying that they do not know, and cannot imagine, all of what heaven will be, but they are both agreed that this resurrection into a harmony of spirit and nature will be an important part of it. Once all of the shadow has gone out of spirits, neither spirits nor nature will be in bondage.

The ways they envision and depict this harmony are too numerous to mention here. Ransom's vision of the Great Game or Great Dance in the closing chapter of *Perelandra*, as well as Anodos's brief experience of such harmony in the last chapter of *Phantastes*, immediately spring to mind. But the writings of theirs which most certainly prove MacDonald's impact are sermons. A sermon of Lewis's entitled 'The Weight of Glory',[35] which has been compared to some of the Church Fathers' writings in its magnificence,[36] is with little doubt Lewis's best non-fiction hint of what lies on the other side of death's door. It is he himself, in fact, who puts it in terms of doors:

> At present we are on the outside of the world, the wrong side of the door. We discern the freshness and purity of morning, but they do not make us fresh and pure. We cannot mingle with the splendours we see. But all the leaves of the New Testament are rustling with the rumour

---

32 PHA, p. 73.
33 See PHA, pp. 117-118.
34 See PHA, p. 184.
35 See WG, pp. 25-40.
36 See Walter Hooper's introduction in WG, p. 18.

that it will not always be so. Some day, God willing, we shall get *in*.[37]

Now this sermon of Lewis's may indeed be highly original and comparable to writings of the Church Fathers, but it is not as original as many readers may first think. It is comprised of many unmistakable echoes of passages from the last collection of sermons that MacDonald published, *The Hope of the Gospel*. Lewis's address, for example, begins by taking issue with the charge that heaven is a bribe. He makes the distinction between proper rewards and mercenary rewards. Marrying a woman for her money, for instance, would be mercenary, he writes, but 'marriage is the proper reward for a real lover, and he is not mercenary for desiring it'.[38] 'The proper rewards', he writes, 'are not simply tacked on to the activity for which they are given, but are the activity itself in consummation'.[39] The point made here is identical to the point that MacDonald makes in 'The Reward of Obedience':

> Let no one start with dismay at the idea of a reward of righteousness, saying virtue is its own reward [...] Would a parent be deceiving his child in saying, "My boy, you will have a great reward if you learn Greek," foreseeing his son's delight in Homer and Plato—now but a valueless waste in his eyes? When his reward comes, will the youth feel aggrieved that it is Greek, and not bank-notes?[40]

A direct connection here is indisputable, as Lewis, in his sermon, even uses the same analogy—learning Greek—to help make his point: 'The schoolboy beginning Greek grammar cannot look forward to his adult enjoyment of Sophocles as a lover looks forward to marriage or a general to victory'.[41] The point that both authors make is the same: that a person learning God's goodness in this life is like a schoolboy learning Greek. To both, the prospect of a future reward (heaven, or the delights of Greek poetry), when set against the 'drudgery'[42] or 'valueless waste'[43] of the present day's grammar lesson, can seem very much like bribery. And their present discipline, when it seems to have so little real connection with the joy of the future reward, will often seem mercenary. The truth, Lewis writes, is that heaven is the 'very consummation' of earthly discipleship, as being able to delight in Greek poetry is the consummation of learning Greek.[44] In both cases the discipline and the consummation are intimately and inseparably connected, though in both

---

37   WG, p. 37.
38   WG, p. 26.
39   WG, p. 26.
40   HG, p. 135.
41   WG, p. 26.
42   WG, p. 27.
43   HG, p. 135.
44   WG, p. 27.

cases the disciple is not always aware of this intimate connection and therefore suspects that the reward is bribery and the discipline mercenary.

But 'as gradually as the tide lifts a grounded ship',[45] Lewis writes, those who keep obeying God and keep believing in the joy of heaven will increasingly know that God's goodness and the joy of his heaven are intimately connected. This goodness and this joy may have necessarily had to have been separated in human experience in earthly life, as Psyche's lover in the myth had to remain invisible for a time,[46] but in heaven, after men have begun to live the song that they would sing,[47] the life and the song will be quickened and the intrinsic harmony between goodness and joy will be made manifest to human experience. Even in this life, the closer one gets to God's goodness is the closer one gets to knowing this accord. As Lewis writes, one 'cannot even begin to know' such harmony except by 'continuing to obey and finding the first reward of our obedience in our increasing power to desire the ultimate reward'.[48] Or as MacDonald wrote before him, 'Every obedience is the opening of another door into the boundless universe of life [...] Each good thing opens the door to the one next to it, so to all the rest'.[49]

As to what may be made manifest on the other side of the last door we know of—that is, physical death—the best way to sum up what they write may simply be to say that one 'gets the girl'. It is Gibbie, the great lover, for example, who eventually gets Ginevra at the end of *Sir Gibbie*, not Donal Grant, the great poet. Gibbie through the course of the novel has lived his song; Donal, at the end of the story, has still a long way to go. Likewise, it is the rusty knight who is married to the white lady in *Phantastes*. It is he who, having slain his dragon, can go singing his song while riding through the forest. Anodos, still learning to slay his passions and learn love, remains single. And if Nature—that which is 'exterior' to souls or spirits—can be spoken of in feminine terms, it is part of a very fitting symbol of the consummation that both authors believed in and portrayed. Once the souls of men and women have come into harmony with God's good love, than all of Nature will be brought into harmony with all redeemed souls. The 'bright shadow'[50] of Christ, having brought wholeness and eternal life to men's hearts, will bring it to all nature. In New Testament terms, the redeeming bridegroom will consummate the marriage and his redeemed bride will experience what Christ's bodily resurrection was the first

---

45   WG, p. 27.
46   See pp. 110-112, above.
47   See pp. 41, 98, 109-112, 147-148, above.
48   WG, p. 27.
49   HG, pp. 137, 143.
50   See SBJ, pp. 179-181.

fruit[51] of: a new harmony between spirits and nature. Spirits will escape their bondage not by a separation *from* Nature, but by a new harmony *with* Nature.

As MacDonald writes in another sermon of the same collection, the redeemed will inhabit a body like Christ's resurrected body: 'a body that will not thwart but second the needs and aspirations of the spirit [...] changed by the interpenetrating of the creative indwelling will'.[52] And with these spiritual bodies we will be brought into 'true and perfect contact with the creation'.[53] And so too in Lewis's sermon: 'When human souls have become as perfect in voluntary obedience as the inanimate creation is in its lifeless obedience, then they will put on its glory, or rather that greater glory of which Nature is only the first sketch [...] We are summoned to pass in through Nature, beyond her, into that splendour which she fitfully reflects'.[54]

One can see this understanding reflected in their fiction. One example, in *The Great Divorce*, is the lizard of lust, that dominates a ghost, being killed, but then being resurrected and changed into a great stallion upon which the ghost, now a man, rides.[55] The liberated man rides and rules a Nature that has been transformed. All of the surrounding plain and forest shakes with the sound of a liberated, singing Nature: 'It was the voice of that earth, those woods and those waters. A strange archaic, inorganic noise, that came from all directions at once. The Nature or Arch-Nature of that land rejoiced to have been once more ridden, and therefore consummated, in the person of the horse'.[56]

A similar harmony, and even greater beauty, is expressed in the vision of the redeemed Sarah Smith, similar to Dante's Beatrice here, whose glorified soul is so intimately connected with her glorified body that Lewis cannot remember if she was naked or clothed. If naked, it must have been 'the almost visible penumbra of her courtesy and joy' which produced the illusion of a 'shining train that followed her across the happy grass'.[57] If clothed, it must have been the 'clarity with which her innermost spirit shone through the clothes' that produced the illusion of nakedness.[58] In this way Smith is a fictional representation of what Lewis writes of in his sermon. She has moved from merely seeing beauty on Earth to doing 'something else which can hardly be put into words—to be united with the beauty we see, to pass into it, to receive it into ourselves, to bathe in it, to become part of it'.[59] Having become

---

51 See 1 Cor. 15.20-23; Rom. 8.23; 11.16.
52 HG, p. 212.
53 HG, p. 212.
54 WG, pp. 37-38.
55 See GD, pp. 85-87.
56 GD, p. 86.
57 GD, pp. 89-90.
58 GD, p. 90.
59 WG, p. 37.

'voluntarily obedient' as the 'inanimate creation is in its lifeless obedience', she has put on 'that greater glory of which Nature is only the first sketch'.[60] Having followed God's love on Earth, she has been made lovely and joyful beyond all imagination in heaven. She has gained the beautiful face that Orual lacked by going in 'beyond Nature' and eating 'of the tree of life'.[61] The transformation that the narrator of MacDonald's *Annals* believed would occur in his wife Ethelwyn has occurred in Smith. The 'loveliness of wisdom and the beauty of holiness' that she gained in earthly life is unveiled and the 'glowing' and 'gathered brilliance' of her lovely soul shines out 'like the moon from under a cloud, when a stream of the upper air floats [the veil] from off her face'.[62]

This harmony of spirits and Nature is the same kind of thing that one finds at the end of *Phantastes*, and near the end of *Lilith* where 'The world and my [that is, Vane's] being, its life and mine, were one [...] I lived in everything; everything entered and lived in me'.[63] New senses, 'hitherto asleep', awake and enable him to be utterly engulfed with the joys that had once only been *suggested* by Nature's beauty.[64]

All earthly things, in fact, not just Nature, will be redeemed and transformed in the heaven that MacDonald and Lewis believed in. In the last chapter of Lewis's Narnia tales, for example, heaven includes all that was best on Earth. All '*real* countries', in fact, are spurs of land jutting out from 'the great mountains of Aslan'.[65] Old friends, familiar cities, even old homes that have been destroyed, find new and better life in this heaven. This helps to show the overall influence of MacDonald upon Lewis, who had once seemed interested in only an escape from Earth, matter and a Nature whom he depicted as Satan.[66] The closing vision of heaven in his last Narnia story resembles a scene that concludes MacDonald's first book, *Within and Without*. In the heaven MacDonald depicts there, Julian and Lily are reunited with their wife and mother. The first sight they see of her is of a 'woman-form, a wonderful mingling of the earthly and the unearthly in its pure beauty' rising up to meet them.[67] As this woman is a wonderfully harmonious mingling of the earthly and unearthly, so would Lewis's heaven at the end of *The Last Battle* come to be.

---

60   WG, p. 38.
61   WG, p. 38.
62   AQN, p. 574. See p. 119, above.
63   LIL, pp. 383-384.
64   LIL, p. 384.
65   LB, p. 226.
66   See p. 22-23, above.
67   WW, p. 192 (V.iii). See p. 50-51, above.

But this 'getting the girl', the harmony and ecstasy between spirits, Nature, a new heaven and new Earth,[68] need not obscure an even greater union which MacDonald and Lewis believed to be the fountainhead of all harmonies and ecstasies. In 'The Weight of Glory', for example, Lewis refers to Augustine's saying that 'the rapture of the saved soul will "flow over" into the glorified body'.[69] The body's and Nature's share in this 'torrens voluptatis'[70] is an overflow from the rapture that the saved soul experiences. And this essential rapture, Lewis makes clear in the same sermon, is a result of our getting in past that door which separates us from the Father and Home of our being:

> We should hardly dare to ask that any notice be taken of ourselves. But we pine. The sense that in this universe we are treated as strangers, the longing to be acknowledged, to meet with some response, to bridge some chasm that yawns between us and reality, is part of our inconsolable secret. And surely, from this point of view, the promise of glory, in the sense described, becomes highly relevant to our deep desire. For glory means good report with God, acceptance by God, response, acknowledgement, and welcome into the heart of things. The door on which we have been knocking all our lives will open at last [...] to be at last summoned inside would be both glory and honour beyond all our merits and also the healing of that old ache.[71]

MacDonald, in a sermon entitled 'The Creation in Christ', calls this getting into the heart of things 'inness'.[72] In another he calls it the healing of that rift caused by evil, that is, 'what springs from myself and not from God' or 'a perversion of something of God's'.[73] It will be the rejoining of a 'stream' to 'its source',[74] an absolute destruction of the one principle of hell: 'I am my own'.[75] It will be moving from things which do not 'satisfy' to a place where souls 'feel quite at home',[76] a place that will not need religion, for 'how should there be law or religion where every throb of the heart says God!'.[77] It will be much more like flying a kite 'with God himself for [one's] playmate' than it is like a 'sermon' or 'ever-lasting prayer meeting', though sermons and prayers

---

68   See 2 Peter 3.13; Rev. 21.1; Isaiah 65.17, 66.22.
69   WG, p. 38.
70   WG, p. 38.
71   WG, pp. 35-36, 36-37.
72   US, p. 431 (second quarter of penultimate paragraph in 'The Creation in Christ', third series).
73   US, p. 619 (last quarter of last paragraph of 'The Inheritance', third series). Lewis underlines in his copy.
74   US, p. 619 (last quarter of last paragraph of the same sermon).
75   US, p. 495 (first half of par. 3 in 'Kingship', third series).
76   US, p. 618 (third quarter of the last paragraph of 'The Inheritance', third series).
77   US, p. 615 (last half of par. 11 in the same sermon).

may have helped get us there.[78] The good and holy Love that God is, which may have seemed like such a 'valueless waste'[79] or 'drudgery'[80] during one's discipleship on Earth will make manifest its intimate connection with the Joy and Beauty that he is.

Or perhaps the best way to sum up MacDonald's understanding of 'inness' is to simply point out that it is getting closer to the God described in our previous chapter. As we quoted MacDonald there,[81] 'the fatherhood of the Father' meets and blends with the 'sonhood of the Son', and we are drawn 'up into the glory of their joy, to share in the thoughts of love that pass between them, in their thoughts of delight and rest in each other, in their thoughts of joy in all the little ones'.[82] Lewis would come to follow him in this understanding, as we can see near the end of the last of his Narnia books when the children are beckoned to go 'further up and further in' to what and who he is.[83]

But as always with MacDonald, he seeks to return readers' attention to the present. It may be good to have a hope of a future welcome into the heart of things, but there is always a priority in his writings on a faith that means getting the heart of things into our hearts here and now. As he writes in 'The Inheritance': 'If [one] knows the Lord, he will not trouble himself about heaven; if he does not know him, he will not be drawn to *him* by it. I would not care to persuade the feeble Christian that heaven was a place worth going to; I would rather persuade him that no spot in space, no hour in eternity is worth anything to one who remains such as he is'.[84] That is, no place or time is worth being in for one who remains without God his Father. We may get further into him in heaven, but for now he wants to get further into us, and have us care more for one another, as with the youth in Melchah's story or Orual in Lewis's version of the Cupid-Psyche myth.

As MacDonald writes, there *is* 'the father's smile' that is the 'perfect reward of the child's' waiting in heaven, and all else that comes with it.[85] There is 'the essential bliss of the creature' that beholds and is beheld by 'the face of the creator',[86] expressed in *Phantastes* as the ultimate reward of Anodos's following the rusty knight: 'if I might wait on him to the world's end, although no smile but his should greet me, and no one but him should say,

---

78   US, p. 615 (second and third quarters of par. 11 in the same).
79   HG, p. 135.
80   WG, p. 27.
81   See pp. 235, above.
82   US, p. 429 (last half of par. 23 in 'The Creation in Christ', third series).
83   The title of chp. 15 of *The Last Battle*.
84   US, p. 614 (first quarter of par. 11 in 'The Inheritance', third series).
85   HG, p. 181.
86   HG, p. 112.

"Well done! he was a good servant!'".[87] But until then, when we have acquired faces with which to bear the beauty of this smile, there is the peace 'at the heart of things'[88] which we can begin to share in. As MacDonald writes:

> So long as there dwells harmony, so long as the Son loves the Father with all the love the Father can welcome, all is well with the little ones. God is all right—why should we mind standing in the dark for a minute outside his window? Of course we miss the *inness*, but there is a bliss of its own in waiting. What if the rain be falling, and the wind blowing; what if we stand alone, or, more painful still, have some dear one beside us, sharing our *outness*; what even if the window be not shining, because of the curtains of good inscrutable drawn across it; let us think to ourselves, or say to our friend, 'God is; Jesus is not dead; nothing can be going wrong, however it may look so to hearts unfinished in childness'.[89]

The way to get *in*, again we see, is through a faith in Christ that means following him through a world of pain, suffering and wickedness, and learning to walk in the gravity and tenderness of his Love until all wicked pride has been put to death.[90] This study, hopefully, has shown how this understanding found its way into Lewis's mind and writing, due in no small part to MacDonald's books. But if one more example is needed, there are these words from Lewis, written just after his description of the 'fountain of joy' that awaits us:

> Meanwhile the cross comes before the crown and tomorrow is a Monday morning. A cleft has opened in the pitiless walls of the world, and we are invited to follow our great Captain inside. The following Him is, of course, the essential point.[91]

---

87   PHA, p. 175. Lewis echoes this understanding in 'The Weight of Glory' when he quotes the verse of Scripture, Mat. 25.21, that inspires the passage in *Phantastes*. See WG, p. 33.

88   US, p. 432 (last quarter of penultimate paragraph of 'The Creation in Christ', third series).

89   US, pp. 431-432 (second quarter of penultimate paragraph of the same sermon).

90   See MacDonald in HG, p. 113, who mentions how getting closer to God, as in Dante's *Paradiso* (Canto 26), means loving one's neighbour more, not less. See also Lewis in WG, p. 40, who writes of the gravity of truth that comes with loving God: that 'Next to the Blessed Sacrament itself, your neighbour is the holiest object presented to your senses'.

91   WG, pp. 38-39.

AFTERWORD

The primary concern of this study, the reader will know by now, has been primary sources. It compares two authors and their works in an attempt to tell the story of one author's influence upon the other.

A good way to help end such a study, however, might be the attempt to put the study itself into context with other scholarship on MacDonald and Lewis. The difficulty in doing so lies in the dearth of book-length studies on both MacDonald *and* Lewis. It is surprising that such a study has not already been attempted, given how long people have known of the important connection between the two. There are many things this study has in common with other studies on either MacDonald or Lewis, but this is the first I know of that attempts a comprehensive (though by no means exhaustive) look at both authors' works together, and on themes that were so central in each man's thinking and imagination.

A book entitled *Essays on C.S. Lewis and George MacDonald: Truth, Fiction, and the Power of Imagination*[1] is a good example of the dilemma. However enticing the title may be to those seeking information on the literary connection between the two authors, each essay in the book is about an aspect of either Lewis's *or* MacDonald's work. No more mention is made in the book's essays of the connection between the two writers than is usually said in the brief references in biographies, which rarely go very far beyond Lewis's attraction to *Phantastes* or his making MacDonald a character in *The Great Divorce*. The only things that really tie the two together in this book is the fact that one essay on MacDonald appears alongside four about Lewis, and the pithy six-page introduction by Cynthia Marshall. It is Marshall alone in this book who notes how the 'distinctive literary texture' of *Phantastes* required Lewis to 'abdicate control as a reader' and submit to the 'charm and mercurial imagery' in MacDonald's book.[2] And it is she alone, apart from whatever connections the reader himself might make, who draws specific attention to the epistemological, as well as religious, experience of 'engulfment' and 'self-surrender' that *Phantastes* provided Lewis with: 'Just as [Lewis] here perceives all "common things" transformed through the light of imagination, so the light of Christianity ultimately affords him his basic vision of existence'.[3] After Marshall's tantalizing introduction, there are no further attempts to draw

---

1 Cynthia Marshall, ed., *Essays on C.S. Lewis and George MacDonald: Truth, Fiction, and the Power of the Imagination* (Lampeter: Edwin Mellen Press, 1991).
2 Marshall, in *Essays on C.S. Lewis and George MacDonald*, p. 2.
3 Marshall, p. 3.

connections between the two authors, or to describe what MacDonald did to Lewis. This study is a thorough attempt to do so, though its primary concern is not Lewis's epistemology, and though it is not as sure as Marshall that reading *Phantastes* was primarily an epistemological surrender to the imagination as such.[4]

Rolland Hein's 1982 study of the ideas behind MacDonald's fiction, *The Harmony Within: The Spiritual Vision of George MacDonald*, is a good example, in microcosm, of how most MacDonald or Lewis scholarship is both similar and dissimilar to this study. Like this study, Hein takes the author's belief seriously and uses it in his analysis of the author's fiction. As he writes in the introduction, it is a demonstration of 'how thoroughly the symbolic terrain of [MacDonald's] imaginative prose is shaped by his theological convictions'.[5] In this respect my study shares much more in common with Hein's than it shares with the Freudian approach of Robert Lee Wolff's *The Golden Key*[6], the Jungian approach of Richard Reis's *George MacDonald*[7], or the psychiatric studies of David Holbrook, who has produced studies on both MacDonald[8] and Lewis.[9] The studies by Wolff, Reis and Holbrook all give prominence to a psychological or subconscious something, such as 'a profound fear of woman'[10] or paranoid schizophrenia,[11] as the most important key to interpreting, or explaining, their fiction. This study, like Hein's, offers another key to interpretation: the religious beliefs of the authors taken seriously.

An obvious difference between this study and Hein's is that this study looks at the connection between *two* authors on a particular theme. Hein

---

4   The fact that Lewis waited many years, until his reason was also convinced, to become a Christian suggests that reading *Phantastes*, however powerful an experience for Lewis, did not result in an epistemological coronation of imagination. See also his address 'Is Theology Poetry?' in WG, written many years after his conversion, in which he states that he does not surrender his mind in believing all that pleases his imagination most. Marshall is without doubt correct, though, to mention how Lewis admitted human reason alone to be insufficient for a deep and lasting faith.

5   Rolland Hein, *The Harmony Within: The Spiritual Vision of George MacDonald* (Grand Rapids: Eerdmans, 1982), p.xvi.

6   Robert Lee Wolff, *The Golden Key: A Study of the Fiction of George MacDonald* (New Haven: Yale University Press, 1961).

7   Richard Reis, *George MacDonald* (New York: Twayne Books, 1972).

8   David Holbrook, *A Study of George MacDonald and the Image of Woman* (Lewiston: Edwin Mellen Press, 2000).

9   David Holbrook, *The Skeleton in the Wardrobe: C.S. Lewis's Fantasies: A Phenomenological Study* (London: Bucknell University Press, 1991).

10   Holbrook, *A Study of George MacDonald and the Image of Woman*, p. 3.

11   Holbrook claims this for both MacDonald and Lewis. See *A Study of George MacDonald and the Image of Woman*, p. 139.

does mention Lewis and there is, naturally, considerable space devoted to the themes of evil and goodness. But the mentions of the connection between Lewis and MacDonald are brief. He uses the connection, in three paragraphs of the introduction,[12] as a starting point in a discussion of MacDonald's fiction, which of course is what the book is about. Lewis is mentioned, outside this introduction, only five more times throughout the book.

And so it is in most all scholarship on either MacDonald or Lewis. Another example is a recent study by Barbara Amell, *George MacDonald and the Logic of Faith.*[13] It is a study similar to this one in that it attempts to prove that MacDonald's faith was much more logical than is generally admitted. Another similarity is that it devotes considerable space (one chapter) to the themes of evil and suffering. But since it is a book about MacDonald, not the connection between MacDonald and Lewis, its discussion of Lewis's ideas on either the nature of faith or evil and suffering is very brief. It may be argued, indeed, that what words she does devote to comparing the two authors[14] are too few to be of much value, but just the right amount to do harm. She uses two sentences of her own to paraphrase the entire meaning of Lewis's *The Problem of Pain* and then proceeds, without quoting Lewis, to make judgements on how this meaning compares with MacDonald's attitude.

Another recent study, by David C. Downing, tells the story of Lewis's conversion and, like this study, notes Lewis's movement from the 'dualism during the war years'[15] to 'the Christian affirmation of both spirit and matter'.[16] But like most other studies it only mentions Lewis's early reading of MacDonald's *Phantastes* as a beginning. What other influence MacDonald's writings may have had on Lewis is not its concern. No more is said about how MacDonald contributed to Lewis's journey to faith, or about how both men kept their faith, or how Lewis's fictional depictions of faith may have been influenced by MacDonald's. The reverse is of course true regarding an unpublished thesis by James Stewart Washick that examines doubt and faith in MacDonald's poetry.[17] Like this study, its concern is faith amidst pain and suffering, but Lewis of course had no influence on MacDonald, so there is no reason to mention him.

---

12   Hein, pp. ix-x.

13   Barbara Amell, *George MacDonald and the Logic of Faith* (Portland: B. Amell, 2000).

14   See Amell, pp. 141-142, regarding pain and suffering.

15   See chapter five in David C. Downing, *The Most Reluctant Convert: C.S. Lewis's Journey to Faith* (Downer's Grove: Inter Varsity Press, 2002).

16   Downing, p. 95.

17   James Stewart Washick, *He Who Fears to Doubt: Doubt and Faith in George MacDonald's Major Verse* (Ann Arbor: University Microfilms International, 1997) [PhD thesis, University of South Carolina].

The point here is that there are many studies that are somewhat similar to this study, but perhaps none that are very similar. The most similar study, in fact, may be a book by Richard Purtill in 1974 that explored the literary similarities between Lewis and his friend Tolkien: *Lord of the Elves and Eldils: Fantasy and Philosophy in C.S. Lewis and J.R.R. Tolkien*.[18] As in this study, there are chapters on the relation between God and evil. It also, like this study, takes the authors' thinking seriously and draws from a wide range of the authors' works. As with this study, one can hope to gain a 'cross-section' of the two authors' thought and imagination.

The works most similar to this one in their concentration on the connection between MacDonald and Lewis have been articles and essays. There is Don King's ten-page article in 1986 on the 'childlike' in MacDonald and Lewis,[19] Gregory Wolfe's seven-page article on 'C.S. Lewis's debt to George MacDonald',[20] Gail Hammond's comparison of the two writers' literary styles,[21] and a two-page comparison of *The Lion, the Witch and the Wardrobe* and *The Princess and the Goblin* by Sally Adair Rigbee.[22] And there is the essay by Cynthia Marshall, mentioned above, introducing a book of essays about either MacDonald or Lewis. Other than these essays and articles, the only other essay this author knows of that examines the relationship between MacDonald and Lewis is Catherine Durie's essay on the two in a book of essays on MacDonald edited by William Raeper.[23]

Durie's excellent essay is particularly important to mention here because of its attempt to stress qualities in MacDonald's writing that did *not* find their way into Lewis's. Because this study's main business has been to document similarities and demonstrate influence, there is the danger of overlooking the differences between the two. As is done here, Durie points out the differences between Lewis and MacDonald on hell and notices, as many others have, the relative ambiguity of MacDonald's symbols when compared to Lewis's 'almost

18   Richard Purtill, *Lord of the Elves and Eldils: Fantasy and Philosophy in C.S. Lewis and J.R.R. Tolkien* (Grand Rapids: Zondervan, 1974).
19   Don King, 'The Childlike in George MacDonald and C.S. Lewis', in *Mythlore*, 46 (Summer 1986), pp. 17-26.
20   Gregory Wolfe, 'C.S. Lewis's Debt to George MacDonald' in *CSL: The Bulletin of the New York C.S. Lewis Society*, 15 (1983), pp. 1-7.
21   Gail Hammond, 'C.S. Lewis and George MacDonald: A Comparison of Styles', in *C.S. Lewis Bulletin* (Dec, 1981).
22   Sally Adair Rigbee, 'Fantasy Places and Imaginative Belief: *The Lion, the Witch and the Wardrobe* and *The Princess and the Goblin*', in *Children's Literature Association Quarterly*, 8 (1; Spring, 1983), pp. 10-11.
23   Catherine Durie, 'George MacDonald and C.S. Lewis', in William Raeper (ed.), *The Gold Thread: Essays on George MacDonald* (Edinburgh: Edinburgh University Press, 1990).

intrusive clarity'.[24]

There is the corresponding danger, in Durie's purpose: that of over-stating certain differences, or of numbering the differences without weighing them. She, for example, claims that Lewis is more severe in his use of symbols than MacDonald, writing that Lewis's images comparing God to an angler playing a fish and a cat pursuing a mouse are less benevolent than MacDonald's 'Great Shepherd' who sends out his 'sharp-toothed sheep-dogs' that bring lost sheep back into the fold.[25] There may be something to this, but Durie does not mention how closely many of Lewis's symbols, especially in his fiction, resemble MacDonald's symbols. She does not mention that MacDonald compares God to a fire that destroys all that is not of its kind,[26] or that MacDonald's great North Wind sinks a ship full of people. Neither does she mention the striking similarity between Aslan's treatment of Aravis in *The Horse and His Boy* and Prince the sheep-dog's treatment of Agnes in 'The Wise Woman'. And while mentioning the 'sheer power and even cruelty'[27] of two of Lewis's symbols used in a piece of non-fiction (his autobiography), she fails to mention the many times when Lewis speaks out against cruelty (his essay against vivisection, for example) and mere power (Letter XXII of *Letters to Malcolm*, for example), or Aslan's many acts of tenderness in the Narnia books. And she forgets to mention how often tender lovers refer to each other as a caught fish or hunted mouse without intending to suggest oppression or cruelty. The phrase 'it took me a long time to reel her in' is not often meant to suggest cruelty, just as a 'cat and mouse game' can often describe the courtship between lovers, or potential lovers, who do not intend to oppress or eat each other. We should be both careful and thorough in our study of authors' symbols, parables and metaphors.

This is not to suggest that Durie may not be onto something very valuable indeed. It is only to suggest the need for a wide and diverse acquaintance with MacDonald and Lewis scholarship, and with the works of MacDonald and Lewis themselves.

In the same book in which Durie's essay appears, there is a cross-section of vantage points that are found in both MacDonald and Lewis scholarship. There are Jungian and feminist interpretations of MacDonald's texts (Edmund Cusick's and Roderick McGillis's, respectively); a discussion of what connection MacDonald's books might have with postmodernism (Stephen Prickett's essay), Charles Kingsley (Colin Manlove's essay), and the Victorian fairy tale (Gillian Avery); as well as David Robb's more traditionally literary look at MacDonald's Scottish novels. The same variety holds true for recent book-

---

24 Durie, in Raeper, p. 179.
25 Durie, p. 171.
26 US, pp. 18-19 (paragraphs 2-4 in 'The Consuming Fire', first series).
27 Durie, p. 171.

length studies of either author, from Timothy Bleecker's unpublished thesis on MacDonald's 'Christian Romanticism'[28] to Doris T. Myer's analysis of Lewis's defence of language against the New Criticism and other deconstructive trends,[29] to the exposed undercurrents of 'jealousy and competition for the Mother' in Holbrook's study of MacDonald's fiction.[30]

The perspective of this study might best be seen in contrast to books like Holbrook's. In Holbrook's study of MacDonald's fiction, Robert Lee Wolff, who saw a phallus around every corner in his interpretation of MacDonald's imagery, is referred to over forty times. Carl Jung is mentioned four times and Sigmund Freud sixteen times. In contrast to these sixty-plus references to psychoanalysts, Holbrook refers to MacDonald's own sermons only once,[31] and this is quoted from a secondary source. Unless Holbrook is waiting to write a book that surveys MacDonald's own thought, it is obvious how little importance he gives an author's conscious beliefs.

This study of MacDonald and Lewis doesn't deny that psychoanalytic, feminist, and other critiques of these writers' works may have something valuable to tell us, but it does deny that they are the only keys to understanding their fiction. It believes the authors' own beliefs and thinking do matter, and has sought to prove here that such things had a great deal to do with how their stories, poems and fairy tales turned out. Like Thomas Howard's 1980 study of Lewis, it attempts to look '*along*' the authors rather than merely looking '*at*' them.[32] However true or untrue MacDonald's and Lewis's beliefs actually are, it takes an excessively dogmatic person to say that they have nothing to do with their fiction. And so this study can be seen as a sort of correction, or counter balance to the studies that, for whatever reasons, ignore these beliefs.

It is also important to remember here, again, that Lewis's contact with MacDonald's literature by no means made him identical to MacDonald. The live influence of an author does not necessarily mean the annihilation of the reader, though it may come to mean transformation through a kind of 'good death', as MacDonald or Lewis might put it. Lewis was no more a carbon copy of MacDonald than MacDonald was of Novalis. Lewis read

---

28   Timothy J. Bleecker, *The Christian Romanticism of George MacDonald: a Study of His Thought and Fiction* (Ann Arbor: University Microfilms International, 1990) [PhD thesis, Tufts University].

29   Doris T. Myers, *C.S. Lewis in Context* (Kent: Ohio State University Press, 1998).

30   David Holbrook, *A Study of George MacDonald and the Image of Woman* (Lewiston: Edwin Mellen Press, 2000).

31   Holbrook, p. 238.

32   See Thomas Howard, *The Achievement of C.S. Lewis* (Wheaton: Harold Shaw, 1980), p. 7. Howard quotes from an essay of Lewis's in which he stresses the importance of doing both things when studying anything. See 'Meditation in a Toolshed' in GDK, pp. 212-215.

many other authors and was a different person. He came to share much of MacDonald's Christian understanding of reality, but Lewis never wrote like a man raised in rural Scotland,[33] as MacDonald never wrote as if he were an Oxford don. MacDonald never attempted the kind of apologetics that Lewis wrote, and Lewis never attempted what David Robb has called a 'Romantic transformation' of the 'commonplace world': a sacramental blending of the familiar that does not need to be transported to, or obviously invaded by, the fantastic.[34] And there are the differences in thought and style that have already been mentioned in this study.

Both writers believed in, or came to believe in, the same distinction between evil fortune and moral evil, the same differences between pride and love, the same tender and severe love of God. Lewis also came to share MacDonald's understanding, or the Christian understanding, of the relation between spirits and Nature. But they never came to write about these things in exactly the same way. The tone and quality of their books are unique, even though they share many things in common. Any reader will notice this. The dream-like maze of images in *Phantastes* is by no means the rock-hard narrative we find in *Perelandra*, however much both books may speak of good death. And there is no one very much like Tibbie Dyster[35] in Lewis's books, however much her homely wisdom may have in common with Professor Digory Kirke's Platonistic understanding of things.[36]

And this really is the best way to get acquainted with the unique individuality of each author's books: to simply read them. This study's main purpose has been to trace influence, to show what two authors have in common. What it

---

33   Robb convincingly counters Lewis's own suggestion (See AL p. 232) that MacDonald's novels, including his Scottish novels, were written simply out of economic necessity. See ROBB, pp. 29-37. For more on this, and an overview of the Scottish novels, see Robb's essay 'George MacDonald's Scottish Novels' in William Raeper (ed.), *The Gold Thread: Essays on George MacDonald* (Edinburgh: Edinburgh University Press, 1990), pp. 12-30.

34   As Robb puts it, MacDonald was able in his novels, 'more clearly and directly than in any other literary medium', to attempt such a transformation (ROBB, p. 30). Lewis's fantasy worlds often contain the homely in close contact with the fantastic, as we have shown, but he never attempted this sort of transformation in a realistically set novel. The closest he gets is in *That Hideous Strength*, but here too the transformation of the commonplace is achieved with the help of another world overtly breaking into our familiar one. It is more akin, in form, to the supernatural thriller that his friend Charles Williams excelled at, than to MacDonald's novels. Robb suggests that MacDonald was able to 'domesticate wonder and strangeness' in the same way that Scott did: by simply drawing the Scotland he remembered living in.

35   See AFH.

36   See LWW.

cannot do so easily, and what it could never do adequately, is to fully convey the differences. It will be noticed how each chapter in this study begins with a quotation from authors other than MacDonald or Lewis. Part of the purpose of this has simply been to help introduce, in epigrammatic fashion, the subject of each chapter. Another purpose has been to show how Lewis has not simply been influenced by MacDonald, but by many writers, as MacDonald himself was influenced by many writers. Most of the quotations, indeed, are drawn from at least one of either MacDonald's or Lewis's own books, and all of the quotations come from books that either MacDonald or Lewis was familiar with. Most all of the works used here were familiar to both authors. One will notice, for example, how similar the situation that St. Augustine describes[37] is to certain events in Lewis's *The Great Divorce*. And so it is not simply the influence of one man upon another, though it is clear that MacDonald had a disproportionate influence upon Lewis. It is the influence of a body of literature, much of it Christian.

But a body, as we have seen, does not mean a mass of equal, interchangeable parts.[38] Another purpose for the quotations has been to emphasise how all of these writers, like MacDonald and Lewis, are at once the same *and* different. At the head of chapter four, for example, there are quotations from Shakespeare, Austen and Tolkien. All three quotes show that all three authors' characters—a king of England, a baronet and a hobbit—suffer, or are dominated by, similar temptations. But no one who has read Shakespeare, Austen and Tolkien, or these three works, will say that they are the same. A Shakespearean history play is not nearly the same thing as one of Miss Austen's novels, and both of these works are vastly different from Tolkien's fantastic prose epic. They have some things in common, but they are all unique.

And so it is with the works of MacDonald and Lewis. They each produced works of art, and in so doing demonstrated what Lewis refers to as 'the principle of art': "'the same in the other'".[39] Both were Christians who shared an essentially Christian understanding of reality. The labour of this study has been to show how MacDonald's influence upon Lewis, more than any other author, helped take him from mere imaginative escapism to a Christian understanding of pain, suffering, evil and God's goodness. It has been to point out elephants standing amidst fern seed, to document what must already be obvious to many: that what they came to believe and write about these things was essentially 'the same'. MacDonald, in an essay on the 'fantastic imagination', writes of how the imagination embodies 'old truths' in 'new forms', and how an author, however wild and strange he makes his

---

37   See title page to chp. 3, above, p. 128.
38   See p. 272-274, above.
39   RPS, p. 3.

fantasy world, has no right to turn the moral law in it 'upside down'.[40] 'It would be wicked', he declares, 'to write a tale representing a man it called good as always doing bad things, or a man it called bad as always doing good things'.[41]

This study has shown how Lewis came to believe in the same essential 'relations of live souls' that MacDonald believed in, and how neither man 'meddled with' these relations in their stories.[42] The essential Love that God is goes beyond mere morality, they believed, especially the dry and dusty morality that they both tasted as children, but God is never less than all good and all loving, they also believed, and never less than absolutely dedicated to bringing people out of their pride to this kind of goodness. No story or book of theirs meddles with this understanding. Lewis followed his master in representing the same kind of goodness that made both their works more than imaginative escape. In this respect the truth of their art is in most essentials the same, and if one becomes convinced that their understandings of goodness are significantly connected with reality, it may be said that it is also a case of God's influence upon them both, and not simply one man's influence upon another, much as light can be described in terms of both particles *and* waves. A man's influence upon another may in fact be an example of a kind of influence God exerts upon many men and women. In this respect, surely it is good to avoid both the 'conception of the poet as the sole source of his poetry',[43] as Lewis and many others noticed long before Barthes,[44] as well as the more recent, deconstructive fashions that increasingly allow no room whatsoever for the poet, his mind, or the song he would sing.

As to how different, or unique, each man's art is, this study will offer no more than what may have already been said in conjunction with its main purpose. And surely the best way to know the individuality of an individual book (or books) is the same way one best knows the individuality of people: not by looking *at* them in a study, or on the dissection table, but by meeting them face to face or mind to mind. Opening the cover of a book and yielding to the stories themselves, like opening a door and yielding to the concrete presence of another, will no doubt help us in this regard, and help us more enjoyably, than any number of studies could hope to do.

---

40   CFT, pp. 6-7.
41   CFT, p. 7; also in ORTS, pp. 313-322. For MacDonald's idea of art and its relationship to truth, see also 'A Sketch of Individual Development' in ORTS. See also ROBB, pp. 20-22.
42   CFT, p. 6.
43   AL, p. 209.
44   See the famous essay 'The Death of the Author', in Roland Barthes, (Stephen Heath, tr.) *Image, Music, Text* (New York: Hill and Wang, 1977).

BIBLIOGRAPHY

PRIMARY SOURCES

Lewis, C.S. *The Abolition of Man*. New York: Macmillan, 1986.
- *The Allegory of Love: A Study in Medieval Tradition*. New York: Oxford University Press, 1973.
- *C.S. Lewis: Collected Letters, Volume 1* (W. Hooper, ed.). London: Harper Collins, 2000.
- *Christian Reflections*. London: Harper Collins, 1991.
- *Compelling Reason: Essays on Ethics and Theology*. London: Harper Collins, 1996.
- *The Dark Tower and Other Stories*. London: Harper Collins, 1998.
- *English Literature in the Sixteenth Century, Excluding Drama*. Oxford: Clarendon Press, 1954.
- *An Experiment in Criticism*. Cambridge: Cambridge University Press, 2000.
- *Fern-Seed and Elephants, and Other Essays on Christianity*. London: Harper Collins, 1998.
- *The Four Loves*. San Diego: Harcourt Brace Jovanovich, 1991.
- *God in the Dock: Essays on Theology and Ethics*. Grand Rapids: William B. Eerdmans, 1993.
- *The Great Divorce: A Dream*. London: Harper Collins, 1997.
- *A Grief Observed*. New York: Bantam, 1976.
- *The Horse and His Boy*. New York: Harper Collins, 1994.
- *The Last Battle*. New York: Harper Collins, 1994.
- *Letters of C.S. Lewis* (W.H. Lewis, W. Hooper, eds.). San Diego: Harcourt Brace and Company, 1988.
- *Letters to Malcolm: Chiefly on Prayer*. New York: Harcourt Brace Jovanovich, 1964.
- *The Lion, the Witch and the Wardrobe*. New York: Harper Collins, 1994.
- *The Magician's Nephew*. New York: Harper Collins, 1994.
- *Mere Christianity*. New York: Macmillan, 1984.
- *Miracles: A Preliminary Study*. New York: Macmillan, 1978.
- *Of This and Other Worlds*. London: Harper Collins, 2000.
- *Out of the Silent Planet*. New York: Macmillan, 1986.
- *Perelandra: A Novel*. New York: Macmillan, 1986.
- *The Pilgrim's Regress: An Allegorical Apology for Christianity Reason and Romanticism*. Grand Rapids: William B. Eerdmans, 1997.
- *Poems*. San Diego: Harcourt Brace and Company, 1992.
- *A Preface to Paradise Lost*. London: Oxford University Press, 1944.
- *Present Concerns*. San Diego: Harcourt Brace & Company, 1986.

- *Prince Caspian*. New York: Harper Collins, 1994.
- *The Problem of Pain*. New York: Macmillan, 1986.
- *Reflections on the Psalms*. London: Harper Collins, 1998.
- *The Screwtape Letters*. New York: Macmillan, 1982.
- *The Silver Chair*. New York: Harper Collins, 1994.
- *Spirits in Bondage: A Cycle of Lyrics*. San Diego: Harcourt Brace and Company, 1984.
- *Studies in Medieval and Renaissance Literature*. Cambridge: Cambridge University Press, 1998.
- *Surprised by Joy: The Shape of My Early Life*. San Diego: Harcourt Brace & Company, 1984.
- *That Hideous Strength: A Modern Fairy-Tale for Grown-Ups*. New York: Macmillan, 1986.
- *Till We have Faces: A Myth Retold*. San Diego: Harcourt Brace & Company, 1985.
- *The Voyage of the Dawn Treader*. New York: Harper Collins, 1994.
- *The Weight of Glory and Other Addresses*. New York: Simon and Schuster, 1996.

MacDonald, George. *Adela Cathcart*. Whitehorn: Johannesen,[1]* 1994 [London: Hurst and Blackett, 1864].
- *Alec Forbes of Howglen*: Whitehorn: Johannesen, 1995 [London: Hurst and Blackett, 1900].
- *Annals of a Quiet Neighbourhood*. Whitehorn: Johannesen, 1995 [London: Strahan, 1867].
- *At the Back of the North Wind*. Ware: Wordsworth, 1994.
- *A Book of Strife in the Form of the Diary of an Old Soul: Daily Writings for Devotional Reflection*. London: Triangle, 2001.
- *The Complete Fairy Tales*. New York: Penguin, 1999.
- *David Elginbrod*. Whitehorn. Johannesen, 1995 [Philadelphia: MacKay, 1900].
- *A Dish of Orts: Chiefly Papers on the Imagination, and on Shakespere* (sic.). London: Sampson Low Marston & Company, 1893.
- *England's Antiphon*. Whitehorn. Johannesen, 1996 [New York: Macmillan, 1890].
- *An Expression of Character: The Letters of George MacDonald* (G.E. Sadler, ed.). Grand Rapids: William B. Eerdmans, 1994.
- *George MacDonald: An Anthology* (C.S. Lewis, editor). New York: Simon and Schuster, 1996.

---

1 *All Johannesen editions of George MacDonald's works cited here are reproductions of much older editions. The older editions are given here, in brackets, at the end of each Johannesen entry.

– *Guild Court, A London Story.* Whitehorn: Johannesen, 1999 [New York: Routledge and Sons, 1886].
– *The Hope of the Gospel.* Whitehorn: Johannesen, 1995 [London: Ward Lock, 1892].
– *Lilith.* Whitehorn: Johannesen, 1998 [London: Chatto & Windus, 1896].
– *The Miracles of Our Lord.* Whitehorn Johannesen, 1995 [London: Strahan, 1870].
– *Phantastes: A Faerie Romance.* Grand Rapids: Wm. B. Eerdmans, 1981.
– *The Portent and Other Stories.* Whitehorn: Johannesen, 1994 [London: Fisher Unwin, 1909].
– *The Princess and Curdie.* London: Penguin, 1994.
– *The Princess and the Goblin.* London: Penguin, 1996.
– *Rampolli.* Whitehorn: Johannesen, 1995 [London: Longmans Green, 1897].
– *Ranald Bannerman's Boyhood.* Whitehorn: Johannesen, 1993 [London: Blackie, 1911].
– *Robert Falconer.* Whitehorn. Johannesen, 1995 [London: Hurst, 1880].
– *Salted with Fire.* Whitehorn. Johannesen, 1996 [London: Hurst & Blackett, 1900].
– *Sir Gibbie.* Whitehorn. Johannesen, 1996 [New York: A.L. Burt, 1900].
– *Unspoken Sermons: First, Second, and Third Series.* Whitehorn: Johannesen, 1997 [London: Strahan, 1867 (first series). London: Longmans, Green, 1886 and 1889 (second and third series)].
– *Within and Without: A Dramatic Poem.* London: Longman, Brown, Green, Longmans, & Roberts, 1857.

SECONDARY SOURCES

Amell, B. *George MacDonald on the Logic of Faith.* Portland: B. Amell, 2000.
Barthes, R. *Image, Music, Text* (S. Heath, tr.). New York: Hill and Wang, 1998.
Bleecker, T.J. *The Christian Romanticism of George MacDonald: A Study of His Thought and Fiction.* Ann Arbor: University Microfilms International, 1990.
Boethius. *The Consolation of Philosophy* (P.G. Walsh, tr.). Oxford: Oxford University Press, 1999.
Como, J.T. (ed.). *C.S. Lewis at the Breakfast Table, and Other Reminiscences.* New York: MacMillan, 1979.

Downing, D.C. *The Most Reluctant Convert: C.S. Lewis's Journey to Faith*. Downer's Grove: Inter Varsity Press, 2002.

Gibb, J. (ed.). *Light on C.S. Lewis*. New York: Harcourt Brace Jovanovich, 1976.

Green, R.L., and Hooper, W. *C.S. Lewis: A Biography*. New York: Harcourt Brace Jovanovich, 1976.

Hein, R. *The Harmony Within: The Spiritual Vision of George MacDonald*. Grand Rapids: Eerdmans, 1982.

Holbrook, D. *The Skeleton in the Wardrobe: C.S. Lewis's Fantasies: A Phenomenological Study*. London: Bucknell University Press, 1991.

– *A Study of George MacDonald and the Image of Woman*. Lewiston: Edwin Mellen Press, 2000.

Howard, T. *The Achievement of C.S. Lewis*. Wheaton: Harold Shaw, 1980.

Jaffe, A. *The Myth of Meaning in the work of C.G. Jung*. Hull: Hodder and Stoughton, 1970.

MacDonald, Greville. *George MacDonald and His Wife*. London: Allen and Unwin, 1924.

Myers, D.T. *C.S. Lewis in Context*. Kent: Ohio University Press, 1998.

Purtill, R. *Lord of the Elves and the Eldils: Fantasy and Philosophy in C.S. Lewis and J.R.R. Tolkien*. Grand Rapids: Zondervan, 1974.

Raeper, W. *George MacDonald*. Tring: Lion, 1987.

Raeper, W. (ed.). *The Gold Thread: Essays on George MacDonald*. Edinburgh: Edinburgh University Press, 1990.

Reis, R. *George MacDonald*. New York: Twayne, 1972.

Robb, D.S. *George MacDonald*. Edinburgh: Scottish Academic Press, 1987.

Schackel, P.J. *Reason and Imagination in C.S. Lewis: A Study of Till We Have Faces*. Grand Rapids: Eerdmans, 1984.

Walsh, C. *The Literary Legacy of C.S. Lewis*. New York: Harcourt Brace Jovanovich, 1979.

Washick, J.S. *He Who Fears to Doubt: Doubt and Faith in George MacDonald's Major Verse*. Ann Arbor: University Microfilms International, 1997.

Wolff, R.L. *The Golden Key: A Study of the Fiction of George MacDonald*. New Haven: Yale University Press, 1961.

INDEX

Achilles 178, 221.

Adam-Eve banishment story 111-112, 118.

Aeschylus 11.

Amell, Barbara 55, 136, 293.

Apuleius 70.

Aristotle 273.

Aslan 68-70, 76, 96, 105-107, 126, 138-141, 156-157, 227, 229-230, 232, 236-238, 240-241, 246, 248-249, 253-254, 258, 260, 267-268, 274-275, 287, 295.

Atilla 221.

Augustine 128, 288, 298.

Austen, Jane 158, 182-183; characters' similarity to Narnia characters 298.

Avery, Gillian 295.

Ayer, A.J. 77-78.

Ball, Sir Robert 8.

Barthes, Roland 299.

Berkeley, George 78.

Bible: Gen. 85, 118, 215; Ex. 111; Lev. 123; Deut. 123, 153; Job 10-11; Psalms 42, 170, 180, 214, 226, 245-246; Isaiah 2, 213, 239, 288; Zech. 226; Mat. 5, 42, 96, 100, 123, 172, 173, 176, 186, 189, 209, 210, 226, 232, 234, 239, 251, 278, 290; Mark 123, 234, 269; Luke 123, 126, 173, 189, 205, 225, 226, 232, 234, 269; John 53, 96, 172, 205, 235, 236, 233, 234, 238, 244; Rom. 96, 236, 286; 1 Cor. 49, 96, 109, 189, 274, 286; Eph. 205, 274; Phil. 96, 226, 232, 236, 238; Col. 274, 278; Heb. 153, 205; 1 Peter 24; 2 Peter 288; 1 John 96, 128, 234, 236; Rev. 164, 210, 239, 246, 288.

Blair, Robert 107-108.

Blake, William: MacDonald's use of illustration for bookplate 107-108; and *The Great Divorce* 150.

Bleecker, Timothy 296.

Boehme, Jacob 31.

Boethius 104, 135-136.

Buddhism 266.

Bunyan, John 2.

Burns, Robert 54, 98, 264.

Capron, Rev. Robert ('Oldie') 16.

Calvinism/Calvinists 32-34, 90, 150-152, 174, 175, 218-229, 242.

Chaucer, Geoffrey 278.

Chesterton, G.K. 20-21.

Child-likeness 83, 97, 242, 244; vs. childishness 83, 244, 249-251; 264-265, 290.

Christ (or the Son) 24, 33, 38, 96, 98, 100, 106, 115, 121, 126, 140, 148, 150, 152-153, 157, 162, 173, 189, 194, 209, 216, 219-221, 223, 224-226, 228, 229-230, 232-243, 244-247, 258, 260, 270-271, 273, 274, 281-282, 285-286, 289, 290.

Church of Scotland 33.

Coleridge, Samuel Taylor 114, 264.

Como, James T. 116.

Confucius 212.

Conscience/Moral Law 58, 59-61, 61-65, 76-77, 80-81, 84-92, 104-105, 210-216, 298-299.

Cowie, G.E. 17-19.

Cupid-Psyche myth 70-76, 110-113, 123, 140, 201-203, 249, 264, 282, 285, 287, 289.

Cusick, Edmund 295.

Dante: depiction of devils in *Inferno* 167; *Purgatorio* 170; 193, 247, 255,

273, 278, 286, 290.
Darwin, Charles 82.
Davidman, Joy, wife of C.S. Lewis: death of 92; 121-123.
Deconstruction 296, 299.
Dickens, Charles 183.
Divine Sonship 216-217, 219-221, 232-236, 271.
Douglas, Gavin 5.
Downing, David C. 54, 293.
Dualism 153, 159-161.
Durie, Catherine 294-295.
Edwards, Jonathan 224-225.
Elliott, Jane 147.
Empiricism 54, 77-78, 120-121.
Enlightenment: German Romantics' rebellion against 32; 54; and Jonathan Edwards 224.
Escapism 27-31, 45-47, 50, 278-282, 287, 298-299.
Feminist interpretations, of MacDonald's works 218, 295.
Fisher, John: on purgatory 170.
Foster, M.B. 147.
Frazer, Sir James, author of *The Golden Bough* 19.
Free will (human) 56-57, 59-60, 146-147, 151, 172-173, 175-177, 206, 269-270, 277.
French Symbolists: 32.
Freud, Sigmund 128, 292, 296.
Goethe, Johann Wolfgang von: quoted in *Phantastes* 133; depiction of devils in *Faust* 167.
Good death 32, 49-50, 114, 126, 137, 147, 146-148, 149-151, 163-165, 175, 191, 202-204, 209; in the Trinity 234; 239-240, 246-251, 261-270, 277, 282-283, 288, 290, 296, 297.
Gower, John 217.

Graves, Robert 22.
Green, Roger Lacelyn, co-author of *C.S. Lewis: A Biography* 5, 45.
Greeves, Arthur 1, 6, 19-20, 45.
Haggard, H. Rider 29.
Hall, Joseph 128.
Hammond, Gail 294.
Heaven 283-290.
Hein, Rolland 292-293.
Heinemann, William 22.
Hell, as state of final damnation 171-178; depictions of 203-209.
Herbert, George 18.
Herodotus 24.
Hesse, Herman 32.
Heywood, Thomas 112-113.
Hichens, Robert 24.
Hierarchy 270-277.
Hilton, T. 82.
Hoffman, E.T.A. 31, 114.
Hogg, James 162.
Homer 58, 221, 284.
Holbrook, David 292, 296.
Holiness (see also 'Joy') 2, 6, 20, 23, 46-47, 96, 119, 136, 180, 212-213, 283-290.
Hooper, Walter, co-author of *C.S. Lewis: A Biography* 5, 45, 126; note in 'The Neccesity of Chivalry' 218; note in 'The Weight of Glory' 283.
Horace 48.
Howard, Thomas 296.
Hughes, Arthur, MacDonald's illustrator 107.
Hughes, Ted, son of Arthur 107.
Hume, David 77-78.
Imagination: and reason 28-29, 114-115; and symbolism 134; 279-280, 298-299.
Incarnation 240-243, 282-283.
Individuation 128-137, 148, 150.

Islam/ Islamic conception of God 228-229, 231.
Jaffe, Aniela 128.
Jena Romantics 31.
Joad, C.E.M. 105, 159.
Job 10-11, 93-94.
Joy ('bright shadow' or 'Holiness') 2, 6, 20, 23, 46-47, 96, 119, 136, 180, 212-213, 283-290.
Jung, Carl 128-133, 135-136, 148-150, 161, 292, 295-296.
Keats, John 46.
Keith, A.B. 65.
Kennedy, John, minister of Blackfriars Street Church, Aberdeen 33-34, 67.
King, Don 294.
Kingsley, Charles 295.
Kirkpatrick, William T. ('The Great Knock') 18-19, 22, 54.
Knoepflmacher, U.C. 165.
Lancelot, Sir 217, 261.
Lang, Andrew 24, 29.
La Touche, Rose 112.
Lewis, Albert (father) 8, 12.
Lewis, C.S.: purchase of Phantastes 1; editor of George MacDonald: An Anthology 1-2, 8, 10-12, 46, 95, 149, 152, 164-165, 180, 189-190, 216-217, 233, 234, 235, 279; preface to Anthology 1-2, 216-217; purpose for writing Surprised by Joy 22; early romanticism 1-2, 19-20, 22-24, 25-26, 28-31, 45, 49-50, 53-54, 279-281; loss of mother at an early age 6-8, 157; childhood faith 7-8; early atheism/pessimism 8-10, 16-19, 22-23, 26-27, 280; Malvern College 8; importance of Unspoken Sermons to 10; boyhood in Ulster 12; Wynyard School 16-18; 90; brief faith at Wynyard 17; Cherbourg School 17-19; passion for the occult 17, 19; struggle with 'false conscience' 18; on faith and feelings 17-18, 115-116, 122-123, 262-264; appreciation of the 'homely' 19; idea of 'Joy', 'bright shadow', or 'beauty of holiness' 2, 6, 20, 23, 46-47, 96, 119, 136, 180, 212-213, 283-290; 'baptism' of his imagination by Phantastes 1-2, 19-20, 23, 53; service in the First World War 20-21, 25; as Oxford undergraduate 20-21; Oxford as inspiration for his poetry 29; attitudes toward nature 19, 22-23, 24, 26, 29-30, 44, 57-60, 87-88, 120-121, 261-266, 272-273, 285-288; 'Clive Hamilton' pseudonym 23; on reason and imagination 28-29, 114-115; ambition to be a poet 31; conversion to theism and then Christianity 53-54; summary of the problem of pain 56; Shadowlands (the teleplay, stage play, and film by W. Nicholson) 92, 143; honest doubt 104-105; on faith as action 111, 115-116, 284-285, 290; on the insufficiency of reason 115-116; on 'respectable' wickedness 193, 196, 214; portrayal of Calormenes 227-232; on the 'Divine Sonship' 236; idea of 'glory' 286-287; The Abolition of Man 56, 64-65, 86, 87; The Allegory of Love 128, 210, 217-218, 247, 275, 297, 299; Christian Reflections 87, 115, 117, 121, 149, 210, 267; Collected Letters, Vol. 1 1, 7, 22, 24-25, 29, 31, 54, 123;

Compelling Reason 89; *The Dark Tower and Other Stories* 267; *English Literature in the Sixteenth Century* 5, 53, 170, 273; *An Experiment in Criticism* 149, 209; *Fern Seed and Elephants* 128, 144; *The Four Loves* 196, 208, 227, 239, 262-265, 273-274; *God in the Dock* 79, 105, 160, 211-212, 216, 266, 271, 273, 296; *The Great Divorce* 149-150, 170-173, 175, 176, 178, 195-199, 200, 203, 205, 208, 246, 249, 260, 262, 264, 273, 286, 287, 291, 294, 298; *A Grief Observed* 90, 92-93, 103, 116, 121-123; *The Horse and His Boy* 139-141, 181, 228-229, 231-232, 248-249, 295; *The Last Battle* 69-70, 72, 77, 126, 182, 228-230, 232, 249, 253, 282, 287, 289; *Letters of C.S. Lewis* 229, 263, 272; *Letters to Malcolm* 126, 154, 170, 245, 295; *The Lion, the Witch and the Wardrobe* 61, 68, 96, 140, 156, 181, 236, 238, 246, 249, 274, 278, 282, 297; *The Magician's Nephew* 61, 90-91, 138, 156-157, 181, 183, 215, 253; *Mere Christianity* 56, 63-65, 67, 79-80, 85-86, 80-81, 85-86, 96, 104-105, 153, 159-161, 193-194, 205, 220, 229, 233, 236, 239-240, 267, 273; 'Ministering Angels' 267; *Miracles* 56, 76-80, 86, 120-121, 160, 220, 236, 241; *Of This and Other Worlds* 149; *Out of the Silent Planet* 68, 215, 249; *Perelandra* 43, 57-58, 71-73, 72, 117, 120, 135-136, 150, 158, 165-167, 180-181, 207-208, 237, 249, 275, 283, 297; *Pilgrim's Regress* 54, 89-90, 212, 237, 249, 267, 282; *A Preface to Paradise Lost* 149, 167, 273, 275; *Poems* 244-245, 251, 254; *Present Concerns* 217-218, 221, 237, 244, 260-261; *Prince Caspian* 68-69, 181, 249, 253; *The Problem of Pain* 9-10, 18, 56-61, 86, 95, 97, 105, 130, 140, 143-144, 149, 151-152, 158, 169, 172-176, 183, 195, 203, 206, 208, 213-214, 233, 245, 247, 266, 274, 279, 293; *Reflections on the Psalms* 207, 214, 216, 220, 226, 245-247, 246, 298; *The Screwtape Letters* 56, 96, 115-116, 155-156, 167, 178-180, 183, 193-194, 198-199, 207, 232, 272; *The Silver Chair* 105, 107, 125, 156, 181, 249; *Spirits in Bondage* 22-31, 36-39, 41, 43-50, 53, 62, 122, 208, 240, 278-280, 282; *Studies in Medieval and Renaissance Literature* 278; *Surprised by Joy* 1, 6-9, 12, 16-21, 45-46, 53-54, 90, 136, 285; *That Hideous Strength* 12, 195, 199-200, 214-215, 249-250, 258-260, 275-277, 297; *Till We Have Faces* 70-77, 109, 111, 113, 123, 140, 195, 201-203, 249, 282; *The Voyage of the Dawn Treader* 181, 246, 267-268; *The Weight of Glory and Other Addresses* 76, 205-206, 233, 273, 278, 283-290, 292.

Lewis, Flora (mother): 6-8, 23, 157.

Lewis, Joy Davidman (wife): 92, 119, 121-123, 143.

Lewis, W.H. (brother) 16; editor of *Letters of C.S. Lewis* 229.

Lindsay, David, author of *Voyage to Arcturus* 179.

Littlejohns, Richard 32.

Love (charity, or *agapē*): beyond thought, imagination and feeling

122; and Screwtape 179; Paul's
description of 188-192; other loves
submitting to 196; in the Trinity
232-235; not simply tender 247;
called 'Gift-love' 264; Gift-love
and Need-love 274; 277.
Lucretius 8-9.
Lyndsay, Sir David 215.
MacDonald, Charles Edward
(cousin) 35.
MacDonald, Charles Francis
(brother) 13.
MacDonald, George: called 'my
master' by Lewis 1; loss of mother
at an early age 6-7, 13-14, 157;
King's College, Aberdeen 10,
31-32; pastor to congregation at
Arundel 10, 35-36; summary of
the problem of suffering 10-11;
rural upbringing in Aberdeenshire
11-14; early death of brothers
13-14; death of Duke Gordon
14; home in Italy 107-108;
preoccupation with death 14-
15; empathy and sympathy with
atheists 15-16; honest doubt 15-
16, 94-95, 101-105; ambition to
be a poet 31; early romanticism
31-32, 38, 54, 114; influence of
German literature 31-32, 38;
'good death' 32, 49, 114, 126,
137, 144, 147, 150, 163-165, 175,
191, 203, 209, 234, 240-241,
247-251, 266-266, 268-270, 276,
282-283, 288, 290, 296-297;
reaction to Calvinist teaching
32-34, 90, 151-152, 174-175, 218,
221-226, 242-243; Blackfriars
Street Church in Aberdeen,
32-33; Missionar church in
Huntly 33; reaction to harsh

Scottish weather 34; training at
Highbury Theological College
34-35; unorthodox preaching 35;
rejection by Stebbing congregation
35; marriage to Louisa Powell
35-36; *Casa Coraggio* 107-108;
lung problems 11, 35-36, 92-93;
attitude towards nature 38, 44-45,
81-84, 88-89, 260-263, 264-266,
286-287; calls to courage 50, 55,
62, 94-95, 96-104, 107-109, 111-
115, 117-120, 289-290; on child-
likeness 83, 97, 242, 249-251,
264-265, 268-270, 290; lecture
tour of northeastern United
States 92; winter in Algiers 93;
eczema in later years 93; stroke
93-94; on faith and feelings 107,
113-115, 124, 264-265; move
to Bournemouth 107; 'corage!'
as family motto 107; on faith as
action 108-109, 111-115, 123,
177, 277, 279-282, 285, 289-290;
accused of emotionalism 114;
dislike of intellectualism 114;
on the imagination and the will
114-115, 279-280, 298; 'darkness'
of later novels 116-117; supposed
loss of faith 116-117; definition
of 'human' 183; on 'seeming'
vs. 'being' 182, 184, 194; on
respectable religiosity 184-188,
193-194, 225-227; on the 'Divine
Sonship' 216-217, 219-220, 232-
235, 271; dreams of a life at sea
224; as a character in Lewis's *The
Great Divorce* 195, 205, 208, 260,
262, 291; *Adela Cathcart* 120,
130-131, 142-143, 219, 237-238,
250-251, 258, 271; *Alec Forbes
of Howglen* 13, 112-114, 141,

144, 154-155, 163-164, 184-185, 191-192, 199, 222, 237, 256-257, 259-260, 279-280, 297; *Annals of a Quiet Neighbourhood* 14-15, 43, 53, 119, 145-146, 210, 287; *At the Back of the North Wind* 67, 100-105, 110, 118, 125-126, 130, 141, 154, 218-219, 237, 253, 258, 276, 295; 'The Castle' 271; 'A Child's Holiday' 258; *The Complete Fairy Tales* 126, 134, 165, 203-204, 248, 266, 268, 299; *David Elginbrod* 12, 142, 183-184, 192, 206, 237, 242, 257-258; *The Diary of an Old Soul* 116, 124-125, 269; *A Dish of Orts* 114, 134, 299; *England's Antiphon* 128, 210; *An Expression of Character: The Letters of George MacDonald* 108, 112; *George MacDonald: An Anthology* 1-2, 10-12, 46, 95, 149, 149, 152, 164-165, 180, 189-190, 216-217, 233-235, 279; 'The Giant's Heart' 130-131, 250; 'The Golden Key' 126, 266, 268; *Guild Court* 136, 143; *The Hope of the Gospel* 5, 12, 146-149, 210, 226, 242, 270-271, 276-277, 284, 285-286, 289-290; 'The Light Princess' 237-240, 265, 268; *Lilith* 108-109, 138-139, 175-176, 178, 203-206, 242, 248-250, 264, 268-269, 276, 278, 281, 287; *Miracles of Our Lord* 216, 219-220, 239, 242, 276-277; *Phantastes* 1-2, 5-7, 10, 19-20, 23, 32, 40, 48, 53, 55, 100, 113, 115, 117-120, 122, 129, 132-137, 140-141, 150, 154, 157, 162-164, 190-192, 203, 209, 237, 242-243, 252-253, 256, 260, 265, 267-268, 276, 278, 281-283, 285, 287, 289-293, 297; *The Porten*t 14,

192; *The Princess and Curdie* 44, 61, 83-88, 90, 205, 219, 250, 253-256, 259; *The Princess and the Goblin* 45, 61-62, 66-70, 72-73, 75, 77, 81-83, 98, 107, 254, 259, 294; *Ranald Bannerman's Boyhood* 13-14; *Robert Falconer* 109, 142, 145, 147-148, 151-153, 157, 162, 175-177, 184-186, 192, 222-224, 228-230, 237, 242-243, 256-257, 268-270, 275, 280; *Salted with Fire* 119-120; 'The Shadows' 131, 133, 141; *Sir Gibbie* 12, 88-89, 98-100, 130, 154, 158-159, 162-163, 186-189, 190, 192-194, 222, 237, 285; *Thomas Wingfold, Curate* 136; *Unspoken Sermons* 5, 10-13, 94-97, 105, 114-115, 126, 128, 140, 149, 152-153, 159, 164-165, 168-170, 174, 177, 183, 189, 192-194, 203, 207, 210-211, 213, 216, 219-222, 224-226, 228-229, 233-235, 239, 241, 244-245, 247-248, 251-252, 265-266, 271, 273-274, 276-277, 281, 288-290, 295; 'The Wise Woman' 203-204, 237, 248, 267, 295; *Within and Without* 31, 36-46, 48, 48-51, 53, 57, 98, 108-111, 122, 144, 147, 242-243, 253, 287, 289.

MacDonald, George, Sr. (father) 12-13, 31, 35; as model for David Elginrod 257-258.

MacDonald, Greville (son, biographer) 12, 92-96, 116, 126, 128.

MacDonald, Helen MacKay (mother) 6, 13-14.

MacDonald, James (brother) 13.

MacDonald, John (brother) 13-14.

MacDonald, Lilia (daughter) 93.

MacDonald, Louisa Powell (wife)

35-36, 39, 92-93, 107.
MacDonald, Mary Josephine
(daughter) 93, 107.
MacDonald, Maurice (son) 107.
MacKay, Helen (cousin) 34.
Maconachie, Rev. J. 34.
MacPherson, James (Ossian) 54.
Maeterlinck, Maurice 32.
Malory, Sir Thomas 218.
Manicheanism 29, 265.
Manlove, Colin 295.
Marshall, Cynthia 291-292, 294.
McGillis, Roderick 295.
Mill, J.S. 212.
Milton, John 24, 112, 138, 167, 180,
181, 198, 273, 275.
Morality/Conscience/Moral Law 58,
61, 63-67, 76, 80-81, 84-91, 104-
105, 210-216, 298-299.
More, Thomas: on purgatory 170.
Morison, James 33.
Myer, Doris T. 296.
Naturalist arguments 77-81.
Nature 283, 285-287, 297; Lewis's
attitudes toward 22-23, 24, 26,
29-30, 44, 57-60, 87-88, 120-
121, 261-266, 272-273, 285-288;
MacDonald's attitude toward 38,
44-45, 81-84, 88-89, 260-263,
264-266, 286-287.
Neo-Platonists (and hierarchy) 273.
New Criticism 296.
Nicholson, William 92.
Nietzsche, Fredrich 91, 115.
North Wind 67, 100-105, 110, 118,
125-126, 130, 141, 154, 218-219,
237, 253, 258, 276, 295.
Novalis (Friedrich von Hardenburg)
31-32, 114, 264.
Occultist tradition 17.
Omnipotence 55-57.

Orpheus-Euridice myth 111.
Oxford Socratic Club 76, 79.
Paul: description of love 188-189; on
the body of Christ's church 274.
Persephone-Hades myth 111.
Pick, J.B. 179.
Plato: 65, 110, 127, 233; Platonism in
Phantastes 129-130; neo-Platonism
and hierarchy 273.
Postmodernism 98, 218, 295.
Predestination 33, 186, 221-222,
229.
Prickett, Steven 295.
Pride 167-169, 178, 180-184, 186-
187, 193-200, 205, 214, 221, 226-
227, 231-232, 240, 242, 250-251,
261, 264, 267-270, 272-275, 277,
280-281, 290, 299.
Prometheus 11, 26, 108.
Pullman, Phillip 181-183.
Purgatory 169-171.
Purtill, Richard 294.
Queen Irene (Mistress of the Silver
Moon, Princess Irene's great-great
grandmother) 61-62, 66-67, 83-
86, 87-88, 91, 98, 100, 105, 107,
118-119, 141, 157, 218-219, 237,
253-254, 259-260, 276, 279.
Raeper, William 33, 35; his Jungian
interpretation of MacDonald's
works 128-133, 135-137, 145-
146, 149-150, 154, 161; author of
George MacDonald 6, 12-14, 31,
33-36, 38, 67, 82, 92-94, 107-108,
116, 123, 126, 129-130, 132-133,
137, 154, 161, 218-219, 223-224,
257, 271.
Reason 58, 62-63, 76-80, 114-116;
and imagination 28, 53-55, 114-
116.
Reis, Richard 292.

Religiosity 34, 184-188.
Resurrection 120-121, 123, 125-126, 241, 283-290.
Rigbee, Sally Adair 294.
Robb, David S. 31, 33, 114, 165, 295, 297, 299.
Rolleston, George 108.
Romanticism: in Lewis 1-2, 19-20, 22-24, 25-27, 28-31, 45, 49-50, 54, 279-281; in MacDonald 31-32, 38, 54, 114.
Rousseau, Jean Jacques 264.
Ruskin, John 82, 112, 167, 255.
Russell, Bertrand 78.
Sadler, G.E., editor of MacDonald's letters 108.
Sappho 2.
Sassoon, Siegfried 22.
Satan 22-23, 27-28, 36, 116, 128-129, 149, 161, 167, 180-181, 198, 245, 275, 287.
Schackel, Peter J. 71.
Schopenhauer, Arthur 19.
Secession Church 33.
Shakespeare, William 114, 158, 273, 298.
Shelly, P.B. 11, 105.
Sidney, Sir Philip 53.
Sinclair, Sir George 31.
Socrates 212.
Solomon 259.
Sophocles 284.
Spenser, Edmund 237, 273.
Stevenson, Robert Louis 162.
Stewart, Colin, MacDonald's brutal school teacher 13.
Swedenborg, Emanuel 31.
Taylor, Jeremy 210.
Tennyson, Alfred 26, 29, 89, 105, 278.

Tolkien, J.R.R. 68, 81, 158, 294, 298.
Trinity: unique Christian doctrine of 233-235, 270-271, 276.
Troup, Robert 32.
Tyndale, William: on Purgatory 170.
Usk, Thomas 210.
Violence: in works of Lewis and MacDonald 248-251.
Von Hügel, Friedrich: on hell 172.
Walsh, Chad 31, 92.
Washick, James Stewart 293.
Wells, H.G. 8.
Will: as distinct from emotions, sense or imagination 46, 110, 113-116, 123, 262-264.
Williams, Charles 297.
Wittgenstein, Ludwig 78.
Wolfe, Gregory 294.
Wolff, Robert Lee 31, 114, 116-117, 128, 292, 296.
Wordsworth, William 5, 114, 264.
Yeats, W.B. 29.
Zoroastrianism 160.

INDEX

OTHER TITLES OF INTEREST

C. S. Lewis

C. S. Lewis: Views From Wake Forest - Essays on C. S. Lewis
Michael Travers, editor

Contains sixteen scholarly presentations from the international C. S. Lewis convention in Wake Forest, NC. Walter Hooper shares his important essay "Editing C. S. Lewis," a chronicle of publishing decisions after Lewis' death in 1963.

"Scholars from a variety of disciplines address a wide range of issues. The happy result is a fresh and expansive view of an author who well deserves this kind of thoughtful attention."
Diana Pavlac Glyer, author of *The Company They Keep*

The Hidden Story of Narnia:
A Book-By-Book Guide to Lewis' Spiritual Themes
Will Vaus

A book of insightful commentary equally suited for teens or adults – Will Vaus points out connections between the *Narnia* books and spiritual/biblical themes, as well as between ideas in the *Narnia* books and C. S. Lewis' other books. Learn what Lewis himself said about the overarching and unifying thematic structure of the Narnia books. That is what this book explores; what C. S. Lewis called "the hidden story" of Narnia. Each chapter includes questions for individual use or small group discussion.

Why I Believe in Narnia:
33 Reviews and Essays on the Life and Work of C. S. Lewis
James Como

Chapters range from reviews of critical books, documentaries and movies to evaluations of Lewis' books to biographical analysis.

"A valuable, wide-ranging collection of essays by one of the best informed and most acute commentators on Lewis' work and ideas."
Peter Schakel, author of *Imagination & the Arts in C. S. Lewis*

C. S. Lewis Goes to Heaven: A Reader's Guide to The Great Divorce
David G. Clark

This is the first book devoted solely to this often neglected book and the first to reveal several important secrets Lewis concealed within the story. Lewis felt his imaginary trip to Hell and Heaven was far better than his book *The Screwtape Letters*, which has become a classic. Clark is an ordained minister who has taught courses on Lewis for more than 30 years and is a New Testament and Greek scholar with a Doctor of Philosophy degree in Biblical Studies from the University of Notre Dame. Readers will discover the many literary and biblical influences Lewis utilized in writing his brilliant novel.

C. S. Lewis & Philosophy as a Way of Life
Adam Barkman

C. S. Lewis is rarely thought of as a "philosopher" per se despite having both studied and taught philosophy for several years at Oxford. Lewis's long journey to Christianity was essentially philosophical – passing through seven different stages. This 624 page book is an invaluable reference for C. S. Lewis scholars and fans alike

C. S. Lewis: His Literary Achievement
Colin Manlove

"This is a positively brilliant book, written with splendor, elegance, profundity and evidencing an enormous amount of learning. This is probably not a book to give a first-time reader of Lewis. But for those who are more broadly read in the Lewis corpus this book is an absolute gold mine of information. The author gives us a magnificent overview of Lewis' many writings, tracing for us thoughts and ideas which recur throughout, and at the same time telling us how each book differs from the others. I think it is not extravagant to call C. S. Lewis: His Literary Achievement a tour de force."
Robert Merchant, *St. Austin Review*, Book Review Editor

Mythopoeic Narnia:
Memory, Metaphor, and Metamorphoses in The Chronicles of Narnia
Salwa Khoddam

Dr. Khoddam, the founder of the C. S. Lewis and Inklings Society (2004), has been teaching university courses using Lewis' books for over 25 years. Her book offers a fresh approach to the Narnia books based on an inquiry into Lewis' readings and use of classical and Christian symbols. She explores the literary and intellectual contexts of these stories, the traditional myths and motifs, and places them in the company of the greatest Christian mythopoeic works of Western literature. In Lewis' imagination, memory and metaphor interact to advance his purpose – a Christian metamorphosis. *Mythopoeic Narnia* helps to open the door for readers into the magical world of the Western imagination.

Speaking of Jack: A C. S. Lewis Discussion Guide
Will Vaus

C. S. Lewis societies have been forming around the world since the first one started in New York City in 1969. Will Vaus has started and led three groups himself. *Speaking of Jack* is the result of Vaus' experience in leading those Lewis societies. Included here are introductions to most of Lewis' books as well as questions designed to stimulate discussion about Lewis' life and work. These materials have been "road-tested" with real groups made up of young and old, some very familiar with Lewis and some newcomers. *Speaking of Jack* may be used in an existing book discussion group, to start a C. S. Lewis society, or to guide your own exploration of Lewis' books.

George Macdonald

Diary of an Old Soul & The White Page Poems
George MacDonald and Betty Aberlin

The first edition of George MacDonald's book of daily poems included a blank page opposite each page of poems. Readers were invited to write their own reflections on the "white page." MacDonald wrote: "Let your white page be ground, my print be seed, growing to golden ears, that faith and hope may feed." Betty Aberlin responded to MacDonald's invitation with daily poems of her own.

"Betty Aberlin's close readings of George MacDonald's verses and her thoughtful responses to them speak clearly of her poetic gifts and spiritual intelligence."
Luci Shaw, poet

George MacDonald: Literary Heritage and Heirs
Roderick McGillis, editor

This latest collection of 14 essays sets a new standard that will influence MacDonald studies for many more years. George MacDonald experts are increasingly evaluating his entire corpus within the nineteenth century context.

"This comprehensive collection represents the best of contemporary scholarship on George MacDonald."
Rolland Hein, author of *George MacDonald: Victorian Mythmaker*

In the Near Loss of Everything: George MacDonald's Son in America
Dale Wayne Slusser

In the summer of 1887, George MacDonald's son Ronald, newly engaged to artist Louise Blandy, sailed from England to America to teach school. The next summer he returned to England to marry Louise and bring her back to America. On August 27, 1890, Louise died, leaving him with an infant daughter. Ronald once described losing a beloved spouse as "the near loss of everything". Dale Wayne Slusser unfolds this poignant story with unpublished letters and photos that give readers a glimpse into the close-knit MacDonald family.

A Novel Pulpit: Sermons From George MacDonald's Fiction
David L. Neuhouser

"In MacDonald's novels, the Christian teaching emerges out of the characters and story line, the narrator's comments, and inclusion of sermons given by the fictional preachers. The sermons in the novels are shorter than the ones in collections of MacDonald's sermons and so are perhaps more accessible for some. In any case, they are both stimulating and thought-provoking. This collection of sermons from ten novels serve to bring out the 'freshness and brilliance' of MacDonald's message."
From the author's introduction

Behind the Back of the North Wind:
Critical Essays on George MacDonald's Classic Children's Book
John Pennington and Roderick McGillis, editors

The unique blend of fairy tale atmosphere and social realism in this novel laid the groundwork for modern fantasy literature. Sixteen essays by various authors are accompanied by an instructive introduction, extensive index, and beautiful illustrations.

Through the Year with George MacDonald: 366 Daily Readings
Rolland Hein, editor

These page-length excerpts from sermons, novels and letters are given an appropriate theme/heading and a complementary Scripture passage for daily reading. An inspiring introduction to the artistic soul and Christian vision of George MacDonald.

Christian Living

The Living Word of the Living God:
A Beginner's Guide to Reading and Understanding the Bible
Rev. Tom Furrer

This book is based on over 20 years experience of teaching the Bible to confirmation classes at Episcopal churches in Connecticut. Chapters from Genesis to Revelation.

Keys to Growth: Meditations on the Acts of the Apostles
Will Vaus

Every living things or person requires certain ingredients in order to grow, and if a thing or person is not growing, it is dying. *The Acts of the Apostles* is a book that is all about growth. Will Vaus has been meditating and preaching on *Acts* for the past 30 years. In this volume, he offers the reader forty-one keys from the entire book of Acts to unlock spiritual growth in everyday life.

Open Before Christmas: Devotional Thoughts For The Holiday Season
Will Vaus

Author Will Vaus seeks to deepen the reader's knowledge of Advent and Christmas leading up to Epiphany. Readers are provided with devotional thoughts for each day that help them to experience this part of the Church Year perhaps in a kore spiritually enriching way than ever before.

"Seasoned with inspiring, touching, and sometimes humorous illustrations .... I found his writing immediately engaging and, the more I read, the more I liked it. God has touched my heart by reading Open Before Christmas, and I believe he will touch your heart too."
The Rev. David Beckmann, Founder of The C.S. Lewis Society of Chattanooga

Called to Serve: Life as a Firefighter-Deacon
Deacon Anthony R. Surozenski

Called to Serve is the story of one man's dream to be a firefighter. But dreams have a way of taking detours – so Tony Surozenski became a teacher and eventually a volunteer firefighter. And when God enters the picture, Tony is faced with a choice. Will he give up firefighting to follow another call? After many years, Tony's two callings are finally united – in service as a fire chaplain at Ground Zero after the 9-11 attacks and in other ways he could not have imagined. Tony is Chief Chaplain's aid for the Massachusetts Corp of Fire Chaplains and Director for the Office of the Diaconate of the Diocese of Worchester, Massachusetts.

Harry Potter

The Order of Harry Potter: The Literary Skill of the Hogwarts Epic
Colin Manlove

Colin Manlove, a popular conference speaker and author of over a dozen books, has earned an international reputation as an expert on fantasy and children's literature. His book, *From Alice to Harry Potter*, is a survey of 400 English fantasy books. In *The Order of Harry Potter*, he compares and contrasts *Harry Potter* with works by "Inklings" writers J.R.R. Tolkien, C.S. Lewis and Charles Williams; he also examines Rowling's treatment of the topic of imagination; her skill in organization and the use of language; and the book's underlying motifs and themes.

Harry Potter & Imagination: The Way Between Two Worlds
Travis Prinzi

Imaginative literature places a reader between two worlds: the story world and the world of daily life, and challenges the reader to imagine and to act for a better world. Starting with discussion of Harry Potter's more important themes, *Harry Potter & Imagination* takes readers on a journey through the transformative power of those themes for both the individual and for culture by placing Rowling's series in its literary, historical, and cultural contexts.

Repotting Harry Potter: A Professor's Guide for the Serious Re-Reader
Rowling Revisited: Return Trips to Harry, Fantastic Beasts, Quidditch, & Beedle the Bard
James W. Thomas

In *Repotting Harry Potter* and his sequel book *Rowling Revisited*, Dr. James W. Thomas points out the humor, puns, foreshadowing and literary parallels in the Potter books. In *Rowling Revisited*, readers will especially find useful three extensive appendixes – "Fantastic Beasts and the Pages Where You'll Find Them," "Quidditch Through the Pages," and "The Books in the Potter Books." Dr. Thomas makes re-reading the Potter books even more rewarding and enjoyable.

The Deathly Hallows Lectures:
The Hogwarts Professor Explains Harry's Final Adventure
John Granger

In *The Deathly Hallows Lectures*, John Granger reveals the finale's brilliant details, themes, and meanings. *Harry Potter* fans will be surprised by and delighted with Granger's explanations of the three dimensions of meaning in *Deathly Hallows*. Ms. Rowling has said that alchemy sets the "parameters of magic" in the series; after reading the chapter-length explanation of *Deathly Hallows* as the final stage of the alchemical Great Work, the serious reader will understand how important literary alchemy is in understanding Rowling's artistry and accomplishment.

Sociology and Harry Potter: 22 Enchanting Essays on the Wizarding World
Jenn Simms, editor

Modeled on an Introduction to Sociology textbook. this books is not simply about the series, but also used the series to facilitate reader's understanding of the discipline of sociology and a development of a sociological approach to viewing social reality. It is a case of high quality academic scholarship written in a form and on a topic accessible to non-academics. As such, it is written to appeal to Harry Potter fans and the general reading public. Contributors include professional sociologists from eight countries.

Harry Potter, Still Recruiting:
An Inner Look at Harry Potter Fandom
Valerie Frankel, editor

The Harry Potter phenomenon has created a new world: one of Quidditch in the park, lightning earrings, endless parodies, a new genre of music, and fan conferences of epic proportions. This book attempts to document everything - exploring costuming, crafting, gaming, and more, with essays and interviews straight from the multitude of creators. From children to adults, fans are delighting the world with an explosion of captivating activities and experiences, all based on Rowling's delightful series.

Hog's Head Conversations: Essays on Harry Potter
Travis Prinzi, editor

Ten fascinating essays on Harry Potter are divided into five sections: Conversations on 1) Literary Value, 2) Eternal Truth, 3) Imagination, 4) Literary Criticism, and 5) Characters. Contributors include the following popular Potter writers and speakers: John Granger, James W. Thomas, Colin Manlove, and Travis Prinzi.

Fiction

The Iona Conspiracy (from The Remnant Chronicles book series)
Gary Gregg

Readers find themselves on a modern adventure through ancient Celtic myth and legend as thirteen year old Jacob uncovers his destiny within "the remnant" of the Sporrai Order. As the Iona Academy comes under the control of educational reformers and ideological scientists, Jacob finds himself on a dangerous mission to the sacred Scottish island of Iona and discovers how his life is wrapped up with the fate of the long lost cover of *The Book of Kells*. From its connections to Arthurian legend to references to real-life people, places, and historical mysteries, *Iona* is an adventure that speaks to eternal truths as well as the challenges of the modern world. A young adult novel, *Iona* can be enjoyed by the entire family.

Poets and Poetry

Remembering Roy Campbell: The Memoirs of his Daughters, Anna and Tess
Introduction by Judith Lütge Coullie, editor
Preface by Joseph Pearce

Anna and Teresa Campbell were the daughters of the handsome young South African poet and writer, Roy Campbell (1901-1957), and his beautiful English wife, Mary Garman. In their frank and moving memoirs, Anna and Tess recall the extraordinary, and often very difficult, lives they shared with their exceptional parents. The book includes over 50 photos, 344 footnotes, a timeline of Campbell's life, and a complete index.

In the Eye of the Beholder: How to See the World Like a Romantic Poet
Louis Markos

Born out of the French Revolution and its radical faith that a nation could be shaped and altered by the dreams and visions of its people, British Romantic Poetry was founded on a belief that the objects and realities of our world, whether natural or human, are not fixed in stone but can be molded and transformed by the visionary eye of the poet. Unlike many of the books written on Romanticism, which devote many pages to the poets and few pages to their poetry, the focus here is firmly on the poems themselves. The author thereby draws the reader intimately into the life of these poems. A separate bibliographical essay is provided for readers listing accessible biographies of each poet and critical studies of their work.

The Cat on the Catamaran: A Christmas Tale
John Martin

Here is a modern-day parable of a modern-day cat with modern-day attitudes. Riverboat Dan is a "cool" cat on a perpetual vacation from responsibility. He's *The Cat on the Catamaran* – sailing down the river of life. Dan keeps his guilty conscience from interfering with his fun until he runs into trouble. But will he have the courage to believe that it's never too late to change course? (For ages 10 to adult)

"This book is a joy, and as companionable as a good-natured cat."
        Walter Hooper, author of *C. S. Lewis: Companion and Guide*

The Half Blood Poems
Inspired by the Stories of J.K. Rowling
Christine Lowther

Like Harry Potter, Christine's poetry can soar above the tragic to discover the heroic and beautiful in such poems as "Neville, Unlikely Rebel", "For Our Wide-Armed Mothers," and "A Boy's Hands." There are 71 poems divided into seven chapters that correspond to the seven books. Fans of Harry Potter will experience once again many of the emotions they felt reading the books – emotions presented most effectively through a poet's words.

Pop Culture

To Love Another Person: A Spiritual Journey Through Les Miserables
John Morrison

The powerful story of Jean Valjean's redemption is beloved by readers and theatergoers everywhere. In this companion and guide to Victor Hugo's masterpiece, author John Morrison unfolds the spiritual depth and breadth of this classic novel and broadway musical.

Through Common Things: Philosophical Reflections on Popular Culture
Adam Barkman

"Barkman presents us with an amazingly wide-ranging collection of philosophical reflections grounded in the everyday things of popular culture – past and present, eastern and western, factual and fictional. Throughout his encounters with often surprising subject-matter (the value of darkness?), he writes clearly and concisely, moving seamlessly between Aristotle and anime, Lord Buddha and Lord Voldemort.... . This is an informative and entertaining book to read!"
        Doug Bloomberg, Professor of Philosophy, Institute for Christian Studies

Above All Things: Essays on Christian Ethics and Popular Culture
Adam Barkman

"Whether discussing Winnie the Pooh or The Walking Dead, this book digs up buried philosophical treasure. Those who don't normally think of themselves as philosophically inclined will be surprised and delighted as Barkman rescues philosophy from dry classroom abstractions and reveals how it fills the glorious messiness of everyday life."
        Dr. Kevin Flatt, Assistant Professor of History, Redeemer University College

Spotlight:
A Close-up Look at the Artistry and Meaning of Stephenie Meyer's Twilight Novels
John Granger

Stephenie Meyer's *Twilight* saga has taken the world by storm. But is there more to *Twilight* than a love story for teen girls crossed with a cheesy vampire-werewolf drama? *Spotlight* reveals the literary backdrop, themes, artistry, and meaning of the four Bella Swan adventures. *Spotlight* is the perfect gift for serious *Twilight* readers.

Virtuous Worlds: The Video Gamer's Guide to Spiritual Truth
John Stanifer

Popular titles like *Halo 3* and *The Legend of Zelda: Twilight Princess* fly off shelves at a mind-blowing rate. John Stanifer, an avid gamer, shows readers specific parallels between Christian faith and the content of their favorite games. Written with wry humor (including a heckler who frequently pokes fun at the author) this book will appeal to gamers and non-gamers alike. Those unfamiliar with video games may be pleasantly surprised to find that many elements in those "virtual worlds" also qualify them as "virtuous worlds."

CPSIA information can be obtained at www.ICGtesting.com
Printed in the USA
LVOW08s0906040215

425647LV00004B/630/P